Treasures of the Royal Armouries
A Panoply of Arms

TREASURES OF THE ROYAL ARMOURIES

A PANOPLY OF ARMS

Edited by Edward Impey
Director General and Master of the Royal Armouries

Published by Royal Armouries Museum,
Armouries Drive, Leeds LS10 1LT, United Kingdom

www.royalarmouries.org

Copyright © 2022 Trustees of the Royal Armouries

All rights reserved. No part of this publication may be reproduced, stored in a retrieval system or transmitted in any form or by any means, electronical, mechanical, photocopying, recording or otherwise without the prior permission of the publisher.

ISBN 978 1 913013 40 0 *hardback*
ISBN 978 1 913013 41 7 *paperback*

Royal Armouries Publishing: Martyn Lawrence
Designer: Robert Dalrymple
Colour reproduction: Typo•glyphix
Printed in Wales by Gomer Press

10 9 8 7 6 5 4 3 2 1

A CIP record for this book is available
from the British Library

Front cover:
Gilt armour owned by Charles I (see entry 59)
Rear cover:
Thompson machine gun (see entry 109)

Contents

7 Foreword by H.R.H. The Earl of Wessex and Forfar

9 Introduction

11 Arms, Armour, History and Culture

29 The Royal Armouries: History and Collection

45 TREASURES OF THE ROYAL ARMORIES

276 Glossary

281 Further reading

287 Acknowledgements and contributors

288 List of entries

BELOW Detail of the stock of a single-barrelled flintlock shotgun from the 'Tula garniture' for Elizabeth, Empress of Russia [see catalogue 88]

Foreword

Describing weapons of war as 'treasures' might, at first glance, seem a little odd, yet that would be to miss their significance. History is essentially the study of people and events in the past, of which wars and battles tend to be the most memorable and engaging. Unfortunately, the story of humans on this planet is inextricably linked with warfare, arms and armour. Fortunately, perhaps the best collection through which to tell their story belongs to the Royal Armouries.

A mixture of items made in this country, captured through combat or presented as gifts to the Sovereign of the day, the Royal Armouries contains arms and armour from around the world collected over several centuries. Apart from being a testament to human ingenuity and imagination, perhaps the most surprising thing about the collection are the extraordinary examples of craftsmanship. Of course, there are plenty of examples of mass-produced, functional weapons, but then again, it is really quite amazing to see the care and attention that went into producing highly personalised and ornate weapons and armour.

This superbly illustrated and researched book tries to capture the essence of the collection, held across various sites, by selecting just a few exceptional items. They are chosen due to their rarity, their uniqueness, their place in the evolution of weaponry or because of the story associated with them. For me, the most remarkable story is that of the humble battle hammer; a small, hand-held weapon used against knights in armour in the Middle Ages which became a symbol of office and today is still carried to denote delegated royal authority, although in the rather more ornate form of a mace. The most famous is perhaps the one used in the Palace of Westminster, specifically the House of Commons, although every regional, county or civic assembly must have one. Most bear little resemblance to their origins in terms of design, although there are exceptions, such as the mace used at the University of Bath, which clearly have a more warlike appearance.

Thanks must go to Dr Edward Impey and Dr Martyn Lawrence for the amount of time and effort committed to compiling *Treasures of the Royal Armouries: A Panoply of Arms*, when the real challenge is always what to leave out and what to keep. However, it must be remembered that these pages only provide a small insight into the Royal Armouries' collection and their associated stories, but if it inspires you to visit even one of their sites then all that time and effort will have been worthwhile.

H.R.H. The Earl of Wessex and Forfar KG GCVO

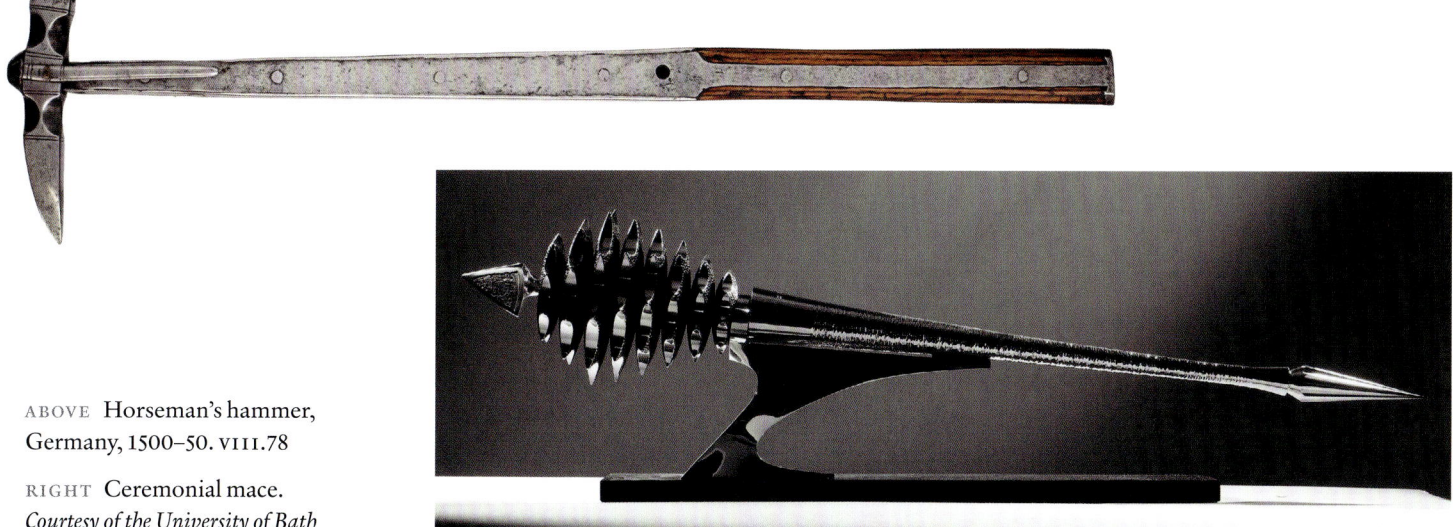

ABOVE Horseman's hammer, Germany, 1500–50. VIII.78

RIGHT Ceremonial mace. *Courtesy of the University of Bath*

I · Introduction

The Royal Armouries is calling this book a 'panoply' – an ancient Greek word for a set of weapons and armour, in English now meaning any showy assemblage of artefacts, usually of military and sporting hardware. This is what it is: a panoply of 115 short articles on items in the Royal Armouries' collection which, amidst hot competition, have claims to exceptional interest. As such, it joins the ranks of the 'Treasures' or 'Director's Choice' publications of many museums and heritage bodies in recent decades, including the Armouries, which published *Treasures from the Tower of London*, accompanying an exhibition in 1982.† It aims, as these do, to show off chosen items from the collection, to enthuse the reader about these special pieces and the subject in general, and to explore its importance.

And important it certainly is: arms and armour have been at the forefront of the reshaping of the geopolitical, religious and cultural map of the globe for thousands of years, and continue to alter or maintain it. To this we can add the contribution of arms and armour and its development, with far greater consequences, to science, technology and manufacture in general. Meanwhile, as many of the entries demonstrate, weapons, armours and associated accoutrements are often items of fabulous craftsmanship or works of art in their own right, and can be enjoyed simply as objects of beauty and wonder. In addition, as items associated with famous or fascinating but little-known events, and worn and carried by people, arms and armour offers a uniquely personal contact with the past. In short, arms and armour, as a branch of material culture into which, arguably, more resources and more ingenuity have been poured and with more far-reaching consequences than any other, is a subject that offers something for everyone.

For some, of course, the subject is tainted by the violent purpose for which most arms are made. This is understandable. So is to question why museums of arms and armour (and almost every country has them) are useful. Whatever your starting point, however, the creation and use of arms and armour are inextricable from the story of humankind, which – devoid of natural weapons or defences such as claws or speed

† Norman, A. V. B. and G. M. Wilson 1982. *Treasures from the Tower of London*, London: Arms and Armour.

Fig.1 | Detail of the 'Lion Armour' [see catalogue 44]

[9]

– has needed to manufacture substitutes. Whilst thinking about arms and armour as a subject in its own right can be avoided, its consequences cannot. Arms and armour, then, is part of our common heritage, and it is the job of museums, particularly the Royal Armouries, to explain and present its collection and the subject in ways that are scholarly, objective, engaging, inclusive and continually improving.

The range of items, however, goes beyond 'treasures', in the sense of beautiful, valuable, bejewelled and precious-metal items. Such things certainly are included, but so are many others associated with past events and people, particular communities and causes, or which serve to illustrate particular technological developments. Among them are the fabulous mid-16th century Italian 'Lion Armour' [44] and a Chinese Ming dynasty sword [15], both pieces of extraordinary technical and artistic virtuosity which also represent important aspects of history and art history. Alongside them, though, we also describe the brutally functional re-hafted scythe blades picked up on the battlefield of Sedgemoor in 1685 [71], a Thompson sub-machine gun, indelibly associated with Ireland in the 1920s and Prohibition-era America [109], and a Norwegian whaling cannon of 1947 [111]. Wittingly or otherwise, the particular enthusiasms of the nineteen contributors, all museum staff past or present, have also played a part in the selection.

The wide definition of 'treasure' is mirrored by the broad chronological, geographical and cultural scope of the material. Items range in date from the 4th century BC [2] to a gun commissioned for the millennium [114], and in origin from Southeast Asia to Glasgow. Nor were all these 'treasures' made for warfare, but also for warlike competition – especially forms of tournament [for example, 25] – or field sports, among them guns [for example, 87], a crossbow [54], a sword [45] and spears [for example, 64]. Others, although squarely parts of the panoply, are not arms or armour at all, but associated equipment: among them are an exquisite set of tools made in about 1690 for Ferdinando, Grand Prince of Tuscany [77], powder flasks, saddles [11, 14, 53], fencing manuals [6, 90] and the Duke of Wellington's telescope [97]. In addition, several paintings, such as a near-contemporary panorama of the battle of Pavia in 1525 [35] and a portrait of Louis XIII of France [66], depict arms and armour in action, being worn, or on display.

The chronological structure allows for major historical events, figures and technical developments to be introduced roughly in order, although it has to be admitted that some objects can only be dated approximately. The entries themselves follow no particular format, but describe the form, decoration and materials of the objects, how they worked or were used (and by who), and offer information about people involved in their manufacture and their original and subsequent owners. They also place the objects in their broader historical context, noting the states, societies and religious environments in which they were created, and the events and broad historical developments in which they played a part. Where relevant, technical features are explained, although in detail only if central to the object's significance. Some specialist terms are explained in the text, but many more in a glossary at the back of the volume. Each entry is illustrated by one or more specially commissioned photographs, and provides a brief bibliography. In most cases more images, details and other information can be found in the Royal Armouries online catalogue [https://collections.royalarmouries.org], accessible via the inventory number supplied for each item.

The 115 entries form the main part of this book. They are prefaced, however, by contextual and introductory material, the first part entitled 'Arms, Armour, History and Culture': this discusses the impact of arms and armour on history, their role in the development of technology, the importance and enjoyment of weapons and armours as fine and applied art, their depiction in art, and their social and religious attributes and significance. Part two, 'The Royal Armouries: History and Collection', is prompted by the inextricable relationship between the study, display and enjoyment of arms and armour in Britain and the history of the Royal Armouries and its precursor organisations. Ours was not a museum created in one fell swoop, from nothing, by one great scheme, with a brand-new apparatus and purpose, as with the National Portrait Gallery or the Victoria & Albert Museum. Rather, it developed organically over centuries thanks to the antiquarian tendencies and showmanship of the practical and warlike bodies that managed the nation's arsenal, both current and obsolete. The work and functions of these forerunners is therefore briefly explained, beginning in the 14th century – the period of the first really useful records – extending to the late 15th century and the first known instances of deliberately showing material to visitors. It then considers the origins of what was arguably, in all but name, a museum in a near-modern sense, in the 16th and certainly the 17th century, its increasing ambition and sophistication as part of a self-conscious visitor attraction in the 18th and 19th centuries, the emergence of arms and armour as a scholarly subject, and its visitors and their experience. Finally, it describes the development of the modern institution, its expansion beyond the Tower of London and the creation of the purpose-built museum in Leeds, and touches on our plans for the future.

As a final but important note, the Armouries, editor and contributors are aware that this text, given its cultural and geographical range, describes items and historical events which may be viewed in different ways by different people. We recognise, therefore, that there are valid alternatives to aspects of our narrative, and that events described here may reflect political, cultural and social attitudes current in the past but certainly not held today by museum staff. We, along with the museum sector overall, are seeking to increase inclusivity in the description and display of our collection.

II · Arms, Armour, History and Culture

Arms, armour, warfare and consequences

It is a truism that the impact of arms and armour on the geopolitical history of the world has been greater than that of any other class of manufactured product. This impact was made, in the main, through warfare, for which arms and armour are the essential tools. It is important to recognise, however, that most wars, even wars with immense consequences, were fought by armies whose actual equipment was equally matched. In such cases outcomes were determined not by the qualities of arms and armour alone, but by other factors such as demography, resources, finance, organisation, tactics, leadership and luck. Indeed this was generally true of large-scale warfare until the end of the Second World War, in which technical innovations on one side were usually matched on the other. The Greek *phalanx* of the 6th century BC [2] and later the Roman legion used much the same weapons as the armies of their enemies, but they were enormously effective because of their training, discipline, and organisation. Likewise, battles in the 18th and 19th centuries was dominated by square and linear formations of well-drilled infantry.

There is, however, a category of conflict in which victory was assured by superior arms and armour, most commonly when the forces of a technically advanced society encountered those of one less advanced: this has been described, for obvious reasons, as 'asymmetric' warfare. Popular insurrections against established authority could also pit ill-armed rebels into hopelessly asymmetric encounters, in which professionally made and professionally handled arms were decisive factors, and brought predictable results: the massacre of the Duke of Monmouth's rebels, by the professional royal army at Sedgemoor in 1685, is a well-known English example [71]. The defeat of the German peasant rebels at Frankenhausen (Thuringia) in 1526 in which over 100,000 died is a well-known continental one; the Andean revolt of Túpac Amaru (1738–81) against the Spanish, which ended in their defeat in 1781, is one from the Americas.

Superior equipment did not, of course, always ensure victory. At Isandlwhana in 1878 better leadership and greater numbers led to the annihilation of a technically superior British army by the Zulus. Generally, however, success came to better equipped armies. The most obvious examples are, roughly speaking, 'colonial', as in the case of Rome, which even before the era of the Empire (from 27 BC), ruled one in all but name, and which at its greatest extent under Hadrian

Fig. 2 | Relief carving of about AD 70 from Mainz (Germany) showing legionaries in combat. The man to the right is shown in the correct semi-crouched position, legs apart, his shield pushed forward for protection and his *gladius* ready for thrusting forward against the enemy. Roman organisation and tactics, together with their use of armour and this brutal close-combat sword, were important reasons for their victories.
Courtesy of the Landesmuseum, Mainz

stretched across three continents from the Persian Gulf to Carlisle and covered 2.5 million square miles. This was created largely by the Romans' gifts for organisation, but also, particularly in western and central Europe, by superiority in arms and armour, famously shown by many scenes on Trajan's Column, depicting the conquest of Dacia (roughly, Romania) in AD 106. The best known and probably the most important weapon in question was the short, brutal sword of the Roman infantry, the *gladius*, of which the Royal Armouries has a superb example [3].

An obvious parallel to the achievement of the Romans, but largely in the East, in the late 12th and 13th centuries and by the last and most terrible of nomadic conquerors, is that of the Mongols. Led by Genghis Khan (*c.*1162–1227), his sons and grandson Kubilai (1215–94) – the 'Kubla' of Coleridge – and Khan of China, by the 1260s they controlled a great swathe of Asia and parts of Europe, east to west from the Sea of Japan to Cracow, and from north to south the Arctic into the Indian subcontinent. Their special weapon was the powerful composite recurve bow made of wood, horn (on the concave side when strung) and sinew (on the back). It was short enough for use from the saddle and strong enough for outstanding range. This and the quality of their ponies gave the Mongols speed with hitting power, and they were backed up by more heavily armoured lancers. But they also owed their success to the abilities of their rulers who organized them and made the most of their strategic and tactical potential. Thus equipped, for generations the Mongols swept the forces of less mobile and skilled opponents before them [5]. Conversely, the reluctance of the Mamluks, Muslim rulers of Egypt and Syria, to adopt hand-held firearms in the late 15th century was a real factor in their conquest in 1517 by the Ottomans, who were pioneering and enthusiastic users of guns [23]. Similarly at the battle of Pavia [35], fought in 1525 between the forces of Francis I of France and the Holy Roman Emperor Charles V, the fully-armoured French knights were brought down by massed gunfire from arquebusiers. The consequences for military tactics were far-reaching, and for Francis they meant humiliation, imprisonment in Spain, and the loss of all 'save honour' [56]. At about the same time and with still greater impact, technical superiority played a part in Hernan Cortés's conquest in Mexico (1519–21). His small army was greatly assisted by local allies, but the steel armour, edged weapons, horses and guns of the Spaniards had a devastating impact on their Aztec opponents who were reliant on stone-age weaponry. Cortés's victory led to no less than the Iberian domination of the whole of South America, Mesoamerica and, at least until the mid 19th century, much of what is now the USA. More recently, the British Empire has probably been the most influential of them all, resulting in English being the second most widely spoken language in the world and British-derived governance and legal infrastructure evident across the globe. This too can largely be attributed to the success of superior arms backed by industrial might, although British forces regularly encountered equally well-equipped opponents on other continents, such as the Sikhs [83] or the Kingdom of Mysore [92, 93], and the Mahdi in Sudan.

Other examples of the decisive role of weapons include the Mexican-American war of 1846–8, the last major conflict between 'western' powers in which the rank and file on one side – the Mexicans – were armed with flintlocks: the Americans won, and annexed Texas, Arizona, New Mexico, California and parts of Utah. In 1839–42 the Royal Navy crushed the defences of the Chinese Empire with their heavy guns mounted on steamships in the First Opium War. In the previous century China had doubled in size by conquering the steppe lands, and, confident in its great military power contemptuously rejected British requests to increase trade. Internal reactions to foreign interference that resulted from this defeat helped to destabilise the Chinese government whose decline ended only in 1949 with the triumph of the Communist regime. In 1853 and 1854 the 'Black Ships', a small steam-powered naval force under the American commodore Matthew Perry (1794–1858), arrived off the coast of Japan, and although they never fired a shot, they forced its government, mindful of the Opium War, to open the country to European business. In this way superior technology paved the way for the Meiji restoration of 1868 and Japan's meteoric reinvention as a military, technological and economic power.

The application of industrial technology to war in the 19th century produced many such 'asymmetric' confrontations. In 1853, at Sinope in the Black Sea, a Russian squadron armed with exploding shells destroyed a Turkish naval force in what became the opening phases of the Crimean War [100, 101]. In the first Matabele War (1893–4) fifty British soldiers equipped with four Maxim machine-guns [104] fought off 5000 warriors, as remembered by Belloc's couplet:

> *Whatever happens, we have got*
> *The Maxim gun, and they have not*

Sometimes the less technologically sophisticated put up a long resistance. The French seized Algeria in 1830 but bitter resistance continued into the 20th century. The military defeat of native Americans by the US government and state militias – the stuff of 'Westerns' but also real history – continued, astonishingly, up to the surrender of the Apache chief Geronimo in 1909. Japan features again in this context with the dropping of atomic bombs, based wholly on technology which only the USA then possessed, on Hiroshima and Nagasaki in August 1945, which led to its surrender and the end of the Second World War.

Territorial gains through warfare and superior armaments, as the above examples show, can change more than territorial possession, transforming not just boundaries but the religion, language, culture and racial mix of vast areas of the globe. Most of the countries which were once part of the Roman Empire speak 'romance' languages derived from Latin, and are Christian because that religion was enforced after 325 by the imperial authorities. Muslim conquest erased Christianity from North Africa, but the reconquest of Spain and Sicily by Italians, Spaniards and French restored its supremacy in those areas. Spanish, of course, a close Latin derivative, was the language established by force of arms and colonial rule from the late 15th century over most of Central and South America, and Portuguese in Brazil. The tide of Muslim conquest after 732 created an immense empire extending from India to the Pyrenees with an immeasurable cultural impact on a vast range of peoples.

A final inescapable point about arms and armour and history, specifically about gunpowder and guns, is its impact on state formation and societal and political structures within them, as opposed to power balances between them. Many historians have pointed out that the sheer expense of artillery, in particular, meant that only wealthy regimes, backed by a mercantile, manufacturing and technical capacity, could exploit its war-winning capacities. This undoubtedly influenced the 'rise of the nation state', in that bigger nations could wield an exponential advantage over smaller ones. The centralising tendencies from the 16th century onward, as evidenced in Renaissance France or the British Empire, undoubtedly owed much to the threat and deployment of artillery: examples from the period described here include the 15th-century 'Dardanelles gun' [18] of a type which helped the well-organised Ottomans assemble their enormous empire, while the Pavia painting [55] is testament to the power of Renaissance artillery. At the same time, within states, a ruler's command of artillery, as historian of science John Bernal has put it, 'broke the independence of the land-based aristocracy as surely as their castles were battered down by cannon balls. The triumph of gunpowder was the triumph of the national State and the beginning of the end of the feudal order': whilst obviously a simplification, the basic premise stands.

The currency of diplomacy

Arms and armour have always been, as it were, at the 'sharp end' of history. But whilst war, as Clausewitz put it, may be 'the continuation of politics by other means', arms and armour have had a role in politics themselves and in avoiding or cementing its results, as tools of diplomacy. This has led to the creation of many of the most impressive items of armour in the Royal Armouries and in other collections across the world. Arms and armour were obviously not the only items put to such use: concubines, plate, ships, works of art, tapestries, rare animals and chunks of territory were all part of the hard currency of diplomacy. Arms and armour, however, have the advantage of being personal: they were worn or used by the recipient, whilst also flattering his or her warlike spirit, sporting prowess, chivalric credentials, classical learning or aesthetic sense, and simultaneously showing off the technical or artistic prowess of the donor nation. Such gifts could be wholly practical, such as the five galley-loads of arms, armour and ammunition sent in 1449 by Philip the Good, Duke of Burgundy to James II of Scotland, as part of the dowry for his niece, Mary of Guelders, who married the king in that year. In 1457, for essentially similar reasons, the duke sent him 'Mons Meg' [17], a gigantic but plainly functional cannon, later used in encounters with the English and their fortifications. More glamorous inter-dynastic representatives in the collection include the 'Horned Helmet', remnant of an armour made in Innsbruck c.1511–14 [30] and given by the Holy Roman Emperor Maximilian to the young Henry VIII: this is not only a fabulous piece of craftsmanship, but again, as arms and armour were so suited, laden with personal messages and meaning, if rather obscure today. The 'Burgundian Bard', a magnificent horse armour of c.1510, was also part of the gift [29]. From further afield is a 16th-century Japanese armour [43], used as a diplomatic gift by the Tensho Mission of 1582–90, a collaboration between prominent Japanese noblemen and Jesuit missionaries to send a group of Japanese Christians to Spain to strengthen ties with King Philip II. The armour was probably presented to him personally at an audience in 1584. One of the museum's greatest treasures is another Japanese armour, one of two given by the Shoguns Tokugawa Hidetada and his father, Ieyasu, to James I of England, supporting an arrangement allowing the English to trade with Japan [58]. In return, the Japanese received a silver-gilt telescope. Telescopes were then at the very cutting-edge of technological development, and indeed this was the first to leave Europe [97]. It was a gift laden with meaning for it was a Protestant gift, and it had been adopted, used and improved by Galileo Galilei who had challenged Catholic orthodoxy about the heavens. Now sadly lost, it attracted a great deal of attention amongst the Japanese and was instrumental in replacing Iberian with northern European and Protestant influence over the authorities of this increasingly important trading and political associate. In an interesting encounter at the Tower of London in 1669, Cosimo III, Grand Duke of Tuscany, a foreign prince on a quasi-diplomatic visit to England, witnessed a gift being prepared to support another diplomatic mission: whilst viewing the Artillery Room in the Grand Storehouse, he saw two Elizabethan cannon being 'furbished up, by the King's orders, to be sent as a present to the King of Fez [Morocco], on occasion of the Earl of Arundel's embassy to that court'. The recipient was Al-Rashid II, emperor of Morocco from 1666–72, and the diplomat in fact the earl's grandson, Lord Henry Howard.

Sporting equipment was equally acceptable. Examples from the collection include one of the eleven Boutet guns given to Charles IV of Spain by Napoleon Bonaparte (then First Consul), to cement the 3rd Treaty of San Ildefonso [1801]: this was a spectacularly one-sided deal by which France got Louisiana (Spanish since 1763, vast, but undefined) and six warships, and Charles little more than the vague promise of an Italian principality [94]. Sporting weapons were also of course exchanged, as today, as personal gifts, but these sometimes had a part-diplomatic intent, such as the flintlock by Bertrand Piraube [73] probably given by Louis XIV to his friend and relative Charles Lennox, first Duke of Richmond and natural son of Charles II.

A connection with the past

A final feature of the relationship between arms, armour and history is their power to connect the viewer – or better still, the handler – with past people and past events. This has been recognised probably as long as arms and armour have existed, and was certainly clear to the designers of displays at the Tower of London from the 15th century, notably of royal armours and paraphernalia. The practice has led to displays of assemblages or individual pieces more like those of relics than as a 'cabinets' or shows of power. This was, for example, the ethos of the 'military' department of the Royal United Services Institute, founded in 1830 and dispersed in 1962: the sword worn by Wolfe at Quebec; the sash which lowered the body of Sir John Moore into his grave at Corunna by the light of 'the lantern dimly burning' and the skeleton of Marengo, the horse which carried Napoleon at Waterloo, were among its treasures. Regimental museums, such as the Green Howards' museum in Richmond (North Yorkshire) emphasise similar things – and effortlessly or subliminally teach history through the connection between items, people and thence the regiment. Such places offer genuine links between things and people, but of course, as with relics – and some *were* relics – many items so displayed had no real connection to the associated person or event: the Holy Lance in the Hofburg in Vienna was certainly not the one that pierced Christ's side, nor was 'the Sabre of Charlemagne' even made at the time of his death. Even the conscientious United Services Institute were guilty of wishful thinking, as in the case of their 'Mortuary' sword (now in the Royal Armouries collection: **68**) of about 1640, spuriously claimed to have been used by Cromwell at the infamous sack of Drogheda (County Louth, Ireland). But again, for those who over many years took it at face value, it has offered a frisson of horror and a very personal connection with an important historical figure.

Arms, armour, science and technology

Potential advantage over an enemy has meant that many aspects of technology were invented, developed, and first applied in the design and creation of arms and armour. Such technologies cover a vast range of scientific discoveries and applications, essentially in the fields of physics and chemistry, and specifically, in those of explosives, metallurgy, ballistics, engineering and medicine, but also crucially in the processes of manufacture. Aspects of these developments are considered below, but when it comes to the application of science and technology to arms and armour itself – even if the actual physical and chemical processes at play were not necessarily understood – a vital imperative was the relentless desire for increased accuracy, range, impact and rate of fire in small arms and artillery. What immediately follows is a brief exploration of the process as it relates to small arms, illustrating the technical development of what for centuries was humankind's most important arm, and at the same time the hand-in-hand development of weapons and technology more generally.

The first handguns were short metal tubes mounted on wooden bars or 'tillers', muzzle-loaded and ignited through a touch-hole [16, 23] with a red-hot iron or 'match' (a smouldering rope end). The potential to actually *aim* the gun by sighting down the barrel, and firing it whilst keeping it steady, was introduced with the matchlock [37, 39] whereby a simple trigger mechanism brought the match down on to the touch-hole or priming pan and ignited the main charge. Although in Europe this straightforward and inexpensive arrangement remained in use until the end of the 17th century (and far longer in other parts of the world) it had many disadvantages: keeping a match burning in proximity to gunpowder had obvious dangers, while keeping it alight was always difficult, impossible in wet weather, and, in the dark, revealed the position of the user. The answer to these problems lay in mechanical systems – lock mechanisms – providing reliable self-ignition on demand. The first of these, perhaps invented by Leonardo da Vinci, was the wheellock [37, 49]; in these, a spring-loaded wheel, wound by hand, spun against a dog-head holding a piece of pyrites and striking sparks into the priming pan giving the first weapon that, once loaded, could be fired at will, and, most importantly, used safely and effectively on horseback. Meanwhile rifling (that is, scoring the inside of the barrel with spiral grooves, causing the projectile to spin in flight and so greatly improving range and accuracy) was being used in sporting weapons from the early 16th century. Accompanying improvements in powder – essentially to the rate at which it burned, and therefore to its propulsive power – made a parallel contribution. The wheellock, however, was expensive and fragile, and from the early 17th century was replaced by the better-known and longer-lived 'flintlock'. Invented in France, possibly by Marin le Bourgeois (c.1550–1634) of Lisieux (Calvados) in c.1610, a shaped flint was held in spring-loaded hammer or 'cock' which could be pulled back ('cocked'), and released on pulling the trigger, striking the flint against a 'frizzen' (a combined steel and pan cover) and generating sparks which ignited the priming powder and thence the main charge [60, 70, and others]. Steadily improved, flintlocks were the mainstay of European armies and sportsmen from the late 17th century until the 1840s, although rate of fire was limited by the number of actions required to load and fire.

Fig.3 | Gunner's Quadrant made for Julius, Duke of Brunswick (1528–89). The long arm of the quadrant is placed into the bore of the gun and the position of the pendulum on the scale, in theory, allows the gunner to adjust the elevation of his piece and thus its range. XIV.19

Early attempts at increasing rate of fire with repeating weapons included the use of multiple barrels, as in the medieval *Ribeauldequin*, or Henry VIII's 'walking staff' [36], although as applied to small arms weight was always a problem and loading time proportionately increased; another method was superimposed charges, whereby, usually, more than one charge of powder and shot were loaded into the same barrel and fired in succession, ignited by ingenious external lock mechanisms or highly risky internal ones. Some medieval cannon were breech-loaders, as small arms could be too, such as the Royal Armouries' gun that belonged to Henry VIII and used a re-usable iron cartridge, loaded at the breech and (originally) fired by a wheellock, in principle anticipating the modern cartridge-based system by over four centuries [37]. More ambitious still were the early attempts at the now-familiar revolver, the first having clusters of barrels rotated against a fixed stock, roughly akin to the 'pepperbox' pistol of later centuries, of which the earliest survival is a three-barrelled model of *c*.1540 in Venice. Still more ambitious were the revolvers made by John Dafte (XII.4745: 70) and Thomas Annely (XII.4745) around 1680 and 1710 respectively, and later Elisha Collier's variant, too complicated for practical use, patented in 1818 (XII.1503). Other systems were also developed, notably the Sienese gunmaker Michele Lorenzoni's (1650–1735) fiendishly complex one of the 1660s, whereby charges of powder and ball were housed in a bulbous magazine at the wrist and loaded successively into the chamber by a pair of levers. An English version of about 1690 is described below [79].

The answer to the flintlock's limitations came with the development of percussion ignition. In its mature form, a copper cap containing fulminate of mercury was fitted to a tube leading to the chamber, struck by a hammer, exploded and ignited the main charge [99]. Highly relevant to the history of the Royal Armouries, important steps in the development of the system were made by its inventor the Reverend Alexander John Forsyth (1769–1843) at the Tower of London in 1806–7 and the collection includes a number of his experimental prototypes [XVI.51A–H]. Significantly, Colt was able to exploit the simplicity of the system to realise his machine-made revolver [103], exhibited at the Great Exhibition of 1851, in turn triggering revolutionary changes in the manufacture of the Pattern 1853 Enfield Rifle Musket at Enfield Lock and elsewhere. Percussion ignition was a crucial prerequisite for the development of the self-contained cartridge and consequently the fully practical breech-loading and machine weapons [104]. It is ultimately seen in the low-cost personal automatic weapons such as the AK47 [112], which for over half a century has been the preferred weapon of regular forces and, depending on your perspective, of the insurgent or freedom fighter worldwide.

When it comes to the impetus given by the development of arms and armour to the advancement, understanding and use of physics and chemistry, gunpowder was arguably, once again, the most crucial factor. Gunpowder itself is made up of 75% by weight saltpetre (potassium nitrate), 15% charcoal and 10% sulphur, although proportions can vary: when touched with a spark or hot iron, the sulphur ignites, the heat causing the saltpetre to release oxygen, enabling the charcoal to ignite. The mixture then burns very quickly, releasing large volumes of gas almost instantaneously, creating an explosion. In a gun, this forces a projectile out of the barrel; in other confined spaces, such as in a grenade or shot-hole for mining purposes, radial expansion does the work, shattering iron, rock or coal or whatever surrounds it. Originating in China, gunpowder was known in Europe and being used for guns by the early 14th century – the English Franciscan friar, Roger Bacon, produced a perfectly workable recipe in 1257 – and within decades manuscript manuals were being produced, such as the Armouries' German *Feuerwerkbuch* or 'Book of Fireworks' of *c*.1380 [13]. The development of their art was linked to alchemy, the equivalent of experimental science in the Middle Ages, so that the link between it and European scientific discovery is practically as old as its use, although its history is hotly debated and much remains unknown. From the 18th century attempts to understand its combustion were a key incentive to the emerging science of chemistry. Antoine Lavoisier (1743–94) was a commissioner on the board of the French government's *Régie des Poudres et des Salpêtres*, and his work led to the discovery and naming of oxygen, earning him the title 'father of modern chemistry'. At the same time internal ballistics (what happens between ignition of the propellant and the projectile's emergence from the barrel) and external ballistics (the motion of the projectile in flight) exercised a whole range of natural philosophers, or what today we would call scientists.

[16] ARMS, ARMOUR, HISTORY AND CULTURE

During the Middle Ages and the Renaissance, work built on that of Aristotle by men such as Niccolò Tartaglia (1499–1557) and his *Novo Scientia* of 1537 and Galileo Galilei (1564–1642) which ultimately encouraged Isaac Newton (1642–1727) to formulate his laws of motion. Benjamin Robins (1701–51), known as the founder of aerodynamics, published his experimental measurements of bullet flight and impact in 1742. Given the professional link between the use of artillery and the understanding of powder and the mechanics of flight, the French artillery schools of the 18th century were the first formal institutions dedicated to scientific and engineering education: important French mathematicians and physicists such as Joseph-Louis Lagrange (1736–1813), Pierre-Simon Laplace (1749–1829) and Gaspard Monge (1746–1818), whose work had implications far beyond arms and armour, were trained by these schools, as of course was Napoleon.

Soldiers themselves began to take more scientific approaches to developing their weapons of all kinds, a notable example being the 1796 Light Cavalry Sword [96] associated with Major-General Le Marchant (1766–1812). Rockets – self-propelled iron-bodied gunpowder projectiles – also interested these new professionals, including William Congreve (1772–1828), emulating those used by the Marathas and Mysoreans in India [92, 93]: they were widely used by British forces in the Napoleonic wars, notably by the navy. As the 19th century progressed artillery became more and more effective, notably with the appearance of the 1862 Armstrong gun [101] and, in 1898, the French 'Soixante-Quinze', the first modern mobile field gun with recoil control [106]. The chemist came to the fore once again in the First World War with the production of new explosives, particularly for artillery, poison gas and ersatz materials. This scientific approach to warfare accelerated and continued relentlessly in the Second World War, applied to conventional weapons, air weapons, and what we now call 'weapons of mass destruction'. The use of projectiles to bring down manned and unmanned aircraft such as the V1 'flying bomb' further advanced the understanding of the physics of flight and projectiles and the application of the scientific method and statistical approaches to operations, to reduce the numbers of 'rounds per bird', accompanied by the use of radar, feedback control and early analogue computers to direct gun fire. It was also an 'arms and armour' context that saw the development of one of the first stored programme computers, the Electric Numerical Integrator and Computer (ENIAC), originally built (and subsequently used) to calculate artillery firing tables, although first used, with still greater consequences, to study the feasibility of a thermonuclear weapon.

Arms and their effects have also prompted many of the most important innovations in medical science. This was so in the ancient Western world, although the great Greek and Roman doctors' pronouncements remained unhelpfully unchallenged, other than in the Muslim world, until the 17th century. By then, field experience, if not experiment, was leading to important developments, such as Ambrose Paré's (1510–90) treatment of gunshot wounds, followed by further advances in surgery, particularly amputation. Later, the Napoleonic Wars saw another surge in surgeons' capacity to save lives. Improvements in nursing, thanks to Florence Nightingale's famous work in the Crimea, not only transformed the survival rates of the wounded but also identified ways of fighting infections which had hitherto accounted for more deaths than the battlefield. Medical progress accelerated, along with evidence-based scientific understanding in general during the First World War, in which the sheer volume of trauma cases prompted enormous advances – in the creation, for example, of blood banks permitting blood transfusion on a large scale, infection control, successful compound fracture treatment, and the birth of plastic surgery. Progress accelerated, once again, in the build up to the Second World War and for its duration, not least through the mass use of sulphonamides, invented in the 1930s, and, from 1943, antibiotics, both of which saved thousands upon thousands of lives, while the latter, ever more advanced, now saves billions. Plastic surgery meanwhile – its potential transformed by the new drugs – moved into a new realm of competence and success. Today, medical science continues to be stimulated by the impact of battlefield trauma treatment, aided, through a kind of ghastly if virtuous circle, by dramatically increasing survival rates.

Perhaps the most obvious and important impacts of science developed in an arms and armour context are those on material science and metallurgy. The deadliness of the *gladius*

Fig. 4 | A cast iron cannon almost certainly made in the Sussex Weald, probably in the reign of Edward VI (1547–1553). It has been at Pevensey Castle (Sussex) since 1587. The technology of casting iron, invented in Germany in the Middle Ages, was driven by the desire to make cheap, strong guns. Put to many other uses from the 18th century onwards, it gave a major impetus to the Industrial Revolution. XIX.280

[3] depended on its steel construction, while the natural composites of the recurved bow were used by horsemen to great effect in Asia. Damascus blades [38] were produced by combining wrought iron with carbon from vegetal matter in sealed crucibles; subsequent controlled cooling and forging at low temperatures reduced brittleness and produced blades that were both strong and held a good edge. Hardened armours protected against arrows, the earliest example in the collection dating from around 1550 (II.82), although the technique had been known since about 1400. From the 15th century cannon were made in wrought iron [17] as well as in cast bronze [18], and their creation and use linked the fields of chemistry, physics, metallurgy and manufacturing processes. The use of cast iron in cannon was a major step. This exploited the blast furnace, developed in the Rhineland in the 15th century, and was first and foremost used for weapons. Cast iron guns were first produced in England at Buxted (Sussex) in 1543, thanks to the presence of iron ore deposits and readily available fuel from the then-abundant Wealden woodland. Although not in general use until the 18th century, the earliest surviving example of 1547–53 is 4.3 in calibre, bearing the initials 'E.R', thought to stand for Edward VI (r.1547–53) – not Elizabeth – has been at Pevensey Castle (Sussex) since 1587.

1Cast iron guns, however, brought with them one of the defining manufacturing problems and advances of the 18th century – the precise boring of their barrels. Vital contributions were made in Geneva by Jean Maritz (1680–1743) who used horse-power to drive boring machines with vertical [1715] and horizontal [1718] axes. In England John Wilkinson (1728–1808) famously used his machine to bore steam cylinders for Matthew Boulton and James Watt, with a precision of fit of 'the thickness of a thin shilling', making a defining contribution to the Industrial Revolution and the whole science and practice of mechanical engineering. The heat generated in cannon boring also prompted Benjamin Thompson (Count Rumford, 1753–1814) to begin fundamental experiments on heat and heat transfer.

As the cast iron example shows, manufacturing is one of the fields in which arms and armour have had the most significant impact outside their immediate use, and the production processes and techniques pioneered by the arms makers, particularly those of interchangeable manufacturing, eventually enabled much that is familiar about modern society. That these things first occurred in the field of arms and armour is not surprising, spurred on as they were by the sheer number of weapons required in warfare between rich and powerful nation states: possibly the first instance of interchangeability, was, as with so many things, in ancient China, where the crossbow used under the First Emperor, Qin Shi Huangdi (Qin ruler 221–210 BC) had a cast bronze trigger mechanism, the first mass-produced military artefact.

In England, related logic began to be applied in the reign of Charles I with a proclamation of 1631 requiring that the guns and edged weapons of the Trained Bands (London's Militia), and initially all government-issued military equipment, were to be standardised, with 'patterns' deposited at the Office of Ordnance at the Tower to serve as three-dimensional specifications. Further rigour was introduced with the formation of the Worshipful Company of Gunmakers in 1637. In France, as early as 1722 French scientist René Antoine Ferchault de Réaumur (1683–1757) advocated the interchangeability of gun parts, although this was not seriously taken up. Between 1768 and 1829, however, it was, on the initiative of Jean Baptiste Gribeauval (1715–89), and this led to the standardisation of artillery and associated equipment, in turn demanding the manufacture of interchangeable parts and rigorous quality control. Honoré Blanc of the St Etienne armoury devised a system of gauges allowing the interchangeability of lock parts for the M1777 musket, and by the end of the 18th century similar techniques were in use in England: the Duke of Richmond's musket (XII.107) of the 1780s had a lock designed by Henry Nock (1741–1804) with some interchangeable components, a practice carried over to the lock of the New Land Pattern Musket which, by 1809, had 'a lock so tallying in all its parts, that any part of one lock may fit another', and was ultimately made by fourteen suppliers. American efforts in this direction accelerated after the War of 1812, with the adoption of the standardised, French-influenced M1819 musket at both Harpers Ferry (West Virginia) and Springfield Armories (Massachusetts) and the development of Thomas Blanchard's (1788–1864) machine-tool system for making gunstocks. By 1844 muskets and rifles with interchangeable components were being made at both Harpers Ferry and Springfield, and further developments in machine tools and the use of gauges, including by Colt, swiftly followed. The principles and practices were applied to making the earliest British standard-issue military rifle, the Enfield Pattern 1853, the first product made at high volume in the United Kingdom with interchangeable machine-made parts. Many of the machine-tools were supplied by R. S. Robbins and S. E. Lawrence of Windsor (Vermont), both originally gunmakers, and the Ames Manufacturing Company of Chicopee Falls (Massachusetts), who also supplied gauge sets – some held today by the Royal Armouries. This combination came to be known generically as 'Armory Practice' in America and 'The American System' in England. These developments facilitated the industrialisation of war and so also its scale, notably in the American Civil War (1861–65) and in the World Wars, but they were also swiftly borrowed by other industries, famously including the making of sewing machines by the American Isaac Singer (1811–75) in the 1850s, and later in bicycles, not least by Ames. The essentials were adopted at the very beginning of the 20th century by Ransom Eli Olds (1864–1950) of 'Oldsmobile' fame, whose first production car used standardised parts, paving the way for the better-known achievements of Henry Ford, William Morris (later Lord Nuffield), Herbert Austin and the vehicle industry thereafter. Applied to manufacturing more generally, these developments made possible the 'consumer society', recognisable in the 19th century and to its full extent in the next, with all the social and economic impacts and consequences this entailed.

Overall, then, it can be said that the technological development of arms and armour has had – and continues to have – an incalculable impact on world economy and society. It has not only driven greater effectiveness, but thanks to the application of arms and armour-derived science, technology and processes, has gone far beyond those purposes for which they were originally developed.

Arms, armour, art and design

The most obvious significance of arms and armour derives from, as discussed above, their impact – what they *did*, that is, the primary purposes for which they were intended. But many items of arms and armour display aesthetic and artistic qualities which not only add another dimension to their cultural importance, but, as will be seen, to the range of their purposes. The following paragraphs briefly consider aspects of the relationship between arms, armour, art and design.

The first issue considered is what have been and remain the reasons for the embellishment of arms and armour. Broadly speaking, these include, perhaps most importantly, the projection of power and status, for which of course wealth, easily demonstrated through arms and armour, was a prerequisite; this could work through creating a fabulous overall impression when worn, or – aided by the nature of the decoration itself – when displayed or depicted. The results can endow arms and armour with another dimension of interest, as examples of 'applied art' and even 'fine art' (items created with a primarily aesthetic intent). The relationship is of course at its closest when such items are designed, decorated or even made by the best artists. At the same time the depictions of arms and armour *in* art can be an invaluable historical source, providing important or unique information as to the original form and decoration of arms and armour, and how it was worn or used. Last but very far from least, the virtuosity and sheer beauty of so many items of arms and armour means they can be enjoyed at an immediate, sensory and emotional level, quite independent of any technical or historical knowledge or interest in their purpose.

A fundamental reason for decorating weapons, particularly hand-held arms and certainly armour, is that they share an intimacy with the user, responding to humankind's almost universal desire to decorate important artefacts. This can take a very light touch, such as minimal engraving to a lock, a sword hilt, or of all but the very plainest armours. However, for the decorative features of an item of arms and armour to dominate its appearance, and in many cases exponentially multiply its cost, other motives are required. The most important of these is essentially to do with the status of the owner or wearer, probably recognised for as long as armour and arms, not least those used for hunting, have been in existence. A famous illustration of arms and armour successfully projecting magnificence and overawing the observer's impression is Homer's description of Agamemnon, king of Mycenae, putting on his fantastical armour:

The greaves first he set about his legs; beautiful they were, and fitted with silver anklepieces … And about his shoulders he flung his sword, on which gleamed studs of gold, while the scabbard about it was of silver, fitted with golden chains.

Much more follows in this vein. Neither Homer nor Agamemnon necessarily even existed, and the *Iliad* was written down long after the historical siege of Troy, but the point holds. Artefacts from the ancient world include the amazing bronze helmet of about 1300 BC from the Elamite Empires (modern Iran), adorned with embossed bronze figures, in the Metropolitan Museum of Art, New York. Roman 'parade' armour, known from sculpture and surviving examples including from Pompeii, could be fabulously elaborate, and was to influence the design of Renaissance equivalents: these were at their most impressive in the 16th and early 17th centuries, an example being the Royal Armouries' Negroli buffe of 1538 [39], the 'Lion' armour of 1550 [44] and the Augsburg burgonet of *c.*1600 [55]. Such things were usable in battle, although they were more vulnerable than plainer armours. They were also more likely to attract attention, as in the case of Parisot, nephew of the Grand Master of the Knights of Malta, singled out thanks to his gilded armour and killed in a hail of shot during the Turkish siege of Malta in 1565. Functionality was, however, subservient to the impression to be made on the spectator. While such armours are not a strength of the Royal Armouries collection, a visit to the Musée de l'Armée (Paris), or the tremendous displays in the *Rüstkammeren* of the Kunsthistorisches Museum in Vienna or the Historisches Museum Dresden, make the point very clearly. However, the Royal Armouries' does include, from a little later, the foot combat armour of Christian of Saxony, made in Augsburg in 1591, a *tour de force* of gilded motifs on a blue-black background [51]; another is the wholly gilded harness made for Henry Stuart, eldest son of James I [59], inherited by Prince Charles, later Charles I, and usually described as his. The field and tilt armour of Elizabeth I's favourite, Robert Dudley, Earl of Leicester, made at Greenwich in about 1575 [46] is another highly decorated armour, made in this case for a nobleman.

A function of decoration could also lie in its content and messages, in addition to overall effect: an example is the armour given to Prince Henry Stuart by an ambitious English soldier and courtier [57]. On this, the life-story of Alexander the Great is depicted in over 200 exquisite vignettes, blatantly urging on the young prince to mighty deeds and associating him, in the eye of the beholder, with one of greatest conquerors of all time. In this sub-category too lies the Armouries' 'silvered and engraved' harness and horse-armour made for Henry VIII in about 1515, decorated with quasi-heraldic motifs celebrating the English alliance with Castile, the intertwined initials of Henry and Katherine of Aragon, and scenes of the martyrdoms of selected saints including St George [31]. Hercules, needless to say, was a popular subject, psychologically lending his strength and prowess to an owner or wearer: examples in our collection include a steel shield or *rondache* dated 1579, with embossed and chiselled decoration depicting eight of his adventures (v.53). Lavish arms and armour could continue to project their owners' status when not in use through their deliberate and showy display, at least to the elite: as will be seen, this was the case with Henry VIII's 'rich weapons' at the Tower of London possibly even in his own lifetime, while at the Schloss Ambras (Austrian Tyrol), hundreds of armours, including from the court of Maximilian and his own, were displayed by Archduke Ferdinand II (l.1529–95) in his *Liebrüstkammer* and *Heldenrüstkammer*. Phillip II of Spain organised a display for similar purposes in the royal palace at Madrid. By 1591, the *Rustkammer* of the Electors of Saxony in Dresden offered a display of figures in parade armour, mounted on wooden horses, and in Vienna a similar arrangement was in place by the middle of the 17th century. It was at least one of the ideas behind this – the celebration of a dynasty, monarch and their pedigree through arms and armour – which led to the creation of the first deliberate displays at the Tower of London.

Whether for warfare or hunting, weapons could also be fittingly lavish for royal or noble use, as is much of the material described in this book. The pistols made in London by a Huguenot maker, Pierre Monlong [81], were intended to appeal to buyers who recognised the prestige to be gained from owning them. Lavish decoration was also applied to items not used by the owner themselves but by their attendants or bodyguards: an Armouries example is the deadly Partizan made for the guard of Louis XIV of France, a fabulous piece of metalwork of blue and gold bearing the king's not-so modest motto *NEC PLURIBUS IMPAR* (roughly, 'second to none') [75]. In a variation on the theme, the Grand Storehouse tympanum [80] adorning the 17th-century Grand Storehouse at the Tower served as a statement about the might of British arms and its monarchs and alluded to the vast stocks of weaponry it housed.

Sporting equipment for the elite was often, as today, highly decorated, and from the middle of the 16th century onwards, the most abundant decorated pieces are guns. An early, if not over-lavish example is the Royal Armouries' antler-veneered German wheellock of about 1535. Other examples include the three guns of the garniture made in 1752 for the Empress Elizabeth of Russia (r.1741–62) at her own workshops at Tula, 100 miles south of Moscow; intended for use by this celebrated huntress, their silver plaques, silver inlay and gilding reflected and enhanced the status of this most unusual monarch [88]. Stone bows – crossbows firing stones or lead bullets – of interest not least in that they were often used by women, including Elizabeth I of England, are often lavishly decorated: the Royal Armouries has a superb mid-18th century example by the Dresden maker Christian Tricks, by tradition once belonging to Maria Leczinksa, Queen Consort of France from 1725 to 1768. Exquisite decoration was, of course, also applied to other field-sport equipment and accoutrements, as varied as a profusely decorated crossbow from c.1600 [54], a pocket set of tools of c.1690 for Ferdinando III de' Medici [77], and a powder flask of c.1580 [53] – all made in England – and an Italian boar spear of c.1600 [64].

The impact of wearing and bearing elaborate armour and weapons in warfare and on great occasions could be replicated in more permanent form in portraiture, whether in painting or sculpture, underlining or laying claim to the subject's military and chivalric attributes, wealth and status. The magnificent armour shown in Titian's lost *Charles V with drawn sword*, known thanks to Rubens' copy of c.1605 [56], made all these points about the most powerful man in Europe. The same is true of the portrait of Charles's son, Philip II of Spain wearing the flower pattern armour made by Desiderius Helmschmied. Tellingly, Phillip spent considerably more on the armour than he paid Titian to paint it. The brilliant gold armour of the young Louis XIII depicted in the Armouries' 'circle of Rubens' picture [66] – and the equipment scattered nonchalantly at his feet – has the same effect, although here the alluring goddess of Victory lends a more light-hearted touch.

In our portrait attributed to Marcus Gheeraerts II (1561–1637) of Robert Radcliffe, 5th Earl of Sussex, a mere nobleman, the simple connotations of his armour are heightened by other references to his valour and knightly status [52]: generally, in the ostrich plumes of his helmet, symbolising bravery, and more specifically in the orange colour of the tablecloth, traditionally associated with courage, endurance and strength. Occasionally the artist's concentration on the armour could inadvertently rather eclipse the man himself: in a portrait of Guidobaldo II della Rovere, Duke of Urbino (duke 1538–74), the celebrated Negroli 'bat-wing' or 'fame' armour is more prominently the subject of the painting than the rather unimpressive duke. The importance a patron could attach to the correct and suitably impressive appearance of armour in their likenesses is illustrated by the future Phillip II's complaints, in a letter to his aunt, about Titian's rather loose depiction of his crisply magnificent Augsburg armour in a portrait of 1550: if there was more time, he said, he would have made the artist go over it again.

Bearing out the power and endurance of these messages was the desire of kings, noblemen and others to have themselves portrayed in armour long after its practical obsolescence, whether based on a family heirloom, a studio prop, or the painter's imagination (there was no need, of course for the sitter to worry about fit or to *wear* the armour, as the painter could simply scale it up or down). An example at the summit of the social scale is the much-copied portrait of William III as Prince of Orange by William Wissing (1656–87) 'wearing' a Cuirassier armour made for Charles I in 1610–20 (for the reality, see **72**). In 1698, Peter the Great, Emperor of Russia commissioned Godfrey Kneller (1646–1723) to paint an outrageous portrait of him in full armour, with similar intent, which he gave to William III. In the 18th century George II, although, as the last king of England to lead troops into battle, with some credibility, was also depicted in armour, as was his son-in-law, William IV, Prince of Orange (r.1711–51). Nineteenth-century enthusiasm for all things medieval once again saw great men portrayed in historic armour, real or imagined, among them Prince Albert, consort of Queen Victoria, although by then prompted more by dreams of medieval romance and chivalry than martial pretensions. Meanwhile, contemporaries, including Napoleon III (Emperor of the French, 1852–70) and his nemesis Wilhelm I (German Emperor, 1871–88),

Fig.5 | Alabaster effigy of Sir Richard Cholmondeley, Lieutenant of the Tower of London 1513–20, in the castle chapel of St Peter ad Vincula, c.1521. It shows a form of armour combining largely late 15th-century English forms with those of the early 16th, such as the rounded sabatons and the one-piece construction of the breastplate. No such armour of this form survives. *Photograph courtesy of Malcolm Mercer*

commissioned their dashing and moustachioed portraits in the semi-functional cavalry cuirasses of the time, a throwback to the earlier tradition. Arms and armour also appear occasionally in portraits of women, for related reasons, such as in an 18th-century portrait at the Château de Chambord (Loir-et-Cher) of a fabulously dressed *Dame chasseresse* with flintlock and hound and dead quarry at her feet. In most depictions of armed and armoured women, however, the equipment is of loosely classical form, alluding to Minerva, Roman goddess of wisdom and the less brutal aspects of warfare rather more than martial prowess *per se*: an example is a depiction of the learned Queen Christina of Sweden (r.1632–64), wearing a plumed helmet, a scaled corselet, and incongruously clutching, instead of the usual spear, a tilting lance. The figure of Britannia, if a personification not a person, has appeared in this attire since the early 18th century, her trident being a reference to British naval power. Royal and aristocratic women were also frequently depicted, especially in the 16th to 18th centuries, 'as Diana', goddess of hunting, wispily clad and variously shown with bow, quiver, occasionally a spear, a horn, hounds and other kit, although the allusion was more to chastity than skill at the chase. A particularly famous example, ironically, is the picture of Diane de Poitiers (1500–66), mistress of Henri II of France, in the Louvre.

A different but important aspect to the relationship between arms, armour, painting and sculpture is the value of artistic representation as a historical source, displaying forms, items or activities otherwise only hinted at in writing, unknown or poorly understood. Perhaps the most obvious category, in a Western European context, is funerary effigies and brasses, the basis as it happens for almost all we know about armour in England before the early 16th century. In some cases monuments serve as a rare source for a particular detail, such as the mail cap worn by Sir William Cantilupe (d.1309) at St Felix's, Felixkirk (North Yorkshire) or the tilting helmet of Sir William Gascoigne (d.1465) at All Saints, Harewood (West Yorkshire). More frequently, however, they represent types that may once have been common but of which few survive: an example from close to home is the armour to the effigy of Sir Richard Cholmondeley at the Tower of London [fig.5], of about 1521.

Paintings, in particular – most effigies have lost any colour they once had – can illustrate the original finishes of armour, notably if once blued, gilded and otherwise decorated but long since the victim of over-cleaning. The portraits of Charles V [56] and of Guidobaldo are examples, and William Dobson's (1611–46) 1644 portrait of the future Charles II, showing an armour in the Royal Armouries collection, another. Works of art can also give an idea of the contexts in which items of arms and armour were used, such as – in a very literal example – a drawing of 1498 by Albrecht Dürer (1471–1528) of a horseman in early Maximilian-style armour and a shallow long-tailed sallet [21, 22], which he later annotated, 'This was the armour at the time in Germany'. So too, for example, do the immensely detailed battle scenes in Mughal manuscripts, such as an illustration in the Ashmolean Museum to the *Hamzanama*, of the 1590s, showing the Prophet's uncle, Amir Hamza, triumphing over a variety of enemies, superhuman, human and otherwise. Most cultures embracing both graphic art and hunting, literate or otherwise, have produced images in many media showing how weapons and other equipment were used in the field, predictable examples being the 17,000-year-old cave paintings at Lascaux (Corrèze, France), or, to make a giant geographical and chronological leap, the 7th-century BC Assyrian Lion Hunt reliefs in the British Museum. Closer to our time, the illustrations in manuscripts of the *Book of the Hunt* by Gaston Fébus of the 1380s, intended partly for instruction, are particularly informative. The Medieval and Renaissance genre of the 'Hunting Tapestry' has also left us many detailed scenes and narratives, such as the fabulous Flemish 'Devonshire Hunting Tapestries' of c.1430–50, in the Victoria & Albert Museum, or the 'Hunts of Maximilian' of 1521–32, in the Metropolitan Museum of Art, New York. Earlier, roughly contemporary, and later Eastern and East Asian art also abounds in enthralling depictions of the hunt, not least, again, in that of the Mughals: among them are the set of late 16th-century illuminations showing the Emperor Akbar (r.1556–1605) variously pursuing antelope, capturing a cheetah and spearing a tigress from the saddle (Victoria & Albert Museum). From a still later period, abundant but incidental information is offered by paintings, such as those of Jean-Baptiste Oudry (1686–1755) or, famously, the many gory close-quarter scenes by Frans Snyders (1579–1657), showing, in terrifying detail, how boar-swords and boar-spears [45, 64] were actually used, and the appalling risks involved. A visit to the fabulous Musée de la Chasse et de

la Nature (Paris), or its partner museum at the Château de Chambord (Loir et Cher), or even their online catalogues, will amply underline the point.

The most direct relationship between art and arms and armour, however, is in the involvement of artists in design, decoration and even manufacture. That this happened is to be expected, given the prestige and cost attached to the finest arms and armour for millennia. Not surprisingly such involvement was a feature of the Renaissance, given the wide range of activities and skills that an artist could boast, or be expected to: Leonardo da Vinci famously bragged about his skill as a military engineer, may have invented the wheel-lock [49], and made futuristic designs for military equipment, including a gigantic crossbow and a form of tank. Michelangelo Buonarotti (1475–1564) designed new defences for Florence's short-lived Republic in 1528–9, thereby taking forward in leaps and bounds the basic principles of European fixed fortifications used until 1914; the Bolognese artist Girolamo da Treviso was killed at the siege of Boulogne whilst working hands-on as a military engineer for Henry VIII. No surprise then that Hans Holbein the Younger (1497–1543), in England at Henry VIII's court in 1526–8 and 1532–40, produced fabulous designs for sword and dagger hilts, and for at least one complete sword, one of which is shown in his cartoon of 1537 for a wall-painting at Whitehall Palace of the king and his father. His work appears on armour too: the engraved and gilded decoration to Henry's garniture for field and tournament (11.8), made in 1540 by Erasmus Kirkenar, Master Workman at Greenwich, includes foliage detail, mermen and lively cherubs based on Holbein's drawings found in his *Englischen Skizzenbuch* ('English Sketchbook') of 1534–38. The actual engraving may have been done by Giovanni di Maiano (c.1486–1542), an important artist in his own right, particularly for his part in introducing Renaissance taste to England. The Augsburg artist Daniel Hopfer (1470–1536) specialised in the etched decoration of armour, such as one of 1536, belonging to Charles V, in the Real Armeria in Madrid, and is thought to be the first to use etching in printmaking: Albrecht Dürer similarly provided decorative designs for the arms and armour of his sovereign, Maximilian I and (incidentally) may have been taught the art of etching by Hopfer. The Flemish artist Adriaen Collaert (1560–1618), also decorated

TREASURES OF THE ROYAL ARMOURIES [23]

Fig.6 | Cast bronze sword hilt made in Italy in the early 17th century, a first-rate if bizarre piece of Renaissance sculpture, and by any standards a work of art. IX.2156

armour himself, and other approximate contemporaries, such as the artists Etienne Delaune, Daniel Hopfer, Virgil Solis and Marcus Gheeraerts the Younger [52], provided source material for armour etchers.

Better still, arms and armour were on occasion not only decorated by professional artists or with their designs, but created by them. Here we might cite the so-called *Furies Gun*, a functioning cannon cast by the Venetian founder Orazio Antonio Alberghetti (1656–90), sculpted by an as-yet-unknown hand, but which holds its own artistically against the most accomplished Renaissance 'fine art' bronzes [90]; it bears an apt inscription, applicable to a good deal of arms and armour, ET POMPA ET USU ('both for show and for use'). A similar case can be made for the cast-bronze sword hilt probably sculpted by Pietro Tacca (1577–1640) in the early 17th century, conceivably for Cosimo II de Medici [fig.6]. The sculptor and goldsmith Benvenuto Cellini (1500–71) tells us in his outrageously boastful *Autobiography* of his highly decorated daggers, 'far more beautiful and durable', of course, than the Turkish models which inspired him. In a few cases an armourer could achieve not only self-evident qualification as an artist through his work, but also the recognition of his peers, a good example being Filippo Negroli of Milan (1510–79) and his brothers, the only members of their profession to be included in Giorgio Vasari's (1511–74) *Lives of the Artists* of 1550, praising his 'work in chasing arms of iron'. Towards the end of the century he was also ecstatically praised by the Milanese connoisseur and historian Paolo Morigia (1525–1604). The best of 17th- and 18th-century wooden horses at the Tower, whilst neither arms nor armour but made to display both, were by the most accomplished English sculptors of the day, including Grinling Gibbons and John Nost, and must qualify at least by association [74]. From a later era, the French gunmaker and brilliant draughtsman Nicolas-Noël Boutet (1761–1833), in charge of the *Manufacture Nationale d'armes à Versailles* after the Revolution and with the near-unique title of *Directeur Artiste*, is also firmly in this category [94].

The most frequent link between artists and arms and armour, however – and as applied to guns in particular from the 17th to the 19th century – was through published designs, either general works applied by gunsmiths to their products, or made specially for them. Prominent among them were Claude Simonin (1635–93), author of *Plusieurs Pieces et Autres Ornements pour les Arquebuziers*, and the Parisian Nicolas Guérard's (1648?-1719) fabulously detailed *Diverses Pièces d'Arquebuserie* of c.1700: both had an enormous influence – Guérard's designs being found on the Armouries 'Simpson' gun [87] and the Tula Garniture [88]. Their contemporary, Jean Bérain (1640–1711) served from 1663 as *Dessinateur de la Chambre et Cabinet du Roi*, effectively chief designer to the court of Louis XIV: the son, interestingly, of a gunsmith, he was a prolific publisher of designs, many made for or used on arms and armour, and some specifically for *arquebusiers*. His designs were also used on weapons for the royal guard [75], mentioned above. Oudry's wonderfully lively works, known through engravings, were frequently used as the basis for scenes and

[24] ARMS, ARMOUR, HISTORY AND CULTURE

Fig.7 | Hilt to a hangar made in Paris in about 1850. It depicts a poacher with his leg caught in a man-trap. In his agony he has dropped his gun, but his powder flask hangs around his neck and the head of a dead duck lolls out of his pocket. IX.5407

vignettes, applied for example to a Viennese flintlock of c.1740 by Hans Georg Schmidt, on which an adaptation of his famous *Fox Hunt* appears on the stock, as it does on the Armouries' Boutet gun given by Napoleon to Charles IV of Spain [94].

The mid 19th century saw a renewed but final flourishing of this practice and of highly decorated gun manufacture. Charles Claesen's (1829–86) gathering together of fantastical neo-gothic and romantic designs in his *Recueil de l'Ornements et de Sujets pour être Appliqués à l'Ornementation des Armes d'après les Dessins des Principaux Artistes* [1857] is an excellent example: it was used in decorating the shotgun made in Paris by Gilles Michel Louis LePage-Moutier [102], for the Great London Exposition of 1862, and won the highest praise in the catalogue – note the title – *Masterpieces of Industrial Art and Sculpture at the International Exhibition 1862*. Other pieces of extraordinary mid-19th century virtuosity in the Royal Armouries collection include the wonderful silver hilt to a hangar (a hunting sword), the combined work of a Prussian goldsmith Jules Wièse (1818–90) and the Parisian goldsmith François-Désiré Froment-Meurice (1802–55), taking the form of a poacher in 18th-century dress [fig.7]. Such creations led the author Victor Hugo to describe Froment-Meurice in an Ode (no less) of 1841 as 'the new Benvenuto Cellini' – high praise indeed.

The artistic properties of arms and armour, and their appreciation as works of art, have also been roundly and unquestionably assumed by collectors and institutions in relatively recent times. This was particularly so in the mid-19th century, when collections of arms and armour were assembled as works of art on the same footing as paintings, such as those of Ralph Bernal (sold at auction in 1855) or Hollingworth Magniac (sold in 1892, but complete by 1867), or the Asian arms and armour assembled by the fourth Marquess of Hertford (1800–70) and the European armour collected by his son Sir Richard Wallace (1818–1890), now part of the Wallace Collection.

The status of such things was underlined by luxury publications, mostly French, such as Léon-Auguste Asselineau's *Meubles et Armures Anciennes* (c.1844) or Alexandre du Sommerard's *Les Arts au Moyen Age* (1838–46), and in the major historical exhibitions such as the South Kensington Museum Loan Exhibition of 1862, which included a large section entitled 'Decorative Arms and Armour'. In the same vein, it is no coincidence that the Metropolitan Museum of Art in New York, a 'national institution and a gallery of art', has one of the finest collections of decorated arms and armour in the world.

Allied to this, the artistic and aesthetic qualities of arms and armour give them the power to excite interest in people who otherwise would pass them by. Sometime in the 1970s the editor's grandmother cut short his would-be learned ramble about a museum exhibit, along the lines of 'yes, darling, but

TREASURES OF THE ROYAL ARMOURIES [25]

isn't it *beautiful*?'. How right. The simple aesthetic appeal of many arms, armours and related items – including dozens described below – offers a straightforward and instinctive route to enjoying them and opens the door to real enthusiasm and curiosity: witness the case of Wallace himself, and the many Fine Art curators who have become arms and armour specialists, including a former Master of the Armouries, Sir James Mann.

In contrast to the kind of fabulously decorated items described above, deliberately beautiful or at least deliberately impressive, it is worth adding that arms and armour, like many functional items, could achieve real beauty through their simplicity and obvious utility. Among these, although aesthetic effect was undoubtedly intended, is the Armouries' South German late-15th century 'Gothic armour for man and horse', the epitome of the 'knight in shining armour' of chivalric legend, beautiful thanks to its sculptural form and lively and superbly executed and very loosely zoomorphic fluting [19]. A very different example is the 28-bore side-by-side shotgun by (and on loan from) Holland and Holland, the London gunmaker, absolutely minimally decorated but of eye-catchingly perfect line and form. Much simpler pieces can also achieve great aesthetic success, if of a different sort, through their obvious blend of successful form and function. This is often the case with swords – perhaps most famously in that of the un-mounted Japanese sword blade (xxvi s.238) – and, dependent on personal taste, the plainest automatic or revolving pistol. The Sealed Pattern 1908 British cavalry sword [107], the last designed for such use, certainly has a form of beauty in its clean and sinister lines, although Edward vii's declaration that it was 'hideous' is a reminder that such things are in the eye of the beholder.

Arms, armour, meaning and symbolism

Throughout history, and clearly since the Neolithic period of prehistory (approximately 10,000–3500 BC), certain items of arms armour were, as can be deduced from archaeological evidence, held not just to be useful, but also to be imbued with sacred and symbolic properties. Roughly speaking these might be said to fall into five categories: first, weapons or armour used for, or put to, a religious purpose, or indeed actually made for one; second, arms and armour for practical use, but which were believed to hold intrinsic spiritual properties and powers which benefited the user; third, arms and armour bearing religious symbols or inscriptions which were believed to endow them with, or call upon, supernatural power; fourth, and closely allied, decoration which proclaimed the religious allegiance and piety of the wearer; and finally, items endowed with a special quasi-spiritual status as symbols of civic pride and nationhood, or as mementos of great men or great events. Arms and armour have also been used for millennia as trophies, commemorating the victory, usually, of one state or dynasty over another. In addition, arms and armour has played a role in creating and identifying particular social groups, demarcating status, and forming the structure of entire social and political systems.

Such properties originate, ultimately, in the capacity of arms and armour to save or take life – both, in most cultures, deemed susceptible to divine intervention – and which could dispatch a warrior or victim from this world to the next. As a result, and thanks to the special skills required, it is not surprising that the makers of arms and armour, in addition to their products, could take on a very special place in society, in mythology and even as deities. Among the superhuman variety are Wayland, the smith and weapon-maker appearing in many of the tangled strands of early medieval Norse and Germanic mythology, and (if perhaps more historically) in Hebrew legend, and concerning a much earlier time, Tubal-Cain, great-grandson of Cain, 'forger of all instruments of bronze and iron' (Genesis 4:22) and held to be the 'first blacksmith'. In Japan, from the 7th century AD the blacksmith Amakuni is credited in legend with the Japanese sword roughly as we know it and having gained immortality through his achievements. As for deities, the best-known in the West are Hephaestus (Greek: Vulcan to the Romans), god of fire and metalworking, and the Norse god Thor, whose hammer, *Mjollnir*, is surely a blacksmith's, and who was implicated in making magical weapons. A rough equivalent from the East is Tvastar, blacksmith of the Hindu gods.

Turning to the use of arms and armour for religious purposes, the most abundant and best-known is the votive use of arms and armour, in particular the former. This could take the form of ritual 'deposition', involving loss, use as grave goods, or display on sacred premises: all these practices were aimed in one way or another to propitiate divine favour, forestall divine displeasure, or equip the dead for the afterlife.

'Deposition' is known in the West from the Neolithic and early Bronze Age onwards, well-studied examples English including that of Great Baddow (Essex) where six flint axes of varying colour and form and a discoidal knife were found carefully arranged together. Bronze axes were deposited at a variety of wetland and dry land sites across Europe, ending the working lives of powerful weapons but enhancing their value as gifts to supernatural beings. Examples from the Iron Age include the timber causeway complex over the river Witham at Fiskerton (Lincolnshire), renowned for its incremental and piecemeal offerings of swords, spears and shields, echoing the more dramatic displays of seized trophies and martial offerings laid on bridge-like structures at the 'type site' of La Tène in Switzerland. In the case of the Witham Valley, the practice continued well into the Middle Ages, demonstrating the perennial allure of votive deposition, even when this had no place in the official religion of the people concerned. In some cases, items were specially made for votive deposition, such as the ostentatious 'super-sized' Bronze Age dirk from Oxborough (Norfolk), impossible to wield, but which magnified the meaning of such blades. Conversely, from the Bronze Age, miniaturisation could create compressed versions of the real thing, condensing their value in a symbolic surrogate, as in those found at the hilltop sanctuary of Nettleton Top (Lincolnshire).

In many cultures arms and armour have been held to be endowed to varying extents with magical powers and intrinsic spiritual significance and even personalities, as not least in having names. In this sphere, swords, of all weapons, hold pride of place, and have done so since their first appearance in the Bronze Age, thanks fundamentally to their beautiful simplicity, deadly effect, and close-quarter operation as an extension of the human arm. Obsolete today, they remain part of the insignia of soldiers across the world, appearing on the badges and heraldry of states and individuals, and in civil life are paired with the scales as a symbol of justice. Instances of swords being held to have magical properties, names and even personalities abound, famously, for example, in the Norse and Germanic legend and literature of the early Middle Ages: as with other cultures that had comparable mythology, we can assume that warriors fully believed their weapons were imbued with magical properties. A well-known literary example from the West is the 'rare and ancient sword' named Hrunting, given to Beowulf by Unferth, and used in his fight with Grendel's mother. This is trumped by King Arthur's sword, variously named in the Middle Ages and of complex etymology but since the 15th century usually called *Excalibur*, along with *Galatine*, given to Sir Gawain by the Lady of the Lake. Among dozens of others are those named in the 11th-century *Song of Roland* – his own, *Durandal*, and *Almace*, belonging to Turpin, Archbishop of Reims. St George's sword, too, had a name – *Ascalon*, today beloved of the war-gaming and fantasy fraternity. In the Muslim world the best known is probably *Zulfiqar* (etymology unknown) of Ali [Ali Ibn Abi Talib], ward and relative of the Prophet, regarded by Shia Muslims as his successor and a crucial figure in Islamic history. No such sword still exists, but it is abundantly represented, with its distinctive double point, in graphics, heraldry and insignia, especially those of Shia origin. For Hindus, the sword *Pattayudha*, weapon of Virabhada, a warlike form of the god Shiva, is probably the most renowned, and has been since at least 1000 BC. Armour, too, could be held to have supernatural powers: examples are legion, but to return to *Beowulf* and Arthur, include the mail shirt the hero wore in fighting Grendel, and (according to 12th-century retellings) the king's 'golden helmet with a crest carved in the shape of a dragon' (later, *Goswhit*), and his shield *Pridwen*.

But for a reader of any nation or culture today, it is Japan that most readily springs to mind in the context of the cultural and spiritual attributes and importance of swords. Since the 7th century AD, the weapons themselves have been famously sharp but strong, with a graceful curve and delicate patterns in the steel, giving beauty to the metal itself; at the same time, their creators and their work have always been solemnised through ritual and ceremony. Once in use, a sword became embedded as a fundamental part of its owner's identity, inextricably interwoven with the status, appearance, codes of behaviour and honour of the *samurai*. A warrior's sword became part of him, and his spirit would remain associated with it after death. Consequently, Japanese swords possess a spiritual essence, almost as if they are living entities in their own right: a particularly famous example was the *Honjo Masamune*, now lost, made by Gorō Nygūdō Masamune (1264–1343). In Japan today, large numbers of historic swords have been carefully preserved, passed down through generations and frequently given to shrines as votive offerings, studied in great scholarly depth, and admired as works of art. Several practicing swordsmiths are ranked as living National Treasures due to their acknowledged place in the cultural heritage of Japan. The popularity and reputation of the Japanese sword has also made it a common and instantly recognisable motif in popular culture.

In the case of arms and armour imbued with or inviting divine protection, or through proclaiming the user's piety, an example close to home is Henry VIII's Tonlet armour of 1520 [34], prepared specifically for what came to be called the Field of Cloth of Gold tournament. It displays St George, patron saint of England, and the Virgin and Child on each side of the great bacinet skull: the images also had the implicit purpose of seeking their blessing and protection, but were also, perhaps, positioned to distract an opponent and deter blows. For similar reasons the cuirass of Henry's garniture for field and tournament of *c*.1515 depicts the gruesome martyrdoms of St George and St Barbara, patrons, amongst other things, of soldiers and those in danger of sudden death. Weapons too could bear such images, including the Royal Armouries' *Messer*, a single-edged sword of about 1500 [26], decorated with images of St Barbara and St Katherine of Alexandria in their capacities as patron saints of knife grinders. Decoration and messages invoking divine protection were not, obviously, confined to European products, but were routinely used throughout parts of the world: the museum's Chinese Ming dynasty sword-hilt of about 1420 [15], associated with Tibet and displaying a blend of Hindu and Buddhist imagery, is a spectacular Asiatic example: the centrepiece of the design is a monstrous visage making up the hand guard, representing themes of the two religions, both of which were intended to give protection to its user. In a variation on the theme are items whose symbolic form or decoration was not only intended to protect the wearer but to proclaim his faith and commitment, as in the case of the late 15th-century Turkish helmet or 'Turban helm' [24], bearing an inscription declaring this faith and allegiance to his ruler. Similarly, the shape and decoration of the Royal Armouries 'Quoit turban' [83], made for an elite Sikh warrior (*Akali*, or 'immortal') in the 18th century, all underlined the wearer's commitment to the faith and the divine favour that ensued, in addition to actually incorporating throwing weapons (the 'Quoits'). Quotations from holy books, on or associated with arms and armour, could also be deemed to increase their effectiveness, such as – to pick two very diverse examples – the paraphrases of Psalm 144 inscribed on the Norse and Germanic '*Benedictus*' swords of the 8th to 12th centuries, or the passages from the Qu'ran traditionally stitched into the quilted cotton armour of Hausa warriors in northern Nigeria.

Some of the items described in this volume (and many others besides) entered the Royal Armouries collection as trophies, or had served as trophies in the past – that is, items captured from an enemy and used as permanent symbols and reminders of the victor's prowess and righteousness. This is probably the most blatant, obvious and best known of the symbolic roles of arms and armour, and is no doubt as ancient as the objects themselves. A famous example of the practice is Delphi, the holiest place in pre-Christian Greece, where the early 5th-century BC 'Treasury of the Athenians', still standing in restored state, was bedecked with captured weapons: an inscription reads, 'The Athenians dedicated this treasury together with the arms and prows [of ships] which they seized from the enemy', referring to the victories over the Persians at Marathon (490 BC) and ten years later, at sea at Salamis. The 'treasuries' of other cities stood nearby, with similar contents. Similarly at the Greek temple and sanctuary at Ephesus (Izmir Province, Turkey), captured weapons were deposited by the representatives of many states, and displayed there in thanks for divine favour. As discussed below, comparable practice was in many ways responsible for the origins of the Royal Armouries museum, and indeed of many others [80]. In more recent times, some countries have run state-managed programmes of distributing trophies across their provinces: a prominent English instance is of the 89 bronze and 875 iron cannon brought back from the Crimea in 1857, many of which were distributed to British towns, cities and overseas territories for public display. Outside Ludlow Castle (Shropshire), for example, stands a two-tonne gun inscribed 'Captured 1855 at Sevastopol' and described at the time as a 'great trophy of national valour'. The exercise was repeated across the country after 1918 – including at Ludlow – although the more complex artillery of the time fared less well outdoors, and ironically many examples were scrapped for the war effort in 1940. Overseas, the Dominion governments too asked London for war trophies for public display, and certainly displayed their own, and sent others to England: indeed, Canada's

III · The Royal Armouries: History and Collection

Arms and armour at the Tower of London in the Middle Ages

state archivist was appointed Controller of War Trophies and responsible for a programme of collection, distribution and display. Using metal from captured guns weapons to make other commemorative items has also had a long, long history: in a British context this has applied most famously, since 1857, in making Victoria Crosses, using bronze from a particular Chinese cannon.

Displaying arms and armour to boost national and dynastic pride was not, obviously, confined to the West. The 6th-century church of Hagia Eirene (Holy Peace) in Istanbul, later enclosed within the outer courtyard of the Topkapı Palace, was used by the Ottomans from 1453 both as an arsenal for their elite infantry, the Janissaries, but also – in a close analogy with the Tower of London – as a place to display military trophies. This included material captured from the Savafid Persians in 1514, from the Mamluk Sultanate of Syria and Egypt in 1517, and from many Christian opponents of Turkish expansion [23]. When the Janissaries were disbanded in 1826, Hagia Eirene became, for a while, a museum – another parallel with the Tower. On similar lines, in 14th – and 15th-century Alexandria, the Mamluk Sultans kept a sacred arsenal of weapons captured in war or received as tribute, including 170 swords from between 1367 and 1436 celebrating the faith and military prowess of the dynasty. The Royal Armouries possesses one of them, dated to the fourteenth century and of Italian origin, bearing an Arabic inscription which translates as 'The pious donation of [the] King al-Ashraf Barsbāy – May his victory be strengthened! In the storeroom [in] the Hall of Victories in … Alexandria the well-guarded' [9].

Since 1996, the organisation's headquarters, most staff and collection items have been based or kept at the purpose-built museum in Leeds. The story of the Armouries begins, however, at the Tower of London, itself originating in one of two castles planted in the newly captured city by William the Conqueror in 1066. Its immediate purpose was as a refuge for the king, his troops, horses and equipment, as a base from which to put down rebellion, and as a permanent physical symbol of Norman rule. With the building of the White Tower – the famous great tower or keep which gave the place its name – the supremacy of this castle was assured, and the other (on the site of what became Baynard's Castle) was soon downgraded. Today the Tower is one of the best-preserved and largest castles in Europe, and unquestionably one of the best-known: unlike most European capitals, whose great royal fortresses have either vanished or been wholly rebuilt (witness the Louvre in Paris, the Hofburg in Vienna, or the Alcázar in Madrid), London's retains most of its medieval defences intact. As a fortress it was a failure: it was several times captured, was hopelessly out of date by 1500, and ceased to serve as a readily usable royal palace in the 13th century. In its other functions, however, it was supremely successful, among them – the most important and enduring – as an arsenal and a place of military administration. In the former lie the origins of the Royal Armouries collection, and in the latter those of the institution.

From the first weeks of its existence, as an improvised earth and timber arrangement in the corner of Roman city walls, the castle housed armed men. The storage and repair of their equipment must then have been part of its daily life: picture the wonderful embarkation scene in the Bayeux Tapestry, of the men carrying hauberks, bundles of swords, following a cart laden with serried ranks of spears and helmets. Note too the wine, equally important, in skins and barrels.

How these activities were managed in the late 11th and most of the 12th century is unknown, although the ancestors of the departments of state which were later responsible for it existed in embryonic form by the reign of Henry II (r.1154–1189), under the household function called the 'chamber' (from the king's most private apartment), and its officers, the chamberlains. From this developed the Privy Wardrobe, a government department responsible for the provision of arms and armour for the king and his wars: 'Privy' differentiated it from the 'Great Wardrobe', responsible for managing a broader range

of possessions, while 'Wardrobe' – *garderoba* in the Latin accounts – derived from its management of the king's clothes and textiles. Medieval kings were frequently on the move, and the Privy Wardrobe staff went with them, although operating a regional network of stores at royal castles and other places across the country; those closest to any real or potential action functioned as points for assembling and distributing arms and armour for official use. The Tower of course was one of them, and by 1325 already had some special status, as John Fleet, Keeper (*custos*) of the Privy Wardrobe from then until his death in 1344, was styled 'clerk and keeper of the king's privy wardrobe at the Tower', suggesting some sort of permanent presence. Its rise to special prominence, however, began in 1338, when it was formally chosen as the fixed home of the Privy Wardrobe, now no longer itinerant: Fleet now became 'keeper of the jewels, armour and other things', including the Mint, and later also 'Keeper of the King's armour in the Tower', aided by assistants, the 'Yeomen of the Kings Armour'. From this time onwards inventories show a standing armoury at the castle. Fleet was succeeded by ten more Keepers, all with broadly similar duties, although after 1361 the Great Wardrobe, housed largely outside the Tower in Blackfriars, was also in their charge. The last Keeper, Simon Fleet, was in office from 1407 to 1415, the year of the battle of Agincourt, although the post survived until 1428.

The work of the Keepers and the castle essentially consisted of the procurement, manufacture, repair, storage, and issue and recall of arms and armour. The Keepers were able to order and purchase material from independent London-based manufacturers – some of whom were from abroad – or imported from the Low Countries, Germany, Italy or Spain; they also had some rights to impress key craftsmen into occasional royal service. In the 1350s, for example, Keeper Rothwell was appointed to

take in London and elsewhere as many armourers, fletchers, smiths and other artificers for the works of armour, bows, bow-strings, arrows, arrow heads ... also to buy 1000 bows, painted and white, 10,000 sheaves of the best arrows with heads hard and well steeled.

He also ordered much else, including chests for storing archery equipment. With the outbreak of the Hundred Years War in 1337, the demands of the English armies which fought at Crécy, Poitiers and elsewhere meant that the quantities of material it handled were truly enormous – those of arrows, for example, frequently running into hundreds of thousands within a few years, such as the 891,912 supplied between 1344 and 1351. Arms and armour were also made in the Tower by permanent employees, including, from the early 14th century at least, armour specifically for the king and his inner circle. These were made by 'King's armourers', such as a certain John de Colonia, active from the 1330s, if primarily a tailor. More ordinary material was also made and repaired in small quantities at the Tower by resident craftsmen and in purpose-built workshops.

Over time the types and quantities of arms and armour issued from the Tower varied considerably, From 1361 to 1377 the Tower was handling smaller quantities of archery equipment but more armour for archers, but thereafter the

Fig.8 | Scene from the Bayeux Tapestry, embroidered in England in the late 11th century and depicting the key events prior to and during the Norman Conquest. It shows Duke William's fleet embarking in Picardy, but could equally depict the movement of arms, armour and equipment at the Tower of London in its very earliest years.
Courtesy of the City of Bayeux

Fig.9 | Engraving of *c*.1864 of the funerary brass of William Rothwell, Keeper of the Privy Wardrobe, the government department which managed the maintenance, procurement and issuing of arms and armour from the Tower of London, the second in a series of eleven in office from 1323 to 1415. The brass, of 1361, survives at the church of Holy Trinity, Rothwell, in Northamptonshire.

Fig.10 | A gun from Castle Rising in Norfolk, on loan to the Armouries. Guns of this form – of wrought iron 'hoop and stave' construction and loaded at the breech – were kept and made at the Tower in the late 14th and 15th centuries. AL 14.1, 3

emphasis shifted, very importantly, to guns or 'ordnance'. The first association of the Tower with gunpowder, however, occurs in the accounts for 1333–4, very early in the history of its use in Europe [13], recording the purchase of saltpetre and sulphur, which can have been used for little else. By the mid 1340s guns were clearly being stored there, as shown by the accounts for 1344–51 under Keeper Robert Mildenhall, who sent ten of them, with powder, ingredients for powder, lead bullets and arrows to be fired from them [13,17, 18], to Calais. Possibly some ordnance was then being made on site, but this was certainly the case by the early 1370s under Keeper John Sleaford (in office 1365–78). The products included guns 'with pots' (that is, wrought-iron breech-loaders), as in those from Castle Rising (Norfolk), the earliest-known guns of English provenance, one of which is displayed in the White Tower [fig.10]. Handguns were also being made there, in their earliest form comprising short iron barrels fixed to the end of long shafts, sticks or 'stocks' – hence the modern term – usually fired whilst propped on a forked rest, in an embrasure or from a parapet [16, 23].

Storing arms and armour within the cramped confines of the Tower was clearly a problem, but its importance is shown by the solution – the invasion of high-status domestic interiors. One example is St Thomas's Tower, otherwise known as 'Traitors' Gate', built in the 1270s by Edward I to house his most important private chambers: here, in the 1270s, hooks were installed for the storage of crossbows [fig.11]. Similarly, in 1382 the bedroom of Richard II's consort Anne of Bohemia, and the Great Hall of the royal palace, were commandeered

TREASURES OF THE ROYAL ARMOURIES [31]

for stores and workshops, while cannon balls had to be hastily removed from the king's apartments before his arrival for Christmas in 1387. By the early 16th century the royal lodgings had been almost wholly given over to munitions storage, and in 1639 a giant warehouse was built within the shell of the long-ruined hall. Meanwhile, its function as an arsenal and supply base had a major impact on other parts of the castle fabric, in particular the eastward extension of the Tower Wharf, begun in the 1330s and completed in 1389, directed by a royal Clerk of Works, one Geoffrey Chaucer (1343–1400) in his day-job capacity.

In the last decades of the 14th century the Privy Wardrobe remained firmly in control, but in the first half of the next it was eclipsed by two new departments – the Office of Ordnance and the Office of Armoury. This was partly thanks to increasing emphasis on ordnance, evident from the 1370s and accelerated by Henry v's campaigns in France, for which vast numbers were issued. Some ordnance was still being made at the Tower, such as by William Gerardson, gunner, and by 1427 their products and others seem to have been kept in an 'artillery house' that probably stood, like its successors, to the north of the White Tower.

With this new emphasis came the emergence of officials who combined practical administrative skills and military experience, such as John Hampton, who occupied, intermittently, the new posts of Master of Ordnance and Serjeant of the Armoury, the former being made a permanent appointment in 1450. The Hundred Years War ended in 1453, but with the outbreak of the 'Wars of the Roses' in 1455, activity ramped up again: in May 1460, for example forty wagons of ordnance were sent from the Tower to Henry vi's central base at Kenilworth Castle (Warwickshire), which continued to be supplied from there. After Henry Tudor's victory over the Yorkist Richard iii, gun-making continued with the aid of Breton gun founders, and the 1495 survey of Sir Robert Clifford, Master of Ordnance 1495–1508, shows that the tower held a large and varied quantity of ordnance.

Other equipment and armour continued to be made at the Tower throughout the remainder of the century. This included material for the king himself and his entourage, and since the very early 15th century the king's principal armourer, firmly based at the Tower, had been referred to variously as 'armourer of the king in the Tower', 'armourer of the body of the king',

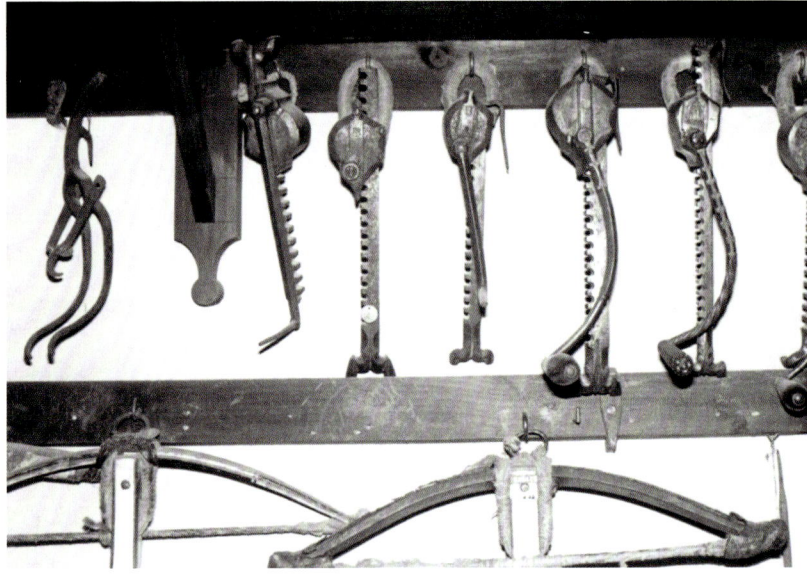

'serjeant armourer of the king', or 'serjeant of the armoury': his tasks included producing and supplying items for the king's own use, oversight of the remaining armour stores, buying in fresh supplies, and organising the production of armour by other London-based craftsmen. John Hill and Martin Pull, appointed 'armourers of the body of the king' in 1408 and 1413 respectively, for example, delivered breastplates, vambraces, rerebraces, helms, and bacinets to the Privy Wardrobe for Henry v's use early in his reign. After the appointment of John Stanley in 1437, the Serjeant of the Armoury was no longer personally involved in manufacture, and his post became purely managerial. He and his juniors sometimes lodged within the castle, as in the case of 'yeoman armourer of the body' in 1437, who had the use of a chamber, kitchen, woodshed, and workshop.

By the end of the century the Offices of Armoury and Ordnance were settled comfortably at the Tower. From 1485, under the supervision of Henry vii's leading supporter and household controller, Sir Richard Guildford of Rolvenden in Kent, they underwent a ten-year period of renewal. This was continued by Clifford, his successor, although for all this, by European standards the king's artillery still left much to be desired.

'Many great cannon': the Tower and its armoury as a showplace, c.1480–1660

The use of the Tower for the storage, manufacture and distribution of arms and armour did not, of course, end with the Middle Ages, but continued, periodically waxing and waning in importance, until the middle of the 19th century. It was this function that was to prompt and permit the deliberate display of arms and armour for which the Tower remains celebrated

Fig. 11 | Part of the armoury at the castle of Churburg, in the South Tyrol, in the Middle Ages the seat of the Matsch family, and since 1537 the Trapps, showing crossbows and cranequins – mechanisms for spanning them – hanging on a rack. Although a modern arrangement, it follows medieval precedent, of a type likely to have been found at the Tower in the 14th century. *Photograph courtesy of Thom Richardson*

today: it also gave the castle a useful purpose, ensuring its survival and dictating the use and design of most of its internal buildings – a reminder that the history of the Armouries is wholly indissoluble from that of the castle and the institution of the Ordnance Office.

As it happens, independent of arms and armour, the story of the Tower itself as a spectacle dates from the building of the gigantic White Tower, designed, above all, to impress: in the Middle Ages it was rivalled as one of the city's sights only by the first stone bridge (completed 1209) and (Old) St Paul's, and is named in descriptions of the city in 1173 and 1324. By the early 13th century the building had gained further prestige through its attribution to the fictional Brutus, supposed founder of the British nation, and by the 1330s to Julius Caesar – a myth that persisted until the 17th century. By 1210 the castle gained further kudos as the home of lions, beasts with powerful royal and heraldic associations, and from the mid-century a whole menagerie, including, in 1259, an elephant. As these were housed in an outer barbican at the western entrance – by the 1530s the 'Lyons towre' – they were easily seen and easily heard, and it was with the establishment of the menagerie that the Tower's history as a 'visitor attraction' can be said to start. The zoo remained in the Tower until 1831 when some of the animals were moved to Regents Park where, from 1847, they were displayed to the public in what became known as the London Zoo by the Royal Zoological Society.

Given the Tower's fame and prominence, it was a short step from showing off the beasts and buildings to showing off the buildings' contents. Displaying the king's jewels made a point about the king's wealth, while weapons and armour – along with the castle itself – demonstrated the military might of the nation and its ruler. The first recorded experience of its effect dates from 1489, when a nobleman and soldier from Franconia (Germany), Wilwolt von Schaumberg (*c.*1446–1510), visited the Tower with his future biographer, Ludwig von Eyb. There they were shown 'many great cannon quartans and a culverin, which shoot forth balls of iron, with many other culverins and stone cannon, the like of which are no longer seen elsewhere': as it happened, alas, the professional soldier from the hard school of ceaseless European warfare was not very impressed. Similar views were opined by the next two known visitors: first, an unidentified Italian visitor, and second, Jacob Rathgar, secretary of Frederick, Duke of Württemberg, who noted that on 22 or 23 August 1603 'his Highness was shown the Tower of London, as well as the Mint and the Armoury therein, which, however is not indeed to be compared with the German armouries, for although there are many fine cannon in it, yet they are full of dust, and stand about in great disorder'. Tellingly, though, Paul Hentzner – another German who visited in 1598 – thought that 'eight or nine men, employed by the year, are scarce sufficient to keep all the arms bright'. Efforts were clearly being made to show things to advantage.

This material was stored in a building on the site of the existing Waterloo Block to the north of the White Tower, possibly that of 1427, and described as a 'house of ordnance' 1497 and in 1501. By 1536, however, it was on its last legs and Sir Francis Flemyng, Lieutenant of the Ordnance, was granted £2,894 to 'erect and new buylde one house wherein all the Kinges Ordinance and Municions may be kepte'. The new structure, built 1545–7, soon known as the 'Long House of Ordnance', timber-framed on a brick base, was at least two storeys high and covered a larger area than any building in the Tower. It is known from an aerial *plan cavalier* of 1597 [fig.12], a print of 1666–7 by Wenceslaus Hollar, and others of the 1680s.

Importantly, this time special 'rackes' were set up for hanging weapons, some in special rooms, 'whereon all the Kinges maieties riche Weapons of his own person should be kepte'; grouping the 'riche' material together would have been convenient, but also facilitated their display. And by now, rather than simply letting curious visitors see the Tower's treasures, their active display seems to have been official and normal practice – witness the order by William Earl of Southampton on 16 September 1539 to Thomas Cromwell, concerning Frederick II, Count of the Palatine (1482–1556), that 'You shall after a visit to Windsor show him the Tower and Ordnance, if you think it advisable'. (The count duly paid his visit and admired the treasury, although made no mention of arms and armour.) In Elizabeth's reign this seems to have become still more routine, as suggested by the Privy Council's order in 1578 to show a certain 'Monsieur Kentell, gentleman of High Almagnye [Germany] the Tower of London and 'suche thinges as are *usuallie* [italics added] shewed therin'. By then, and probably from Henry VIII's time, visitors were shown the

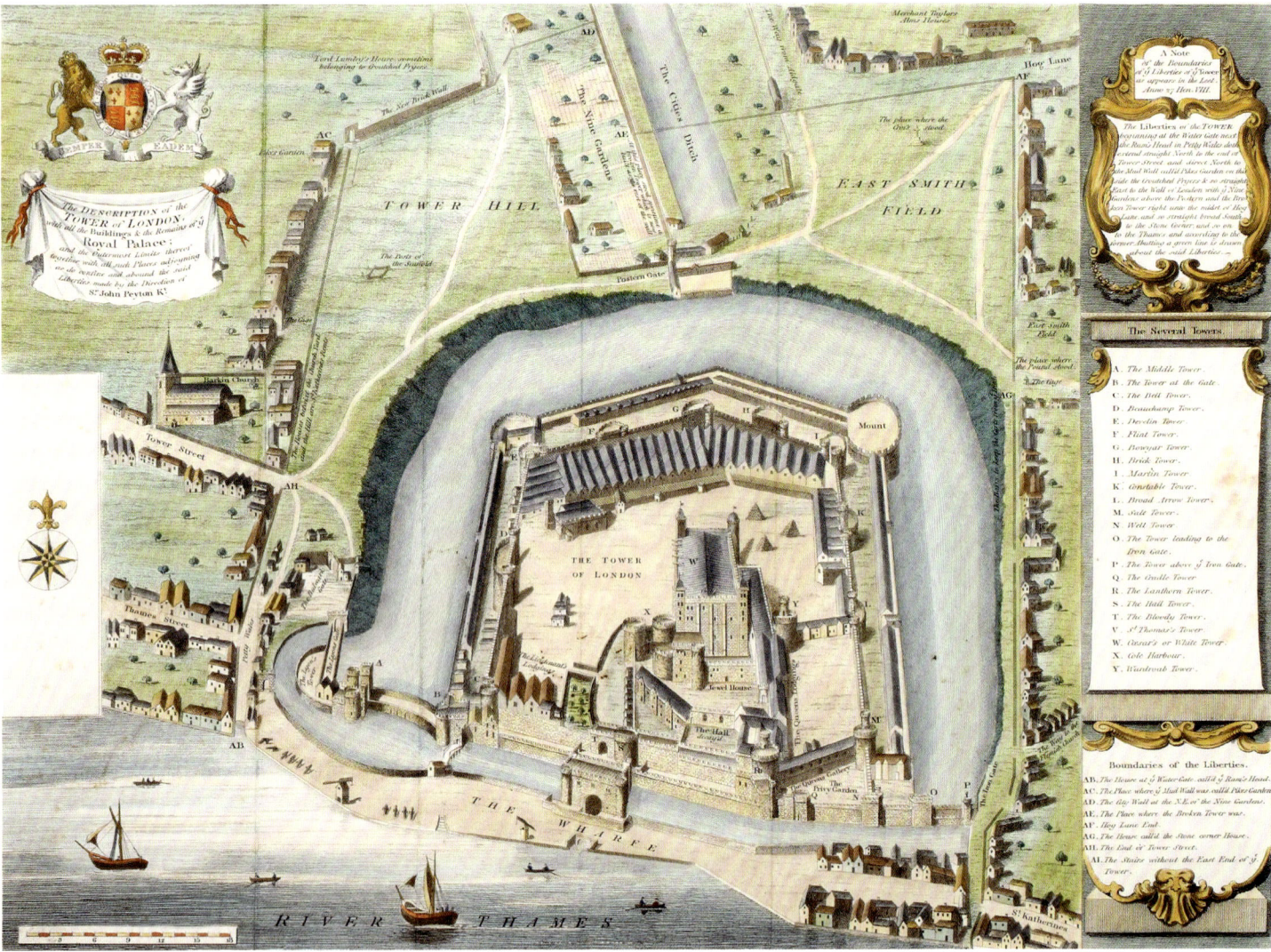

sights by the Yeoman Warders. They were originally employed as the King's gaolers at the Tower; from 1550 they were permitted to wear the full-dress uniform of the Yeoman of the Guard, and in the 17th century became known as 'beefeaters'. Their role was fundamentally important in the development of the Tower as a showplace, giving scripted tours, and taking separate fees for showing off the various sights, although at least in the next century Ordnance staff had a role too: in 1688 the Deputy Keeper of the Armoury was paid £52 10s in compensation for what he might have earned from 'shewing the Armoury – being the most considerable perquisite of the Plais, Occasioned by the Demolishing of the ye Old Storehouse'. As today, tours were enlivened by occasional deviation from the facts. By at least 1686, for example, the 'Holy Water Sprinkler' – a Henry VIII-period *Morgenstern* (a long-handled spiked mace) fitted with three guns, which is still on display in the White Tower – was billed as the late king's 'walking staffe'; visitors were told of an occasion when, carrying it in disguise on a nightly perambulation, the king was arrested by his own guard (who, being 'bluff', 'King Hal' pardoned with a few jokes) [36]. Other items were given spurious or 'wishful-thinking' provenances, such as a large field armour of 1540 (again, still on display), by the 1620s, described as the armour of John of Gaunt (1340–99), a famously tall man; the 'Horned Helmet' [30] was held at least from 1638 to have belonged to Will Somers, the king's jester, thanks to its comical appearance.

Facilitated and encouraged by the special accommodation provided for the king's 'riche weapons', the cult of Henry VIII was already evident at the Tower in his own lifetime, but it was under his daughter Elizabeth I that this came into its own, with a heavy emphasis on his own arms and armour and his supporting cast's. Most visitors who left records were clearly pointed to items such as the lance of Charles Brandon, Duke of Suffolk [32], the king's friend, jousting partner and brother-in-law. Among them were Lupold von Wedel in 1584, and John-Ernest, Duke of Saxe-Weimar who in 1613 noted

[34] HISTORY AND COLLECTION

Fig.12 | Engraving of 1742 reproducing a lost original of 1597. The many-gabled building occupying the whole of the far side of the inner ward, to the north of the White Tower, was the 'Long House of Ordnance, built in 1545–7. Its enormous size illustrates the importance of the Tower of London as an arsenal in the 16th century.

'Two cannon of immense size, made of wood, which Henry VIII took with him to strike terror into the enemy before Boulogne'. In the last months of the queen's reign the Duke of Würtemberg was intrigued to see 'the long barrel and stock which belonged to the last King Henry, father of her present Majesty; this he is said to have carried on his saddle, and it may be compared with a musket'. An anonymous Polish visitor of 1633 was shown 'Henry VIII's sword, so heavy that two men could hardly lift it' – another reference to the king's physical prowess.

For unofficial, personal visitors, viewing this material was unlikely to be cheap, and indeed it did not become affordable for regular visitors until the mid 19th century. In 1599 the Swiss physician Thomas Platter had to make eight different payments, the first, of three shillings, in one of the armouries in the White Tower, 'to a keeper in attendance', adding up to twenty-one shillings in total; Lady Judith Barrington spent eleven shillings visiting the place in 1639, and in 1660 the Scottish soldier of fortune General Patrick Gordon's collective payments amounted to no less than thirty-three shillings – enough to pay a workman for four months. Nevertheless, by the early 17th century the Tower was receiving less exalted people, as revealed in lines by Henry Pecham (1578–1644), author of *The Compleat Gentleman* of 1622. They ask:

> 'Why do the rude & vulgar so hastily post [go] in a madnesse
> To gaze at trifles, and toyes not worth the viewing?
> And think them happy, when may be shew'd for a penny …

Pecham went on to name items such as 'The lance of John a Gaunt and Charles Brandon's still in the Tower'. By the middle of the 17th century, therefore, complete with special displays, guided tours, fees and a good social mix of visitors, the stage was set for the more sophisticated display of arms and armour over the next two centuries.

'A mere assemblage of curiosities'?
A museum in all but name, 1660–1895

The Tower's function as a showplace rapidly came to the fore after the Restoration even as it began to give ground as an arsenal to places such as Chatham and Woolwich. By then, however, the Tower Armoury's displays were, overall, already more sophisticated than the 'mere assemblage of curiosities' to which John Hewitt, Ordnance Storekeeper, feared arms and armour was relegated in the public mind in the 1840s. The word 'museum', however, was never formally part of the organisation's title until 1983 (although it may have been loosely described as such by staff and visitors): in its pre-1983 incarnation it was simply the 'Tower Armouries'. Since the word 'museum' was first used in its modern sense with the foundation of the Ashmolean in 1683, it can be said that the activities and public offer at the Tower, at least from the 1680s, constituted a museum in all but name – both in 17th-century and modern parlance. Nevertheless, the year 1660, with the return of the Stuart monarchy, was to have momentous consequences, and ushered in a new chapter in the history of arms and armour at the Tower.

The Interregnum of 1649–1660, the short-lived republican era that followed the defeat and execution of Charles I in 1649, saw the sale of most of the king's fabulous art collection and the seizure and almost total destruction of the state regalia and plate (kept at the Tower) and the Crown Jewels. Fortunately, arms and armour fared rather better, although much was lost, including all but the famous 'Horned Helmet' of the armour given to Henry VIII by Maximilian I [30]. Moreover, during the Interregnum, the Tower not only remained open to well-heeled visitors, but its armoury gained new material brought from Greenwich Palace, including 'rich Gilt Armors of his Late Majesties' [59]. By 1660, ten armours, each mounted on 'a horse of wood' and representing royalty and noblemen, had been housed in the Lieutenant's house (the 'Queen's House'). These were at least occasionally shown to visitors, notably the Dutchman Lodewijck Huygens in 1652, who was the first to note 'a room where horse armour used in former times was stored on wooden horses with armed men on them. There were two suits of armour worn by Henry VII and two worn by Henry VIII.'

This display was the origin and inspiration for what is now referred to as the 'Line of Kings', one of the most celebrated and enduring displays, if in successive guises, in the Tower's history. Quasi-public access followed in 1660, perhaps through the personal intervention of Charles II, who visited the Tower in August 1660: its propagandist potential, emphasising the continuity of the English monarchy, the legitimacy of his own dynasty, and skating over the brief anomaly of the past eleven years, cannot have been lost on him. On his orders William Legge [75], Constable of the Tower and soon to be

TREASURES OF THE ROYAL ARMOURIES [35]

Master of the Armouries, compiled *A View & Survey of all the Armour ... remayneing at the Tower of London, Taken in the month of October 1660*. In August 1661, Willem Schellinks, a Dutch artist, took a guided tour of the Tower. In the Long House of Ordnance he saw

... behind a rail the body armour of several Kings and their horses' armour ... lined up in a row, of very ancient and uncommon fashion, but all well looked after and kept polished. According to their keeper, there is the armour of Prince Henry, King Henry VIII, King Henry VII, Edward III, Charles I, Edward IV, Henry VI, the Duke of Gloucester, Charles Brandon, Duke of Suffolk, and that of William the Conqueror.

In 1685 two new horses were commissioned from Grinling Gibbons (1648–1721) to carry Charles I and Charles II [74], complete with the kings' sculpted heads. Three years later the display was moved from the House of Ordnance to the first floor of the New Armouries (built 1663–4), and gained seventeen new horses, once again carved by some of the best English sculptors of the time [fig.13]. It was seen there in 1694 by the Saxon pastor Heinrich Benthem, and described as a 'Place where the Kings of England are in full Proportion on Horseback, with the proper armour they use in battle'. On the death of William III in 1702 his horse and effigy were added:

George I belatedly joined them in 1750 and George II, the last king to be represented, in 1768. The display moved to a new building (the 'New Horse Armoury') in 1826, back into the White Tower in 1883, was 'banished' (so far as it survived) in the 1960s, partially reappeared in the late 1990s, and is represented today by an 'evocation' of 2013.

Meanwhile, by the end of the 17th century the 'Horse Armoury' had been joined at the Tower by three other major arms and armour spectacles – the 'Spanish Armoury', the 'Small Armoury' and the 'Artillery Room'. The contents of the Spanish Armoury, were, it was claimed, taken from the Spanish Armada of 1588. The display had been assembled by Ordnance Office staff in 1676 in a building near St Peter ad Vincula, thereafter called the 'Spanish Weopen House', before being re-displayed in a room in 'Coldharbour', the inmost ward, to the south of the White Tower. The main purpose of the display, mostly of material allegedly intended for defeating, torturing and oppressing the vanquished English, was also broadly propagandist, trumpeting England's invincibility and her enemies' perfidy – Catholics in particular. In fact it included nothing from the Armada and was effectively a 'cabinet of curiosities', in the manner of numerous private and corporate equivalents then fashionable in London and elsewhere: indeed the 'Spanish' material was openly accompanied

Fig.13 | Pen and wash drawing by the artist and caricaturist Thomas Rowlandson of 1809, showing the 'Horse Armoury', when housed on the upper floor of the New Armouries. A Yeoman Warder explains the sight to his varied party of four. The armour to the right is probably the 'Giant Armour', at the time associated with John of Gaunt. 1.45

by such varied things as re-hafted scythes captured from Monmouth's rebels in 1685 [71], four 'Danish clubs' and ten 'Hercules clubs' (whatever they were) and prestigious material associated with Henry VIII, including a gun-shield [39] and his 'walking staffe' [36]. In 1779, on the outbreak of another war with Spain, it was enhanced with a mounted figure of Elizabeth I addressing the troops at Tilbury in the Armada years. In 1837 the watered-down display, renamed 'Queen Elizabeth's Armoury' in 1832, was moved to the lower chapel in the White Tower, a room still often called the 'Spanish Armoury'. It survived in various guises until the 1980s.

The other displays were in the Grand Storehouse, built in 1688–91 on the site of the 16th-century Long House of Ordnance to the north of the White Tower. This was a magnificent structure, easily the most architecturally distinguished of all post-medieval buildings at the Tower, of brick with stone dressings, with a central bay crowned by a pediment and a tympanum depicting a panoply of arms carved in deep relief [80]. It housed the 'Small Armoury' – so called because it held small arms – an incredible tableau made up of thousands of weapons and a mass of elaborate wood-carvings arranged in 1697 by John Harris, resident of Eton (Berkshire), gunsmith and 'Furbisher to the King'. Among its many frames all dressed with weapons, the *pièces de resistance* included an 'organ' with pipes made out of brass blunderbusses and pistols, a 'fiery serpent', a 'seven-headed monster' and – as noted by Ralph Thoresby, historian of Leeds – 'shields, pyramids and trophies'. In 1698 the Emperor of Russia, Peter the Great, attempting an 'incognito' visit to England (not a great success – he was nearly seven feet tall) was shown the displays and compared them favourably with those in St Petersburg. Its celebrity was to remain undiminished, and 1713 it was described in the anonymous *British Curiosities* as 'one of the greatest Curiosities in its kind, being admired by all strangers'. Later, the historian of London William Maitland described it as a sight 'no one ever beheld without Astonishment … not to be matched perhaps in the world', and others followed in a similar vein.

Tragically, the Small Armoury displays were destroyed when the Grand Storehouse burnt down in 1841, without – astonishingly – any known drawing or image ever having been made of the more elaborate pieces. An impression of the effect, however, is given by a lithograph of 1822 [fig.14], by Harris's much-altered arrangement in the King's Guard Room at Hampton Court Palace, and by the modern 'Hall of Steel' at the Royal Armouries Museum in Leeds, designed by Bob Weller and Alistair Pether in 1995–6.

The fourth excitement, on the ground floor of the Grand Storehouse, was known as the 'Artillery Room', and displayed the great guns of the 'Train of Artillery' – the endless traffic jam of cannon and supply wagons that lumbered after the army in the field. In the early years the weapons on show were ready for use in battle, as some just had been against Monmouth's rebels in 1685. But many were clearly shown essentially as curiosities, such as 'a mortar that shoots 9 several Shells at a time' and 'an Engine for shooting several Musket Balls at once' and, however incongruously, 'a Rack to Extort Confessions', conjuring up images of the Tower's brutal past. From the beginning, however, the contents as a whole were intended as a powerful statement of British military might, bolstered by guns and other trophies captured around the world. Some of this material was also destroyed in 1841, although fortunately much had been moved to Woolwich Arsenal, founded a few years before in 1696: a number of items, including a rectangular-sectioned 16th-century three-barrelled bronze cannon, another breech-loading cannon of 1542 (both made for Henry VIII) and the 'Namur' mortar of 1692 can be seen in the White Tower today.

None of these displays, however impressive and delightful, were meant to actually inform people about arms and armour in general or about any particular item: indeed, the first object labels at the Tower accompanied a redisplay of the Line of Kings in 1826, and in this the Tower Armoury was now falling a little short by 'museum' standards even of the time. But from the early 1820s this was all to change, and by the end of the century, whilst still not termed a museum, the Tower Armouries were on a par in didactic intent with the British Museum, the National Gallery (founded 1824) or the Victoria & Albert Museum [1852]. It was recognised in print as 'the national collection of arms and armour', and was approaching them in prestige. A prerequisite for this was of course understanding the subject itself. The serious historical and typological study of arms and armour had been begun only towards the end of the previous century by Francis Grose (1731–91) in his fascinating *Treatise on Ancient Armour and Weapons* of 1786. Nevertheless, the figure usually considered

Fig.14 | Lithograph of 1822 showing the interior of the Small Armoury on the first floor of the Grand Storehouse. Note the columns, pilasters and festoons made up of muskets, lances and pistols. A Yeoman Warder discusses the spectacle with a visitor. 1.145

to be the father of the subject is Samuel Rush Meyrick (1783–1848). He was one of a busy circle of antiquaries and collectors including Francis Douce (1757–1834) and Sir Walter Scott (1771–1832). Meyrick formed his own collection in London and at Goodrich Court (Herefordshire), and in 1824 published *A Critical Enquiry into Antient Armour*, advancing the subject in leaps and bounds and confirming him as the country's best-known authority. At the Tower, however, unsung Ordnance staff, generally under a Principal Storekeeper, had already been patiently studying the collection and the subject more generally, ultimately to Meyrick's benefit. The first of note was Robert Porrett (1783–1868), appointed in 1795. It was probably thanks to Porrett that in 1821 Meyrick began his association with the Tower, after writing to the Constable, the Duke of Wellington, about the current state of the ancient armour there. He pointed out its poor display and the lack of information offered, presciently suggesting that the Tower Armouries could become (effectively) the national 'museum of armour'. Meyrick recommended that the collection be improved 'for the purposes of the Government, the historian and the artist, and to afford the public an instructive and pleasing gratification in contemplating the skill and ingenuity of remote periods'. His first recommendations were ignored – perhaps thanks to his unflattering description of the Tower displays as 'a subject of ridicule', and by demanding appointment as 'Master of the Armouries' in return for services – not an attitude that Wellington appreciated. In 1826, however, again supported by Porrett, Meyrick's offer was accepted and he set to work. Among other things he rearranged the Horse Armoury in its new home after 1825, presenting men and horses chronologically and, so far as possible, in period-appropriate dress. William the Conqueror lost his musket, and the princes and noblemen removed in 1688 were reinserted. Meyrick also added James II, omitted of course in 1688 [72] but by the 1820s acceptable as a historical figure, although tellingly displayed a little apart from the rest of the royal bloodline.

Meyrick's thinking also influenced the Office's view of the Armouries' purpose and its duties to the public. In 1821 he suggested that the Armouries could become a 'museum' [sic], anticipating the formal adoption of the term by 162 years, and encouraged the Office of Ordnance to admit more 'ordinary' visitors. Thanks largely to price reductions, along with steps to improve the 'visitor experience', numbers rose from 10,200 in 1838 to 94,973 in 1840 and steadily increased thereafter. From 1841 visitors could also buy the Tower's first official guidebook, *The Tower: its history, armouries and antiquities*, by John Hewitt, Porrett's gifted subordinate, and whose *Ancient Armour and Weapons in Europe* [1845] took understanding of the subject far beyond where Meyrick had left it. Then, from 1859, the amount of information available in print was transformed by his *Official Catalogue of the Tower Armouries*. The size and range of the collection was also expanded through gifts and purchase, including of material from Asia and Africa, amongst them the large and important collection of Indian arms and armour presented by the East India Company in 1853. These were specially selected to provide diverse examples from across the subcontinent, and included pieces from the royal armoury of the Sikhs at Lahore.

Further changes followed the Crimean War (1853–56), including the dissolution of the Board of Ordnance and the transfer of its charges, along with the Armouries, to the Secretary of State for War (or the War Office). The changes were led by the playwright, historian and friend of Meyrick, James Robinson Planché (1796–1880): as Meyrick had done, he wrote to the authorities as a private citizen, describing the Tower Armoury as 'disgraceful', and eventually, in 1868, obtained a commission from the War Office to rearrange the collection. By 1888 the vision of Meyrick and Planché had been realised thanks to the Ordnance Office and the efforts of the Tower Armouries staff. Whilst their initial arguments for the appointment of a curator had fallen on deaf ears, within a few years this had come to pass, ushering in, it might be said, the era of the modern museum.

The national museum of arms and armour, 1895–2020

Impressive as the work of Meyrick, Planché and the storekeepers had been, a turning point in the Armouries history was the appointment in 1895 of Harold Lee (1844–1932), from 1892 the 17th Viscount Dillon, as the first Curator of the Tower Armouries, on the death of Head Armoury Keeper (a recently created post) William Brailsford. Both Meyrick, Planché and later even the Secretary of State for War had recommended the appointment of a 'curator', meaning – however unfair to Porrett, Hewitt and their ilk – a distinguished scholar of both

Royal Armoury in the Tower of London

intellectual and social standing and whose responsibilities, unlike the 'keepers' and 'storekeepers', would be confined to historic arms and armour. The new post was created in 1895, eased by the earlier encouragement of the British Museum, and offered to Dillon thanks to work he had already done as a consultant. An ex-soldier and historian of armour and military dress, Dillon was a major figure in the establishment art world, serving as a trustee of other museums, as President of the Society of Antiquaries (1897–1904), and in other prominent capacities. His research had a very practical side, involving dismantling gunlocks to understand their mechanisms, and disassembling, reassembling and wearing armour to study how it actually worked. He wrote over fifty papers on arms, armour and related subjects, and published his *Illustrated Guide to the Armouries, Tower of London* in 1910 – not quite a catalogue (although an outline, unpublished catalogue was prepared at the same time), but an abundantly useful handbook nevertheless. Some of his work appeared under the pseudonym 'Armadillo'. He led the Armouries to a new stage in its progress to modernity: armour and weapons were displayed according to the techniques of the day, with labels and a guidebook describing them, while behind the scenes, early collections management regimes were put in place.

In 1903 the War Office, for some reason puzzled by its new responsibility for a collection of historic arms and armour, tried to transfer it to the British Museum. This would have wiped out the Armouries as an independent entity, but the attempt was prevented by the terms of the British Museum Acts, and instead, in 1904, the Tower of London, and with it the Armoury, was transferred from the War Office to the Office of Works. Its relevant responsibilities were later inherited by the Department for Culture, Media and Sport [1997], the Royal Armouries' sponsoring Department since that time.

Charles ffoulkes (1868–1947) followed as curator in 1913. He was invited by Dillon, who was impressed by his early work on armour-making, to 'take over the Tower'. It was an unusual position in having, as ffoulkes put it, 'a nominal salary, no age limit and no fixed hours of duty'. He stuck it out, however, and retired at 70 in 1938. Like Dillon, whose ancestor Sir Henry Lee was Master of the Armoury under Elizabeth I, ffoulkes could claim an ancestor in service of the Armouries. This was one Captain Thomas Fowke, 'Warden of the White Tower' in 1581 and later 'Keeper of the Queen's Muskets, Calivers and Dags in the Tower of London', one of Lee's subordinates.

ffoulkes was a practical man and an accomplished draughtsman and sculptor, skills which helped him follow in Dillon's footsteps. He studied how armour was made and functioned, and published *Armour and Weapons* (1909) and *The Armourer and his Craft* (1930) – the first serious, and still the only full-length, study of the subject. Most importantly for the Armouries, in 1917 he published the two-volume *Inventory and Survey of the Armouries of the Tower of London*, the first and last modern printed catalogue of the Tower collection. Like Dillon, ffoulkes bought very little, but he was also a ruthless de-accessioner, firmly believing that the Armouries should concentrate on the 'historical collection of European arms and armour for which the Tower has so long been famous': notably, in November 1914, the large collection of Asian material collected in the 19th century and a few pieces of Greek armour were transferred to the British Museum, although sparing the 4th-century BC Cumae panoply [2]. Following the Board of Ordnance tradition of shedding unwanted stores, in May 1917 ffoulkes rid himself of the material forming a purely decorative backdrop in the White Tower: dismissed as 'a quantity of broken gunlocks, sword blades and hilts, ramrods etc … of no technical or historic value', and cheerfully handed over thirty-six hundredweight of 'scrap' to be melted down for the war effort. Further disposals followed in 1926 and 1928. As it happened, though, losses were outnumbered by acquisitions, largely through carefully cultivated gifts and the acceptance of historic collections from other state bodies, although there had been a nasty moment in 1913 when it was proposed that the Armouries should hold only pre-18th century material. These acquisitions kick-started the vast enlargement of the collection in the 20th and 21st centuries, among them several items described below. The first transferral, in 1914, was of two Greenwich armours (one being **48**) from Windsor Castle and 'thirteen pieces of the armour of Henry VIII'. In 1925 the ownership and responsibility for no less than 32,000 pieces of 'obsolete' equipment from 175 'War Office establishments' across the British Isles were transferred to the Armouries – a wonderful bonus more than doubling the size of the collection, but creating a perennial headache for the Royal Armouries registrars. In 1927, thanks to ffoulkes' initiative, the Royal Artillery Institution transferred over 700 pieces from their museum, the Woolwich Rotunda, and through related processes, hundreds of historic small arms were received from the Royal Military Depot at Weedon Bec (Northamptonshire) and the Enfield Small Arms Factory (London): these were eventually assembled in 1935 as a study collection at the Tower, a forward-looking initiative for the time. On the public-facing front, ffoulkes was responsible for a major redisplay of the White Tower, occupying all floors (not just, as previously, the top two). The building reopened in April 1916, now exclusively displaying arms and armour of 'the period roughly speaking from 1470–1900'. Heavy ordnance was exhibited in the basement, small arms on the entrance floor, with the 'weapon room' and 'sword room' occupying the first, and the 'Horse armouries' and 'Tudor room' the second.

In parallel with all this, ffoulkes had been a prime mover in setting up what was to become the Imperial War Museum, of which he was appointed as full-time curator and secretary, in March 1917, remaining there until 1933, leaving his Armouries work to weekends. Fittingly, in his last few years at the Tower, the title 'Curator of the Armouries' was changed, with the king's consent, to 'Master of the Armouries', last used in 1670, and held by the museum's Chief Executive today. After leaving the Tower ffoulkes wrote of his experiences in his delightfully anecdotal memoir of 1939, *Arms and the Tower*.

ffoulkes's successor was Sir James Mann (Master 1938–1962), veteran of the First World War and an art historian. However, he built on childhood interests to become an established expert on arms and armour by his mid-twenties. He was at various times, among many other things, Deputy Director of the Courtauld Institute, Keeper of the Wallace Collection, President of the Society of Antiquaries and Surveyor of the Royal Works, and was knighted in 1948. Having seen off the ghastly suggestion by fellow historian F. H. Cripps-Day to 'abolish the idea of the Tower as a museum & and get rid to Whitehall, South Kensington a lot of museum stuff', war broke out and his work concentrated on moving the collection to safety. Much of it eventually went to Hall Barn, a country house near Beaconsfield (Buckinghamshire), and some to Wales, where it was intermittently displayed at Caernarfon Castle (Gwynedd). Meanwhile the Tower was closed to visitors and most of the White Tower made over for recreational purposes to the troops stationed there. Reopening began in 1946 and was complete by 1962, with uniforms 'and objects of military interest' on the entrance floor, military and sporting firearms on the first floor, and Asian material on the second.

Under Mann the collection continued to expand, with occasional but invaluable help from the National Art Collections Fund, as in the case of material from the 19th-century Beriah Botfield collection from Norton Hall (Northamptonshire), and William Randolph Hearst's at St Donat's Castle (Glamorgan), which included a wonderful sporting gun of 1646 by Jean Conrad Tornier [69]. Mann also produced a user-friendly version of his popular guide to the arms and armour at the Wallace Collection and related content for the official Tower guidebooks. Most importantly, perhaps, whereas his predecessors had provided the core arms and armour expertise themselves, Mann brought others onto the staff, notably Russell Robinson, Norris Kennard, Bill Reid and Claude Blair – all of great distinction in their fields – and skilled craftsmen Edward Smith and Arthur Davis, who for the first time provided a conservation and restoration function. The new team were soon raising the international profile of the museum: Mann drew on his vast array of overseas contacts to organise exhibitions including *Armour of Kings and Captains* [1949] from the Austrian national collections, *Armour made in the Royal Workshops at Greenwich* [1951] and *Arms, armour and militaria lent by the Duke of Brunswick and Lüneberg* [1952]. From 1953 staff were able to publish in the journal of the newly formed Arms and Armour Society, edited by Armouries staff or others closely involved. Meanwhile, from 1957, what soon became the International Committee of Museums of Arms, Armour and Militaria (ICOMAM) began bringing together scholars from across the world at its annual conferences, enabling the advancement of the subject on an unprecedented scale.

Mann's work was continued by his successor, Dick Dufty (Master 1963–76), an architect, art historian and distinguished scholar. Importantly, he secured the revived position of Master as a full-time post, and in 1967 appointed Howard Blackmore, author of numerous works on small arms and artillery, as Keeper of Firearms. In 1970 Alan Borg, subsequently Director of the V&A and the Imperial War Museum, joined the staff as Keeper of the Blades. Dufty also began the recovery of the Asian collection, lost to the British Museum in 1914, at the behest of Russell Robinson, the first English scholar to publish seriously on Japanese armour. Robinson curated an exhibition of Japanese armour at the Tower in 1965, and reinstated the Asian gallery in 1970. Dufty's successor Nick Norman (Master 1977–88) took matters a step further by organising the museum's first international touring exhibition, *Treasures from the Tower of London*, displayed in Norwich, Cincinnati and Toronto in 1982–3. He also supported major ventures such as the purchase of the 3rd Earl of Southampton's armour in 1983 (II.360) and securing of the English Civil War armoury from Littlecote House (Berkshire) in 1986 [67]. In 1983, the National Heritage Act, enacted in 1984, completely recast the status of the Armouries, among other bodies. It created a Board of Trustees, charged in headline terms with 'the general purpose of maintaining and exhibiting a national collection of arms, armour and associated objects'. The first chair was the remarkably distinguished William Sidney, Viscount De L'Isle (1909–91), whose part in drafting the Act secured the Armouries' status as an independent museum. Thanks to discussions led by his trustee, Arthur Wellesley, 8th Duke of Wellington (1915–2014), and the agreement of Her Majesty the Queen, the Armouries gained its formal prefix – 'Royal' – in 1985.

Meanwhile, from 1977 onwards Norman had begun to consider expanding beyond the Tower and to investigate potential venues. This materialised just after Norman's retirement, under Guy Wilson (Master 1988–2002), with the opening of a new museum at Fort Nelson in Hampshire. Taking its name from the nearby monument to Lord Nelson, begun in 1807, it formed part of a screen of forts built from 1859 covering the landward approaches to Portsmouth and its dockyards, vital to the defence of the country, its trade routes and empire: the perceived threat was from France, resurgent under the Second Empire of Napoleon III, which in 1859 had launched a warship, *La Gloire*, outperforming any British counterpart and making invasion a possibility. Controversial from the start, by July 1860 the press were calling the forts 'Palmerston's Follies' (after Henry Temple, 3rd Viscount Palmerston, the Prime Minister responsible). In the event, the French threat subsided, and apart from a variety of activities in both World Wars, the Fort played little part in national defence and was abandoned by the Ministry of Defence in the 1970s. In 1978 Hampshire County Council, recognising its historical importance, bought the site, restored it and opened it as a visitor attraction in 1984. Four years later, the Royal Armouries took a lease on the site to display its growing collection of artillery – highly appropriate, as the fort was designed both to resist artillery and to be defended by it. The

Fig.15 | Aerial view of Fort Nelson from the south-east. Built in the 1860s as one of a chain of forts defending Portsmouth from landward attack, since 1989 it has been used for the display of most of the museum's artillery. The enormous tent-like structure is the Artillery Hall.

interpretation of a historic site added a whole new dimension to the Royal Armouries' responsibilities. With it came the opportunity to display items, or their exact equivalents, as and where they were intended to be used, such as the 7-inch 'Armstrong' Rifled Breech Loading (RBL) gun [101], a revolutionary design of *c.*1860 (and the only one to survive in firing condition) which occupies one of four Haxo casemates designed to take them. Today, demonstration firings are carried out by the Portsdown Artillery Volunteers. The 68-pounder smoothbore and 64-pounder Rifled Muzzle Loader (RML), converted from smoothbore, also represent types originally intended for the Fort's main armament which are now displayed in positions designed for them. Meanwhile the eccentric Irishman Robert Mallet's (1810–81) 'Monster' mortar [100], designed in 1857 and intended for besieging roughly contemporary Russian defences in the Crimea, is a particularly apposite exhibit now facing the Portsdown Hill Road. In 1989 the existing steel and Teflon-clad 'Artillery Hall' was built on the Parade Ground, and, with the support of the Heritage Lottery Fund, further improvements followed in 2011–13, including the 'Voice of the Guns' gallery, housing some of the museum's more spectacular pieces. Among them are the 'Dardanelles gun' [18], and the 'Iraqi supergun' [115], a German Second World War 88-mm 'Flak' gun and a British 3.7-inch equivalent of the same era.

The Fort Nelson initiative notwithstanding, the biggest event of the era, and indeed the single boldest public-facing development in the history of the museum, was the creation of the Royal Armouries Museum in Leeds. The origins of the project, as with the Fort, lay in the lack of space at the Tower which allowed only 13% of the collection to be displayed, while the aspirations of The Historic Royal Palaces Agency (now HRP), from 1989 responsible for the castle's overall management, played a part as well. Thinking began again in earnest in 1988, and swiftly focused on 'moving some of the collection north to provide better geographic distribution' and choosing a location with 'affinity', that is, 'an area appropriate to our subject', spawning the short-lived idea of moving the hunting collection to a vacant country house. The museum's ambitions were set out in 'Strategy 2000', presented to the Trustees in June 1990, by which time a site at Sheffield – Meadowhall, close to the M1 – had been offered and found favour, thanks to 'affinity' with the steel industry, the outline support of the Sheffield Development Corporation, and ease of access. Conceptually led by Wilson, the architect Derek Walker (Derek Walker Associates) and a hand-picked design team, the project swiftly developed: the main themes for the galleries were identified and the need for performance spaces, including a tiltyard, agreed. An estimated footfall of at least 500,000 visitors a year was anticipated. Detailed proposals for redisplay of the White Tower and other parts of the Tower of London were prepared in parallel. In the event, changing circumstances brought the Sheffield venture to a close, but the interest it generated prompted overtures from other northern cities, including Leeds, with whom a deal was struck in 1991. The location selected was a brownfield site between (what was then called) Clarence Dock – two linked canal basins of 1850 and 1890 on the Aire and Calder Navigation – and the River Aire. By 1992 £28.5m of public money had been secured, subject to the remaining £14.5m being raised, as indeed it was, from the private sector. The design was again led by Derek Walker, incorporating much of the earlier thinking. Work began on site early in 1994. The objectives of the architectural brief were 'to create a friendly and welcoming building which reflects the quality and excitement of the collections and displays within'. It also asked for a 'radiating' layout, with a central circulation spine from which the galleries could be visited in any sequence. The result is what we see today: its main components are the 'Hall of Steel', galleries dedicated to 'War', 'Hunting', 'Oriental', 'Tournament' and 'Self Defence', along with two lecture theatres, dedicated live interpretation and performance spaces, and the celebrated Tiltyard, in addition to the usual behind-the-scenes apparatus. Until the financial crisis that began in 2008, the museum kept a stable of horses, a kennel of hounds and a mews of hawks, participants in the live interpretation programme. Meanwhile, reviving an earlier Armouries ambition to have a presence in America, in 2000 negotiations opened with the emerging Frazier Museum in Louisville, Kentucky, where the Royal Armouries went on to display many items from 2004–14.

The museum in Leeds was opened by Her Majesty the Queen on 30 March 1996 to a fanfare of acclaim, if also to a few moans about 'Disneyfication', and has been the headquarters of the organisation since. As such the Armouries was the first National Museum based outside London, and was trumpeted at the time as both the 'first example in the arts of the government's Private Finance Initiative' and museographically strikingly innovative.

One more major development, however, was yet to come, thanks to the decision in 2002 to gift the Pattern Room collection to the Royal Armouries. This had its origins in Charles I's Proclamation of 1631, although the earliest probable survival of a 'sealed pattern' is a musket (XII.38) dating from the late 17th century. The service operated from the Tower whilst it remained a major centre of gun-making and assembly, but when superseded by the Royal Small Arms Factory at Enfield in the 1850s, it moved there. Over time it was enlarged by the addition of allied, enemy and technically interesting weapons and accoutrements, and the systematic collection of additional historic items. With the closure of Enfield in 1988, both function and collection were moved to the Royal Ordnance Factory in Nottingham and housed in a new building; this soon closed as well, putting the future of the 'Pattern Room' in peril. The problem was resolved by the energies of museum staff and the intelligent collaboration of the Ministry of Defence and the Department for Culture, Media and Sport with its gift to the Royal Armouries. From 2005 the collection has been housed in Leeds, thus combining the pre-1850 pattern items, those of 1853 to 1988, and the museum's other small arms, to form what is probably the largest historic small arms assemblage in the world. For the Royal Armouries this was a momentous development: in addition to enriching the galleries, the collection serves not only as a key resource for historical research, but also for the work of defence and security agencies, giving the organisation a unique, practical and highly relevant function over and above the usual purposes of a museum.

Since 1996, boosted in 2005 by the Pattern Room acquisition, and despite the difficulties caused by the 2008–11 financial crisis, the Royal Armouries as a whole has achieved its central aims of appealing to the public, building on its status as a centre of arms and armour scholarship, and ensuring its long-term sustainability. At the heart of this of course is the collection: mixing the legacy of the national arsenal, arms and armour of the English monarchy and the fruits of two centuries of collecting, has made it one of the greatest arms and armour collections of all. Although its unique strength is in its sheer range, from a European-American perspective it is one of the 'big five', alongside the Musée de l'Armée in Paris, the Hofjagd und Rüstkammer of the Kunsthistorisches Museum in Vienna, the Real Armeria in Madrid and the Metropolitan Museum of Art in New York, although other fabulous collections abound. This is both a great privilege and a great responsibility. The task of the trustees and staff of the Armouries and its sponsoring government department is to ensure that their institution lives up to its collection and its potential for public benefit. This is our stated intention. Our Master Plan for the future aims to create an organisation and a public offer fit for today's diversifying, demanding and expanding audiences, in keeping with a subject and collection of such importance, appropriate to an organisation with such a fascinating pedigree, and to make the future the longest period in its history.

Amando et Fidando Troppo, son rouinato.

TREASURES
OF THE ROYAL
ARMOURIES

1

Dagger axe (*ge*) and scabbard

China, Warring States period (*c.*4th century BC) · XXVII.290

The emergence of stone-bladed weapons, forerunners in form and function of their metal-bladed successors, dates from the Neolithic period in China, between about 10,000 and 1700 BC. Under the rule of the Shang and Zhou dynasties (1600–1050 BC and 1050–256 BC respectively), advances in casting made bronze-bladed weapons a standard part of the Chinese warrior's equipment. Principal among these was the 'dagger axe' (*ge*), so-called thanks to its broad, double-edged dagger-like blade, but which projected, as in an axe, at a near-right angle from the wooden or bamboo haft: it was fixed in place by lashing its long, broad tang to the side of the haft and by a rearward projection that passed through it. Hafts seem to have varied in length from around 1.5 m to over 4 m, and were capped at the base with a metal ferrule. From the Shang dynasty to the Han period (206 BC – AD 220) dagger axes were the most common form of close-quarters weapon, used by infantry, chariot riders and cavalry, largely due to their suitability for both slicing and hacking.

The development of the weapon, and the arms and armour industry in general, had taken off in the Eastern Zhou dynasty (770–256 BC), particularly during the 'Warring States' period (475–221 BC) which preceded the unification of China, to last for several centuries, under the First Emperor Qin Shi Huang (221–210 BC). Competing regimes prioritised the improvement and manufacture of military equipment to support their bids for control, prompting swift advances in metallurgy and production methods. Surviving examples from this period, manufactured in large quantities in state-controlled workshops for widespread issue, are abundant. The bronze blades were often inscribed with the names of the government overseers and the craftsmen who had made them, as a way of assuring quality control. States took a rigorous interest in monitoring production and controlling distribution, as this was often key to their grasp on power.

This example is a survival from this fraught but dynamic era, and illustrates an important stage in the weapon's evolution. Whereas previously the blade had been longer and broader than the tang, this was later, as here, lengthened and equipped with flanges and perforations, allowing firmer attachment to the haft. Remarkably, in this case the original scabbard has survived. It is made of lacquered wood and decorated with swirling, smoke-like depictions of running animals, birds, and men armed with spears picked out in red.

These details give a pleasing personal touch to this mass-produced item.

From the later Zhou period a separate spear head was often fixed to the top of the haft, the two blades combining to form a halberd (*ji*) which could be used both to cut and thrust. By the Han period, a *ji* was made in iron in a single piece and took a much slimmer, spiked form. As iron and steel began to supplant bronze in arms manufacture from the later Warring States period onwards, the dagger axe gradually fell out of common use; by the Eastern Han dynasty (AD 25–220) it had been supplanted by the more versatile halberd and the increasingly popular sword. Their long history and importance, however, ensured the continued use of jade examples in prestigious burials well into the Han period and beyond.

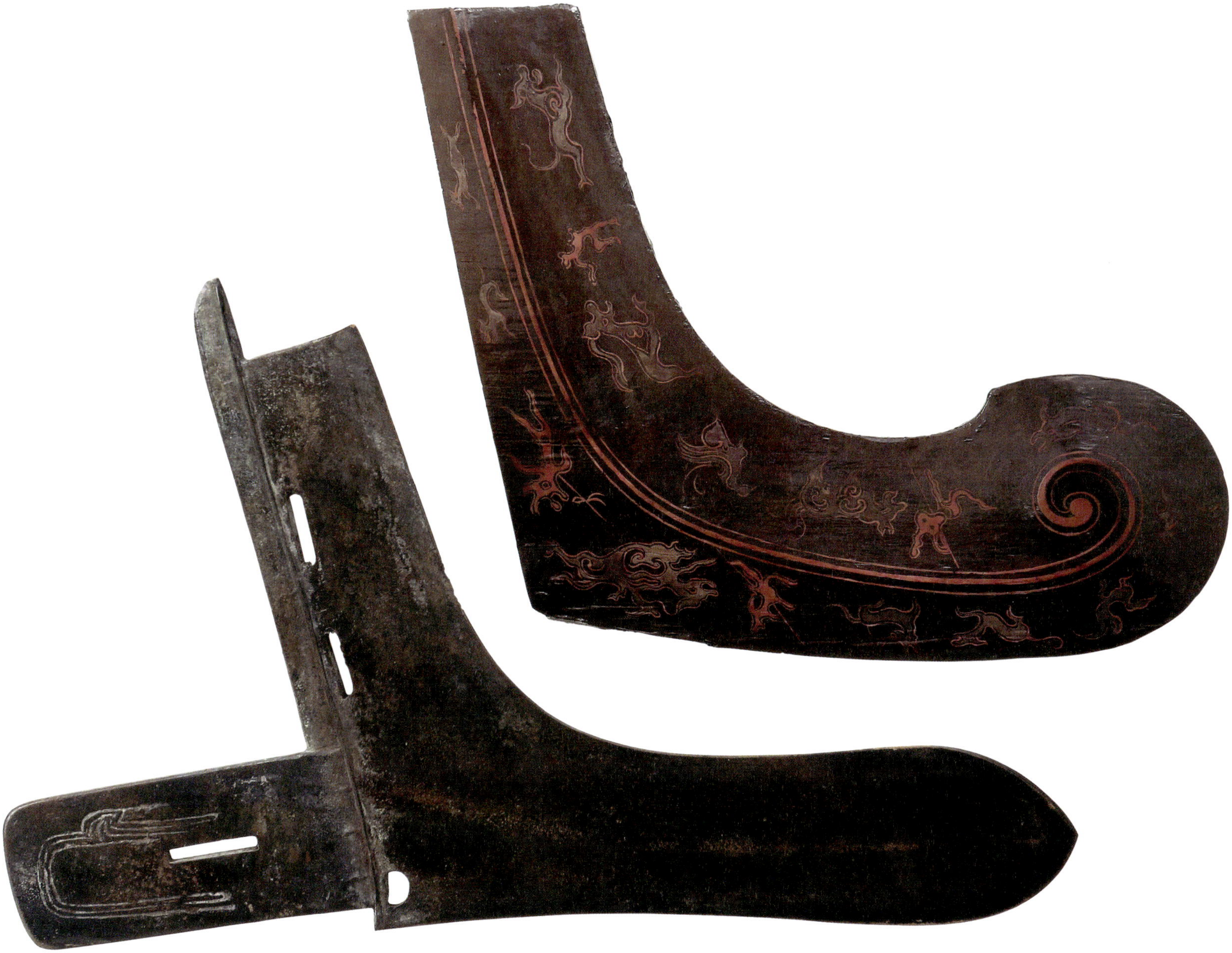

2

Bronze 'Cumae' armour from southern Italy

Southern Italy, 4th century BC · II.197

Armour – clothing and headgear designed to protect the wearer from weapons and missiles – seems to have been used at least in Mesopotamia from as early as the third millennium BC. The Royal Armouries oldest example, however, made of bronze, dates from much more recent times (about 375–325 BC) and is known as the Cumae armour, from the place in Campania, southern Italy, where it was probably found. In form it prefigures some of the key characteristics of more recent and particularly medieval armour, much more familiar to most people, and is one of the best examples of its type outside Italy. Bronze-making expertise capable of producing arms and armour first appeared in the Near East during the fourth millennium BC, then gradually spread to other regions across the Mediterranean, including Greece and the Italian peninsula. The establishment of Greek colonies in southern Italy and Sicily from the seventh century BC led to the adoption of Greek hoplite military tactics and equipment in the pan-Mediterranean region that became known as *Magna Graecia*. In Italy the Etruscans and probably other Italian native peoples followed suit.

The Cumae armour consists of a helmet, a square breast and a back plate, a belt, a pair of greaves, and a pair of thigh defences. The helmet, fitted with decorated side wings, is of a form known as Samno-Attic which continued to be used in Italy long after similar styles of helmet had passed out of fashion in mainland Greece and across the wider Hellenistic world after the death of Alexander the Great. When the assemblage was first published in the *Illustrated London News* in 1853 it included a spear head, a sword and scabbard and another fragment, perhaps an ankle defence, now lost. It is probable that the helmet, cuirass, belt and greaves belong together and have survived because of the funerary tradition in *Magna Graecia* of burying warriors with their arms and armour, unlike in Greece itself where they were traditionally deposited at sanctuary sites. Given its form and quality, we can assume that the armour was worn by a rich and prominent citizen of a city state.

The story of how finds from Etruscan, Greek, and Roman tombs entered European collectors' markets in the 19th century is of interest in its own right. In this case the armour was purchased by the Ordnance Office at the Tower of London in 1853 at the sale of the collection of the Count of Milan who presumably acquired it from the excavations at Cumae organised by Prince Leopold of the Two Sicilies, Count of Syracuse (1830–60). At that time a total of twenty-one tombs at Cumae were reported to have been opened from which a variety of artefacts had been recovered and dispersed amongst private and public collections. This purchase, however, caused something of a stir when it became known that the Ordnance Office and British Museum had competed for it at auction. Questions were asked in Parliament and senior Ordnance Office officials were criticised. As a result, Sir Henry Ellis, Principal Librarian of the British Museum, wrote to the Board of Ordnance demanding advance notice if it intended to buy anything similar in the future – items of this period being, he said, the prerogative of his Trustees. This chastening experience probably explains why the Armouries acquired no further Mediterranean antiquities until the 21st century.

3

Roman sword and scabbard mounts

Germany, c.AD 50–120 · IX.5583

Describing the use of the sword (*gladius*) the Roman writer Vegetius wrote in his *De Re Militari* ('Concerning Military Matters') around AD 400: 'A stroke with the edges, though made with ever so much force, seldom kills, as the vital parts of the body are defended both by bones and armour. A stab, on the contrary, though it penetrates but two inches, is generally fatal.' A relief from Mainz, of about AD 70, nicely illustrates his point: it shows a legionary standing semi-crouched behind his shield, left leg forward, whilst delivering a lethal forward thrust.

This particular form of sword – so called after four found at Pompeii, and so necessarily made before the city's destruction in AD 79 – has been found throughout the Roman Empire, including in Britain. It differs from its predecessors in having a parallel-edged blade and a short point, making it suitable for both cutting and stabbing: carvings from the Adamklissi monument in Romania, of AD 109, and from Mainz in Germany of about AD 70 (CROSSREF p. 12) show it in use. The shortness of the blade shows how frighteningly close-up 'close-combat' was. Why this particular type of sword appeared in the middle part of the first century is unknown, but its capacity to punch through armour suggests it was prompted by the civil wars following the Emperor Nero's death in AD 68, in which armoured legionaries fought each other, and the numerous other conflicts of the period, some involving armoured opponents.

The blade in this case, made of iron, is pointed for the last 76 mm, the tip being reinforced for the last 31 mm. The grip is lost, but was of wood, bone or ivory. Fascinatingly and unusually, the forte of the blade has 'C.VALERI[I] PR[IMI] / C.VALERI[I] PRI[MI] inscribed on one side and > C.VALERI[I] C.RANIU[S] on the other, *i.e.*, C[aius] Valeri[us] Pri[mus] and C[aius] Raniu[s], who were probably successive owners. *Primus* indicates that the first was a centurion, an officer commanding about eighty men. The wood and leather scabbard

[50]

has long since perished, but its embossed and punched-out bronze mounts, originally tinned, survive; the locket plate has two panels, one bearing the figure of a helmeted warrior, and the other a winged Victory writing on a shield hanging from a palm tree; the chape bears another winged Victory holding a palm leaf, and had an ornate palmette with scrolls mounted above it. There is also a collar attachment. The punched-out shapes allowed the white metal to stand out starkly against the dark colour of the scabbard itself.

The sword and scabbard mounts were discovered in a moment of great good fortune by an amateur archaeologist, Wolfgang Johe, on the spoil heap of a hasty excavation in 1971–2 at Wiesbaden, Germany, site of a Roman spa and stronghold (*Aquae Mattiacae*). The Royal Armouries purchased the sword at the Christie's sale of the Axel Guttmann collection of ancient arms and armour in 2004, and it remains the museum's only *gladius*. As such it has the task of representing one of the most efficient military machines of all time – the Roman Legion in its heyday.

4

A Viking sword for a child

France, late 9th to early 11th century · IX.5610

Weapons have probably been made for children, whether as toys or for training, for as long as they have existed. Identifying them as such needs to be approached with caution, as size alone is no proof, but in this case not only the shortness of the blade at 630 mm, but crucially the grip at 76 mm, makes the case very clearly. Its scale apart, the sword is a classic 'Viking' period example, constructed exactly as in the full-size item. The hilt has a pommel of strongly pronounced, 'brazil-nut' form, in use from the second quarter of the 9th century through to the early 12th, if not later. The cross is of a Viking type known as a *gaddhjalt* ('spikehilt'). The narrow blade is double-edged and tapers slightly towards a short, rounded point, with much of its wooden scabbard, together with probable traces of its leather covering, still adhering to it. It was found in the river Seine near Rouen in Normandy, which explains its excavated condition, typical of a river find. Very probably it belonged to someone of Viking descent, one of the *Northmannii* or Normans, who had been ceded the city by the French King in 911.

Fortunately the sword retains its original cast copper alloy shield-shaped scabbard chape, pierced in the shape of a bird, which helps to approximate its date and origin. The established term for this particular design is the 'Birka-falcon' – although not necessarily representing a falcon – as most examples, along with a mould for making similar ones, have been found at the site of Birka: this was a fortified town on the island of Björkö on the east coast of Sweden, an important Baltic trading centre during the early Middle Ages. This comparatively rare form of chape was connected with a warrior elite involved in trading through the Baltic and Eastern Europe, although most examples have been found in Lithuania, with only a few outliers from Western Europe (such as this one), one from the Île de Groix off the Breton coast and another, allegedly, from York. On this basis the sword can be dated to between the late 9th and the early 11th century, and perhaps to the first half of the 10th. It appears to be the earliest known medieval child's sword.

In the Middle Ages boys of noble birth were expected to begin their military training before the age of ten, and there are numerous instances of children being presented with swords: Henry V owned one by the age of nine, and Henry VI was given eight of them at the same age, with 'some greater, some smaller, for to learn the King to play in his tender age'. Surviving medieval children's swords are, however, extremely rare, perhaps amounting to six or seven examples, four of which are in the Royal Armouries collection, the latest from the 15th century. Whilst these were deadly weapons, boys as young as the two Henrys would not have actually fought in battle – the contemporary chronicler Jean Froissart, for example, noted that the ten-year old John of Gaunt was then 'too young to bear arms'. Once in their teens, however, they certainly did: Edward III was fourteen when he commanded his first expedition against the Scots in 1327, whilst his son, Edward the Black Prince, famously 'won his spurs' at the battle of Crécy in 1346 at the age of sixteen. And it was not just about boys, as Joan of Arc relieved the siege of Orléans (1429) at the age of about seventeen, and was wounded by an arrow in the process.

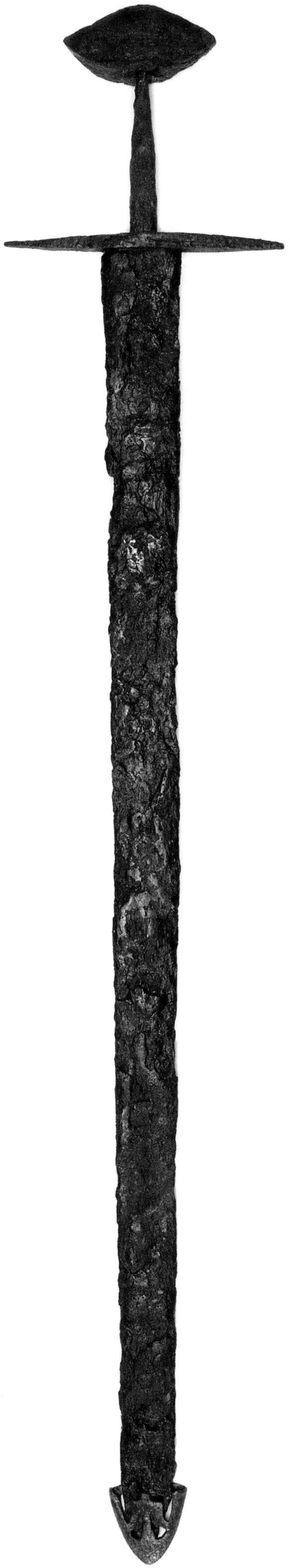

5

Helmet (*zhou*) from China or Central Asia

China or Central Asia, probably Yuan Dynasty (13th-14th century)
XXVIA.192

The expansion of the Mongol Empire began under Genghis Khan in the early 13th century, and by the middle of the following century constituted the largest contiguous land empire in history, extending from the Black Sea to the Sea of Japan and from Siberia to India. From 1271–1368, Kublai Khan, grandson of Genghis Khan, was also able to successfully unite and incorporate the whole of China into the empire, establishing the Yuan dynasty and ruling as Emperor Shizu until his death. As such, he was able to exert immense cultural and political influence across the continent.

At first sight the helmet is of fairly typical Chinese or Central Asian form – a bowl-shaped cap to which was attached, as indicated by the row of small holes around the brim, a mail or fabric neck-guard (perhaps reinforced with iron plates) with a short brim providing some protection to the face, and a raised plume holder at the top. However, unlike most Asiatic helmets, especially Chinese and Tibetan examples, it is made in one piece. A close look also reveals that the whole outer surface is covered in silver inlays of scrolling foliage, Chinese-style lions and Tibetan Buddhist lamas (priests), in a stylised form used from the 9th to the 14th century: intricate and beautiful, the style and subjects of the decoration are indicative of the growing spread and influence of Tibetan Buddhism throughout China and Central Asia under the Yuan Dynasty. Further evidence of this influence is readily apparent in the 15th-century 'Ming' sword [15].

The helmet is also important in representing the basic rounded conical form used for many centuries across vast swathes of Eurasia. After their conquests, the Mongols and their successor states integrated to varying extents with the subjugated peoples of their empires, prompting bilateral cultural, technological, and philosophical exchange. This facilitated the widespread use of this helmet style throughout their sphere of influence. Evidence of this can be seen when comparing this helmet with the late fifteenth-century Turkish helmet [24], which shows continued use of the style dominated by the rounded hemispherical bowl despite the temporal and geographic distances that separate the two pieces.

This helmet, probably worn by a wealthy Yuan military officer, beautifully illustrates these aspects of the Mongols' success.

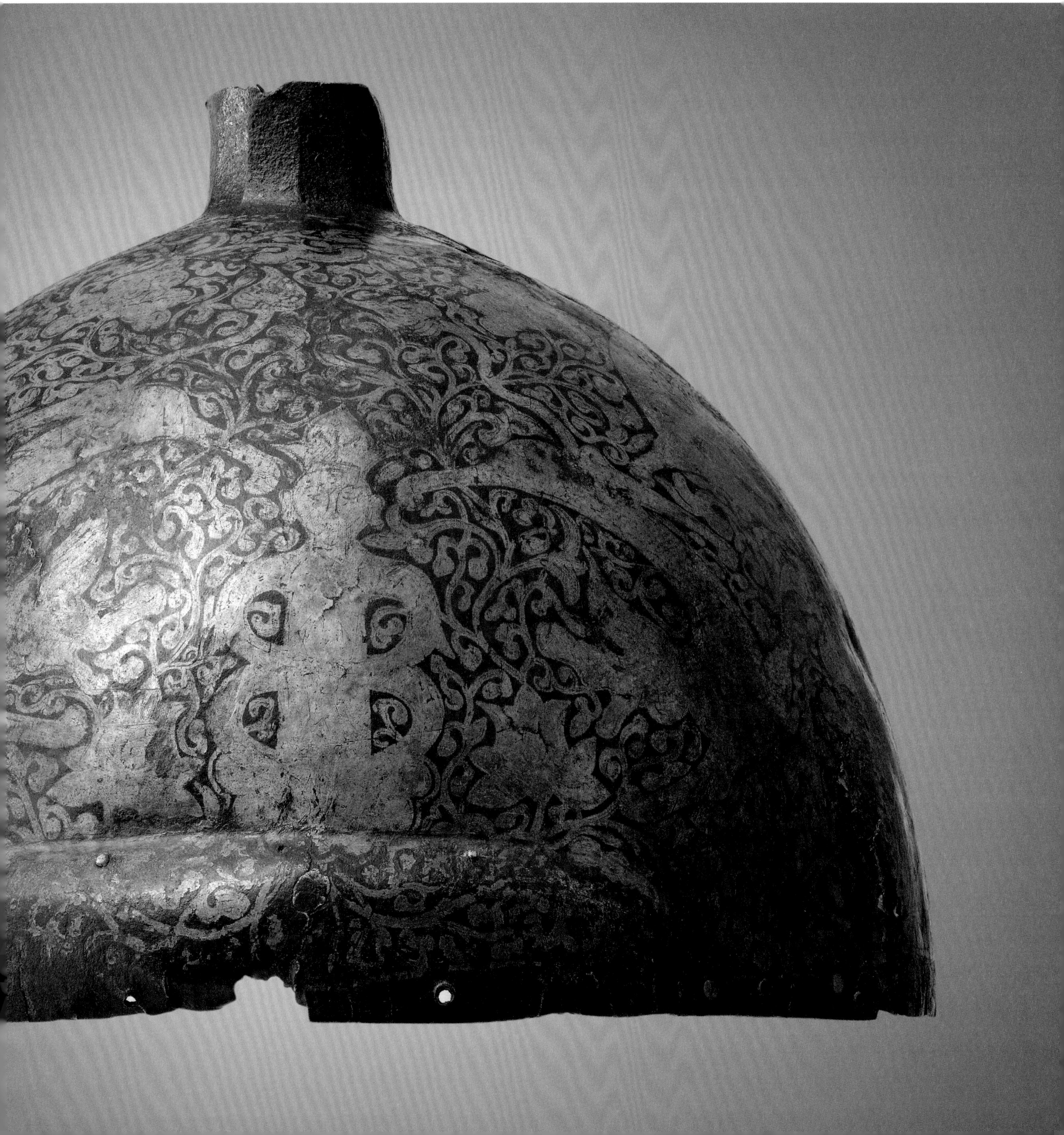

6

Late medieval German fencing manual

Germany, *c*.1320–30 · MS I.33

Fechtbücher or 'fight books' were self-defence manuals, produced in Europe during the later Middle Ages and the Renaissance. Most survivals are from German-speaking lands – hence the German term – and follow a tradition begun by the 14th-century master, Johannes Liechtenauer (d.1389), probably from Lichtenau near Nuremberg. The tradition continued to evolve well into the 16th century and successive masters added their own glosses and flourishes.

This example, Royal Armouries MS I.33, made in Germany in the early 14th century, is the earliest known, pre-dating Liechtenauer by several decades and teaching a different style of combat. It is also the only *Fechtbuch* to describe fencing with sword and buckler (a small shield) alone, as most show the use of many different weapons. As the illustrations show, this style of fencing, which included seven basic guards (referred to here in Latin as *custodes*) was fast, athletic and highly sophisticated.

The book is sixty-four pages long, made up of colour illustrations with explanatory text, describing over thirty-six different sequences or 'plays'; the text is in Latin but uses German technical terms, such as *schiltslach* (shield-strike). For reasons unknown, the combatants in the illustrations are described as a priest (*sacerdos*), who takes the lead role in most sequences, and a student (*scolar*). In the last two pages, the student is replaced, again without explanation, by a woman named Walpurgis. Close examination of the manuscript reveals it as the work of several artists and at least two scribes, although presumably guided by a single author.

The earliest mention of I.33 places it in an unnamed monastery in Franconia (Bavaria, Germany) in the mid 16th century and describes it as 'very old': recent thinking based upon artistic style and Walpurgis's clothing suggests a date of about 1320–1330. Since then the manuscript has had a colourful history, including seizure from the monastery as a spoil of war in the mid 1550s by Johannes Herbart von Würzburg, fencing master to Friedrich Wilhelm, Duke of Saxe-Weimar. Not surprisingly – recognising the importance of his prize – von Würzburg inscribed his own name on it before passing it to his master. From Friedrich Wilhelm the manuscript passed to the dukes of Saxe-Gotha, and was listed in 18th – and 19th-century catalogues of their library. At various times it has suffered from fire damage, neglect, the attentions of graffiti artists, been dis-bound, and lost several pages. From the 16th to the 19th century the manuscript was discussed in numerous German scholarly works on fencing, which, tantalisingly, include possible references to the missing pages. In 1936 it appeared in an exhibition accompanying the Berlin Olympics, but then disappeared until 1950, when it turned up at Sotheby's in London and was bought by the Tower Armouries.

Battered as it is, the manuscript is a beautiful, fascinating and wonderfully preserved reminder of the importance attached to the martial arts, then considered one of the sciences, in the Middle Ages. Today, renewed interest in European martial arts, the European *Fechtbuch* tradition, and the recent publication of this example in facsimile, has ensured that it remains at the forefront of discussion and debate. At the top of the featured illustration, from folio 3, the Priest takes up the 'First' or 'Under-Arm' position on the left, whilst the Scholar opposes him with the position of 'Half Shield'. Below, the Priest attacks and engages the Scholar's sword in a bind.

Notandum hic primitus p[r]ima custodia videl[icet] sub. **G** custodia p[r]ima recta d[icitu]r una
obsessio vo[cata] halpschilt. Et sic illo sta[n]do obsesso q[ui] nō... v. contrariū p[r]ime halpschilt langorem sem-
sub ben n[on] ducit aliā plagam qu[am] p[er]petrat de alterslieben
p[er]cussiones qu[e] p[er] su[per]bia[m] attinge[re] n[on] pot[est]. In m[od]icu[m] cap[ut] sit
p[re]ciosum. Si obsesso m[od]o pr[ae]d[i]c[t]o cu[m] in vade[re] vis tu[n]c. Si obmittit gen[us]
cōtrar[iu]m vt inf[ra] sep[tim]um 3[um]

Dum du[cit] halpschilt cedit sub gladiu[m] q[uo]d scutu[m]
su gradib[us] est recipit c. sit e stichslac.
sic ligat caliter sm[en] sut b schilslac.

Notandum q[uod] qui iter sup[eri]us dux[it] plag[am]
gam post ap[...] sine schilslach. si ẽ g[e]n[us]. sic
aut m[od]o eod[em] sit illo faciedo Et religat ā caelat.

Nota q[uod] p[r]ima custodia videlic[et] sub brach[io] p[er] obsess[...] et t[...] ua[...] eu[...]sch q[ui] obsid[ent]
eu[...] ead custodia p[er] p[er]fecte p[r]ima[m] custodia[m] obsid[...] m[...]ch[...] eu[...] regat custodia p[ri]m[a] ca[...]
posto[re] obsid[...] p[er] obsione q[ua]da[m] que p[...]ammo g[...]ard[...] eu[...] p[osto]re q[uo]d vō halpschilt
diss[...] eu[...] m co q[uo]d gladiu[m]. Sic b[ra]ch[ium] g[ra]diu[m] sup[er] scutu[m] tulit q[ue] m[a]nu reg[ui]t scutu[m]
tandi o m[anu] recipit gla[dium].

7

Mail sleeve from the Hundred Years War

Probably Germany, about 1345 · III.17

The long reign of Edward III (1327–77) was a tumultuous one for England. For almost all of it England was at war, both with the Scots, and most significantly with the French in the first phases of the Hundred Years War. Edward's reign was marked by some of England's greatest successes on the battlefield, including Crécy (1346) and Poitiers (1356), but also by the Black Death which devastated its population. Unlike some kings of England, Edward was blessed with male children, Edward the Black Prince, Lionel of Antwerp, John of Gaunt and Edmund of Langley, and it was between their heirs that the Wars of the Roses would be fought for the succession a century later.

The outbreak of the war coincided with the permanent establishment of an armoury at the Tower, under the office of the Privy Wardrobe, which acquired, kept and issued arms and armour. The accounts of the Keeper, John Flete, for the early years of the war document the procurement of military equipment for Edward's armies, and the issue of their equipment for campaigns. The mail sleeve described here is one of the very few pieces to survive in the armoury from its earliest years at the Tower. We can date the sleeve to that period because of a change in the construction of mail in Europe. Mail, formed of interlocking iron and sometimes latten (copper alloy) links, is first recorded in Iron Age Britain, and was adopted and spread by the armies of Imperial Rome to Europe and beyond. Most Roman and early medieval European mail, where it survives in good enough condition to study, is of 'half-riveted' construction, that is of alternate bands of links individually closed by rivets, alternating with others, usually hammer-welded and solid. By the second half of the fourteenth century that style of mail had been replaced across Europe by all-riveted mail, without any solid links. The earliest documents of the Tower armoury date precisely to the period when the change from one style to the other was taking place and allow us to date this mail sleeve and a small number of mail garments of the same construction, to the period before 1350.

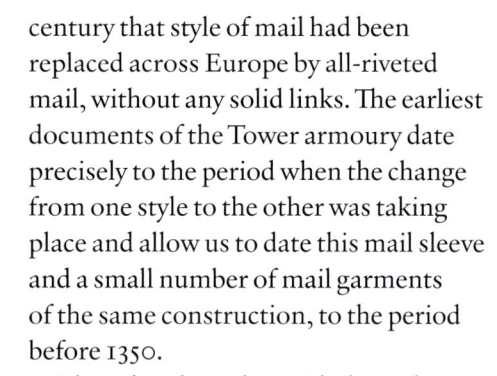

They also show that with the widespread adoption of the first solid-plate body armour, the 'pair of plates', in the fourteenth century, the full mail shirt or habergeon ceased to be worn beneath plate body armour. It was replaced by a mail collar, sleeves and 'paunces', a mail skirt and brayette or groin defence supported at the waist by a belt, all of which together protected with flexible mail the parts of the body that were difficult to protect with plate armour. Though very few of these medieval mail garments were signed by their makers, Flete's accounts record the armourers from whom he procured them in the late 1330s, ready for Edward's first expedition to Flanders in 1339–40. Like the great helms, bacinets and plate defences for the body and limbs, a small minority were purchased from English armourers such as Geoffrey Winchcombe, William Hales and Richard Sutherland, a few likewise from the armourers of Lombardy, but the vast majority were imported from makers from Cologne, Utrecht, Middelburg, Maastricht and other north German and Flemish centres. They set, or perhaps simply continued, a pattern of importing armour from mainland Europe into England which persisted until the seventeenth century.

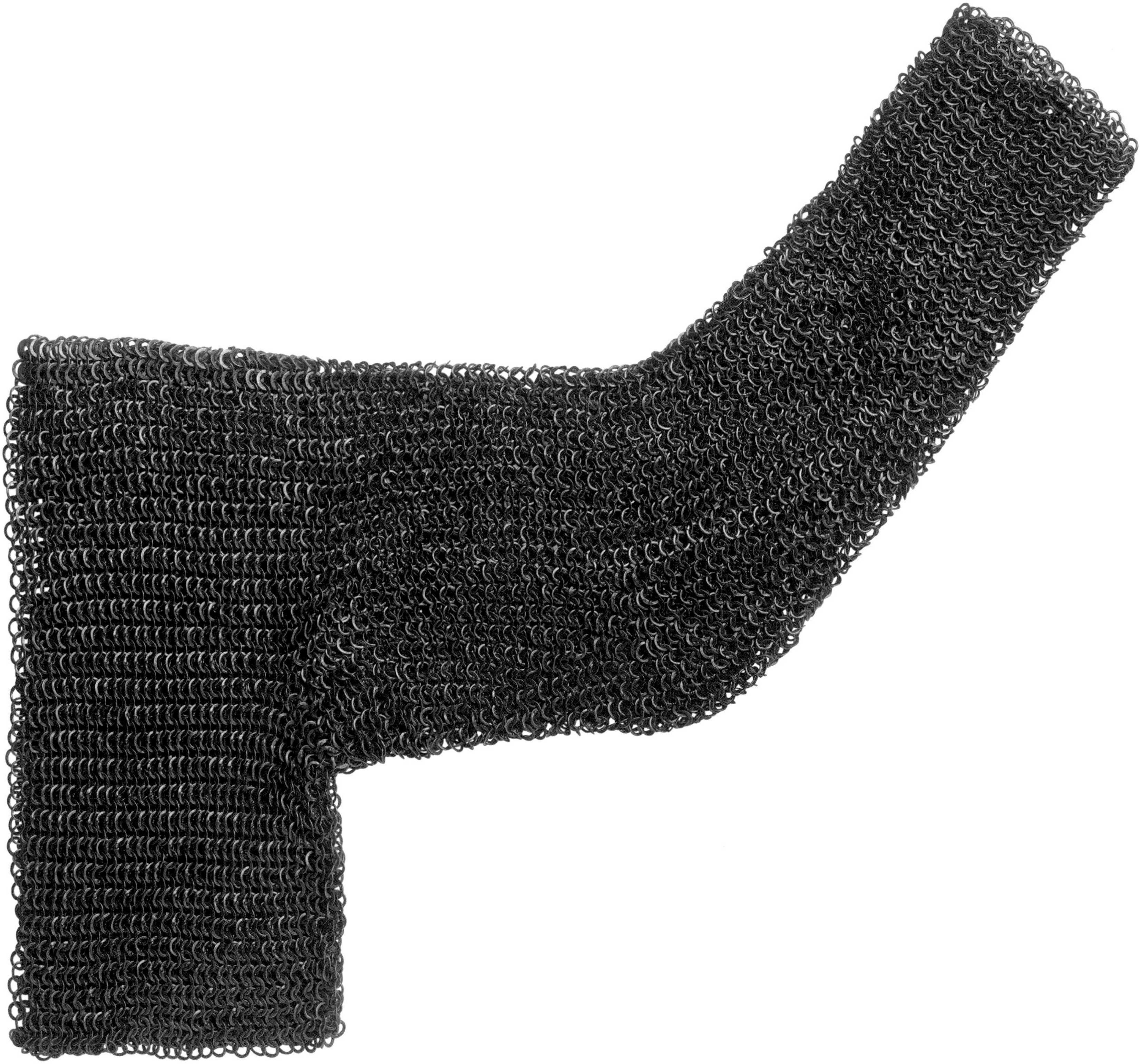

8

Great Helm

Possibly England, mid 1300s · iv.600

The knightly 'Great Helm' is probably the most widely recognised item of European armour of all time. Thanks perhaps to its stern and functional appearance, it was regarded as a symbol of military prowess, status and virtue from its introduction in the 12th century until long after its obsolescence. As such it appears in a wide range of contexts including funerary effigies, seals and paintings, whilst in heraldry it became an essential part of the full achievement of arms: in Germany the great helm and its crest took on such importance that they could take the place, on a seal, of a full coat of arms itself. Today, however, only about twenty genuine examples exist, making this a very rare and important object.

Developed from existing open-face head defences with the addition of rudimentary face-guards, by the middle of the 13th century the great helm, known at the time in Anglo-French circles as the *heaume*, had taken on its archetypal flat-topped form: it was made of several large plates riveted together, and completely enclosed the head. Vision was provided by a horizontal sight with a short bar between the eyes for better protection, although the jousting variant omitted the bar. Despite providing a good level of protection, these helmets had their limitations: the French biographer of Louis ix of France (r.1226–70) mentions that at the battle of Al-Mansourah in Egypt he gave the king his own kettle hat (*chapel de fer*) in exchange for his master's *heaume*, to allow his suffocating master to 'have some air'. In addition to the danger of stifling, the great helm was vulnerable to downward blows, thanks to the angular design and flat top-plate. As a result, during the second half of the 13th century it took on a more tapered form, better able to deflect a blade or missile, and by about 1350 it had become larger and deeper, extending downwards so that the bottom edge rested on the shoulders. Numerous medieval representations, most usefully in effigies, show that by about 1300 the great helm was often worn over a tighter-fitting visor-less bacinet, providing a double layer of protection.

Only two other mid-14th century great helms survive in Britain: those of Edward the Black Prince (d.1376), displayed in Canterbury Cathedral since the Middle Ages, and of Sir Richard Pembridge (d.1375), formerly in Hereford Cathedral and now in the National Museum of Scotland: all three have the sophistication of flanged sights worked out from the lower and upper edges of the face plates to protect the eyes, and of cross-shaped holes at the front for the attachment of a toggled guard-chain securing the helm to the belt or body armour. These features strongly suggest that they all came from the same workshop, and in spite of the establishment of the 'Company of Heaumers' in London in 1347 making an English origin possible, a Flemish or German origin is more likely.

At some point, probably in the 16th or 17th century, the helmet came back into its own in the context of the funerary 'achievement', a widespread practice in medieval and early modern Europe whereby weapons and armour were hung over the monuments of prominent men. Initially restricted to those of warriors, the practice was swiftly adopted by others wishing to endow themselves with a chivalric background. The prestige of the great helm made it particularly suitable for such use, an attribute which in this case ensured its survival.

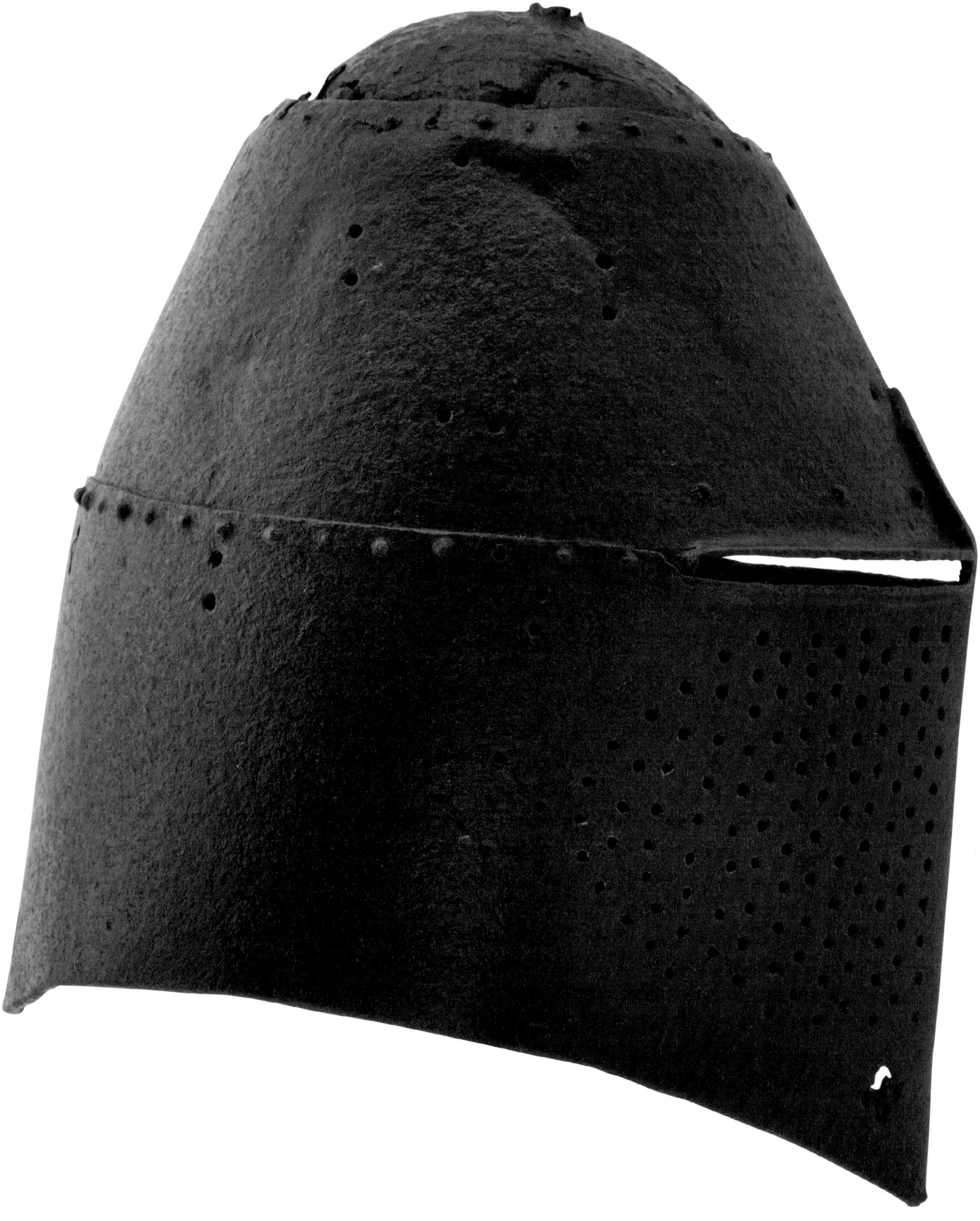

9

Sword with Arabic inscription

Probably Italy, late 14th or early 15th century · IX.950

The beauty of a sword may be due to its decoration, or, as with this late 14th – or early 15th-century example, largely to its form alone. In this case, its attractions and interest are amplified by its extraordinary story, known from the Arabic inscription on the forte of the blade. In English this reads:

Pious donation of [the] king al-Ashraf Bārsbay – May his victory be Strengthened! – in [the] storeroom [in] the Hall of Victories in the frontier city [of] Alexandria the well-guarded, of what he has acquired in [the] month [of] Muharram [in the year] six and thirty eight hundred [August–September 1432].

This identifies it as one of over 170 known swords obtained by the Mamluk sultans, rulers of a state founded by the former slave-soldiers of the Egyptian-based Ayyubid dynasty, who overthrew their masters in the mid 13th century. They received the weapons through capture, as diplomatic gifts or tribute payments, which were then inscribed by the sultans on giving them to their arsenal at Alexandria: at least eleven separate batches of swords reached the arsenal by this means between 1367/8 and 1436/7. This particular item is from a gift precisely enough dated to suggest it was given as tribute to Sultan Barsbây (r.1422–38) by John II, King of Cyprus, Jerusalem and Armenia (r.1418–38), following the Mamluk defeat of his father, King Janus, and in recognition of the sultan as his overlord. The inscription does not help with the date of the sword itself, but the distinctive blade form is donated by the Mamluks in 1368/9, implying that the sword was of some age when bequeathed in 1432, or that this particular form was produced for a number of years. Its marks, as with others in the batch, suggest an Italian origin.

In addition to its extraordinary history, the sword is also important thanks to its place in the development of the weapon itself. This lies in the inclusion of a guard for the forefinger, the first step in a series of developments that what would lead to the increasingly complex and protective hilts of the later 15th century and beyond. Such guards are first depicted in about 1350 and most commonly associated with cutting swords, either those of falchion form or others with single-edged blades. By looping the forefinger over the unsharpened ricasso, a swordsman was better able to align the edge when cutting, but the position made the finger vulnerable, a problem dealt with by this hook-like guard, later to become a closed ring. The form of guard also helps in thrusting, for which the long, narrow, stiff blade, slightly swollen and thickened at the very tip, was well adapted. Exceptionally well-balanced and light in the hand, this would have been highly effective in combat, which – along with its simple elegance and royal provenance – made it a fitting tribute offering and a fitting addition to Barsbây's arsenal.

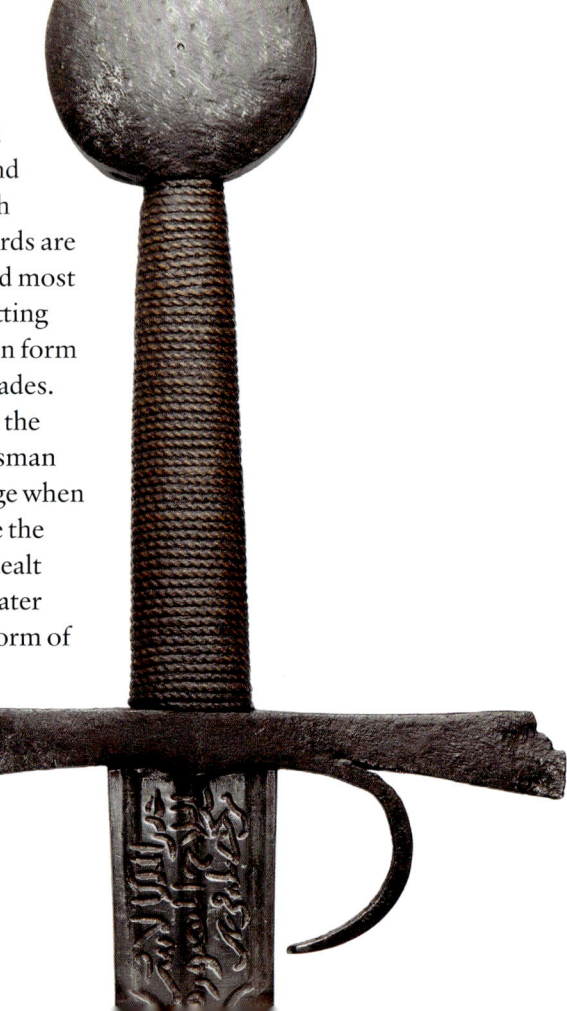

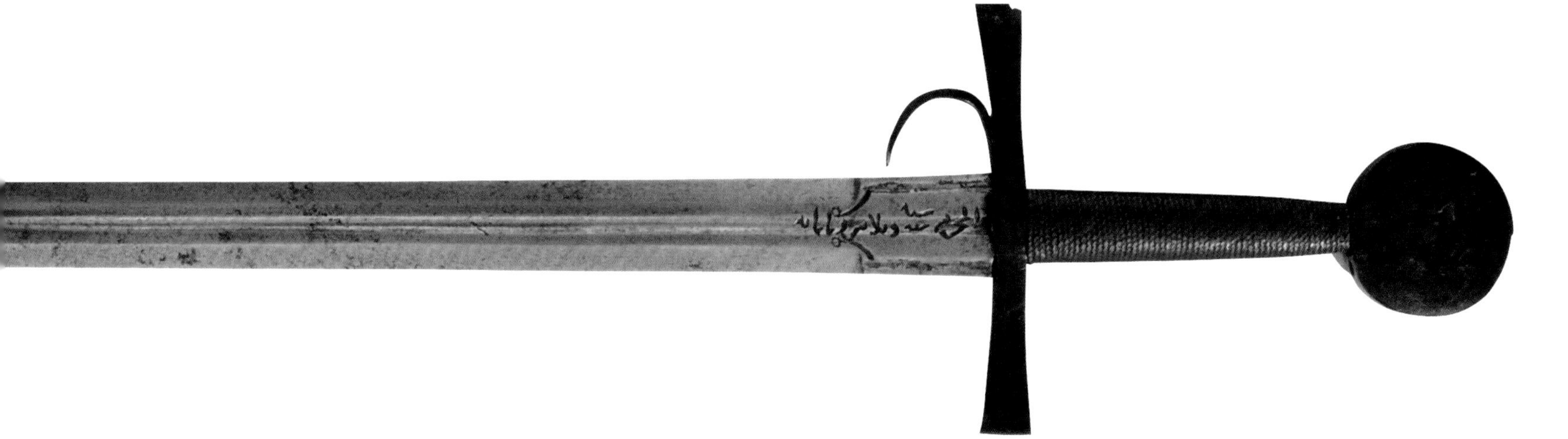

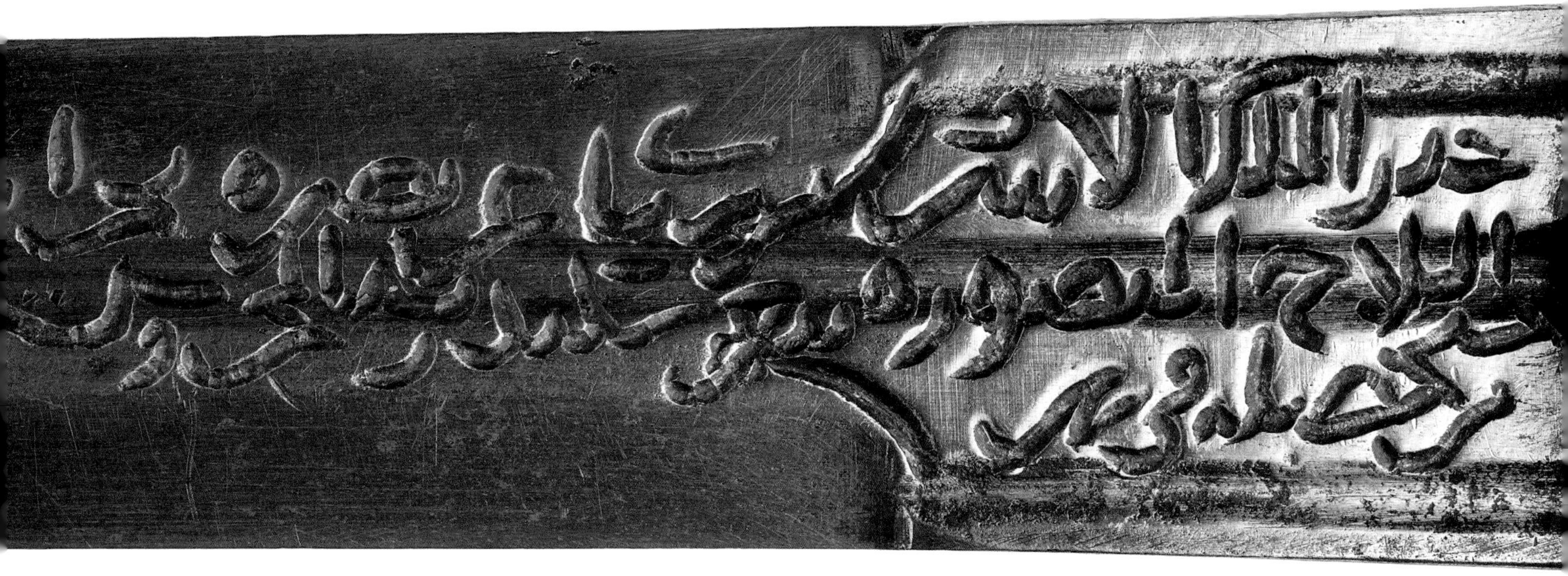

10

The 'Lyle' bacinet

Northern Italy, late 14th century · IV.470

By the second half of the 14th century the great helm had largely been relegated to the tournament, and replaced on the battlefield by the bacinet. Skilfully raised from a single piece of metal, the shape of the bacinet's closely fitting skull was perfectly designed to deflect missile and weapon strikes, and some were made more impressive with the addition of eastern-looking flutes radiating from the apex. Sweeping back from the face, the sides of the bacinet were angled to give maximum peripheral vision.

Unlike the rigid face-plate of most great helms, many bacinets were fitted with a pivoting visor, which, when raised, instantly allowed free vision and breathing. Of numerous different forms, by the late 14th century the most common style featured a conical snout or muzzle, known today (for obvious reasons) as the 'pig-faced' or 'hounskull' bacinet, the latter from the German '*Hundsgugel*' or 'hound's hood'. Widely represented in art of the period, their ubiquity has earned them the cachet of an 'international type' in the view of some arms and armour scholars. As with the skull, the conical snout deflected blows from the face, while carefully designed boxed edges around the sights and mouth kept points away from these vulnerable openings.

Popular though it was, however, the visored bacinet, with its sight thrown far forward of the face, gave a poor field of vision, especially when looking up or down, leading to the increasingly common use of detachable visors: this improved visibility and airflow when engaged in physically demanding close-quarter combat on foot, but posed obvious risks: several accounts relate how the 17-year old prince Henry (the future Henry V) was injured in the face by an arrow after lifting or removing his visor at the battle of Shrewsbury in 1403.

Rather than being worn over a separate mail coif, from the first quarter of the 14th century it became increasingly common for bacinets to be fitted with aventails of densely woven mail over a quilted textile lining. Attached to the helmet by a leather band fitted over a series of pierced staples or '*vervelles*', these were designed not only to protect the neck but also as an extra defence for the shoulders. Easily removable for repair and cleaning, the aventail was secured in place by a twisted cord or metal wire which passed through the holes in the *vervelles*. The 'Lyle Bacinet' is of particular importance in retaining what appears to be its original mail aventail, incorporating a double row of decorative copper-alloy rings.

Written, pictorial and sculptural sources show that many bacinets were lavishly decorated, with applied copper-alloy or occasionally silver gilt bands around the main edges of the visor and on the skull above the face opening. In an age in which knighthood and faith were inextricably linked, these often featured religious symbols, such as the Christogram 'IHS' (a Greek abbreviation of 'Jesus'), believed to protect the wearer. Others were fitted with decorative stuffed leather or textile rolls known to contemporaries as '*orles*' or 'circles', encircling the skull. Aventails were sometimes given a textile covering known as a '*vrysoun*' incorporating richly embroidered designs using geometric or sometimes heraldic motifs. Some accounts even mention bacinets encrusted with pearls and precious stones.

The exact origin of this supremely rare and important item is unknown, but until the 1920s it belonged to the Trapps at Churburg castle (Italian Tyrol), still the most significant collection of European medieval armour in private hands, and perhaps (before 1504) to the castle's previous owners, the Matsch family. In 1939 it was bought by the ship owner Sir Archibald Lyle and given to the Tower Armouries in 1946 in memory of his two sons, one killed at El Alamein and the other in Normandy.

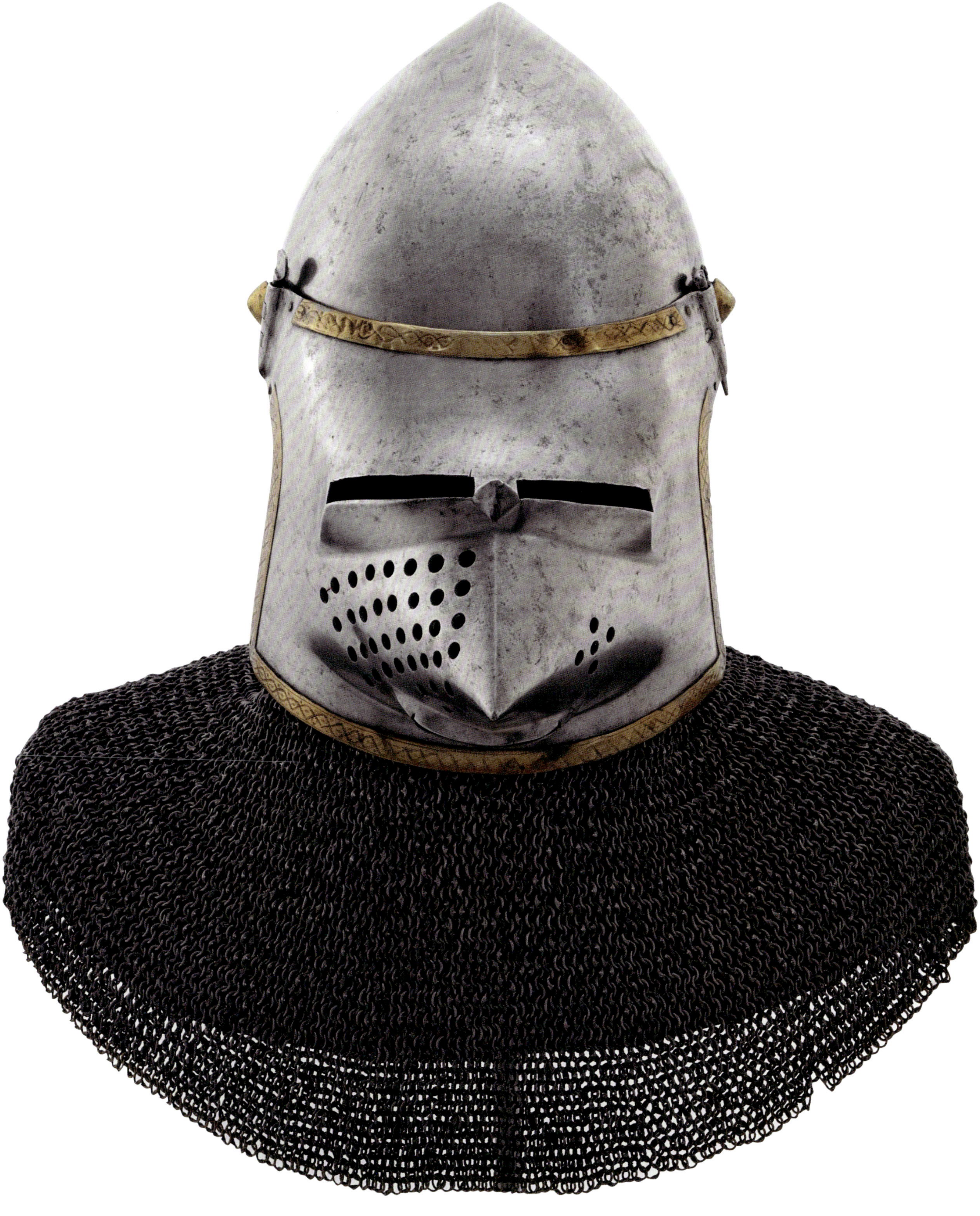

11

Jousting saddle for the '*Hohenzeuggestech*'

Germany, *c*.1400 · VI.94

With the appearance of a gigantic skeleton, this saddle must be one of the world's oddest looking pieces of armour. It was made in Germany in about 1400 for a very particular form of jousting. The sport itself, although more familiar today than for centuries thanks to its resurgence over the last thirty years, may still need a little introduction. Essentially, jousting involved a contest between two horsemen, fought as a series of charges or 'courses' with a couched lance (held level, under the right arm), the aim being to strike the opponent as accurately and as hard as possible above the waist. Victory was determined by increasingly complicated scoring systems. Beginning as training for warfare as much as sport in the mid 11th century, contestants' arms and armour were at first those used on the battlefield (and they faced similar risks) but by 1450 equipment had evolved to become entirely specific to the sport. Over the same period many different forms of jousting had developed. From the late 14th century, most were variations of the safer 'Joust of Peace', using rebated (blunt), coronel-tipped lances and specialised armour, and the more dangerous 'Joust of War', using pointed lances and armour similar to that worn in the field. All, however, made for an exciting spectator sport, showing off the strength and courage of horse and rider, horsemanship, skill at arms, armour and wealth as none other could. No wonder so much time, money and ingenuity were spent on the necessary equipment.

One of the specialist forms of joust developed in the German-speaking lands in the late 14th century was the '*Hohenzeuggestech*', or 'joust in the high saddle'. Saddles were designed to raise the rider as much as six inches above the horse's back, lessening the chance of the horse's head being struck or interfering with its rider's aim. This example, in common with most others, is made of wood with a covering of rawhide; it weighs 16 kg and retains traces of paint that formerly covered all its outer surfaces.

The horseman's seat was formed by two rigid rings, and in the place of the more familiar pommel, the high front or '*arçon*', protected his lower torso and groin. The huge sweeping plates formed a harness around the knight's legs, holding him in a braced, almost upright position. This made it practically impossible for him to be unhorsed, and provided more effective protection than leg armour and tassets; it is a reminder that jousts of this form pre-dated the introduction of the 'tilt' – the long barrier between the opponents to prevent collision. As such, these saddles were also used in the *mêlée*, a form of 'tourney' fought between groups or teams of men according to many different rules, in which the legs were equally vulnerable.

Bought by the Ordnance Office in 1854, the earlier history of this saddle is unknown, although its form reveals its rough provenance and date, thanks to evidence from the handful of other survivals, to be found in Switzerland and Germany. What is clear, however, is that it was repeatedly used in both joust and *mêlée*, as revealed by lance-holes and sword-cuts to the front and to edge of the *arçon*. It is a rare reminder of how brutal certain forms of tourney could be, and the elaborate and ingenious means that were devised to protect participants and their horses.

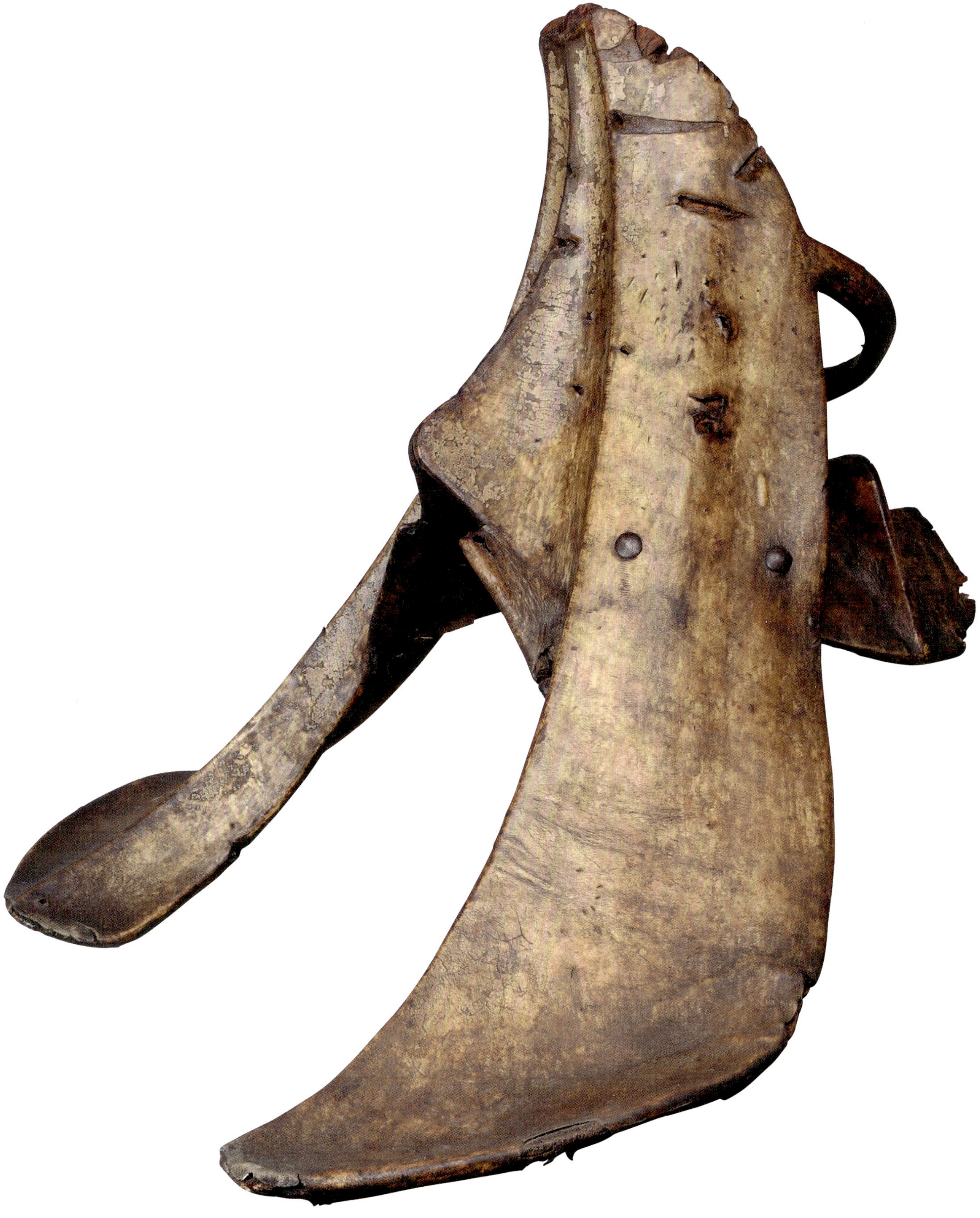

12

The 'Warwick' shaffron

Possibly England, *c.*1400 · VI.446

'His horse is slain, and all on foot he fights', cries Catesby in Shakespeare's *Richard III*, and the king himself, more famously – and more than once – 'A horse, a horse, my kingdom for a horse!'. Dismounted, King Richard's prospects on the battlefield, despite his protestations, were fatally weakened; for the mounted warrior protecting his horse was almost as important as protecting himself. Although always rare, horse armour is known from the 3rd millennium BC in Mesopotamia and was widely used by late Roman and Byzantine cavalry. In Europe its use died out from the 6th century, but was revived in the 12th, in the form of a mail cloak like a horse-blanket extending over the head and neck, with the addition, by the 1260s, of steel or leather plates protecting the horse's head and chest. These respectively formed the 'shaffron' and the 'peytral'. By the mid 15th century, armours were made up of large plates for the body, a laminated crinet for the neck, and a shaffron, and at least one example, made in 1480 for the future Holy Roman Emperor, Maximilian I, covered the animal's legs and entire body with articulated plates. Such armours, known as 'bards', might look hopelessly heavy, but, at 26–32 kg weighed about the same as that worn by the rider. They were particularly fashionable in the first half of the 16th century, but from then on progressively covered less of the body and finally only the head. They were abandoned in the 1630s.

The 'Warwick' shaffron, datable to the early 15th century on the basis of similar examples, is the earliest surviving piece of European medieval horse armour. It is made of a large main plate of steel covering the whole front of the face, with raised dome-like areas over the eyes, pierced with holes, while other holes allowed the horse to breathe. Larger openings at the top made way for the ears, while three pairs of larger holes at the top of the side plates are for attaching the crinet. Its enormous size owes to the need to accommodate a thick layer of padding attached to the inside. Fascinatingly, the piece has taken a series of blows from a range of weapons, showing that it has been used: these include a long gash over the left eye, possibly caused by the point of a sword or spear, a large dent over the right eye, perhaps dealt by an axe or sword, and two cuts to the central keel, the upper one struck with some force. On the left brow a small, square puncture was probably made by a bodkin-headed arrow, as was another dent nearby.

The shaffron and other associated pieces were seen at Warwick Castle by the antiquary Sir William Dugdale in 1656, who heard of a tradition associating it with the legendary pre-Conquest hero, Guy of Warwick. Dugdale was sceptical, writing that 'I rather think they are of a later time', but it is wholly possible that it had been there since the 15th century, and that it belonged to Richard Beauchamp, 13th Earl of Warwick (1382–1439), whose magnificent gilded latten effigy, in full armour, lies in sight of the castle in St Mary's church. One of the greatest and wealthiest knights of the Middle Ages, Beauchamp travelled and campaigned in England, France, Germany, Russia and the Holy Land, and it is reasonable to think that the shaffron went with him and played a part in his exploits.

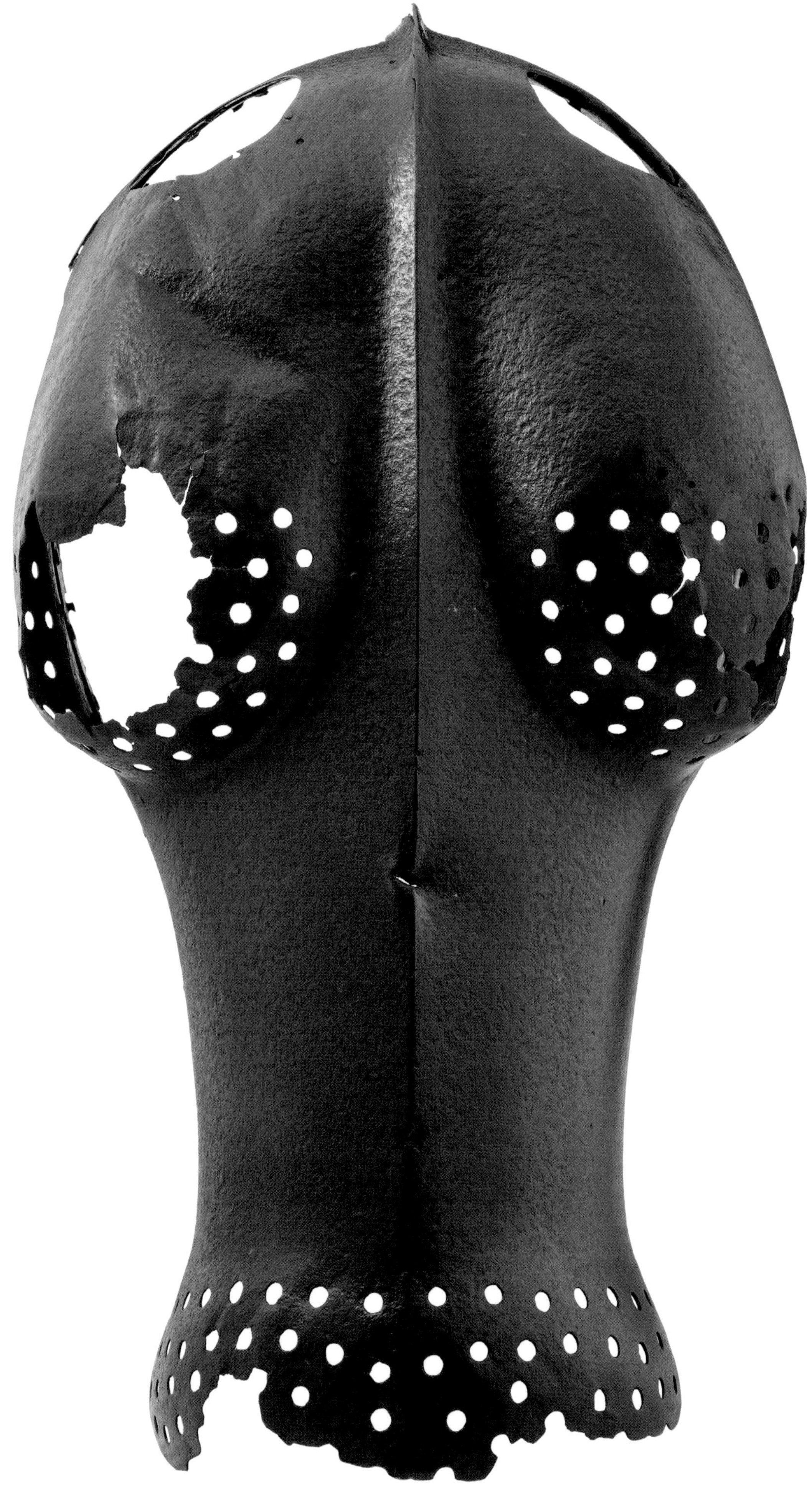

13

A 15th-century 'Book of Fireworks'

Germany, first quarter of the 15th century · Feur 1

Gunpowder, along with the wheel and the printing press, is one of the most important technical developments of all time. It revolutionised warfare, hunting and self-defence, and had an incalculable impact on the course of history. Invented in China, perhaps as early as the 12th century, gunpowder is made up of 75% saltpetre (potassium nitrate), 15% charcoal and 10% sulphur, although the proportions can vary: when touched with a spark the sulphur ignites, the heat from which causes the saltpetre to release oxygen, enabling the charcoal to ignite. The mixture then burns very fast, releasing large volumes of gas almost instantaneously, creating an explosion – which in a gun, forces the projectile out of the barrel.

Although almost certainly used earlier in China, guns were introduced in Europe in the early 14th century, and an example of about 1400 is described below (16). By then, manuals for the manufacture and use for this still-experimental weapon were no doubt in circulation, but the first known example is this *Feuerwerkbuch* or 'Book of Fireworks', the text of which originated in Germany in the 1380s. The author is not named, but by the early 15th century he was held to have been a friar and alchemist called (in Latin) *Niger Berchtoldus* or 'Black Berthold', and credited with the actual discovery of gunpowder itself while attempting to turn lead into gold. Other stories, however, abound: a later copy of the *Feuerwerkbuch* (dated 1444) made for the future Holy Roman Emperor Frederick III (r.1452–93) states instead that he was a Cistercian monk, that he made the discovery in 1380, and for which he was condemned to death in 1388; another contemporary source claims instead that he was executed by Wenceslas, King of Bohemia (r.1378–1419) in 1389. While Berthold was clearly not the inventor of gunpowder, it is clear from these sources that he was indeed the book's initial author, and that it was passed down and copied by later master gunners and their apprentices, who added their own notes about the composition of gunpowder and its use. Some seventy copies are known to exist, dating from about 1400 to 1450; the majority are in German and Austrian libraries, and this is the only example in the United Kingdom. It appears to have originated in Swabia (South Germany) in the first quarter of the 15th century. The first part consists of a standardised text, and describes an allegedly new type of gun called the *Steinbüchse*, capable of firing heavy stone balls over long distances, and a new form of gunpowder, compressed into pellets, called *Knollenpulver* ('lump powder'), a process which avoided the separation of its ingredients in transit. The second part, in a different hand, on different paper and post-dating Berthold, contains a master gunner's comments and notes on the previous text and the illustrations. The third part consists of fifty-four colour illustrations, some of which show a master gunner, clearly identified by his red hat adorned with a feather or brush, conducting a siege and supervising the preparation of gunpowder and various incendiary devices. Other illustrations show various types of cannon and gun-boring machines, as well as siege equipment such as scaling ladders, large shields or pavises, and various types of cart. In the image shown, of a siege, the master gunner has just fired a large cannon and the shot is about to strike the battlements, while incendiary darts fired from a handgun and crossbows rain down on the rooftops. The defenders, also armed with crossbows, are about to return fire.

The Tower Armouries acquired the Firework Book in 1950, but the history of its ownership before the 1860s is unknown. Today it has a special place in our collection, representing the craft of gunnery, its equipment and attendant trades in their first century, and the painful processes of trial and error through which they developed.

lxxxvj

14

Dragon saddle from the Order of St George

Probably Austria or Hungary, early 15th century · VI.95

The saddle was an essential piece of a medieval knight's equipment and it could be as expensive, valued and lavishly embellished as any other. Very few survive: this example, rarity apart, has the distinction of accomplished and lively decoration, and probable association with one of the great European chivalric orders and two of the greatest monarchs of the period.

The saddle's main structure is of wood, a complex, dramatic creation of bold sweeping curves, with a high bow at the front, and at the rear two buttock-shaped semi-circles set at an angle to the tree (the base of the saddle) forming the cantle; the tree itself is pierced with slots for the girth (the larger one) and stirrups, and holes for further straps holding the saddle in place. The main decoration is scribed into broad bone panels, the scored lines being emphasised by black staining, giving the impression of relief, and depicting elaborate foliage and winged, snarling dragons; the effect is heightened by inlays of black, red and green mastic. On either side of the pommel a scroll is held at the top by a hand and below in a dragon's mouth, inscribed in gothic lettering: on the right side it reads, in south German dialect, 'ich hoff des pesten / dir geling' (I hope the best fortune may attend you), and on the left 'hilf got / wol auf sand jorgen nam' (Help God! Forward in the name of St George). Contrasting with these pious words, the scrolls at the back of the cantle perhaps less helpfully declare that 'im ars / is vinster' ('in the arse it is black'). At the point of the bow is a cross of St George. It was probably made not just specifically for its owner, but also to fit a particular horse, and intended for use in hunting, parade or the tournament rather than warfare.

'Orders of chivalry', meanwhile, were exclusive groups of knights and noblemen, usually centred around a monarch and bound together by common oaths, often with a political and military purpose, and mostly formed between the early 14th and the late 15th century: among those extant today is the Order of the Garter, founded in 1348 by Edward III. In 1408, the King of Hungary, Sigismund, later Holy Roman Emperor (r.1433–7), founded the Order of St George to bolster his position at home and to help resist Turkish expansion: membership initially included twenty-one prominent Hungarian barons but was later extended to foreigners including Duke Ernst of Austria; Vitautas, Grand Duke of Lithuania; Christopher, Duke of Bavaria who later became King of Denmark, Sweden and Norway; and Vlad II, Prince of Wallachia in 1431. Vlad subsequently became known as *Dracul*, 'the Dragon', and his son, Vlad Draculea (d.1476), 'the Dragon's son', was the inspiration for Bram Stoker's gothic novel, *Dracula*. The saddle's association with the Order is suggested (fairly convincingly) by the decoration and inscription, placing it among a group of twenty-two similarly decorated examples mostly of central European origin. Some of these can be linked to particular individuals, such as those in the Kunsthistorisches Museum in Vienna linked to Albrecht, King of Hungary (r.1437–9), also featuring the saint (on horseback), and to his son and successor but one, Ladislav V (r.1444–57).

Certainty eludes us, but it is quite possible that the Royal Armouries' saddle was presented to Henry V, king of England, in 1416 by Albrecht's father-in-law, the Emperor Sigismund, along with membership of the Order, when he visited England and was himself admitted to the Garter. If so, Sigismund's gifts would have been very much in keeping with the practice of the time and reflected the renewed prestige of the English monarchy following Henry's victories in France.

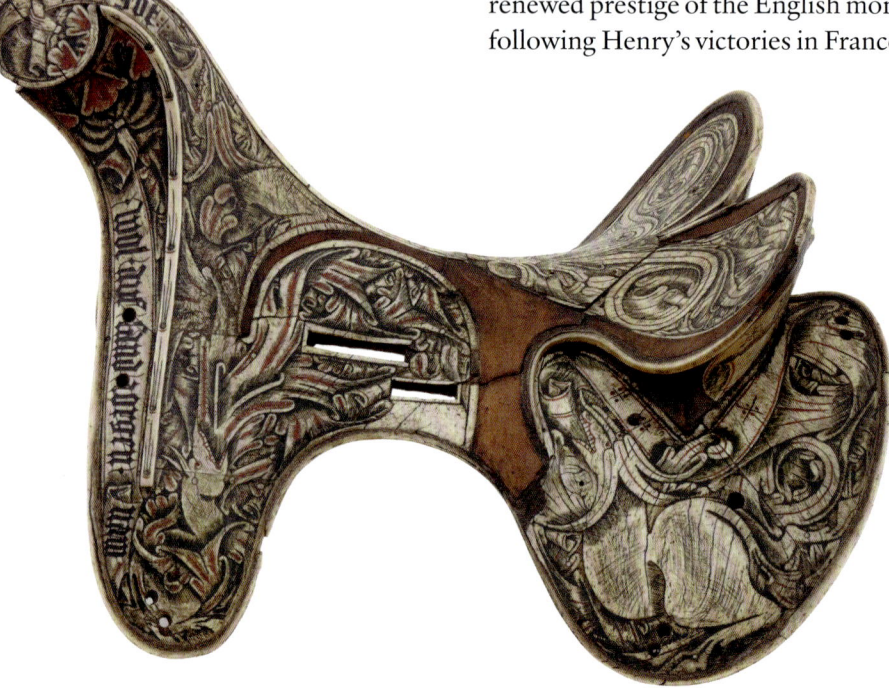

[72]

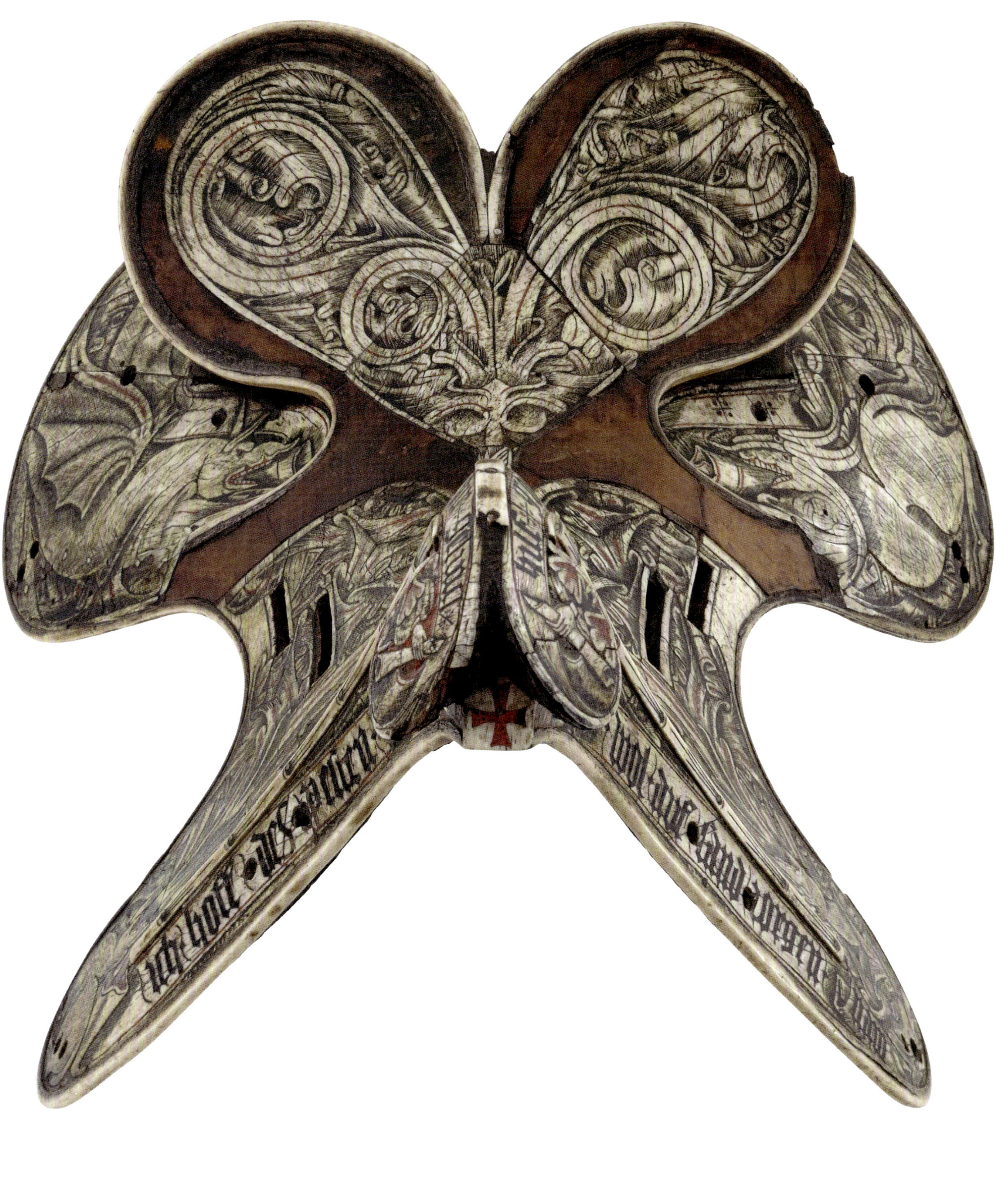

15

The 'Ming' sword

China, about 1420 · XXVIS.295

The Ming dynasty ruled China from the fall of the Mongol Yuan in 1368 until its replacement by the Qing dynasty in 1644, and produced some of the finest technical and artistic creations in Chinese history. This sword is among the best-known and most prized of the Royal Armouries' holdings. Dating from about 1420, the hilt and scabbard are lavishly decorated with gold, silver and semi-precious stones. They were clearly made for a *jian*, a straight-bladed, double-edged blade, militarily obsolete by the time of the Ming dynasty but still prized for ceremonial and presentation purposes and as a status symbol in diplomacy and politics. The existing blade, although medieval, fails to match the hilt in quality, and is probably a later Tibetan replacement of the same form.

The centrepiece of the design is the monstrous face forming the hand guard, which appears to be devouring the blade. This kind of image, common to both

Hindu and Buddhist mythology, is found across China, India, Tibet and much of South-East Asia. It can be interpreted in several different ways, including as a so-called 'wrathful-one' (a destroyer of demons in Buddhist mythology, sent to guide the soul and clear a path towards enlightenment), or a personification of the cycle of creation and destruction, and the inevitability of death and rebirth. Generally though, it is considered to be a symbol of protection and good fortune. In Sanskrit, the ancient Indian language associated with Hinduism and Buddhism, the image is called a *Kirtimukha*, which translates as 'Face of Glory', whilst in Tibetan it is *Chibar*, which means 'That Which Resembles Nothing'.

The *Kirtimukha* or *Chibar* is accompanied by other Buddhist images. Across the pommel are displayed the eight Buddhist symbols of Good Augury, the *Ba Jixiang*: the Wheel of Law or *Dharma*, the standard, the treasure jar, the pair of fish, the endless knot, the lotus, the parasol and the conch shell of victory. There is also a Sanskrit inscription halfway down the scabbard which translates as 'Honorific/Precious Sword'. This is the last of the Seven Jewels of Royal Power, the others being the Precious Wheel, Precious Jewel, Precious Queen, Precious Minister, Precious Elephant and Precious Horse – all symbols of monarchy.

The ornamentation of the hilt and scabbard is very similar to that of two other Ming dynasty objects associated with the Tsurphu monastery in central Tibet, the head of which was a tutor to the Yongle Emperor, third of the Ming dynasty (r.1402–24), and was said to have returned in 1409 with gifts from the Emperor himself. An earlier exchange of gifts also took place in 1407. These similarities, the exquisite ornamentation and the overall Tibetan style and Buddhist imagery, suggest that the sword was also manufactured in the Yongle court for use as a diplomatic gift: the recipient was probably an allied Tibetan ruler, or one of the powerful Buddhist Monasteries whose influence had slowly extended into China under the Mongol Yuan dynasty (1271–1368). As such the sword constitutes not only a fabulous piece of ornamental metalwork and (as Ming weaponry is so rare) an exceptional survival, but also a supreme example of the magical and religious significance with which arms and armour are so often imbued.

16

The 'Danzig' gun

Probably Poland, *c.*1350–1430 · XII.11833

Gunpowder and its origins have been mentioned previously in describing the 15th-century gunners' manual, the *Feuerwerkbuch* (13): although it had several roles in warfare, and others in industry, its use in guns, as its name implies, was the most important. In Europe, the gun first appears in an illustration to the treatise *Concerning the Majesty, Wisdom and Prudence of Kings* (*De nobilitatibus, sapientiis et prudentiis regum*) written in 1326 by Walter de Milemete for the instruction of the future Edward III. This was a curious-looking vase-shaped affair that fired – as was sometimes the case for over a century – not cannon balls but darts, similar to crossbow bolts. In one form or another, however, guns were used in warfare in the 1330s, and by the end of the century were a standard piece of any army's equipment. The best-known type is the 'bombard' – a heavy cannon – but others, such as the 'Danzig gun', portable and useable by an individual, were just as important. Capable of piercing any armour of the period, they eventually replaced the bow and crossbow on the battlefield and were the ancestors of modern small arms.

This example, named for its probable find spot at Gdańsk in modern Poland (Danzig in German), is exceptional for its early date, its sculptural qualities and its diminutive size. Comparative and metallurgical evidence suggests that it was made between *c.*1350 and 1450, at a time when the city was ruled by the Teutonic Knights, a military order, and possibly for them. Comparators for such an early gun are few, the closest being the similarly decorated 'Mörkö gun' from Sweden and one recovered at Tannenberg Castle in Hesse (Germany). As with most handguns of the period, this weapon has a socket to fit a wooden haft or tiller which contemporary illustrations show varying in length from a short handle to a full-length staff. It was, as most guns were until the 1850s, a muzzle-loader. In other words, the powder was poured down the barrel, and the shot, followed by wadding, pressed home with a ramrod; a small charge of powder was then put into the 'pan' – a hollow on the top of the barrel – which was then lit with a 'match' – the smouldering end of a saltpetre-impregnated cord. This in turn set off the main charge via the touch-hole, linking the pan to the inside of the barrel. Although at 183 mm long this gun is both unusually short and, at 12 mm or.47 bore, of small calibre, it is nonetheless a lethal weapon, probably as powerful as a modern handgun using low velocity ammunition. Highly decorated as it is, however, it may have been seen more as a piece of sculpture rather than a practical weapon.

Structurally, it consists of a single bronze casting, hexagonal in section. Its most striking feature is its anthropomorphic decoration, dominated by the theme of the human head: the pan is formed into the gaping mouth of a clean-shaven human face, with the vent at its centre, whereas the muzzle is surrounded by four bearded faces with long hair. These match common representations of Christ and/or John the Baptist, but are as likely to depict the mythical 'wild man' or 'woodwose' of northern European folklore, who appears abundantly in medieval art, architecture and literature (perhaps most famously on the 'Bellarmine' jugs of the 16th and 17th centuries). We will never know the sculptor's intent for certain, but whether expressing piety or evoking the brute strength of the 'wild man' at the business end of the weapon, its decoration would have made some sense.

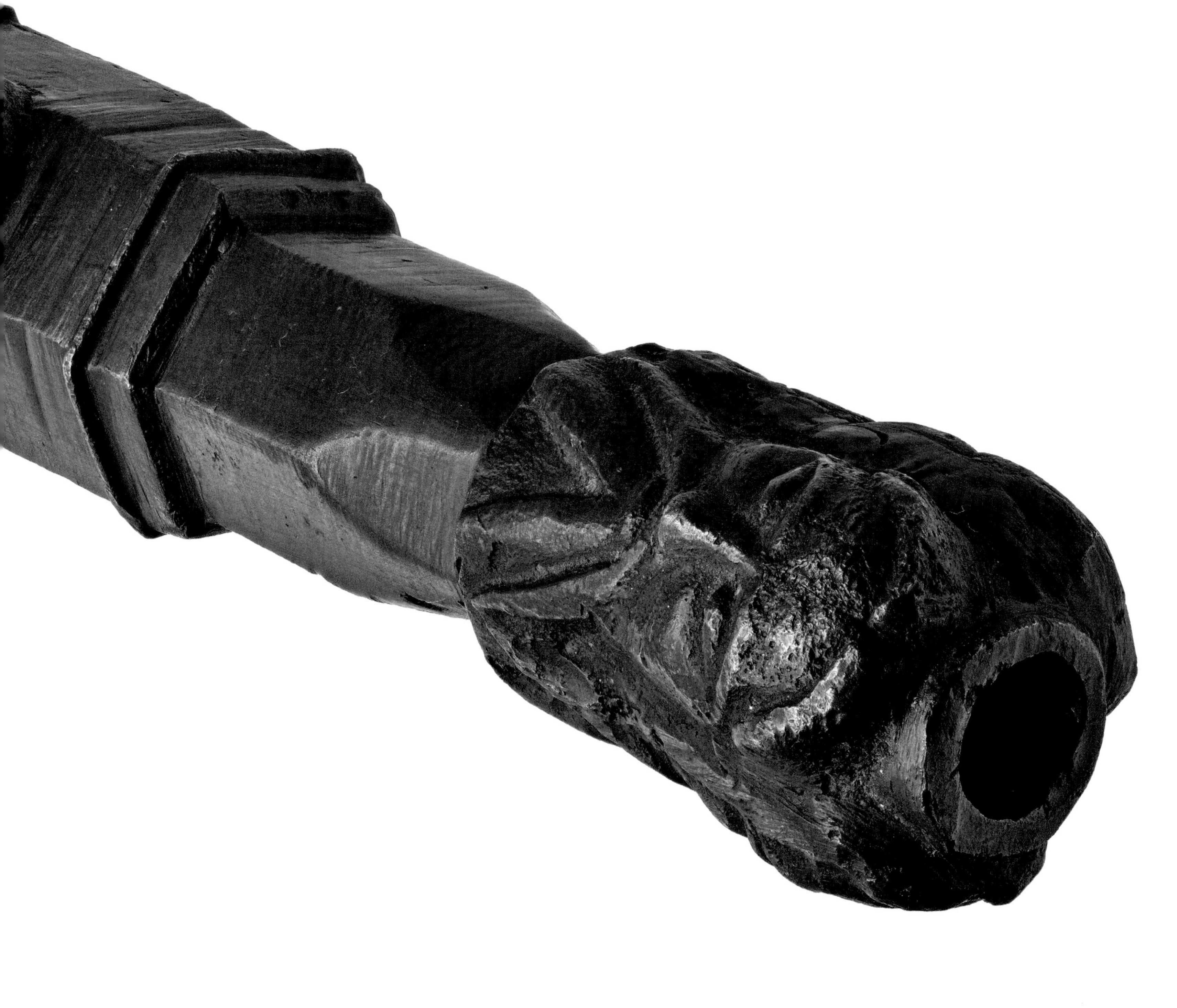

17

Mons Meg, a 15th-century iron bombard

Belgium, 1449 · XIX.13

Mons Meg, displayed at Edinburgh Castle, is the most spectacular, largest and the best-known medieval siege gun or 'bombard' in the British Isles. Its name owes to its place of origin, the city of Mons in modern Belgium, and the 15th-century practice (for reasons unknown) of naming great guns by variants of 'Margaret'. Mons had been held since 1432 by the powerful and cultivated Valois Dukes of Burgundy, and it was Phillip the Good (r.1419–67) who commissioned Mons Meg. It was delivered by the arms dealer Jehan Cambier in June 1449 at a cost of 1536 *groot pond*, equivalent to approximately £450,000 today. As with most bombards, Mons Meg consists of wide barrel and narrower powder chamber, in this case respectively 2.68 m long internally with a bore of 50 cm, and 1.13 m long inside with a bore of 13 cm. The barrel was made up of twenty-five flat wrought iron strips, fitted longitudinally around the circumference of a wooden core or 'mandril', and then wrapped around by thirty-four iron rings, hammered together edge to edge whilst red hot and which then shrank on cooling: the technique was used, by then alongside casting, into the 16th century, but it was this process, thanks to its similarity to wooden barrel-making, that gave gun 'barrels' their name. The powder chamber, ingeniously joined to the rear end of the barrel, is also of wrought iron, but hammer-welded together to create a single massive forging. The existing carriage, made in 1935, based on an image of the gun of about 1600 carved on an inner gateway to the castle, is of a form designed for firing – the barrel being elevated or depressed by the insertion or removal of wooden wedges – rather than for transport: on campaign, the gun was carried on a special iron-bound cart, and was originally fired from a massive timber bed or, in medieval French, '*affust*'. The gun used stone shot, 150 kg in weight, six of which are displayed beside it, and at an elevation of 45 degrees it had a range of two miles. In 1457 the Duke sent Mons Meg, ammunition and a crew to his ally James II of Scotland '*pour soy en aidier à ses affaires*' ('to help him in his work') of driving the remaining English from Scotland. Thereafter, normally kept in Edinburgh, Mons Meg served in various campaigns and for saluting, until damaged by an over-powerful charge in 1681. By then, however, the gun had acquired celebrity status which ensured its preservation, and following the failed Jacobite rising of 1745 was taken, for propagandist reasons, to London. At least by 1810 it was on display in the Grand Storehouse at the Tower: it was described in a guidebook as 'An immense large iron cannon, brought from Edinburgh Castle, called Mount's Meg; it is of such amazing dimensions that two men may go into its mouth'. In 1822 George IV, at Edinburgh in the voluble company of Sir Walter Scott, was persuaded that this great symbol of Scotland's past should be returned. Ten years later it was shipped to Leith, and with bands playing, flags flying and military honours made a triumphant progress to the castle. Today it stands at the very summit of the fortress, and, appropriately enough, next to St Margaret's chapel.

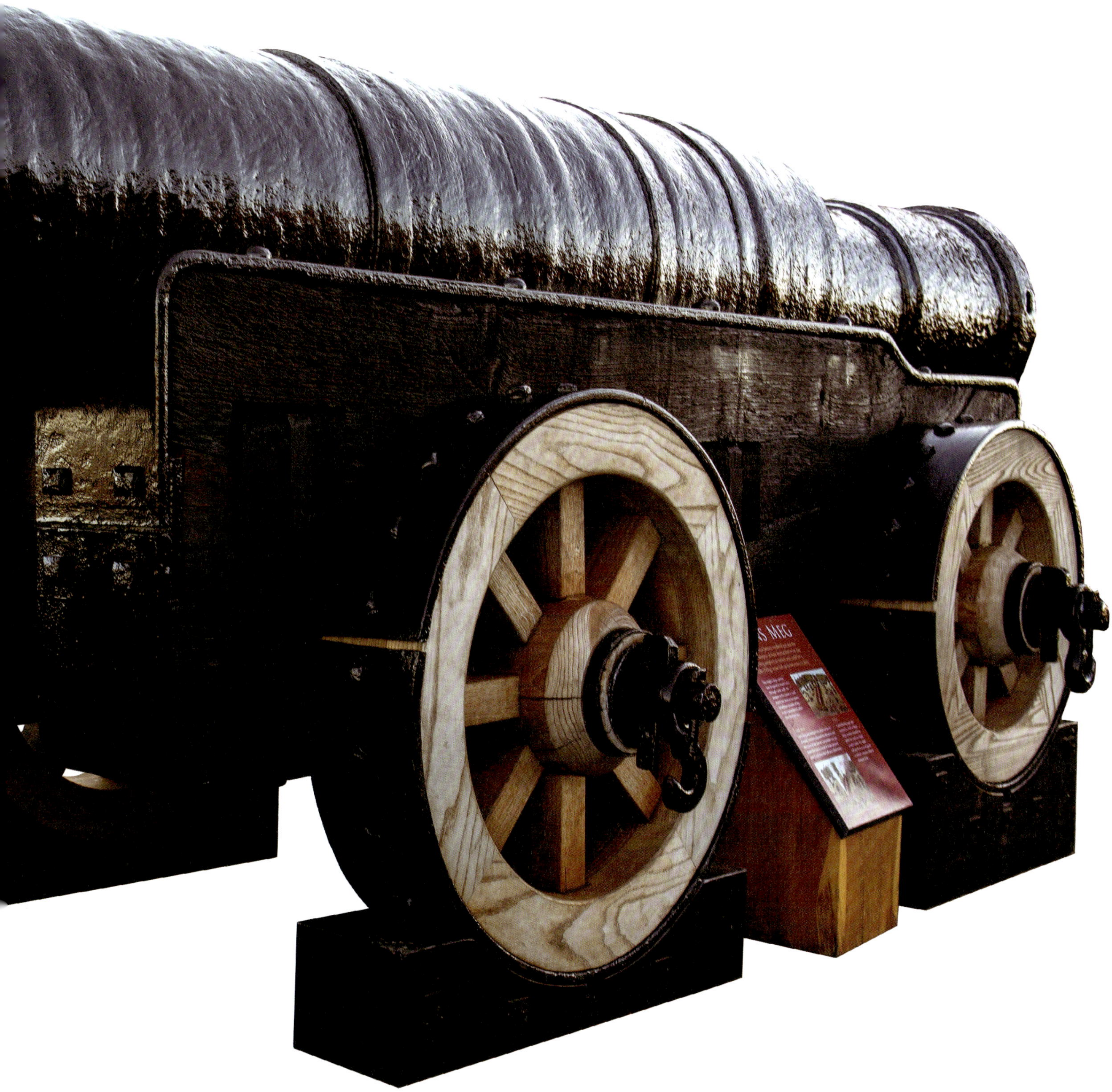

18

The great bronze 'Dardanelles' gun

Turkey, 1464 · XIX.164

In 1453, the city of Constantinople, the capital and almost all that remained of the eastern Roman Empire, was captured by the Ottoman Turks under Sultan Mehmet II ('The Conqueror'). His successors built up – and then, after the 17th century, gradually lost – the vast Ottoman Empire, extending from central Europe to the Persian Gulf, and ruled it until 1922 from the city, officially known from 1930 as Istanbul. Mehmet's victory had been helped by a battery of gigantic cannon made by a Christian Hungarian bronze-founder, Orban (only a few years after Mons Meg, but of very different construction), which blasted great breaches in the city's Roman walls. The Royal Armouries' gun, similar to Orban's and ordered by the same Sultan, is the earliest to survive, the only example outside Turkey, and one of the largest medieval cannon ever made. An inscription on the muzzle tells us it was made by 'Munir 'Ali ... in the year 868 [1464]', so this time clearly by a Muslim: the Ottomans were learning fast. Normal practice suggests that it was cast near its place of deployment, in this case Mehmet's new fort at Çimenlik, near Çanakkale on the southern bank of the Dardanelles, the narrow strait between Europe and Asia linking the Mediterranean and the Black Sea; there it formed part of a battery, mirrored by another 750 m away on the other bank, putting all traffic on this strategically vital seaway at their mercy. Ingeniously, the gun itself is made in two parts, partly (given its total weight of 19.95 tons) for ease of transport, but also to make casting simpler; the two parts, one the powder chamber and the other the barrel, were joined by a screw, turned by capstan bars inserted into a ring of sockets at both ends of each section. In action, the gun was laid on a massive timber bed, with the butt end backed against masonry to take the recoil – essential, as the projectiles were gigantic stone balls 63 cm in diameter, weighing about 306 kg. Simple but devastatingly powerful, this gun and its companions remained in commission well into the 19th century, seeing action in the Anglo-Turkish war of 1807–9, crippling six British warships and causing over 100 casualties. In the 1820s some of them were mounted, with European advice, on modern traversing carriages, and it was then that instructions for use were inscribed on this gun, in Turkish, near the touch-hole. By the 1850s, however, they were scrapped, and the gun's survival owes to the army officer and antiquarian, Lieutenant Colonel (later Major General Sir) John Henry Lefroy, who began negotiations to acquire it for the Royal Military Depository, later the Rotunda Museum, during the Crimean War. The deal was sealed during the state visit of the Turkish Sultan, Abdul Aziz Han, to England in 1867, and – now billed as a present to Queen Victoria – the gun reached its new home in 1868, from where it went to the Tower in 1929 and in 1989 to Fort Nelson. It is shown here in its former outdoor setting but is now displayed in the 'Voice of the Guns' gallery. As Lefroy put it in 1868, this great cannon 'testifies to the former energy and power of the Ottoman race, as no other military monument does, and reminds us of an event which has had a greater influence on the politics of Europe than almost any other in the same period – the fall of Constantinople'.

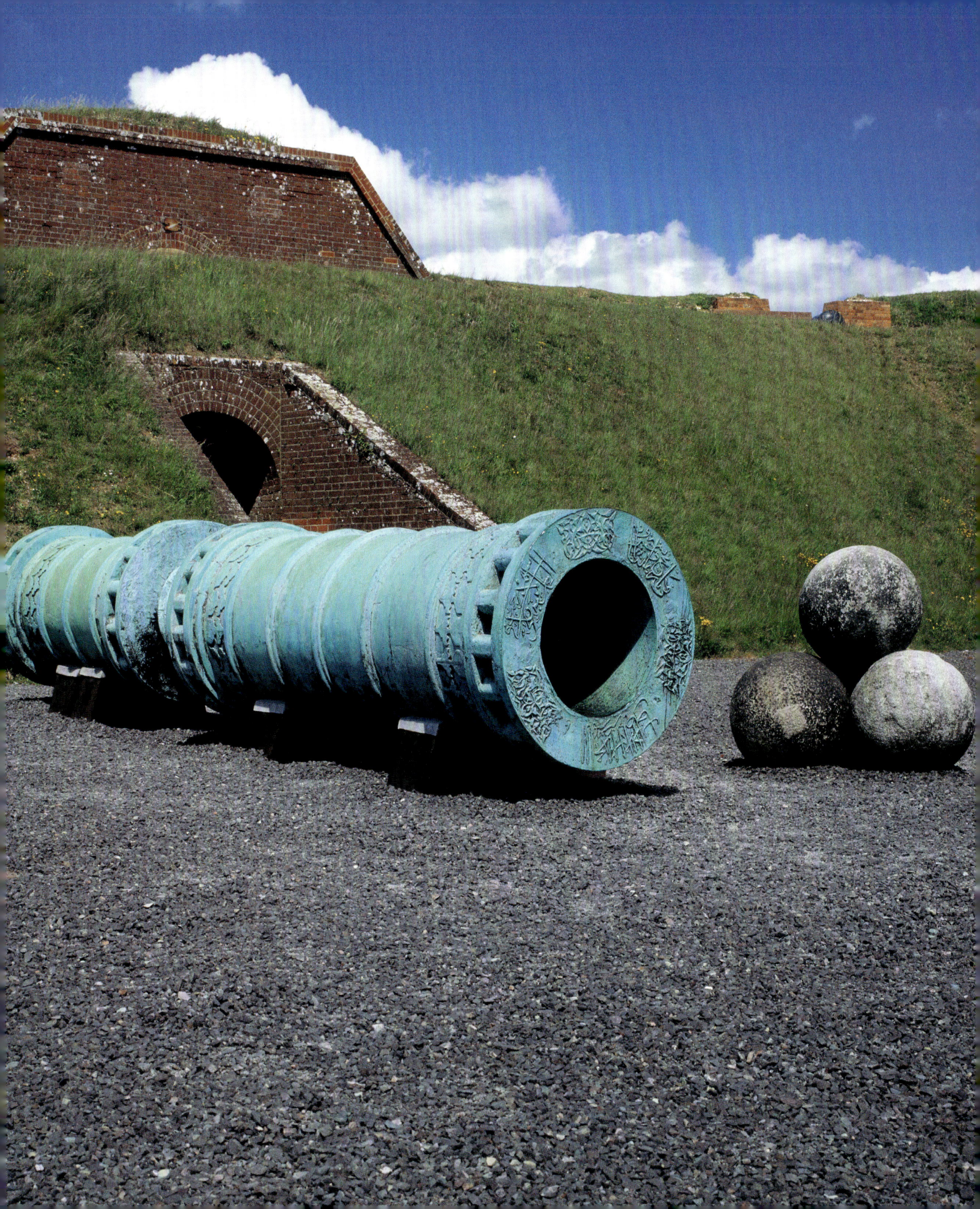

19

Gothic armour for man and horse

South Germany or Austria, late 15th century · II.3, III.69–70, III.1216, III.1300, IV.15, VI.148, VIII.9

German High Gothic armour of the late 15th century, the best known of all medieval styles, has long been considered the supreme achievement of the armourer's art. First applied by 19th-century collectors, the term 'Gothic' drew parallels between the sharply defined lines and cusped edges of such armour and the pointed arches, spires and pinnacles of contemporary architecture. Veritable 'sculpture in steel', it was this that 19th-century artists, such as the pre-Raphaelites John Everett Millais (1829–96) and John William Waterhouse (1848–1917) preferred to depict in scenes from history and legend.

Fascination with Gothic armour continues, but very few complete late-15th century examples have survived: as happened at the Tower on the accession of Henry VIII in 1509, medieval assemblages were frequently swept away as obsolete, to be replaced with pieces fit for modern Renaissance warriors. As a result many existing knightly armours, including this one, are made up of original fragments, roughly contemporary in date, augmented by components restored or reproduced by dealers and collectors. Of the original pieces in this case the back plate is particularly fine, its narrow wasp-like waist and radiating flutes echoing in steel the tightly fitting male doublet, emphasising or simulating the wearer's slender figure and ideal 'v-shaped' torso. Its asymmetry reveals an indulgence in the unorthodox, also occasionally found in contemporary European architecture. The helmet is of particular interest as a product of the noted Treytz dynasty of armourers of Mühlau, on the outskirts of Innsbruck, where, provided with fast-running water to power their polishing mills and good access to raw materials, a colony of armourers had long been established; under the patronage of Archduke Sigismund of Tyrol (r.1427–96), Innsbruck itself had become an important armour-producing centre, and was to be the base of Emperor Maximilian I's imperial court armoury from 1507.

The accompanying horse armour is equally remarkable. Although partially restored, it is exceptional in being one of only three Gothic bards to have survived: one of these, made in about 1450 by the Milanese armourer Pier Innocenzo da Faerno, possibly for Frederick III, Holy Roman Emperor (r.1452–93), is in the Vienna City Museum; the others are in the Wallace Collection, London and the Deutsches Historisches Museum, Berlin. Comprising a shaffron, crinet, peytral and crupper plates, the armour's large surface area provided ample scope for embellishment, in the form of fluting and cusped edges reminiscent of bats' or dragons' wings. The bard also incorporates embossed decoration in the form of a lion's head on the peytral and, with a touch of humour, a lizard or dragon as the tailpiece. According to tradition, the bard was originally the property of Prince Waldemar VI of Anhalt Zerbst/ Köthen (l.1450–1508), and certainly it remained in the armoury of the dukes of Anhalt until sold in the early 20th century. Fitting its status and rarity, it was swiftly acquired by the businessman, politician and newspaper magnate William Randolph Hearst (the inspiration for the eponymous character of Orson Wells' *Citizen Kane*), from whose estate it was bought by the Tower Armouries in 1958. It was displayed along with the man's armour, made up by Armouries staff from pieces in the museum's collection. Together they epitomise the popular image of the 'knight in shining armour'.

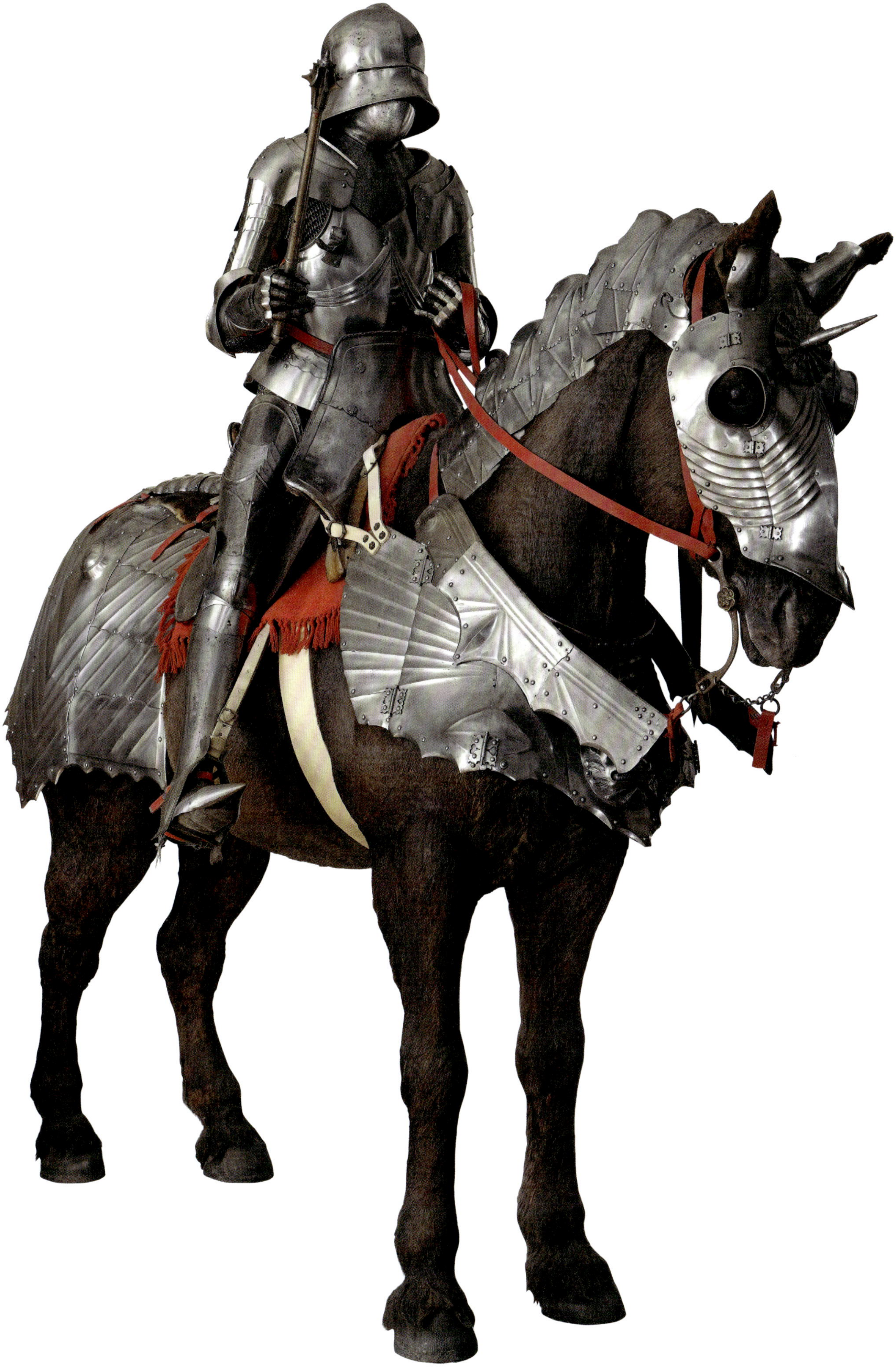

20

The Writhen Hilt sword

Germany, *c.*1480 · IX.949

This remarkable weapon is a 'hand and a half' sword, made in Germany in the late 15th century, and originally the possession of a rich, high-status individual – unknown, alas, but militarily active or wishing to appear so. It was intended for a wide range of uses: primarily for show, in parade and other largely propagandist and social occasions, on foot or on horseback, but exceptionally also in combat and hunting. Its defining feature is the twisted or 'writhen' form of the hilt and quillons, giving the type its modern name. The grip is of oak, carved in the form of a gnarled stave or entwined vine stems, flowing into the gilt bronze pommel and straight quillons, themselves sculpted to resemble three spirally entwined stems.

Part of the sword's appeal is its rarity, as only two others are known, one from around 1500 in the Museo Militar in Lisbon, bearing the mark of Johann Wender, a famous German maker, and the other in a private collection. Others, however, are represented in medieval art, including in two English images – one a mid-15th century rood screen at St Helen's Church, Ranworth, in which it is wielded by St Michael, and the other, a little later, identifying St Catherine at Filby (both in Norfolk). Another appears in an illumination to a manuscript history of Berne (Switzerland) of the 1480s, showing the election in 1212 of the Holy Roman Emperor Frederick II as King of the Romans. One is also clearly shown in one of the five Flemish tapestries of *c.*1500 in the Great Watching Chamber at Hampton Court Palace, bought by Cardinal Wolsey and depicting scenes from Petrarch's *Triumphs*: it is worn, sheathed, by a knight in *The Triumph of Time over Fame*. These illustrations show that the type was known in Switzerland, the Hapsburg lands and in England.

The sword's main appeal, however, is its form, serving as a reminder that medieval swords, even relatively simple ones, were status symbols as well as tools of war, and could be powerful signals of wealth, power and prestige. Not surprisingly, fine medieval swords have been much sought after by dealers and collectors, and this is no exception. Its first such owner was Frederick Spitzer (1851–90): born in Vienna, supposedly the son of a grave digger, after a brief stint in the army he began dealing in art and antiques in London and later in Paris. Spitzer became widely known as Europe's premier art dealer, with a particular interest in medieval and Renaissance pieces, and attracted many illustrious clients including Baron Adolphe de Rothschild (1823–1900) and Sir Richard Wallace (1819–90), whose outstanding collection of arms and armour remains intact at the Wallace Collection in London.

From Spitzer the Writhen Hilt Sword was acquired by William Randolph Hearst [19]. The Royal Armouries acquired the sword soon after Hearst's death in 1951, and displayed it first at the Tower, and then, since 1996, at Leeds.

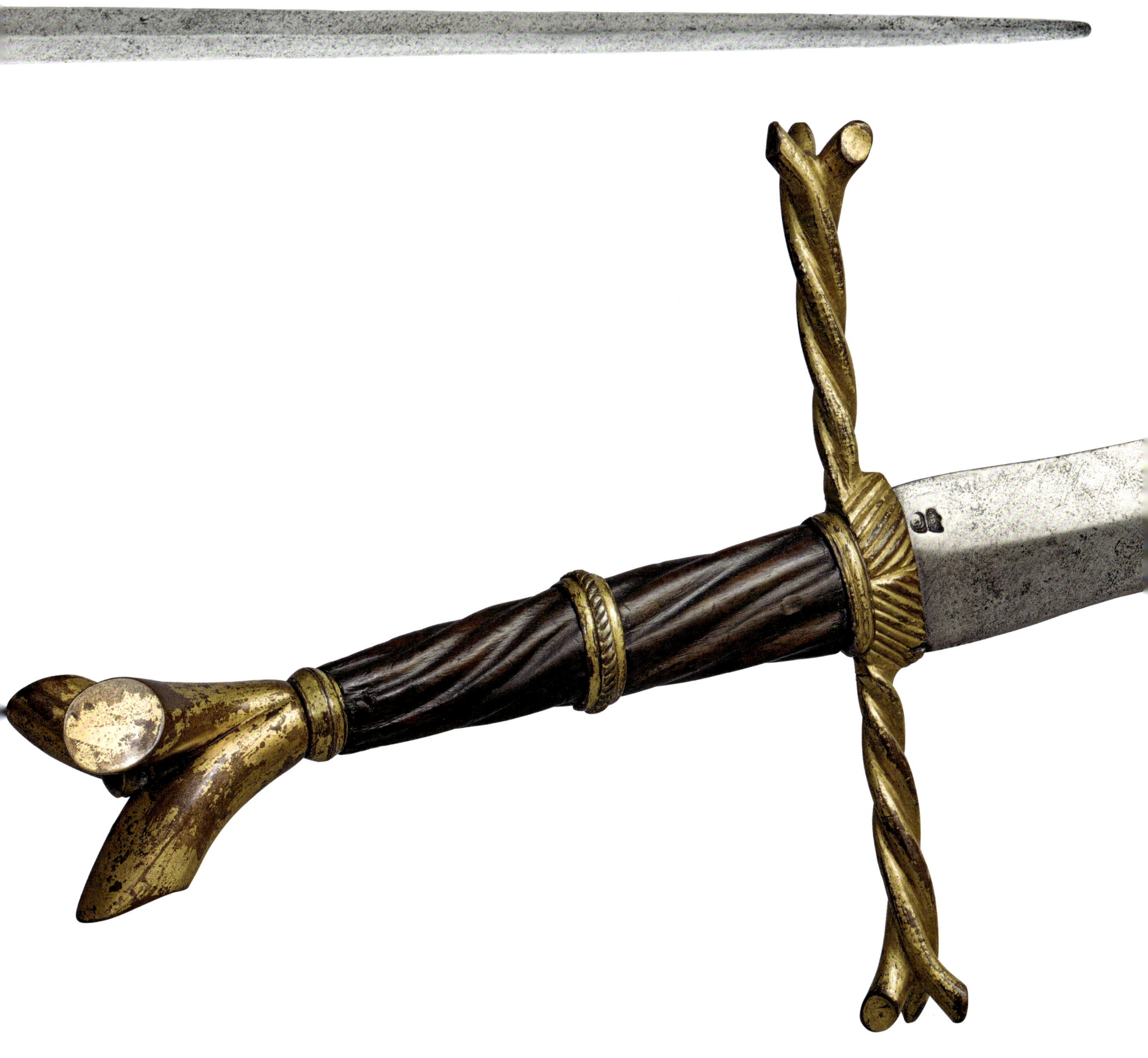

21
Painted sallet

Germany, c.1495 · IV.12

The sallet was one of the most popular helmet types of the late Middle Ages, used across Europe for well over a century. It evolved as an off-shoot of the bacinet along with the '*barbuta*' during the late 14th century, an early reference to one ('*azalata*') occurring in an Italian chronicle of 1389. Originally distinguished from the bacinet by its short upturned tail over the back of the neck and lack of mail aventail, by the 1430s a number of regional styles had appeared and the term therefore applies to a wide range of forms. In Italy, the sallet or '*celata*', sometimes also called a '*barbuta*' today, exhibited deep sides and either a rounded, T-shaped or spectacled-style face opening, resembling the 'Corinthian' helmets of ancient Greece. Towards the end of the 15th century the Italian sallet developed into a more elegant form with shallower sides and tail swept back over the neck. These features may have been introduced from Germany and demonstrate the widespread exchange of ideas in the armour-making industry.

The sallet enjoyed its greatest longevity in the German-speaking lands of Central and Eastern Europe where it was worn on the battlefield until the 1520s. Albrecht Dürer's famous drawing 'A Rider in Armour' (1498) shows an armour in the early Maximilian style with a shallow long-tailed painted sallet, beneath the very telling annotation, 'This was the armour at the time in Germany'. In the tournament the sallet lasted longer still, and in its final form (the '*Rennhut*', after the German-style joust called the '*Rennen*') it was made until about 1600. Sallets became increasingly popular in Germany during the 1440s and 1450s, and by 1460 had become the dominant form. Unlike many high-quality examples which were polished to a mirror-like finish, more cheaply made or 'munition-type' examples were often left rough and 'black from the hammer' – hence the term 'black sallet'. To enliven their appearance, many were brightly painted with bold and sometimes elaborate designs featuring the face of an animal or a monster.

This helmet is exceptional in retaining its painted decoration in the form of a flame-like pattern over the skull and chequered squares charged with stars, portcullises and a knot-work design on the sides and visor. Although originally from Schloss Ort in Austria, the heraldic devices bear no relation to its owners and may be purely decorative. Some sallets, however, were decorated with colours and emblems associated with a particular town or individual, such as an example in the Imperial Armoury in Vienna which bears a red and white chequerboard design and the place name 'ULM' on the tail. Like other 'black' or painted sallets the skull, tail and visor of the Royal Armouries example have been pierced with numerous small holes, arranged in pairs, which may have been used for the attachment of a decorative or protective textile cover. Compared to the more restrictive armet, which fitted closely around the head, these lightweight and versatile helmets provided complete freedom of movement and allowed the wearer to see and breathe with ease. In combat they could be quickly drawn down over the face, whilst their design allowed them to be pushed back on the head for an improved field of view. This ensured their widespread and long-lasting use by all ranks of soldiery from archers to the mounted knight.

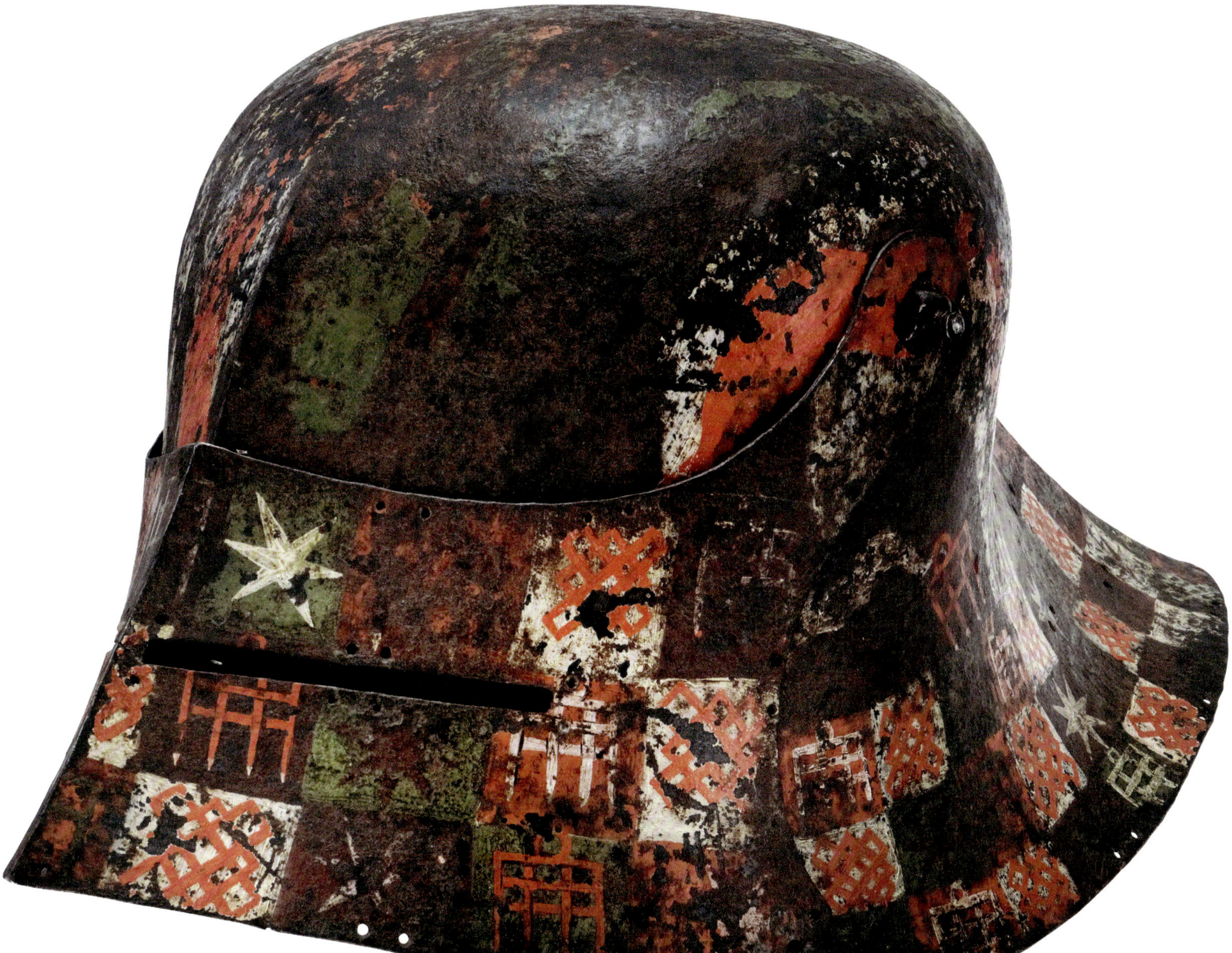

22

Milanese sallet belonging to a knight of the Order of St John

Italy, c.1490 · IV.424

In the 13th century, northern Italy – Milan in particular – became the leading centre of European armour production, a position retained until superseded by German workshops at the turn of the 16th century. In 1288 the Lombard writer and poet Bonvesin de la Riva noted not only the 'abundance of smiths, who everyday make armour of every kind' but also that merchants were distributing it across Italy and beyond. Organised into major commercial companies supplying both princely and basic 'munition quality' armours, Italian armourers exported armour throughout Europe and, crucial to their success, tailored their products to match local styles.

Whilst Milanese armourers had established workshops in Brescia, Ferrara, Modena, Mantua, Venice, Urbino, Rome and Naples, Milan remained the main place of manufacture, and the base of several famous armourer dynasties. The best known was the Negroli, descendants of the famous Missaglia family of armourers, whose outstanding technical skill and beauty ensured that their work was sought after by some of the greatest princely courts in Renaissance Europe. One of them, Filippo (c.1510–1579), is widely regarded as one of the greatest armourers of the age and briefly re-established Milan, in the face of German competition, as the leading centre of armour production.

Bearing a maker's mark of a pair of crossed keys beneath an open coronet, the Armouries' sallet has been attributed to Domenico Barini detto (known as) Negroli (d.1526). The son of Giovanni Barini, who had been employed by the Missaglia, Domenico had established himself as a highly skilled master armourer by the late 15th century. In 1504, alongside his son, he established a business with Sebastiano Negroni da Ello detto Missaglia and over the next nine years dominated the market in the production of princely quality armour. This sallet belonged to a knight of St John, as it came from the arsenal in Rhodes, the Order's headquarters from 1310 to 1522.

Formed out of a single piece of steel, the beauty of the helmet lies in the subtle observation of the anatomy of the human skull, whilst the elongated tail creates an aesthetic S-shaped curve both along the lower edge and the back of the neck. A gilt copper-alloy border has been applied around the edge incorporating Greco-Roman style egg and dart and acanthus leaf motifs, whilst a plume holder faced with an engraved gilt copper-alloy shield has been fixed to the centre front. Though some earlier 15th – century armours had their main edges adorned with applied decoration, this practice did not become widespread until the end of the century. Whilst frequently encountered in Italian paintings of the period, such as by the Florentine artist Davide Ghirlandaio (1452–1525), surviving examples are comparatively rare. Two other sallets, also probably by Domenico Negroli, are now in the Real Armeria in Madrid and exhibit finely detailed gilt copper-alloy bands. Richly ornamented sallets covered in velvet and fitted with highly elaborate gilt mounts were particularly popular in Venice and are often described as '*alla Veneziana*'. Frequently refurbished, such 15th-century helmets continued to be worn in the city's pageants well into the eighteenth century, either as striking symbols of public office or simply for lavish display.

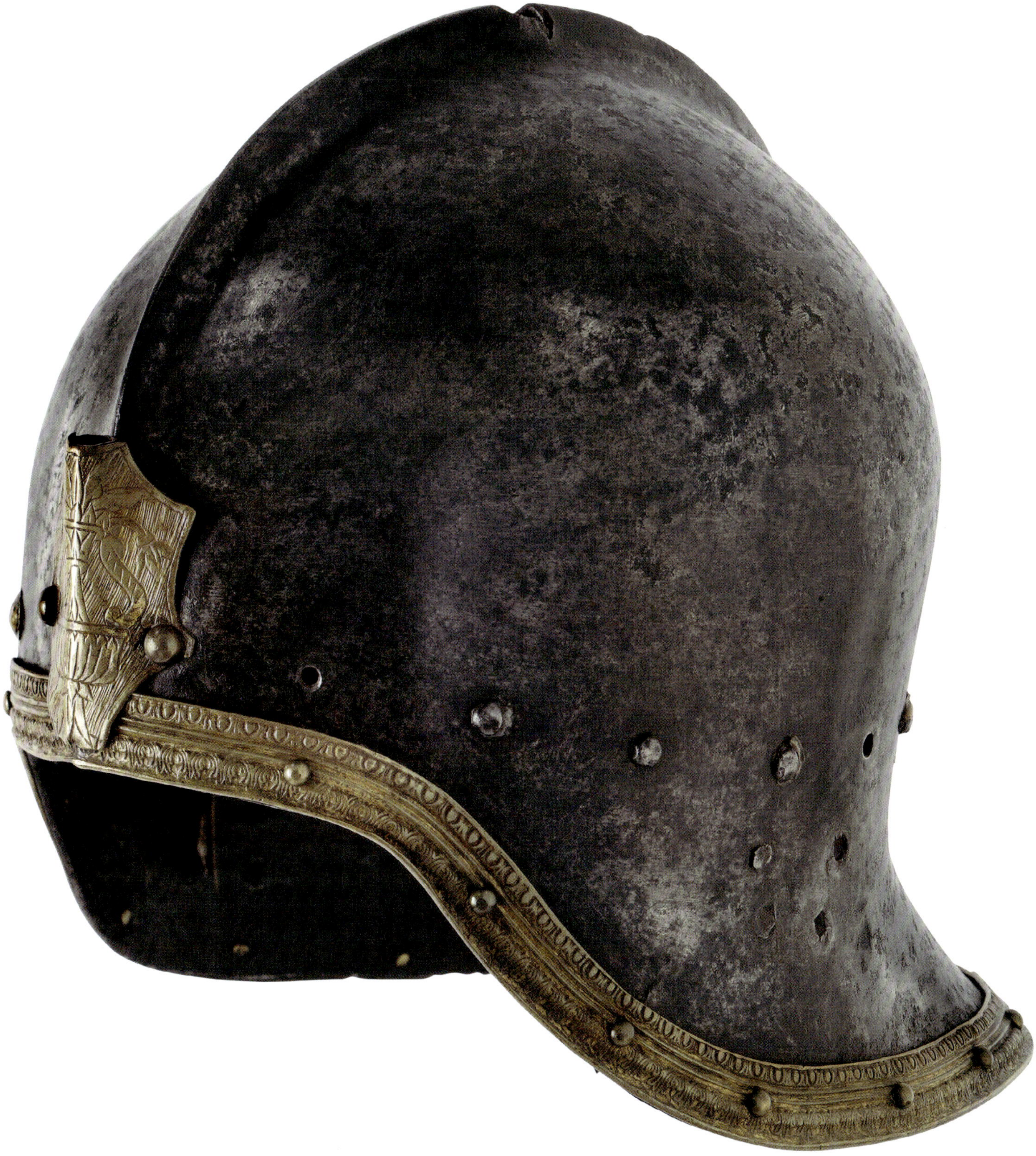

23
Mamluk handgun from Syria
Syria, late 15th century · XXVIF.245

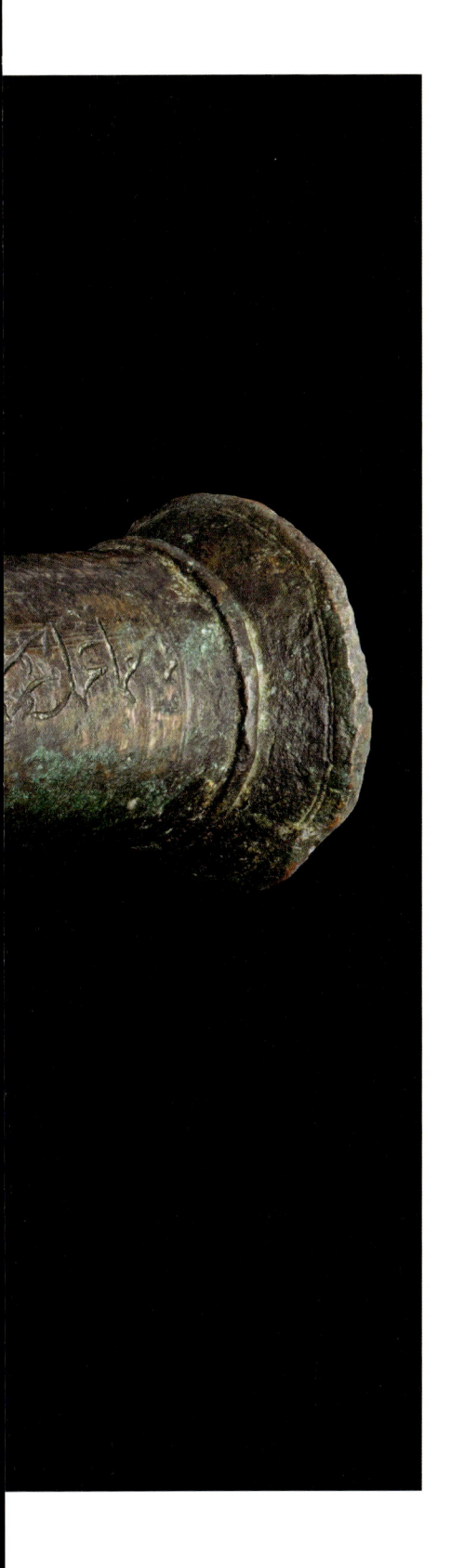

The expansion of Islam, both as a faith and as a catalyst for state formation, is one of the most extraordinary stories of world history. It began in the 620s, with the creation of a group of co-religionists following the prophet Muhammad, and within a century, zeal, military skill and a succession of victories had created an empire of linked states stretching from the Pyrenees to India. Numerous dynasties waxed and waned in the succeeding centuries, among the most important being the Ottomans; others included the Mamluks, rulers of Egypt and Syria from the mid 13th century until 1517, under whose rule this small bronze hand-held gun was made in the 15th century, one of the earliest in the Muslim world. Only 240 mm long, it takes the form of a barrel and a narrower powder chamber, giving it the appearance of a miniature bombard. Originally it was attached to a wooden stock or tiller by an iron spike, still partly surviving. The inscription on the side of the gun reads 'mimma 'amala bi-rasm al-maqarr al-'ali Kertbay al-Ahmar', declaring that it was made under the auspices of his highness Amir Kertbay al-Ahmar, 'al-maqarr al-'ali' being a title frequently bestowed on high-ranking emirs and viziers of the Mamluk sultanate: he was probably the prefect of Cairo of that name under Sultan Qaitbay (r.873–901; 1468–96), then *silahdar* (master of the training of troops) and later Viceroy of Syria under Qaitbay's successor, Sultan al-Nasir Muhammad (r.901–4; 1496–8). In both form and manner of operation, it strongly resembles one illustrated in a Mamluk military manual known as the 'St Petersburg *Furusiyya*', dated 1474, being held by the tiller, propped on a rest, and discharging a single round shot.

As the manual and other written records clearly show, the Mamluks were no strangers to firearms. Until the last decades of their rule, however, they used them far less than other Muslim powers, notably the Ottomans, thanks to their fundamental identity as elite mounted warriors who valued horsemanship above all, and trained rigorously with the bow and lance. It was these skills which were prized by the Egyptian-based Ayyubid dynasty who they had initially served, enabled them to overthrow them, and allowed them to defeat the apparently invincible Mongols at 'Ayn Jalut in 1260. Comparative stability followed in Egypt and Syria, which the Mamluks successfully defended against all comers, so that widespread use of portable firearms by infantry would have been not only an unwelcome but an apparently unnecessary challenge to a way of life that justified the Mamluks' role and power. Only when the very existence of the dynasty was threatened by the Ottomans and the Portuguese, did the Mamluk sultans create firearms units, including a favoured corps of black slaves, to counter those of their opponents.

Yet these necessary decisions provoked wrath, hostility and even violence amongst the Mamluk elite, and it was partly his enthusiasm for firearms, and the consequent rebellion of the nobility, that led to Sultan Al-Nasir Muhammad's assassination in 1498. The forward-thinking Amir Kertbay, however, apparently continued in an unpopular attempt to modernise the Mamluk army by establishing four firearms battalions in Damascus, where this handgun was probably made, but he too died in 1498. Although the Mamluks made further and urgent attempts to increase the power of their artillery and integrate trained arquebusiers into their armies, these efforts were inadequate and too late, a failing which helped the conquest of the Mamluk sultanate by the Ottomans, then still sweeping all before them, in 1517.

24
The Turban helm
Turkey, late 15th century · XXVIA.142

The many forms of the medieval Muslim warrior's arms and armour owed partly to their Arabian origins, and partly to the adaptation of forms and practices used by their neighbours and the peoples they defeated. Overall, Muslim armies made much use of cavalry, and their armour tended to be light and flexible, based on mail and textiles, reinforced with scales or plates; their weapons included the powerful recurve bow, but otherwise their repertoire of weapons was similar to that of the west, although strikingly different in form and decoration.

The helmet shown here, often referred to today as a 'turban helm', was common throughout the Islamic world from the mid 14th century to the early 16th century, and is probably of Ottoman or Aq Qoyunlu origin. The skull of the helmet (that is, the upper part) is formed from a single piece of steel and extended down to eye level, below which further protection was provided by a mail aventail. As shown here, the two apertures at the front are eye-holes, while the vertical band between them and the holes beside it mark the site of a nasal that could be raised for better vision or lowered to protect the face.

Around the brow of the helmet, picked out in silver against a gold background, is an Arabic inscription which translates as 'Glorifier of the faith, victorious, triumphant king, to him be lasting glory, prosperity, wealth, power, peace, health and wealth', referring to an unnamed sultan, possibly Yaqub bin Uzun Hasan (r.1478–90) of the Aq Qoyunlu. Above this is the fluted surface, which bears a delicate floral decoration, surmounted by a second inscription derived from a popular poem of the time which reads, 'To its owner good fortune, peace, and health throughout his lifetime as long as the doves coo'. Such inscriptions are common on Islamic arms and armour, often taken from the Qur'an or prayers, both judged to be just as good a defence against the enemy as the armour itself, or (as here) poetry and references to the exploits of the armour's owner. Given the decorative potential of Arabic script, it often provided the principal graphic ornament to an object, although geometric forms and motifs from nature such as floral scrolls and wild beasts were also used.

Overall, with its fluted sides and finial, the helmet has a distinctly dome-like, architectural appearance, but it also closely resembles a turban – hence its modern name. Although intended for use by heavy cavalry, the shape led to its adoption by certain Darvish groups who normally wore them, at war, in place of their habitual turbans, which were wound around the head with a specific number of folds, representing an important mystical number. Helmets of this form thus became a symbol of faith as much as of armour, and a sign that the wearer was a holy warrior conducting a holy war.

At some point, possibly the result of a victory over the Aq Qoyunlu, this helmet found its way to the Hagia Eirene, a Byzantine church in Constantinople converted into an arsenal after 1453, and later enveloped by the Topkapı Palace. It served both as a working arsenal and as repository for captured arms and armour, and from 1727 a military museum, but in 1839–40 much of its contents were sold to a Genoese scrap merchant under the modernising Sultan Abdul Medjid I. Fortunately, many items, including this turban helm, were saved from destruction and went on to form the core of several important museum collections around the world through in the later 19th and 20th centuries.

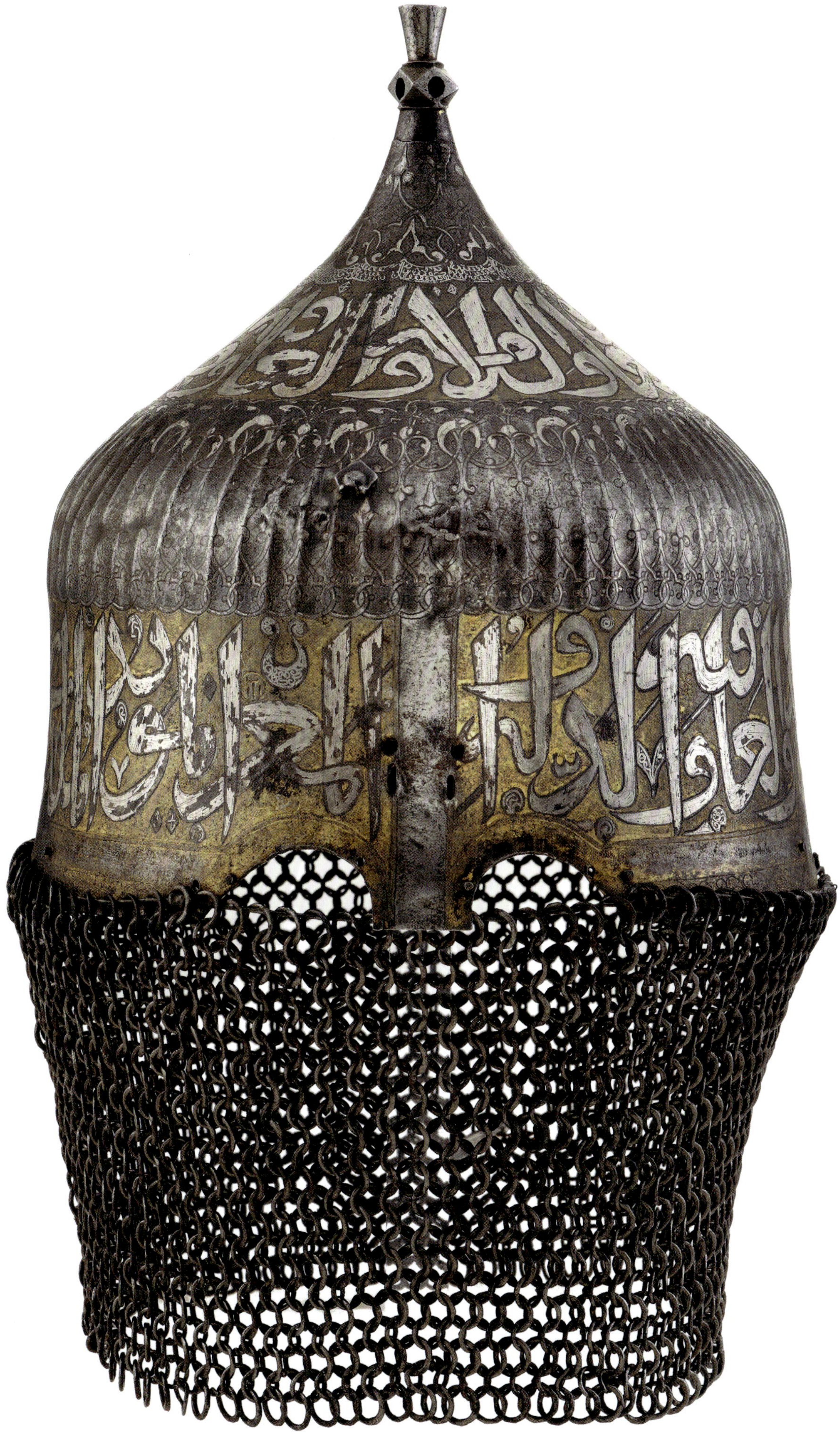

25

Rennzeug jousting armour

Germany, late 15th century · 11.167

Maximilian, son of the first Hapsburg Holy Roman Emperor Frederick III, succeeded in 1493 as Archduke of Austria, was confirmed as Emperor in 1508, and ruled until his death in 1519. Two marriage alliances – his own in 1477 to Mary, heiress to the rich and powerful Duchy of Burgundy, and that of his son Philip to Joanna of Castile and Aragon – made his family the most important in Europe. Maximilian's grandson Charles V (r.1519–1557) ruled over a vast confederation that included Spain, the Low Countries, most of the German-speaking lands, much of Central Europe and parts of the Americas.

Physically brave and a highly skilled warrior and sportsman, Maximilian distinguished himself on the battlefield and in the tournament, and for adroit political reasons took a great personal interest in all things chivalric, later earning him (from 1810) his soubriquet 'the Last Knight'. Not surprisingly, he took a keen interest in armour, and the fictional work *Der Weisskünig* (*The White King*), written partly by the Emperor – the thinly veiled holder of the title role – contains an engraving showing him directing his armourers at work, probably in the workshop of Conrad Seusenhofer at Innsbruck. Prompted by these interests, he commissioned some of the period's finest examples of tournament arms and armour, of which this *Rennzeug* harness is one of many survivors, intended for use in the *Anzogenrennen*, or 'bolted-down joust', a German variant of the 'Joust of War' that emerged in the late 15th century. This took the form of a competition between two participants, either in an open field or an enclosed list, but with no tilt (barrier), armed with sharp lances. The objective, derived from older forms of the joust, was to unhorse the other rider, and in doing so break the lance against the large wooden shield fixed to the front of the armour. This is beautifully illustrated in Maximilian's book on the subject, the *Freydal*.

As this style of joust evolved, so necessarily did a specialist form of armour, inspired by the heavy cavalry equipment favoured in parts of Germany at the time. This *Rennzeug* harness comprises a long-tailed sallet and bevor, the latter being bolted directly to the breastplate with a protruding bolt at the centre, onto which the large wooden leather-covered grand-guard can be secured in place, protecting almost all the upper body. The breastplate is also bolted to the backplate by means of hinged metal shoulder-straps and hinged locks on the flanks. The right-hand side of the armour bears the lance-rest and queue, while the bottom supports a waist plate, six heavy skirt lames and a pair of knee-length tassets to protect the thighs. A large vamplate, or handguard for the lance, serves to protect much of the right-hand side of the body, while a pair of shaped knee defences called *dilgen* hung loosely over the saddle, as leg armour was omitted in this variant of the *Rennzeug*.

Solid, serious and life-preserving as all this was, this harness and its ilk provided for showy, theatrical and mechanically induced effect. Great chivalric poets of the age described how, when struck in the correct place, '*volant* [flying] pieces' (additional plates covering the brow of the sallet and the front of the vamplate) flew apart in an explosive fashion, giving the illusion of shattered armour flying through the air. Astonishing at the time, for Maximilian's admirers in the late 15th and early 16th century these 'exploding' armours were one of his armourers' outstanding achievements, part of chivalric spectacle rivalling those of Arthurian legend.

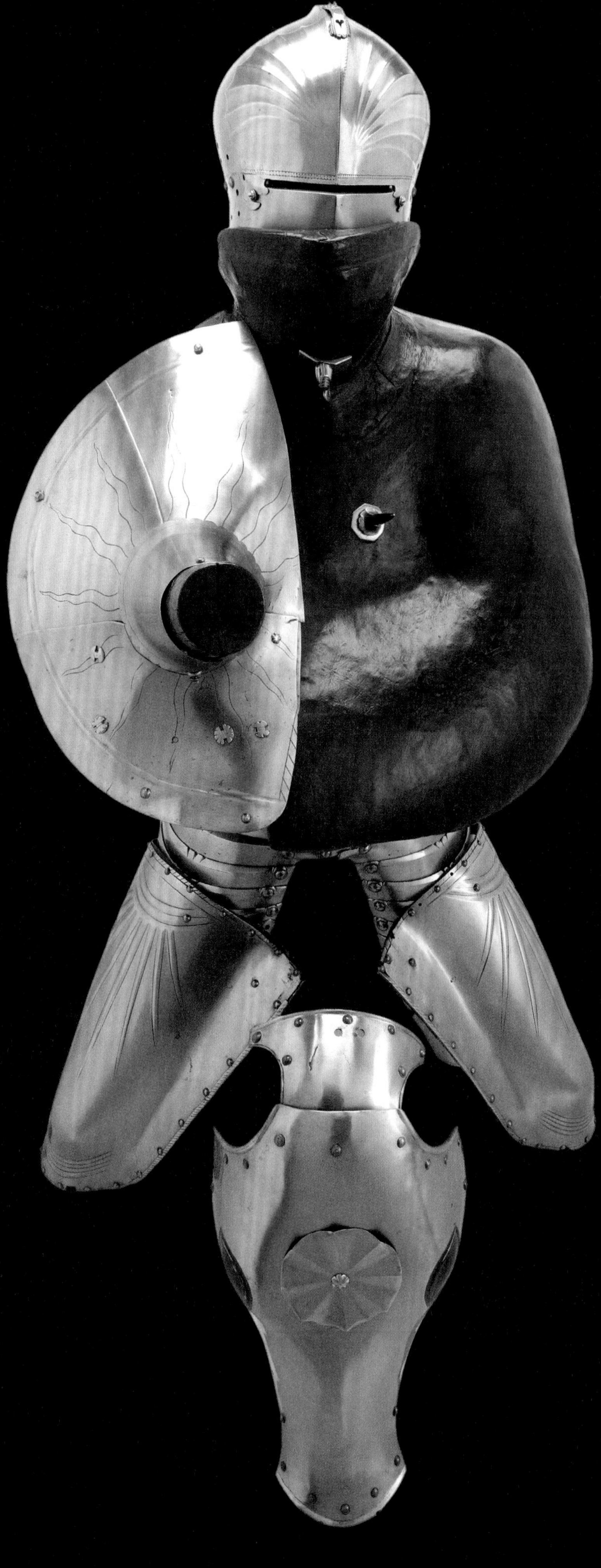

26
Messer (sword)

Possibly Germany, *c*.1500 · IX.634

The *Messer* (German for 'knife') was a type of sword popular in the 15th and 16th centuries. Larger versions (sometimes known as *grosse, langes* or *Kriegsmessers*) were a particular feature of the German-speaking and German-influenced areas of Europe, and appear in Flemish and South German illustrations between 1490 and 1520.

What differentiates a *Messer* from other forms of sword is that whereas most sword blades narrowed at the tang, tapering up through the grip to be hammered in place over the top of the pommel, the tangs of *Messers* were of full width throughout. Grips, usually of wood, were placed either side of the wide tang, like a sandwich, and the whole assemblage riveted together, as in a machete or a modern steak knife. With no structural need for a pommel, grips were sometimes 'beaked' at the end, to stop the hand from slipping, and covered with a cap. The 'beak' in this example has broken off and the cap is missing, but traces remain, along with those of a leather covering. Fortunately, a drawing of 1793 records the weapon when complete. The quillons, also riveted through the quillon block to the blade, are counter-curved, with the forward quillon forming a knuckle-guard with a scrolled end, and the rear ending in a serpent's head.

As is often found on the more numerous single-handed versions of swords with these hilts, the blade is single-edged and slightly curved. The curve, breadth and relative thinness of the blade are well suited to effective cutting, further aided by a point of balance quite far down the blade (225 mm from the hilt) with its flat grip assisting good edge alignment. The grip's length enables two hands to be used, probably necessary for a weapon of this size and weight (1460 g).

As the *Messer* probably developed from the peasant knife of the Middle Ages, it did not necessarily carry the status of the knightly, two-edged sword. Surviving examples are therefore comparatively rare, despite their frequent appearance in contemporary illustrations. This one, however, is no ordinary *Messer*. In addition to their decorative shape, the quillons are etched and gilt with foliate scrolls, which continue onto each side of the forte of the blade. Here, panels contain depictions of St Catherine, patron

[96]

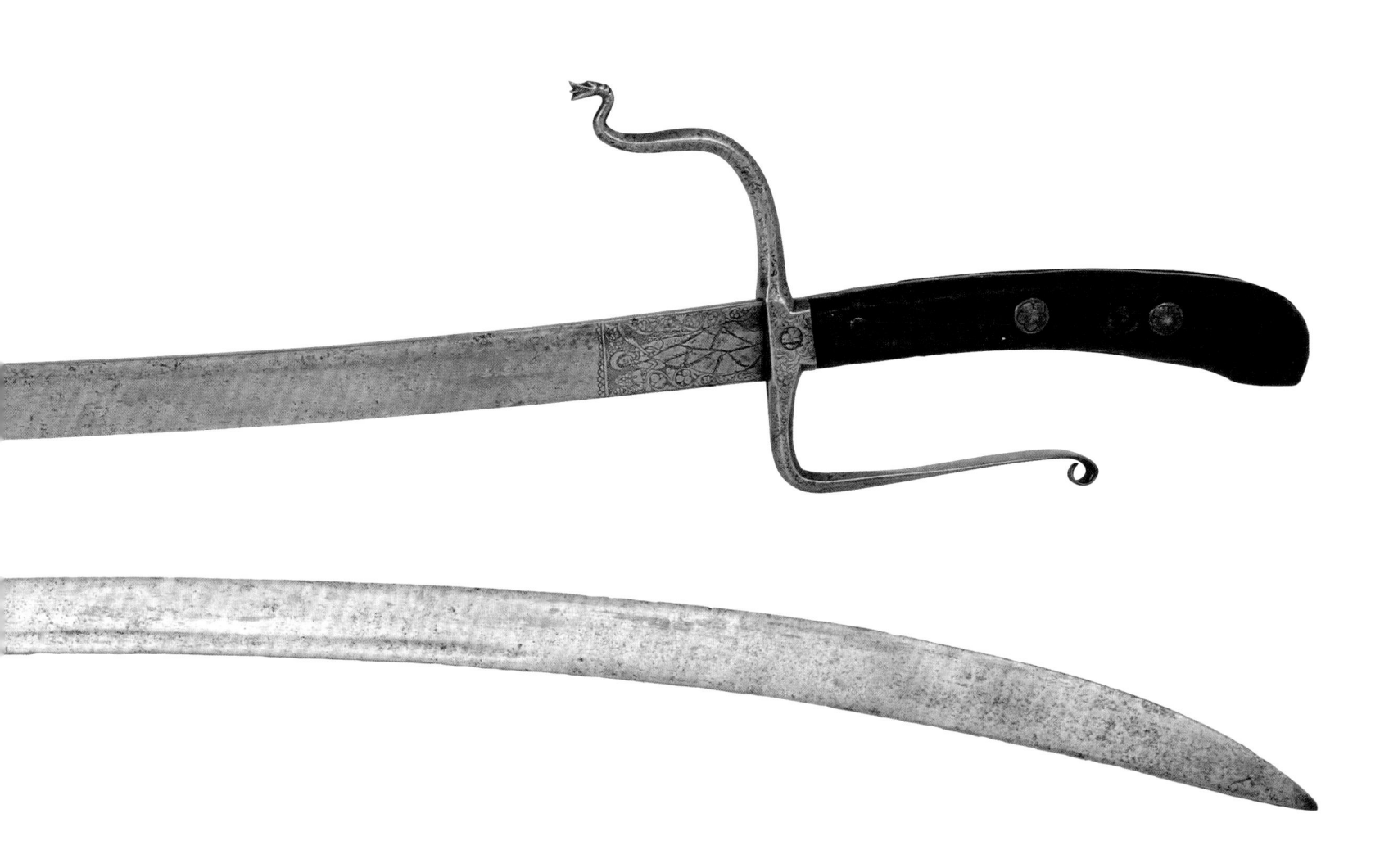

saint of knife grinders and sharpeners, and St Barbara, patron saint of soldiers, armourers and military engineers.

These saints, given their attributes, seem entirely appropriate, but the presence of St Catherine may also be due to an association with Katherine of Aragon: certainly it has plausible links to Henry VIII, in the form of the etched and gilt Tudor Roses, supported by simple roses on the remaining original grip rivets, decorating each side of the quillon block. A similar weapon is also depicted on Henry VIII's contemporary 'Silvered and Engraved' armour [31]. The blade, as indicated by its maker's marks, is possibly from Solingen. If it was owned by Henry, it then made its way to France, where it was first noted at the Musée de l'Artillerie in Paris by J. B. L. Carré in his *Panoplie* (1783): possibly Henry had given it to the French court. It probably came to England after Waterloo and was on display at the Museum of Artillery at the Rotunda in Woolwich by 1862. It transferred to the Tower Armouries in 1927.

27

Italian 'ear dagger'

Probably Italy, *c.*1500 · X.258

Daggers have been used for millennia in most parts of the world, and their overall design, blades, hilts and fittings take an endless variety of forms. Some, such as the 'ballock dagger' (also euphemistically known as the 'kidney dagger'), with its phalliform grips, and the 'rondel dagger', with its disc-shaped guard, have been named for prominent features of their design. The term 'ear dagger' is another, used since at least the 16th century in France ('*poignart à oreilles*', or 'dagger with ears'), thanks to the two flattened discs or plaques in place of the usual pommel and their resemblance to a pair of ears. The 'ears' themselves are circular, outward-splayed, with inner medallion-like faces of gilded cast brass, each decorated in Renaissance style with a female bust in a circle of palmettes and lilies. The outer faces are formed of six alternating discs of ivory and brass. The grips are formed of narrow ivory plaques riveted in turn to flat brass strips and then to the flaring tang, which increases in thickness towards the 'ears'. The exposed edges of the tang are part of the grip itself and are etched and gilt with floral scrolls. The guard consists of a slender rondel spacer, faced with ivory and brass, while the asymmetrical ricasso is etched and gilt with masks, foliage and guilloche decoration in the Renaissance *all' antica* style.

The origins of the 'ear dagger' are interesting but puzzling. Weapons known today as the 'double ear' type were being cast in bronze in Luristan (western Iran or Persia) as long ago as 1200–800 BC, and were again being made in the region in the 4th and 6th centuries AD: conceivably, then, following the Arab conquest of Persia in 641, the victors may have found a weapon to their liking and reproduced it themselves, including, soon, in North Africa. What we do know is that daggers of this form were being made in Iberia after its invasion in 711, led by the North African Nasrid dynasty (rulers of the Caliphate of Granada from 1231 until 1492), throughout the Ottoman empire, and as far east as Afghanistan: several Iberian examples from the 14th century onwards survive, decorated in the Hispano-Moresque style, which combined Islamic and Christian-derived forms with Islamic decoration. Arab power in Spain finally collapsed with the capture of Granada in 1492 – the culmination of the Christian recapture of Muslim Spain, the *Reconquista*. But by then this attractive and apparently effective form was being produced in Italy, particularly in Venice and its hinterland, where it was described as '*alla Levantia*' ('from the East'; a cultural as well as geographical designation). In 16th-century Venice they were known as '*pugnalle* [daggers] *alla stradioti*', in reference to the Albanian and Dalmatian mercenaries in the city's service – again, as the Balkans were under Muslim control – implying at least a contemporary assumption of unfamiliar origin.

It is also clear that, from the 1490s until the mid 16th century, the 'ear dagger' enjoyed limited but exalted use in other European countries. Richly decorated examples were made in France for Francis I and in England for Henry VIII between 1525 and 1550, by the famous maker Diego de Çaias. Presumably because of its unusual appearance, the 'ear dagger' – like the falchion – appears in several 16th-century depictions of biblical events and grisly Eastern martyrdoms. They also appear in a number of royal portraits, including one of the Emperor Charles V of *c.*1530, two of Edward VI as Prince of Wales, one by William Scrots (*a.*1537–53) at Windsor Castle, and the other, by 'Master John', in the National Portrait Gallery. The same weapon is displayed in both.

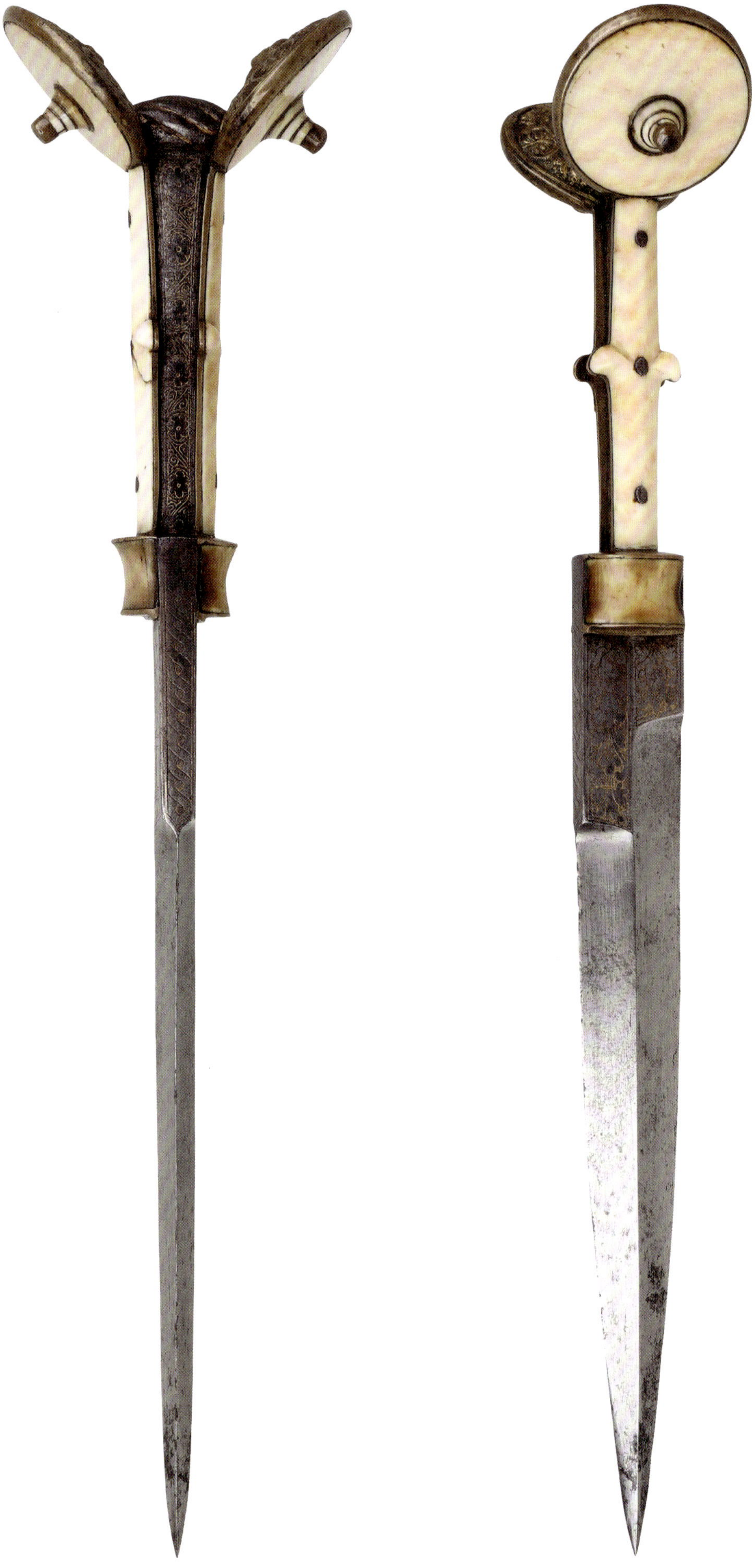

28

Mamluk sword and Ottoman scabbard

Blade probably Syria, late 15th-early 16th century. Mounts probably Turkey, 16th century. · XXVIS.293

One of the greatest advances of all time in the art of warfare was the use of cavalry, which emerged on the Eurasian steppe as early as 2000 BC. From this time on, successive hordes of steppe horsemen emerged from Central Asia and overran swathes of territory, and groups including the Scythians, Parthians, Huns, Turks and Mongols went on to establish new states and empires. Many of the later ruling powers who descended from them adopted and disseminated the religious and political structures of Islam, which emerged in Arabia in the seventh century and spread across large areas of Asia, North Africa and southern Europe at an astounding pace.

Despite the overwhelming reliance on the bow, the steppe horseman had other weapons for close – quarter combat. For a rider moving at speed a single-edged, curved blade was more effective than a straight sword, lending itself to smooth, slicing cuts as opposed to the thrusting and chopping motions suited to a straight, double-edged blade; the curvature meant that only a short section of the edge was in contact with the target at any one moment, thereby inflicting greater damage. The development of the curved, single-edged sword for use on horseback may have occurred in Central Asia as early as the seventh century. By the 15th century its use had spread across much of Asia as the preferred weapon of Muslim cavalry.

Early Islamic examples showing the initial graduation from the straight, double-edged sword towards the curved form are extremely scarce, but happily this example is one of them. The blade is single-edged for most of its length and only slightly curved, with an unobtrusive edge along the back of the lower section. Its shape is the precursor, in its basic form, of the later Turkish *kiliç* blade. Its appearance aligns it with a group of 15th-century Mamluk blades housed for centuries in the imperial armoury in Constantinople and which remain there today: they were taken there by the Ottomans after engagements with Mamluks in Syria and Egypt during the late 15th and early 16th centuries, culminating in the defeat of the Mamluk Sultanate at Raydaniyah in 1517. The blades were later remounted with a variety of different hilt forms by Ottoman craftsmen to appeal to Turkish taste, as was this one: the scrolling gilt foliate ornamentation visible on the hilt and scabbard fittings is typical of the style which decorated many of the rich weapons emerging from the workshops of the Ottoman court during the 16th century. The empty indentations visible on the mounts probably housed precious or semi-precious stones. The hilt, scabbard clasps and chape are in fact remarkably similar to another set attached to one of the sacred swords in the Topkapı Palace in Istanbul, said to have belonged to Abu Hasana, 'Scribe of the Prophet of God', companion of the Prophet, and is thought to have been remounted by court craftsmen around 1560.

Like many edged weapons produced by skilled artisans in South Asia, Persia and the Levant, this blade has a distinctive crystalline pattern resembling watered silk, an inherent feature of the crucible steel or '*wootz*' from which it is made, originating in South India, Sri Lanka and Central Asia. This was produced by combining wrought iron with carbon from vegetal matter in sealed crucibles. Controlled cooling and forging at low temperatures reduced brittleness and produced blades that were strong and held a good edge. As Damascus was well known for producing weapons with such blades, perhaps including this one, the effect – due to properties of the raw material – is often misleadingly referred to as 'Damascus steel'.

29

Henry VIII's 'Burgundian Bard'

Belgium, c.1505–10 · VI.6–12

This spectacular horse bard was probably commissioned by the Emperor Maximilian I, either for himself or his son Philip I, at some point between 1505 and 1510. It consists of a shaffron for the horse's head, a crinet for its neck, a peytral for the chest, crupper for the rear and flanchards for the sides, along with reins and saddle steels. Almost every surface of the bard is intricately decorated with bold embossing and etched with finer detail. The decoration incorporates various symbolic images such as the firesteels ('E'-shaped, hand-held tools for striking sparks) and raguly crosses (formed as if of roughly trimmed branches) of the Burgundian Order of the Golden Fleece, revived by Maximilian when he inherited the duchy on the death of Charles the Bold in 1477. Elsewhere, the bard's surface is covered by the swirling boughs bearing pomegranates, both the badge of the House of Aragon and Maximilian's personal emblem. Similar designs appear in fretwork on the rein guards, and the crinet is engraved with a pattern of overlapping feathers. Originally, the entire surface was silvered, of which traces survive, and at least partly gilded.

Although Maximilian had established his court armoury at Innsbruck, one of the foremost centres of armour manufacture in Europe, the upper rear plate of the bard's crupper bears the 'M' and crescent of Guillem Margot, based in Brussels, then part of the duchy of Burgundy. The gilding and etching of the embossed decoration is attributed to Paul van Vrelant, a Fleming who so impressed Henry VIII that he soon found employment in his new armoury at Greenwich. Like van Vrelant, the 'Burgundian Bard' also found its way to Henry VIII. Maximilian was a shrewd politician and strategist and spent much of his reign seeking to consolidate his position in Europe by securing alliances against his enemies and rivals, particularly the French. His interest in England, still on the periphery of European politics, began during the reign of Henry VII and was renewed following the accession of Henry VIII and his marriage to Katherine of Aragon.

To cement these alliances and bonds of friendship, and to some extent convey his own magnificence and that of his court, Maximilian became a prolific giver of diplomatic gifts. He commissioned pieces for relatives, diplomats, foreign rulers and dignitaries, all in an attempt to secure their loyalty and support against his enemies. It is likely that Henry received the 'Burgundian Bard' as just such a gift. Even though it is unlikely to have been commissioned for the king himself (implied by the absence of any of his personal emblems, such as the rose or portcullis), the fact that it was 'second hand' would not have diminished the impact of such a gift: rather, presenting an armour from his personal collection was a clear indication of Maximilian's regard for Henry and his desire to secure the English king's support for his military and diplomatic ambitions.

[102]

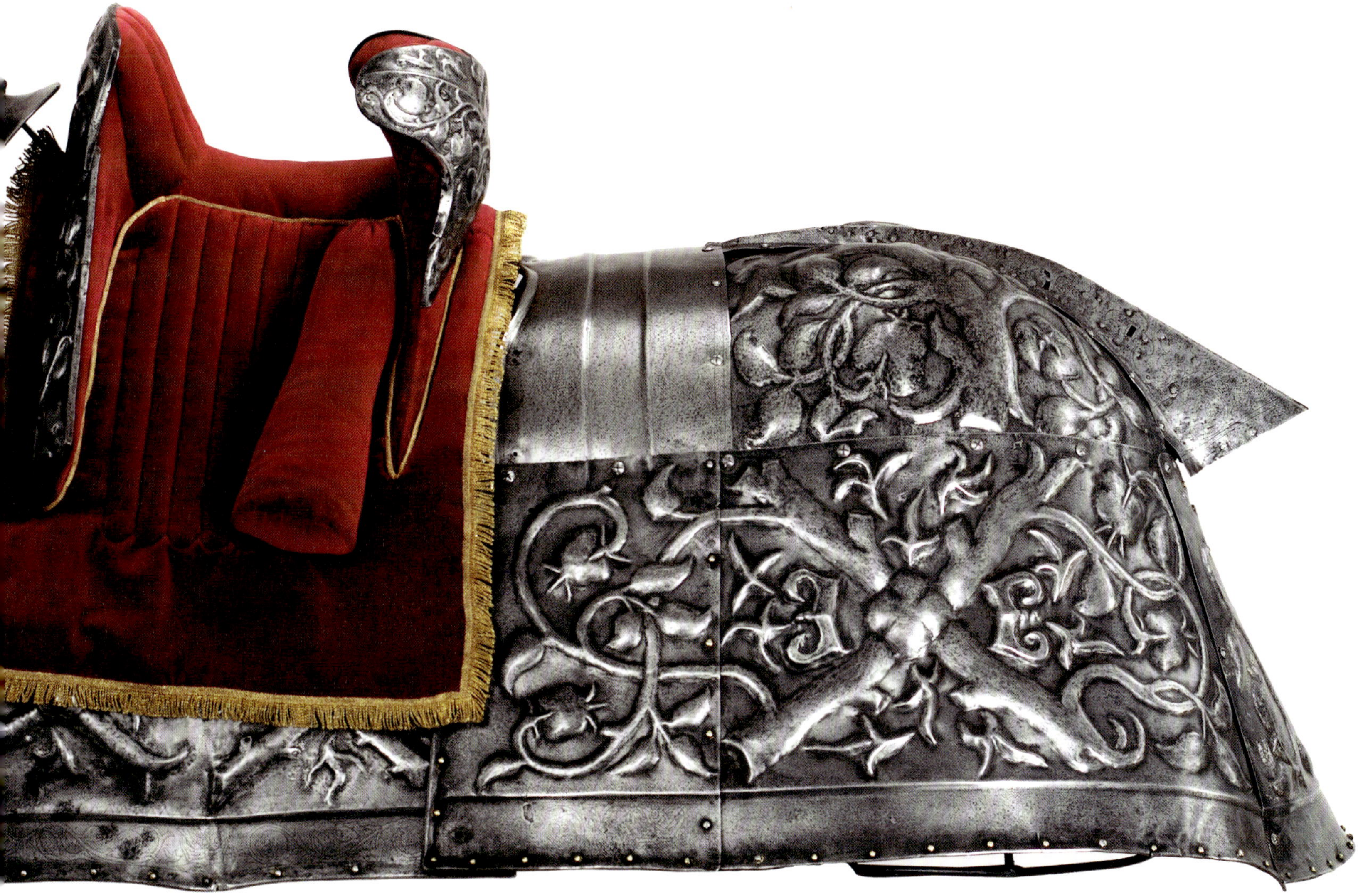

30

The 'Horned Helmet'

Austria, *c*.1511–14 · IV.22

The 'Horned Helmet' has been among the best-known treasures of the Royal Armouries and its precursors since the 17th century. Since 1996, its use as the motif of the museum in Leeds, blazoned about the building and on 'brown signs' by the roadside, has made it the most widely recognised item in the collection. It is also one of the most puzzling, and the subject of exceptionally prolonged, interesting and heated scholarly debate.

From the early 19th century it had been known that in 1511 the Holy Roman Emperor, Maximilian I ordered his court armourer, Konrad Seusenhofer of Innsbruck, to make three fine armours, decorated with pierced and gilded silver panels laid over fine velvet, one as a gift for the young King Henry VIII. The present was traditionally identified as the 'Silvered and Engraved' armour for man and horse [31], but in 1965 the great arms and armour scholar Claude Blair showed it to be a product of the king's own newly established workshops at Greenwich. At the same time, crucially, Blair identified the horned helmet as the only surviving fragment of Maximilian's gift, preserved (no doubt thanks to its curious appearance) when the rest was scrapped at the end of the English Civil Wars. Much remained to be explained, however: why the grotesque mask, the hooked and dripping nose, the brass spectacles, and above all the pair of naturalistic ram's horns? Why would the emperor send the new king of England such an extraordinary confection? The traditional answer – that it had belonged to Will Somers, Henry's court fool – no longer held water, and Blair suggested that its peculiarities were prompted by some sort of in-joke between the two monarchs. Ten years later, however, Dr Alan Borg, then the Armouries' Keeper of the Blades, queried the Maximilian association and argued that the helmet had been ingeniously made up of unrelated 16th-century pieces at a later date. The great scholars then locked horns, and Blair systematically countered Borg's questions and conclusions. Much still remained in doubt, but the intensity of these exchanges was such that for forty years few dared broach the subject again.

In 2009, however, Graeme Rimer studied the helmet anew and published his arguments in great detail. The study agreed with Blair on structural and practical grounds that the helmet was essentially all of a piece, bar the horns. He noted that the mask compares very closely with the face of the *Schellenunter*, or Knave of Bells, which appears on a playing card by Peter Flötner, a German artist of the first half of the 16th century, without horns but complete with a close-fitting hood, hooked and dripping nose, stubbly chin and 'rivet' spectacles. From the late 15th century the fool had been well-established as a figure who demonstrated that human failings were common to all, further popularised by Sebastian Brandt in his extended poem *Das Narrenschiff* of 1491 ('The Ship of Fools'), translated into English in 1509. Henry VIII is likely to have been well aware of it, and would have grasped the meaning conveyed by Maximilian's gift – that all men, however mighty, are capable of being foolish. Subsequently, in 2016, Pierre Terjanian of the New York Metropolitan Museum of Art noted a loosely similar 'fool'-faced helmet depicted in the near-contemporary Thun sketchbook. Possibly there were a number of such objects in existence at the time. Horns, however, fail to appear in the Thun drawing or in any known representation of a fool and with their connotations of cuckoldry would have given Maximilian's gift a rather risqué edge: the explanation is that whilst the horns are finely made, they are crudely attached additions, probably from the shaffron of a contemporary horse armour.

There is no record that Henry ever wore the helmet, and although the horns were clearly fitted before his death in 1547, we do not know why or by whom. Much else awaits discovery or may never be known – features that add to rather than detract from the interest of this unique and remarkable item.

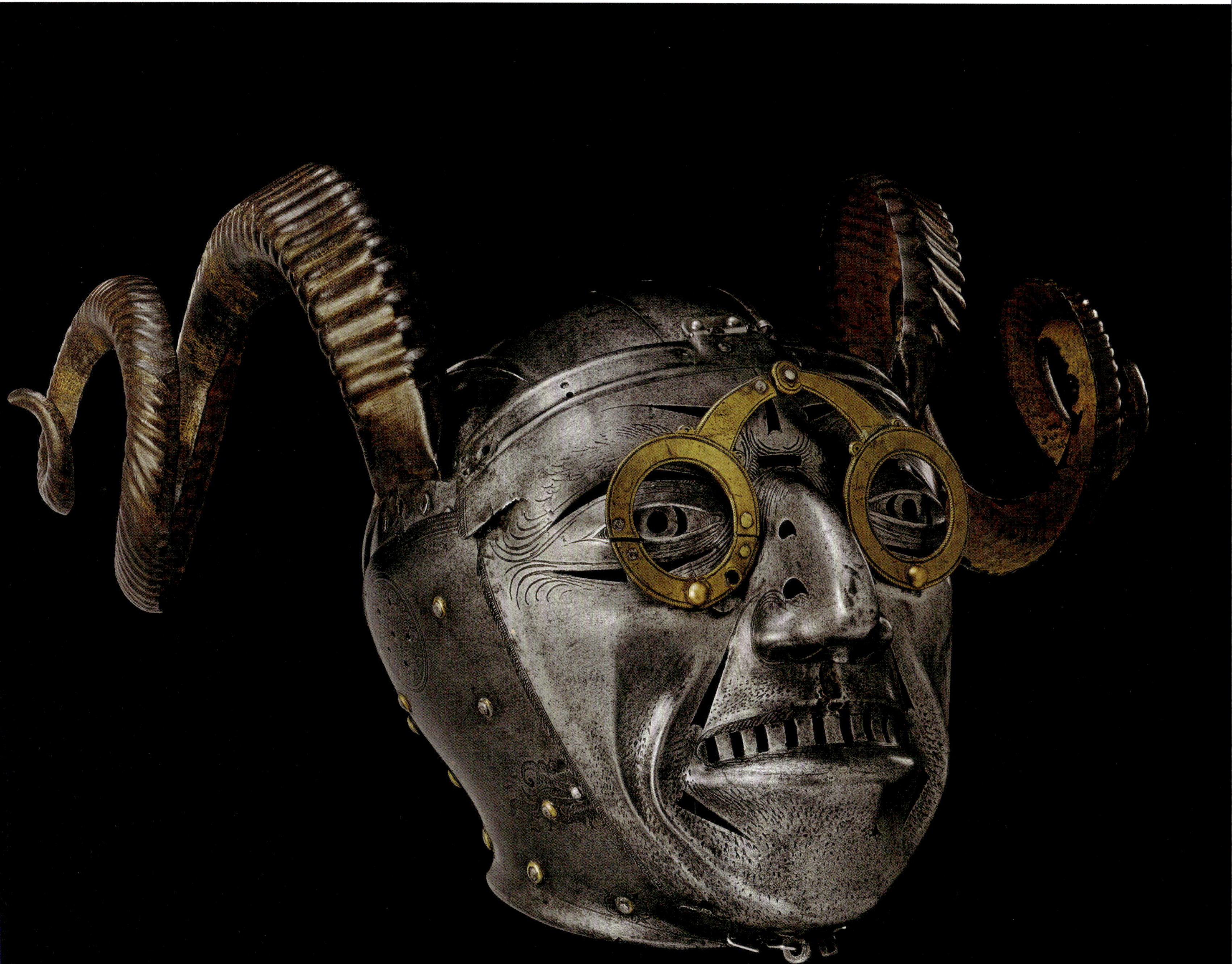

31

'Silvered and Engraved' field armour made for Henry VIII

England, *c.*1515 · II.5, VI.1–5

Armour was made in England throughout the Middle Ages, but as Maximilian I's gift [29] starkly emphasised, continental armour, particularly from Germany and Milan, far outshone the English product, and rich customers routinely placed their orders abroad. The young Henry VIII, fascinated by all things military and chivalric, and fiercely status-conscious, felt this deficiency very keenly: as Maximilian had done in 1504, he decided to establish his own elite manufactory, and so work began on an armoury mill near his palace at Greenwich in 1511, safely beyond the control of the London Guilds. By 1512 Milanese craftsmen had been installed, although swiftly replaced by Flemings and Germans, known as 'Almains'. Thereafter the Greenwich workshop dominated prestige armour-making in England until the 1620s.

The first known Greenwich product was the man's armour to the 'Silvered and Engraved' harness, matched with a bard made in Flanders, both of 1515, and both decorated in England by the king's 'harness gilder' Paul van Vrelant, for which he was paid £66 13*s* 4*d* in 1516. In form, the armour consists of an armet, full armour to the upper body, with a fashionable base or skirt, suitable for foot-combat or, with the front and rear panels removed, for use on horseback, and armour to the legs, terminating in elaborate sabatons. The bard consists of the usual shaffron, crinet, peytral, flanchards crupper and saddle-steels. Despite its popular name, all the outer surfaces of the harness were originally gilded, although today only patches of the silvering (which for metallurgical reasons underlay gilding) survive. The armour was also abundantly engraved, a process that preceded the silvering and gilding. A dominant theme is the dynastic alliance and prospects of Henry VIII and Katherine of Aragon, daughter of the powerful Ferdinand II of Aragon and Isabella of Castile, seen most prominently through their gilded initials, linked by lover's knots, set around the border of the base (skirt). Meanwhile the Spanish-English alliance, cemented by their marriage, is represented by Tudor roses and Katherine's badge of ripe pomegranates, the sheaf of arrows of Aragon and (on the sabatons) the castle of Castile and the Tudor portcullis. Alongside these references to earthly status, the king's piety is also expressed through his motto *'Dieu et Mon Droit'* ('God and my right'), engraved around the border of the bard, and through abundant representation of St George and St Barbara. Both appear on the cuirass; on the breastplate, a fully armoured George stands over the prostrate dragon, while on the back a haloed Barbara stands beside a tower, her most common symbol. St George appears again on the bard (peytral) with the vanquished dragon, both he and his horse wearing armour similar to the 'Silvered and Engraved' itself; the saint's judgement by the pagan king Dacian is then followed by his racking, boiling in a life-size brazen bull, and his final beheading. Elsewhere on the bard, St Barbara watches the building of her tower, before being taken into captivity, tormented and finally decapitated. In all scenes, the figures are clothed and equipped in early-16th century style, with the occasional nod to imagined Asian headgear. All in all, the 'Silvered and Engraved' is remarkable as a piece of technical and artistic virtuosity and as an early product of the Greenwich workshops. It is also an enduring symbol of the confidence and ambition of the twenty-four-year old King, and which projects his image of himself almost as powerfully today as it did in the 16th century.

32

'Charles Brandon's lance'

England, early 16th century · VII.550

'Charles Brandon's lance' has been one of the sights of the Tower of London since at least the 1580s. Its importance lies in its construction, size, the history of its display, the particular aspects of the tournament and ceremony it may represent, and its early association with Brandon, Duke of Suffolk, Henry VIII's friend, brother-in-law and fellow jouster.

The lance is made from a baulk of close-grained pine, sawn lengthwise into two parts, each then partly hollowed out at the grip end and reassembled, enclosing a void. The exterior was then shaped, possibly on a lathe, decorated with twelve flutes, gessoed, and the shaft, it seems, entirely gilded. At a later date it was overpainted with the existing scheme of black, white, red and yellow. The eight-faceted steel head was once gilded too, although it is unlikely to be original.

At 4.36 m long, and with a diameter of 185 mm just forward of the grip, the lance is exceptionally large, and at 8.87 kg exceptionally heavy. In these respects it is only matched or exceeded by five survivors in the Real Almeria, Madrid. Made for the future Charles V before 1519, these are as much as 4.70 m in length and elaborately painted. Size and weight would have made all of these useless on the battlefield and impractical for jousting, while the careful construction (at least of Brandon's lance), their lavish decoration, and indeed their preservation, imply they were not intended for violent or one-off use.

This leaves their actual purpose unclear, although there are two main possibilities. The first is suggested by accounts of international tournaments from the early 15th to the mid 16th century, in which exceptionally strong and skilful jousters rode the length of the lists with giant lances, perhaps held upright, as a stunt preceding the main event. At a joust in Paris in 1514 the English chronicler Edward Hall watched an Italian champion run 'a corse … to his great honour' with a tapered lance *c.*225 mm thick at the butt – bigger than Brandon's – and a similar feat was performed by the celebrated jouster Sir Nicolas Carew at Greenwich in 1517. At least one 15th-century source suggests that such lances may also have been 'run at the ring', that is, couched and aimed at a suspended target. The second possibility, hinted at by Spanish sources, is that such oversize lances were not carried on horseback at all. Instead, they were borne on foot by squires for symbolic and stage management purposes, placed like flagpoles or totems to mark out the ends or corners of the tiltyard. They could, of course, have been used for both purposes, if not others as well. In the 16th century hollow lances were known (variously spelt) in English and French as '*bordons*' and in Spanish as '*bordonasas*', perhaps from the medieval organ pipe of the same name. Outsize versions were known as 'great' or '*grosse*' bordons.

Whether the lance really belonged to Brandon is unknown. His famed prowess in the lists would certainly have prompted the connection by 16th-century Yeoman Warder guides, who would have been informed, even remotely, by Edward Hall, and an audience which knew his *Chronicle*. Nevertheless, the association does date from the first-known mention of the lance, in August 1584, by Lupold von Wendel from Pomerania, who was shown 'a lance, used in English wars by a Zoffoger ['Suffolker']'. This was a time when people who knew Brandon were still alive and could have made or contested the claim. A real connection, then, remains a possibility. Apart from occasional associations with (the famously tall) John of Gaunt, or even Henry VIII, the lance has been labelled as Brandon's ever since – albeit, since the late 19th century, 'by traditional association'.

[108]

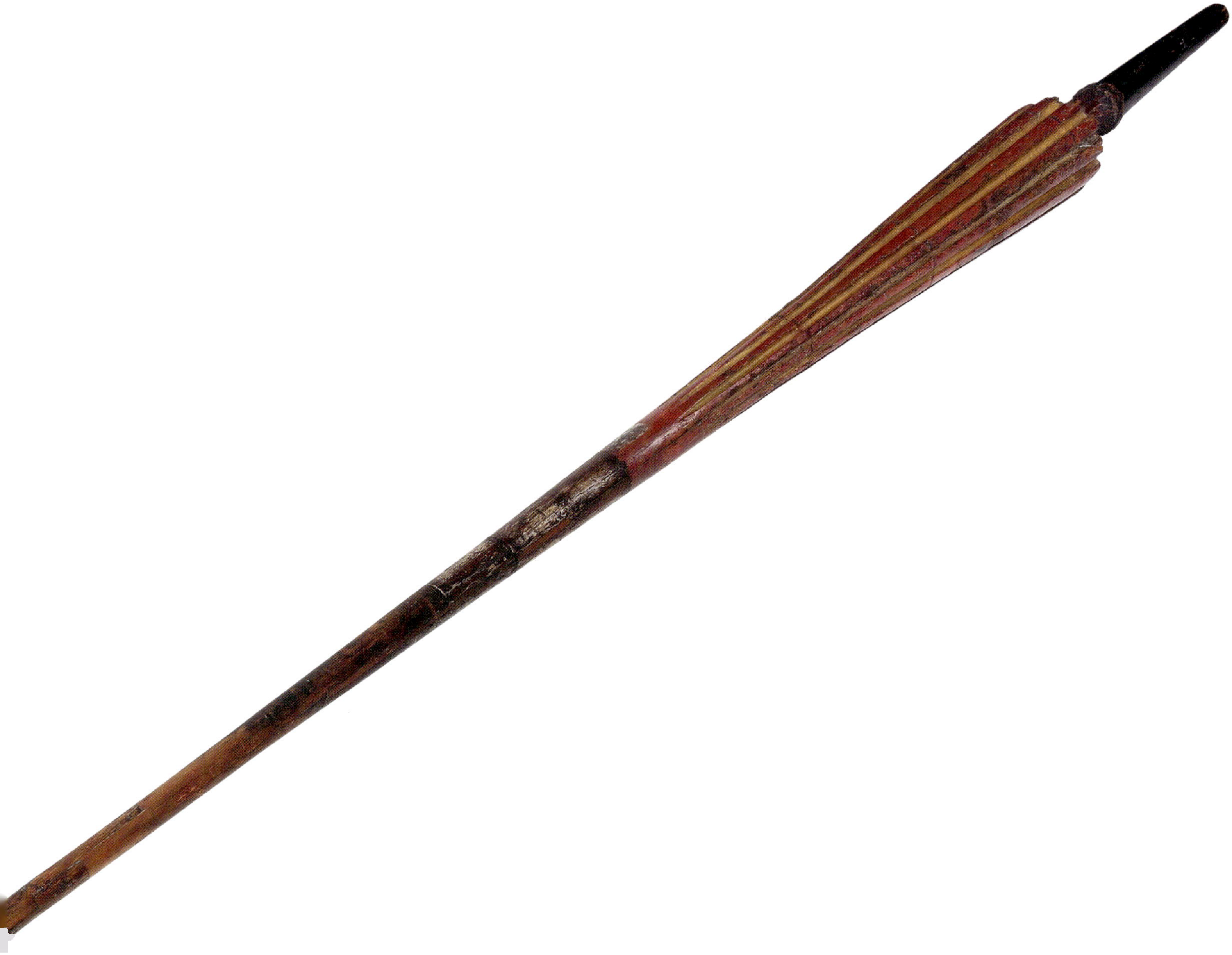

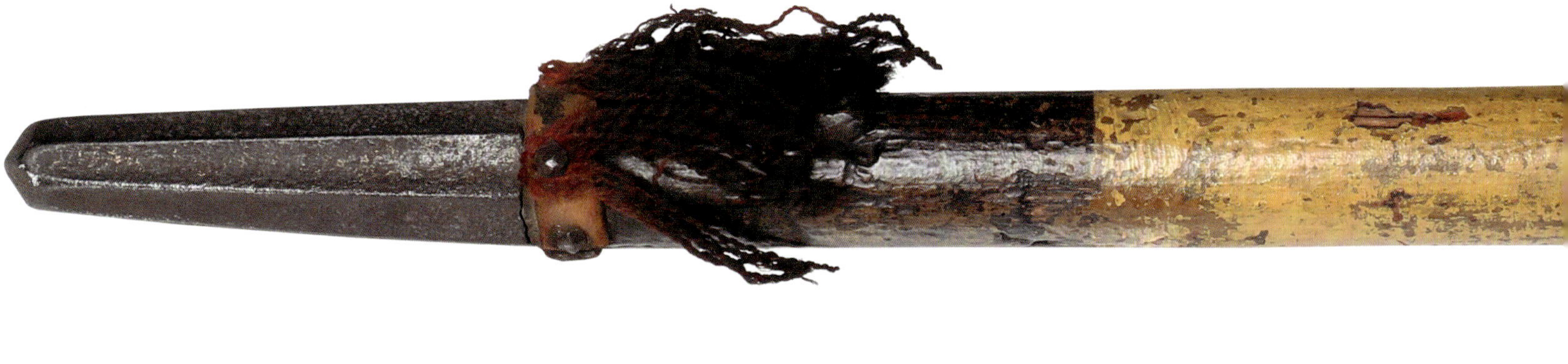

33

Foot combat armour for Henry VIII

England, 1520 · II.6

In the early 16th century the two greatest powers in Europe were the French, ruled after 1515 by Francis I, and the vast Holy Roman Empire, particularly after the accession of Charles V in 1519. Frequently at war with each other, both were interested in an alliance with England, which fitted Henry VIII's ambition to increase his country's influence on the European stage. Despite his desire to emulate his ancestor Henry V on the battlefield, a peace accord was signed in 1514 with Francis I, and within a few years a great meeting between the two kings was being planned for 1520. It was to be held in English-held territory between Ardres and Guines, near Calais, with the aim of securing harmony between the two realms and 'Universal Peace' in Europe. Known to posterity as 'the Field of Cloth of Gold' or the '*Champ du Drap d'Or*', the three-week event included tilts, tourneys and finally combat at the barriers on Friday 22 and Saturday 23 June.

Henry's newly established armourers went to work, and the result was this, the so-called 'foot combat armour' – one of the most important in the Royal Armouries collection. The maker was probably the master armourer Martin van Royne, with his team, and it is thought that the armour is one of the first to have been made by him at the 'Almain' armoury in its temporary home at Southwark. One of only four of this type surviving and comprising 235 separate parts, it is a remarkable piece of engineering, designed to protect every part of the body. As with all tournament armour, the wearer sacrificed a certain degree of mobility for enhanced protection. At 42.6 kg, roughly twice the weight of a normal field armour, it incorporates laminated defences over the inside of the elbow joints, the backs of the knees and, remarkably, the upper thighs, groin and buttocks – the most difficult parts to protect and for which mail usually sufficed. All parts interlock and articulate using turning joints, slots and sliding rivets to allow a good range of movement, yet no gap is left which a weapon might penetrate.

Just two months before the agreed date for the festivities in May, Francis directed that the specification for the 'foot combat armour' was changed. This was reported to Henry by his agent Sir Richard Wingfield: 'As tochyng the combatt at the barrier, ther is lefft out, these wordes following, wt. pieces of avauntage, And in stede therof is sett in Tonnelett & bacinett'. This made the nearly finished armour redundant. It was left (as recorded in the 1683 Tower inventory) 'rough from the hammer', that is, without being polished, let alone decorated: the present bright appearance of the armour results from years of cleaning with brick dust and army-issue Rangoon oil by 19th-century wardens. In its unfinished and latterly unintended state the armour was remarked upon by Tower visitors from the 1690s, partly for its technical virtuosity: a description of 1761 noted that the joints in the hands, arms and thighs, knees and feet 'play like the joints of a rattlesnake and are moved with all the facility imaginable'. It has always appealed, of course, thanks to its association with Henry VIII, a man in the prime of his life, whose athletic build and height the 'foot combat armour' so closely reproduces.

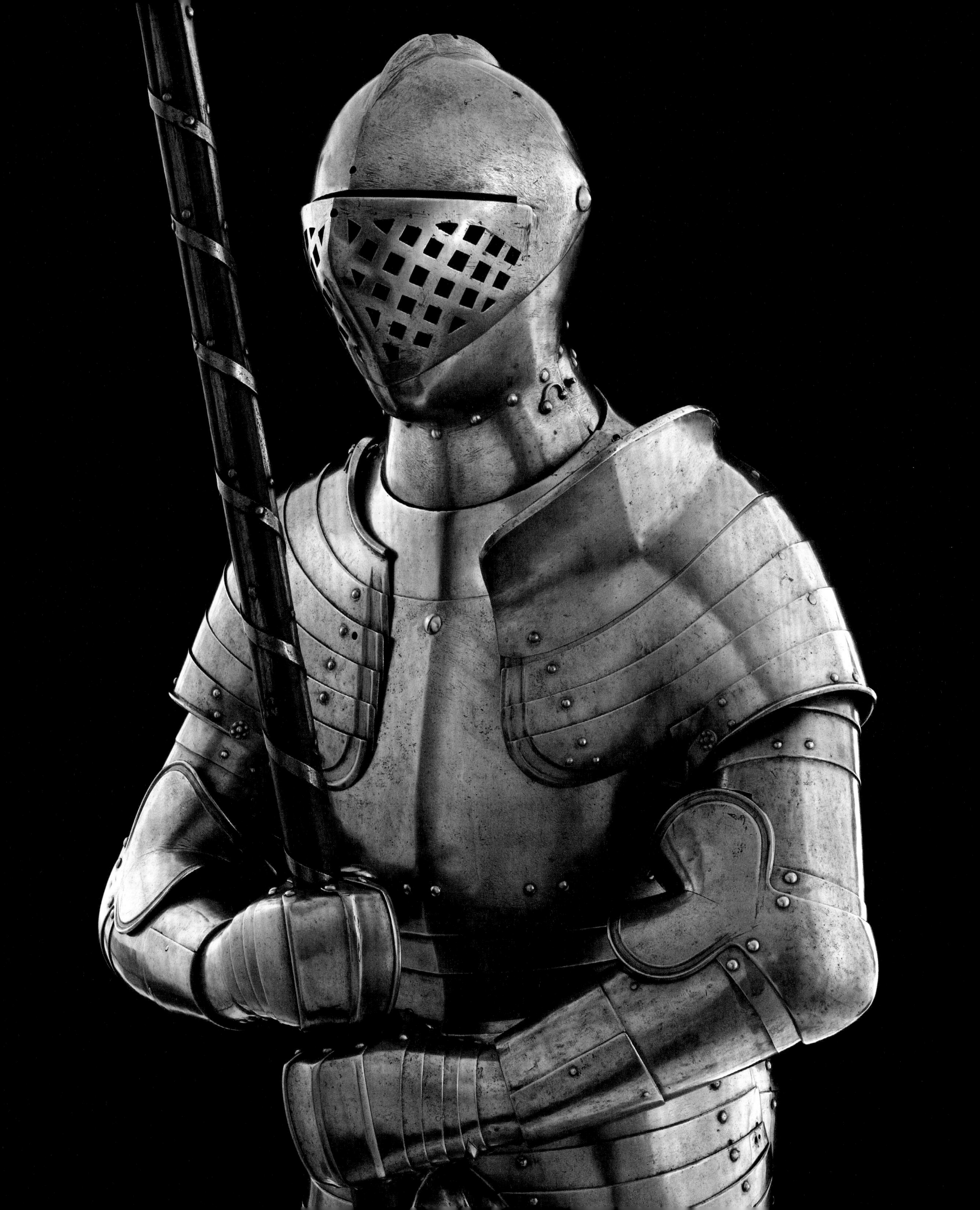

34

Tonlet armour for Henry VIII

England, 1520 · II.7

Fought in an enclosure between two contestants, foot combat used a variety of weapons including throwing spears, swords and axes. Although death in such combats was extremely rare, by the late 15th century a three-foot high barrier was introduced down the centre of the enclosure as a safety measure. Initially, the foot combat appears to have been fought in ordinary field armour, but by the mid-15th century, if not before, the equipment started to become increasingly formalised, and extra defensive elements such as the laminations over the inside of the elbow had appeared by the 1430s. By c.1490 a new type of armour had been developed, possibly in the Burgundian-Habsburg court in Brussels, but still similar to 15th-century field armour. Primarily worn in the German-speaking regions of Europe, the armour included a distinctive long hooped skirt, known as a tonlet (from the Old French *tonnel*, barrel) and a great bacinet strapped or screwed to the cuirass. As the armour was only worn on foot, there was no need to incorporate a cut-out for a lance on the right pauldron, and the pauldrons were symmetrical. In addition the cuisses, usually left open in order to provide more sensitive contact between rider and horse, were fully enclosed with multiple articulated lames protecting the back of the knees.

With the Field of Cloth of Gold fast approaching [33], the English postponed the meeting with Francis I from May until June. This was partly for political reasons but also, according to Cardinal Wolsey, because of 'the difficulty of providing transport and armour'. With the original 'foot-combat armour' now set aside unfinished, Henry's armourers had just over two months to produce another, including a tonlet, according to the new French specifications. With such limited time, they were forced to assemble an armour by adapting several existing pieces and producing others from scratch. Of the pre-existing pieces the bacinet, bearing a Milanese armourer's marks, may have originally been designed for the tourney in which the combatants fought with clubs or rebated swords. In order to make it suitable for the foot combat, additional pierced plates were inserted into the sights whilst a narrow reinforcing band was riveted to the top edge of the visor. The legs and vambraces were adapted from a pre-existing Italian or German field armour with additional articulated lames inserted to protect the inside of the elbow. Tellingly, the leg harnesses have open cuisses and retain a slot for the spurs at the base of the heel, something quite unnecessary for a foot combat armour but essential for a horseman. The cuirass was also adapted (from an Italian or Flemish field armour), and only the pauldrons and tonlet itself were made new.

Once everything was complete, the entire armour was etched. Due to the rush, this involved at least two or three individuals with varying levels of skill. Some of the roughest work, featuring both conventional foliate and scale designs in addition and more symbolically charged Tudor roses, is on the tonlet. A more skilled hand etched the roundels of St George and the Virgin and Christ Child on the pauldrons, whilst the collar and garter of the Order of the Garter showcase the greatest skill. Originally gilded and deep blue or black, the armour would have created a striking effect, echoing the expensive and highly fashioned silver – and gold-embroidered black damask and velvet clothes listed in Henry's Great Wardrobe. In the event, the armour proved as effective as it was impressive, a contemporary noting that the 'two valyaunte kynges' fought 'with such force that the fier sprung out of their armure'.

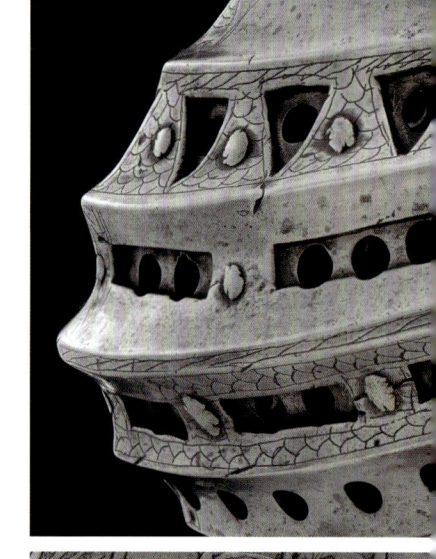

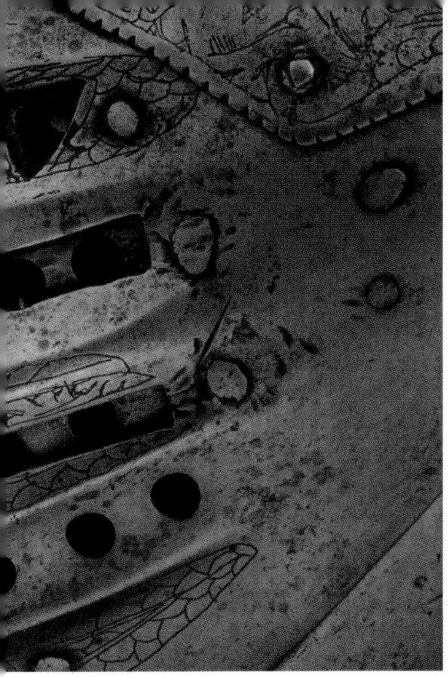
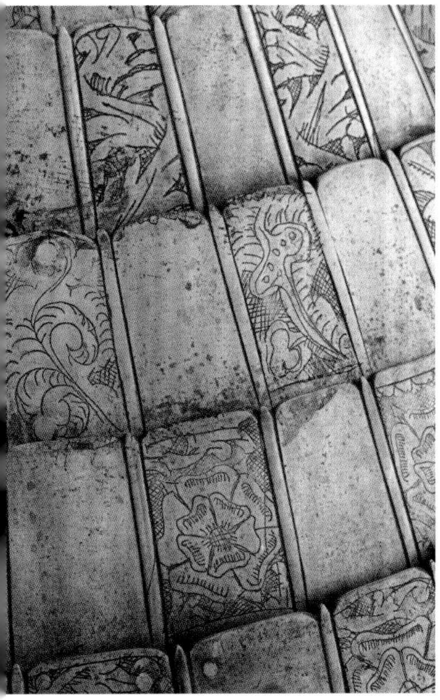
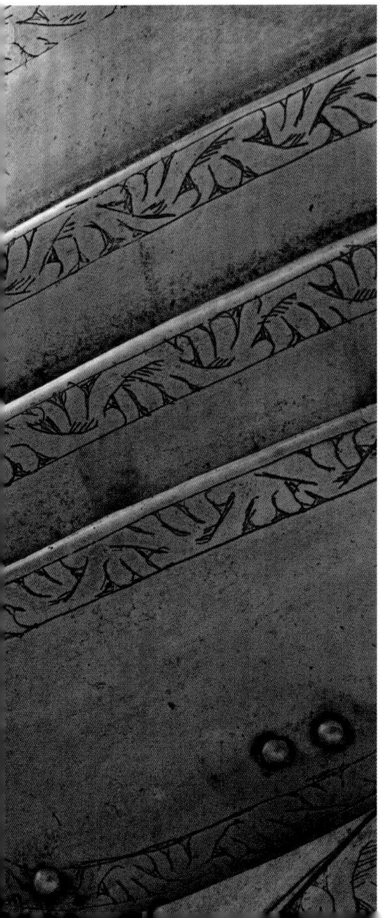
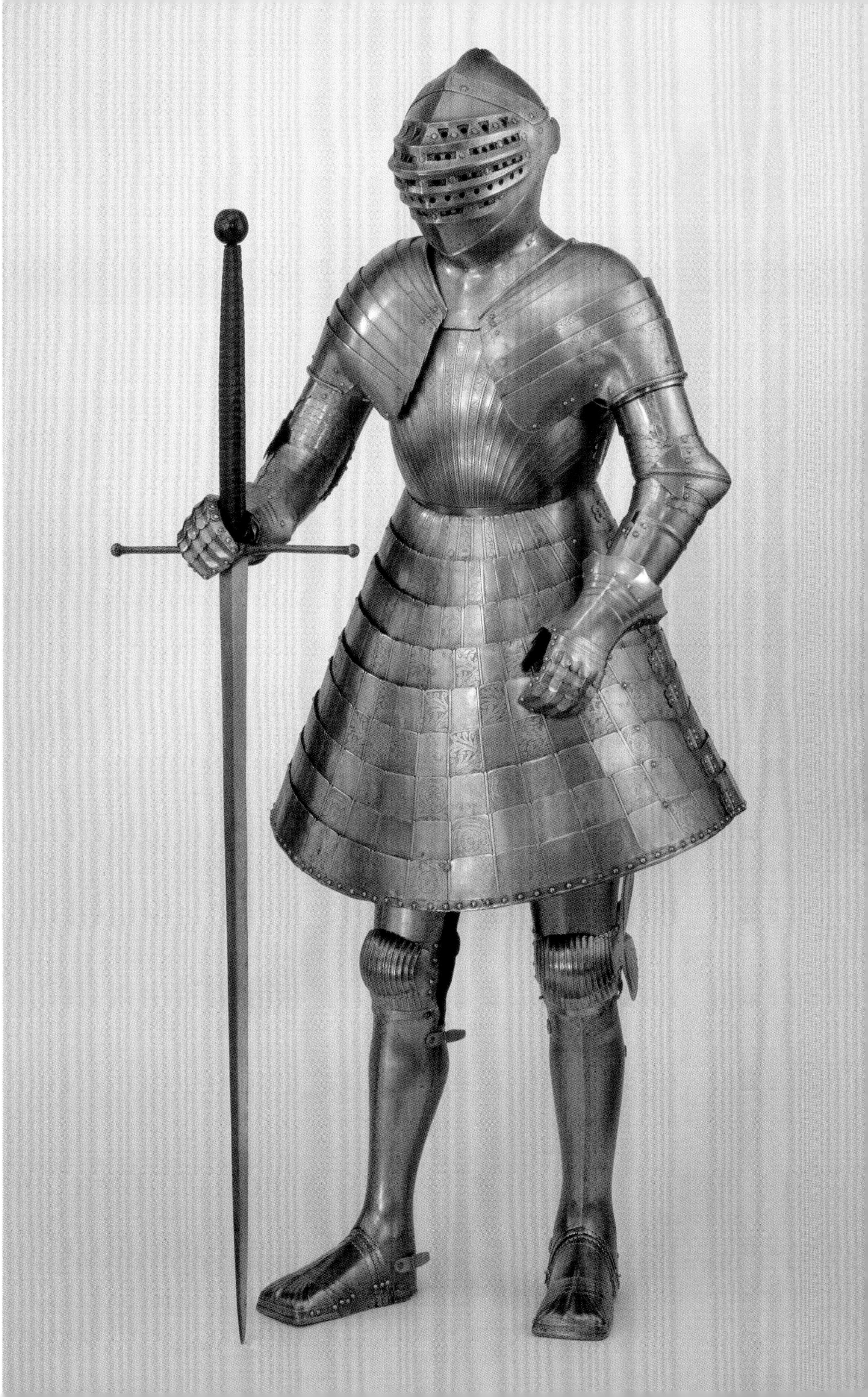

35

Painting of the battle of Pavia

Italy or Spain, in or soon after 1525 · 1.142

'De toutes choses ne m'est demeuré que l'honneur et la vie qui est saulve', or 'Of all I had, only honour and life have been spared': words written by Francis I, king of France, in a woeful letter to his mother in March 1525. His plans for Italian domination ended, and now the bitter captive of his arch-rival the Holy Roman Emperor Charles V, things indeed looked bleak. Disaster had struck in a great battle beneath the walls of the north Italian city of Pavia on 25 January, the stages of which unfold – if, rather confusingly, all at once – in this near-contemporary oil painting by an unknown Italian or Spaniard. France and the Empire shared a border and were natural rivals, and for decades had been at each others' throats, not least in Italy, where both had had interests since the 1490s. Rebounding from a series of setbacks, in 1524 Francis led his troops to victory in the north, seized Milan, pursued the Imperial forces southwards to Pavia, and there set about besieging them: his men set up camp on an island in the River Ticino (shown at the top of the picture) and within the protective walls (red brick, running diagonally across the scene) of the Visconti family's vast pleasure park of Mirabello to the north. Between the two, with the Imperial eagle fluttering above it, lay the city itself: the cathedral, major buildings and the part-modernised defences, can all be made out. Batteries of great bronze guns face it across the moat, and the flashes of return fire from the breached and crumbling walls can be glimpsed through the smoke. But help was soon at hand for the garrison, most importantly a relieving army which arrived in early February under the veteran soldiers Charles de Lannoy and Fernando d'Ávalos, Marquis of Pescara (labelled, lower centre '*El Marchese di Peschiera*'). After a few weeks of skirmishing (see Francis, in gilded armour, his horse caparisoned with *fleurs de lys*, top left), on the 23rd the Imperial troop massed and broke through the park wall (as shown), initiating a confused, bloody but eventful struggle, the French being led by the king in person. In the final stages Francis and his mounted and fully armoured knights were confronted by pikemen and, crucially, by the Imperial arquebusiers: named after their weapon, the arquebus, a smoothbore, matchlock shoulder-mounted gun, heavy and slow to load but capable of penetrating armour, these were the men of the hour; cornered between them, woodland and other obstacles, in a scene reminiscent of Crécy or Agincourt, the flower of France's armoured chivalry were brought down from afar by humble men whose eyes they never met. Unhorsed, Francis fought on foot, but was swiftly captured. The battle was a setback for French ambitions in Italy and a personal catastrophe for the king. But Pavia's lasting legacy was to prove the power of infantrymen armed with firearms over the fully armoured horsemen, who, socially and tactically, had dominated warfare for centuries. The lesson was slowly learned, but within a century they had disappeared from the battlefield. This painting, while not an eye-witness account – nor, in the age of Leonardo and Raphael, a great work of art – provides a vivid, incident-packed, personal and fascinating window onto a key few hours in European history.

[114]

INSVLADE GRAVALON
GRAVALONE
FRANZESI
SAN LAZAR
LATORRE CHE FI FOCO IN SIGNODEL SOCCORSO
PAVIA
EL CONTE DI GIARVA
DVCA DEBORBON
S GALEAZO VISCONTE
S FEDERICO DA BOZOL
EL MARCHESE DEL GVASCO
EL MARCHESE DI PESCHIERA
EL BARCO DI PAVIA
SPAGNOLI ET ITALIANI
EIGRANDE ASSEDIO FACTO APAVIA DAL CHRISTIANI SSIMO S FRANCESCO RE DIFRANCIA FINALMENTE COME PIACQVE ADIO FV PRESA SVA MAIESTA DALLO EXERCITO IMPERIALE QVESTO FV AVENTICINQVE DELMESE DI FEBRARO 152

36

'Henry VIII's Walking Staff', a 'Holy Water Sprinkler' with three guns

Possibly England, early 16th century · XIV.1

Henry VIII's enthusiasm for weapons technology is well known and extended to ingenious combinations of guns with spikes or blades. Makers, meanwhile, were equally keen to produce such things to demonstrate their ingenuity and versatility, but many, like the early 17th-century 'axe-pistol' in the Armouries collection, were of little practical use. This example, however, has a thoroughly workmanlike appearance, at first sight that of a mace, with a long wooden haft (for two-handed use) and roughly cylindrical steel-cased head with a spike pointing forward and nine others protruding radially from the sides. As such it takes the general form of the '*morgenstern*' ('morning star'), a two-handed mace, sometimes with a star-like spherical head – hence the German term by which they are usually known. In England and Germany the cylindrical-headed version was known in the 16th century as the 'Holy Water Sprinkler' and '*Weihwasserwedel*' thanks to a loose similarity to the liturgical item, in so far as the spikes may be said to resemble spurts of water. These weapons were widely used by infantrymen in Europe, particularly in German-speaking lands, but seem to have been particularly favoured by the English in the early part of the century. Shorter and usually finer ones were also used by cavalry.

This weapon, however, is distinguished by its all-steel head and the three short gun barrels fitted into it, each originally fitted with a sliding cover to secure the priming powder and a second cover, swivelling on the central spike, to close the muzzle. These were fired with a loose match (sulphur-impregnated cord glowing at one end), very much in the manner of a medieval handgun, and, if awkward to use, would have been roughly as effective as a later 16th-century pistol. The connection with Henry VIII is clear from its Tower provenance and the mention in the 1547 inventory of Henry's goods of 'Holly water sprincles with gonnes in thende – vii', and another, probably this one, with 'thre gonnes in the Topp'. While this is a particularly fine example and of royal provenance, others are known, for example in the Hofjagd – und Rüstkammer, and in German they merit their own term, *Schiessprügel* ('shooting mace').

By 1599 it was noticed at the Tower, along with other items of Henry's personal armoury, by the Swiss traveller Joseph Platter, and after 1660 it was displayed in the 'Spanish Armoury', largely composed of items allegedly captured from the Armada in 1588 but doubling as a kind of 'cabinet of curiosities'. By then the object was already a favourite among Tower visitors, and was known from at least 1686 as 'King Henry ye 8ths Walking Staff': such was its appeal that from the late 16th century it was claimed to have been his weapon of choice, carried on nightly perambulations about the city 'in one of the cotes of his gard', and by 1787 Yeoman Warder guides were telling their charges that this led to the king's brief imprisonment for carrying an offensive weapon by the watch: the king, however, far from punishing his captor 'applauded his resolution, in honestly doing his duty'. The fame of the weapon also led to its appearance in artistic representations of the king and his era, for example in Henry Monro's *The Disgrace of Wolsey* (1813), now in the Tate: here a spiked mace, thrown to the ground by the irate monarch, lies in the foreground by an upturned stool. Something of a curiosity when made, it is interesting, if not surprising, that that the 'Walking staff' has continued to attract the attention of myth-makers and the public ever since.

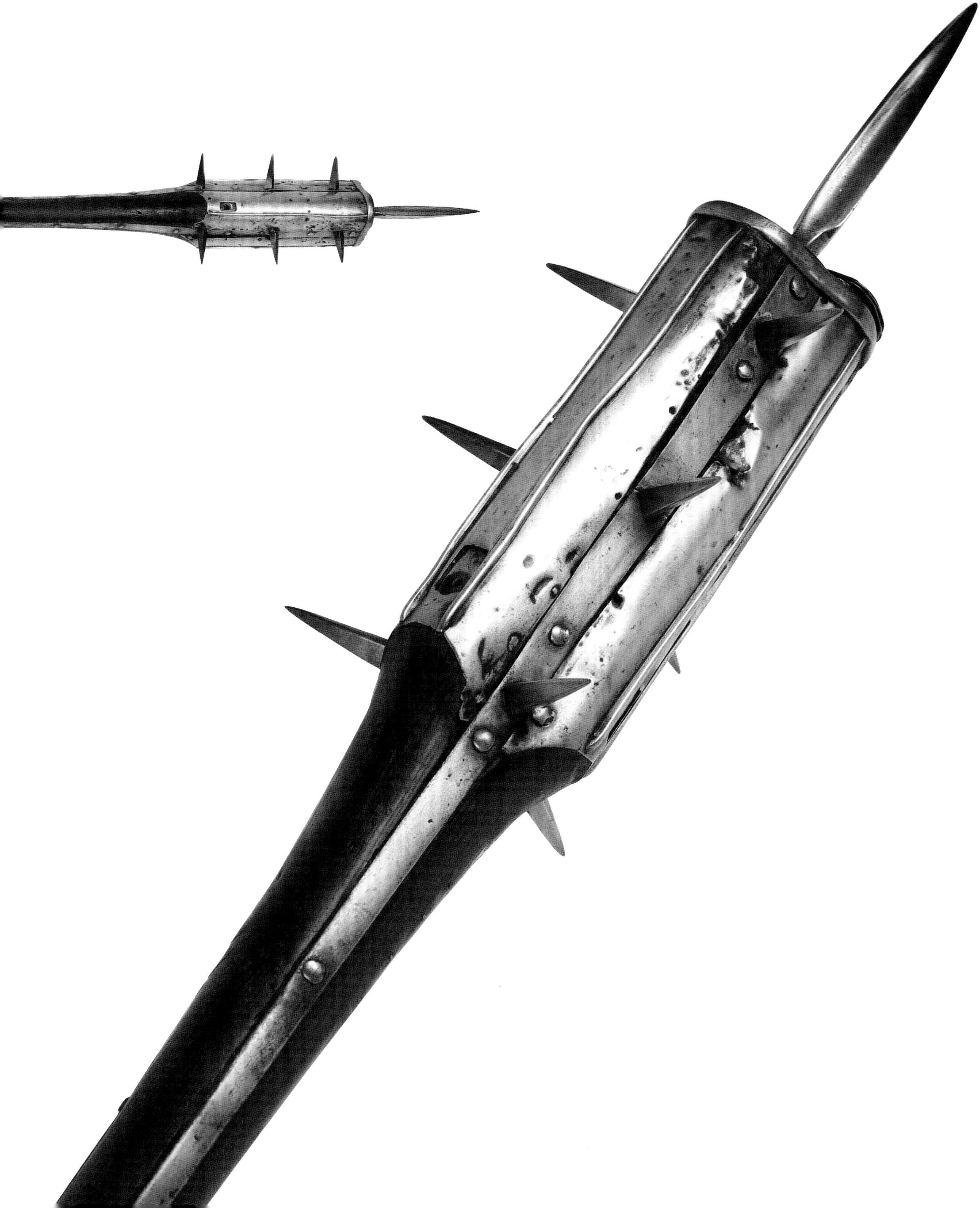

37

Breech-loading gun belonging to Henry VIII

England, 1537 · XII.1

This remarkable gun, dated to 1537, has the distinction of being technically precocious, a superb piece of craftsmanship, a former possession of Henry VIII, and an item proudly displayed to the Tower of London's visitors by the Royal Armouries' precursors since the reign of Elizabeth I. As a weapon, it is remarkable for being a breech-loader; that is, loaded through an aperture at the rear of the barrel rather than, as was the case with most guns until the 1860s, the muzzle. The advantages lay in simplifying the loading process and in increasing rapidity of fire – in all eras one of the gunsmiths' most compelling ambitions – and making it easier to load whilst prone, useful both in war and sport. In this case the breech mechanism, of 'trap door' form, comprised a hinged lid or 'block', lifted to allow a re-usable iron cartridge, pre-loaded with powder and ball, to be pushed forward into the chamber; as such it is the earliest dated example of an arrangement used intermittently, although always outnumbered by muzzle-loaders, until the late 19th century. The original ignition system, as shown by the aperture left by its removal, was a wheellock, whereby a hardened spring-driven wheel spun against a piece of pyrites, striking sparks and igniting the powder in the priming pan; invented c.1500–10, in 1537 this remained an innovative and expensive arrangement. In this case it was replaced by the existing matchlock, for reasons unknown, in the 17th century. The delicately carved walnut stock becomes angular towards the butt, allowing it to be held closely to the cheek and it originally sported a velvet-covered pad for greater comfort. For most of its length the barrel is fluted in the manner of an architectural column, but this ends towards the breech in a raised ring, beyond which 'HR' (*Henricus Rex*; King Henry) is written in relief, alongside a Tudor rose: then, located next to the trap door, is the square-sectioned chamber, engraved with the date 1537, and then the breech block itself, adorned with acanthus scrolls and inscribed 'WH'; this was possibly for William Hunt, 'keeper of the Kings handguns and demi-hawks' from 1538, which tallies with other features to imply that the gun was made in England. Beyond that is a copper-alloy plaque, bearing an engraved and much-worn image of St George and the dragon. The date and initials, meanwhile, conveniently link the gun to the written record: very probably this gun is the 'chamber pece in a Stocke of woode lyned in the Cheke with vellet' inventoried at Westminster after Henry's death, described by a Swiss visitor in 1599 as a 'pistol … which could be loaded at the breech … very like a musket', and listed in the 1691 Tower inventory as 'King Henry the Eights Carbine'. Henry was interested in firearms and their development, and at one time owned over 300 breech-loading small arms, probably more than any other contemporary prince. This one, however, and a similar companion (XII.2) are the only survivors. The fine decoration and small 30-bore calibre imply sporting use, including target shooting, for example at the 'bordes to be shotte at' set up for the king at Windsor Castle in 1537. Game shooting with guns was then in its infancy, but in 1538 Henry and his friends are known to have shot duck – probably on the water – near Greenwich, and this gun and its like were well adapted for such use. The accuracy of the gun and its user are not recorded.

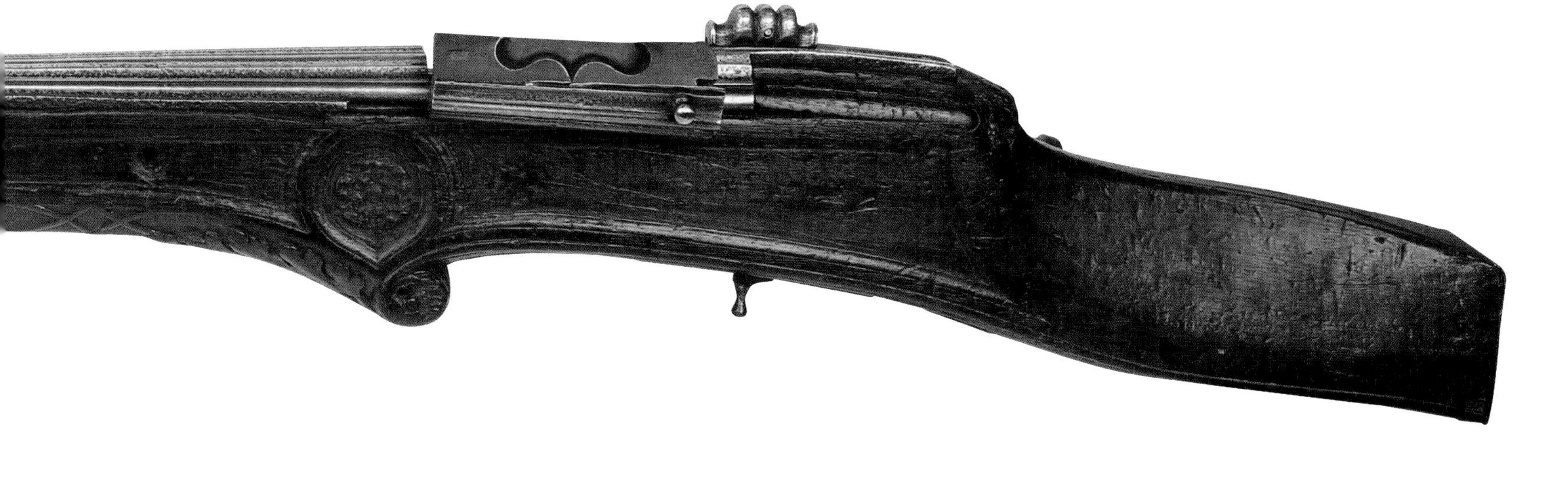
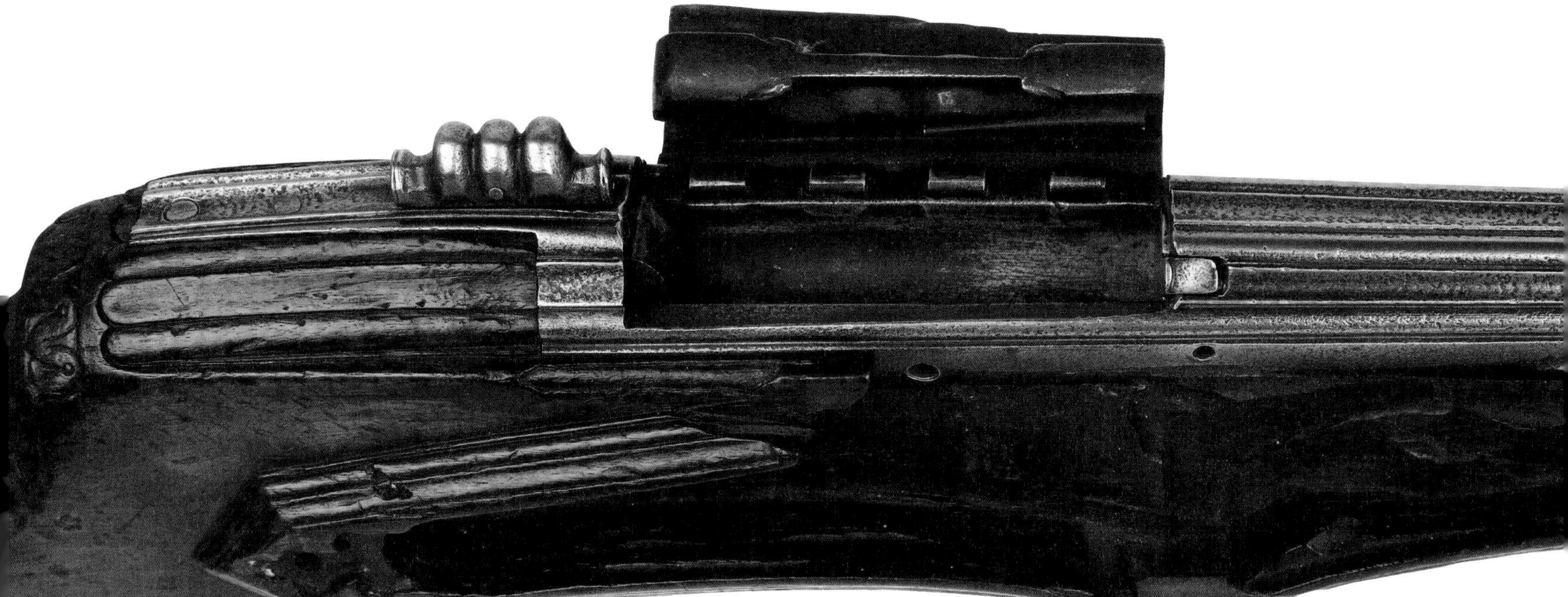

38

Buffe for a burgonet by Filippo Negroli

Italy, 1538 · IV.477

One of the most impressive ways whereby the surface of armour could be decorated was to give it a three-dimensional finish through embossing. Also known as *repoussé*, this involved laying the metal plate on a bed of firm but soft material such as pitch, before hammering out a relief design from the reverse. The plate was then turned over and the detail refined or 'chased' with chisels and punches. The technique was used in antiquity, and perhaps first revived, at least technically, by 15th-century armourers in Germany. However, as the Renaissance was born in Italy it is not surprising that embossing '*all antica*' was first adopted there, including by the greatest armourers. One of these, sometimes but wrongly credited with its invention, was Filippo Negroli of Milan (c.1510–79), under whom the technique rose to an art form in its own right: tellingly he was the only one of his profession mentioned in Giorgio Vasari's famous and highly selective *Lives of the Most Excellent Architects, Painters and Sculptors from Cimabue to Our Times* (1550).

This 'buffe', or lower face defence, part of a richly decorated burgonet, justifies their praise. Inscribed PHĨ ET FRÃ / DE NEGROLIS · F (*Phi[lippus] et Fra[tres] de Negrolis f[aciebant]*; 'Philip Negroli and brothers made this'), and with the date MD XXXVIII (1538), it is one of only eight pieces signed by the man himself and the first to acknowledge the contribution of the younger brothers. Structurally, the buffe is of three parts: the collar of three plain lames and fixed chin plate, and the faceplate, hinged at the sides, embossed in life-size relief with nose, wrinkled at the sides, masterfully sculpted, with a downturned mouth and protruding lower lip; to the sides of the face acanthus leaves in high relief, still partly gilded, spread backwards to the ears. Originally a rich peacock blue, contrasting brilliantly with the gilding, the main surfaces have oxidised to a deep russet. The other surviving parts, the peak or brim of the helmet, in the form of a satyr-like mask, and the two cheek pieces, respectively in the Bargello in Florence and the Wallace Collection in London, are equally lavish.

Owned until 1631 by the Dukes of Urbino, the helmet may have been made for Francesco Maria della Rovere (duke 1508–16 and again 1521–38), perhaps on his appointment as Captain of the 'Holy League' against the Turks in 1538. A known customer of the Negroli, he was also painted by Titian wearing a very similar helmet. The appeal of embossed armour derived from its use in antiquity, including in the decoration of cavalry helmets incorporating naturalistic beard and moustachioed face-masks; wearing the Renaissance version, princes took on the mantle of ancient virtue and heroism, cementing their legitimacy to rule and command. As too in ancient Greece and Rome, whilst used in ceremonies and as quasi-theatrical costume and to convey specific messages, embossed armour also served on the battlefield, as the weight and thickness of the buffe implies.

From the della Rovere, the helmet at least passed to the Medicis of Florence, and was acquired at the breakup of their collection by John Campbell, 2nd Marquis of Breadalbane, soon after 1780. The buffe, now on its own, then passed through two other private owners, and was bought by the Tower Armouries in 1949. Sad as it is that the surviving pieces are separate, this can be said to reflect the value attached to them, now and in the past, as *objets d'art*, rather than of art simply applied to armour.

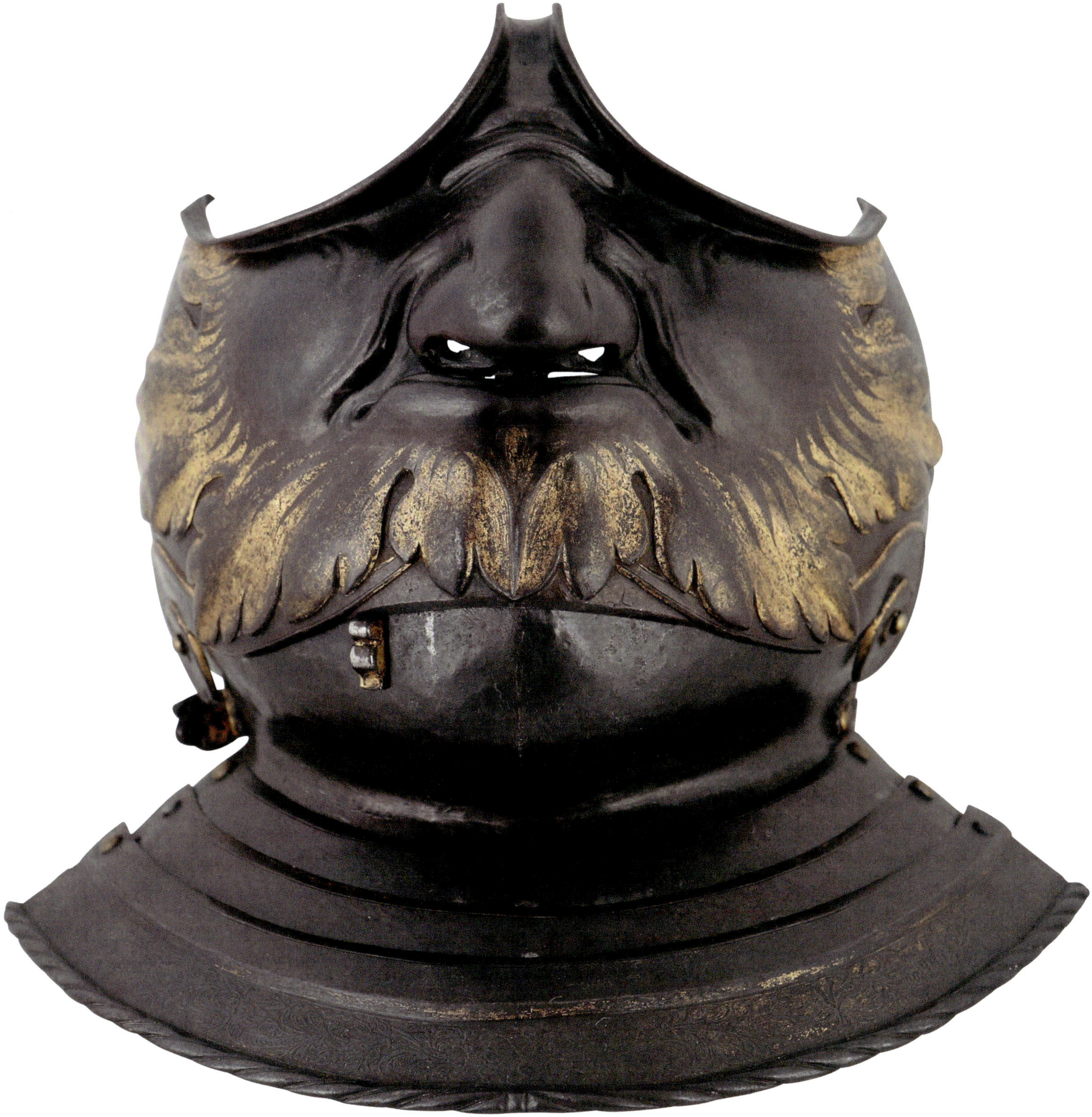

39

Gun shield belonging to Henry VIII

Italy, *c*.1540 · v.39

Along with Henry VIII's 'walking staff' [36], this 'gun shield', also belonging to Henry VIII, is another example of an intriguing 'combination' – in this case of circular metal shield (or 'target') with a small handgun firing through an aperture just above its centre. Shields of this type (another existed in which the gun fired through the boss) are known for their connection with Henry VIII, and the 1547 inventory made after his death notes thirty-five of them, described as 'targets steilde [i.e., steel-covered] wt gonnes'. Pieces recovered from the *Mary Rose*, wrecked two years earlier, show that Henry had once owned several more. Today, sixteen survive in the Royal Armouries collection and others in public collections abroad. Who made them is something of a puzzle, but a possible answer may be found in a letter of March 1544 to the English ambassador to Venice in which a Maestro Giovanni Battista of Ravenna offered the King 'several round shields and arm pieces (*rotelle et imbracciadore*) with guns inside that fire (*tirano*) upon the enemy and pierce any armour.' At least some of Henry's shields, however, may have been made in England, perhaps by converting existing infantry shields.

Eleven of the surviving examples are of the same basic design and are around 50 cm in diameter. Those examined in detail are made of two layers of wooden strips arranged at ninety degrees to one another for strength, faced with iron or steel plates, and lined on the inside with woollen fabric. The shield incorporates a metal mesh viewport, much as in a modern riot shield, allowing the user to remain in cover whilst operating the gun, mounted directly below it. The gun itself is a small pistol-sized handgun with a helically fluted barrel of roughly 'cannon' form, mounted to an iron bracket on the inside of the shield. Technically speaking it is a breech-loading 'chamber piece' with a pivoting U-shaped breech, into which a pre-loaded iron or steel cartridge was inserted, and secured by a transverse pin, chained to the gun for safekeeping, allowing it to be loaded behind the shield and quickly reloaded by inserting a fresh cartridge. The gun was fired by a match held in a 'serpentine' holder fitted to a bracket on the inside of the shield, ingeniously arranged for operation with one hand, thus (in theory) allowing the user to load or wield a sword with the other. This is one of only three with a decorated central plate, depicting the Roman hero Mucius Scaevola after capture by the Etruscan king Lars Porsena, plunging his hand into the flame. Scaevola's deed appears frequently on arms and armour as a symbol of loyalty and courage, but in addition, perhaps, in this case, because fire would appear to spurt from the user's left hand.

While it has been suggested that that the shields were meant for a personal bodyguard, the plain appearance of most examples, and the use of cumbersome and dangerous (and cheap) matchlock ignition suggests that a combat function was intended, as does the discovery of a number of them on the *Mary Rose*. In almost any imaginable situation, however, the gun could only have been fired once and its extra weight would have made the shield all the more unwieldy. Possibly, not least because shields were rarely used on the battlefield by the time of Henry's reign, it had some specialist function, such as in siege warfare or onboard ship; possibly its actual effectiveness depended more on its menacing appearance than on practicality. As with his 'Walking Staff', however, we can be certain that Henry appreciated his gun shields for their novelty and ingenuity, and they too were displayed at the Tower from at least the reign of Elizabeth.

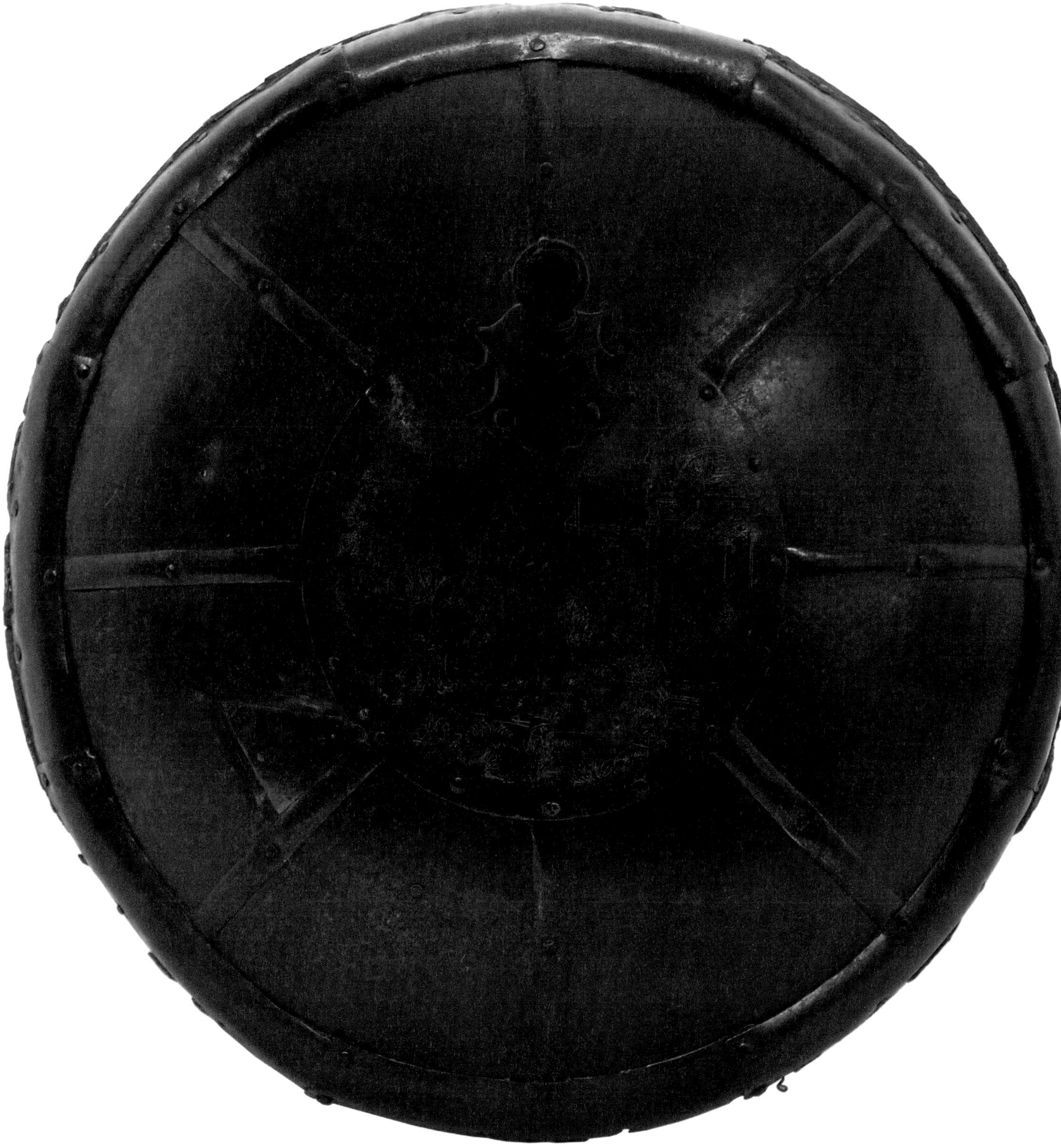

40

Garniture for field, tilt, tourney and foot combat

England, 1540 · II.8

By 1540, the date engraved on this armour, the obese, forty-nine year old Henry VIII was no longer the handsome and fit man who had competed at the Field of Cloth of Gold twenty years before [33]. Yet the king still hungered after the personal adulation and attention that competition could bring, and vanity alone presumably motivated him to appear in a new armour to impress his new queen, Anne of Cleves, whom he had married in January that year. Regarded by many as the greatest of Henry VIII's garnitures, it may well have been made in time for the May Day tournament held in May 1540 at the Palace of Westminster. This four-day event included tilts, tourneys and foot combats over the barriers and was probably the last that Henry VIII ever staged, although there is no record that he actually took part. A related armour, once in the Royal Armouries collection but since 1916 at Windsor Castle, seems to have been made for the wedding, and was subsequently adapted for the king's use at the siege of Boulogne in 1544.

The armour as seen from the front was designed to accommodate the King's considerable bulk but to flatter his figure by skilful tapering at the waist and hips, although his true size is fully evident from behind. The maker was the Master Workman of the King's Greenwich Armoury workshops, Erasmus Kirkenar, probably from Germany or the Low Countries, who had first arrived at Greenwich in about 1518, and at some time after 1521 taken over from Martin van Royne. In 1547, then at Greenwich, the 'complete harness' was described as the 'parcell graven and gilte with all manner of peces of advantage for the felde Tilte Turney and fote'. Most of these survive, although the horse armour is now represented only by its shaffron. Unusually, the king was supplied with two of each component. One of these was unique to Greenwich armours: a concealed inner breastplate, strapped to the body and bolted to the cuirass and plackart (lower breastplate) to take some of their weight and that of the arm defences. In contrast, the groin defence or 'cod piece' was deliberately prominent, such that in later centuries women reputedly stuck pins in the lining to increase their fertility; it has attracted the attention of other visitors for centuries.

The armour was embellished with narrow etched and gilded borders, mostly filled with rather conventional scrolling foliage. Those on the two sets of tilt reinforces, however, are much broader. They are based on designs by Hans Holbein the Younger in his *Englischen Skizzenbuch* ('English Sketchbook'; 1534–8), now in the Kunstmuseum in Basel, Switzerland: the triton, mermen, and mermaids to be found on the armour are all among them. The decoration may have been carried out by the Florentine artist Giovanni da Maiano (c.1486–1542), who had worked for Cardinal Wolsey at Hampton Court and for Henry at Greenwich Palace in 1527; an alternative is one Francis Quelblaunche, from 1539 employed as 'gilter and graver if the Kinges harnis'. The armour was made in the last years of a particular stylistic tradition at Greenwich, superseded by the use of a Tudor rose and knot pattern with recessed bands and borders containing etched strapwork and foliage.

41

Basket-hilted sword and Wrexham buckler

Sword: England, blade possibly Germany, *c*.1540;
buckler, England or Wales, *c*.1540 · IX.4427, V.21

The unprotected sword-hand of an ordinary infantryman was extremely vulnerable in combat, and from the late 15th century was increasingly effectively protected by additional guards around the hilt. Some eventually covered most of the hand in a protective 'cage', generally called a basket hilt. This one is probably the best preserved of a small and important group of an early form of the hilt, known to be English and attributed to the reign of Henry VIII. It was found on the northern foreshore of the River Thames, under Southwark Bridge, in 1979.

The hilt, made of iron, has a two-piece brazed hollow spherical iron pommel, decorated with eight applied, longitudinal iron ribs, each brazed in place. The guard is composed of round-section fire-welded bars and has a pair of straight quillons, and a flattened oval-sectioned wooden grip. The straight, double-edged blade has the dark patination associated with river finds and there are nicks on both edges. Traces of an inlaid mark – possibly a running wolf – in copper alloy remain on the blade. Significantly, the remains of a sword with a very similar hilt was found on the wreck of Henry VIII's warship *Mary Rose*, helping to support the generally accepted dating of the type. The hilts also appear in mid-16th century paintings, such as a portrait attributed to Gerlach Flicke (fl.1545–58) of Palmer (probably William), one of the Gentleman Pensioners, Henry VIII's royal bodyguard of 1548.

Regularly used in conjunction with swords of this type, 'bucklers' are small, functional, concave shields, both to parry an opponent's blows as well to strike him. Of various shapes, including circular, all share a central grip at the back. This example is made of a wooden core reinforced with a series of concentric steel rings, fixed by rows of brass rivets, their heads creating a decorative effect, encircling a conical iron boss with a projecting spike. The back is lined with pigskin tooled with a cross-hatched pattern.

The buckler is one of a unique type known to have been manufactured in the area around Wrexham (Clwyd) on the English-Welsh border, extensively used by infantrymen and civilians from the late 1440s until 1580, although only thirty-one now survive. The association with Wrexham is well-established, and illustrated by the mention in the 1547 *Inventory of King Henry VIII* of 'twoo wreckesham Buckelers'. Some Welsh buckler-makers, however, moved to London to work for the king, such as Geoffrey Bromefeld, appointed 'the kinges boucler maker' in 1530–1. Of the surviving examples made for Henry, the finest – gilt, etched and decorated with the Tudor royal arms – is in the Musée de l'Armée in Paris. Such grand examples were probably intended as gifts, but were also for members of Henry's royal bodyguard: they are borne (along with basket-hilted swords) by various members of Henry's retinue in *The Embarkation of Henry VIII at Dover*, painted in about 1545–50. In the near-contemporary companion picture, *The Field of Cloth of Gold*, another page bears a buckler suspended from a sword-hilt and slung over the forearm. The paintings also show that bucklers could be carried, presumably by a strap or thong looped around the grip, suspended from the hilt of a sword or a belt at the hip.

[126]

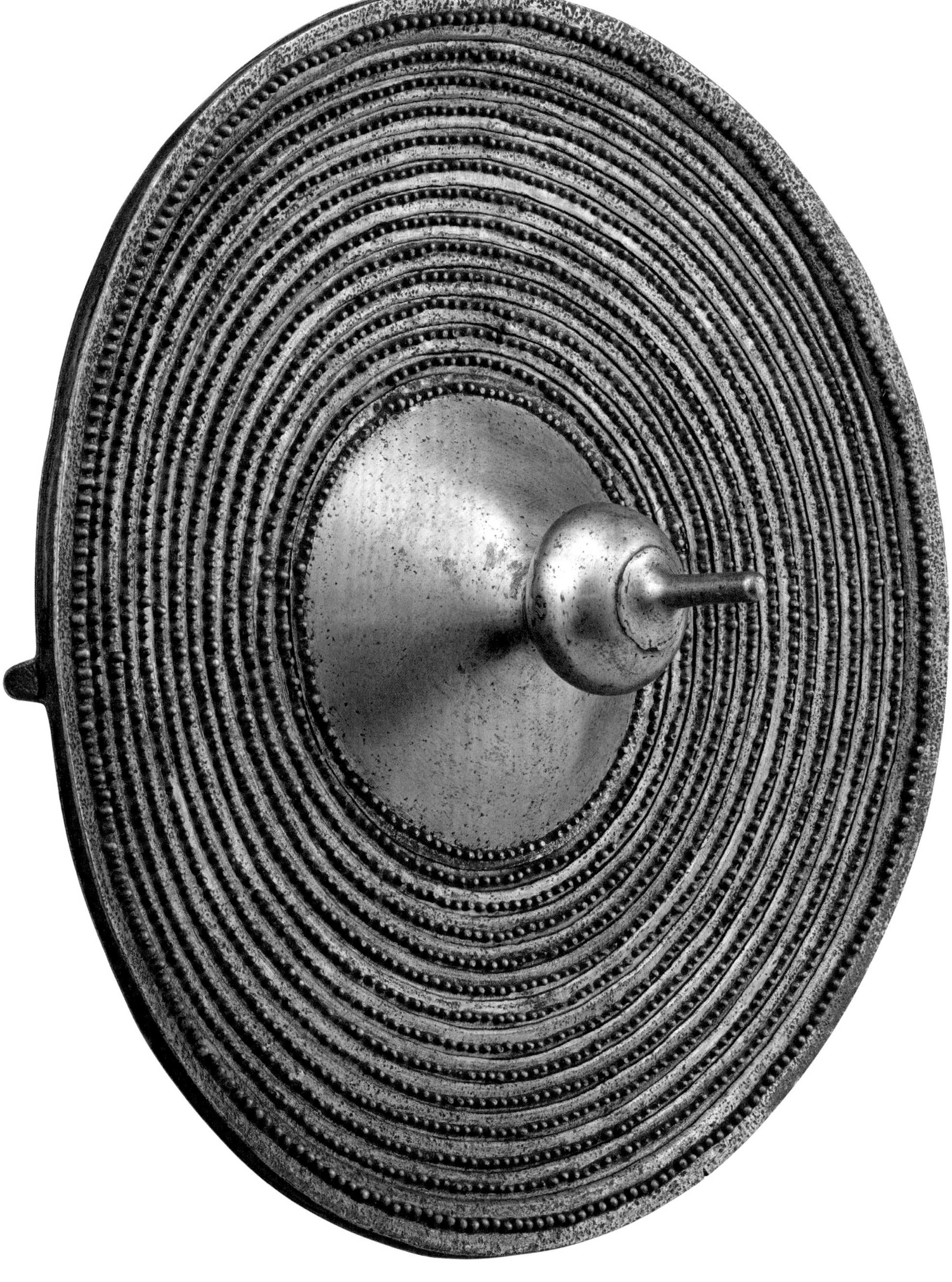

42

Longbow stave from the *Mary Rose*

England, *c.*1500–40 · XI.103

The longbow is perhaps the most famous of all weapons used by English medieval armies, and was their most important projectile weapon from the 13th to the mid 16th century. Although far from exclusively English, and far from guaranteeing invincibility, the famous victories at Crècy (1346), Poitiers (1356) and Agincourt (1415) were due largely to successful archery. Not one medieval longbow, however, is known to survive, and the earliest examples are those recovered from the wreck of the *Mary Rose*. Laid down in 1509, the ship herself was one of Henry VIII's first naval commissions, and of carrack form, with high 'castles' at the bow and stern. Famously, whilst serving as George Carew's flagship in an engagement with the French in the Solent on 18 July 1545, she heeled over, took on water and sank with almost all hands. Fortunately for us, the accumulation of silt over the wreck meant that much of the ship survives, along with a vast treasure of equipment and arms and armour, of which this bow is an example.

Unstrung and unadorned this item appears unremarkable – a single 185 cm round-sectioned length of yew wood, tapering towards its ends from a broader mid-section. Yew naturally combines flexibility with great strength, a factor enhanced by how the bow was made: the staves were cut from the outside of tree trunks or big branches, allowing them to combine both older, harder, more rigid (and redder-coloured) heartwood and softer more flexible (and pale) sapwood. Using the hardwood to form the inner face or front of the bow meant that on bending it provided resistance through compression, while the sapwood provided resistance through tension. Bows varied, obviously, in exact length and thickness, but the most powerful apparently had a draw weight of up to 81 kg, meaning that its user had to be immensely strong; indeed, skeletons found on the *Mary Rose* show that training from childhood actually distorted an archer's bone structure. The bow would have been strung, with the cord itself fitted to horn 'nocks' at each end (now both lost), and the archer provided with arrows, of which over 3,500 were found on the ship. So equipped, a trained archer was capable of shooting ten to twelve arrows per minute over a distance of 230 metres, each capable, under the right circumstances, of piercing mail and plate armour. Its replacement on the battlefield by guns, only completed in the 17th century, owed more to the relatively minimal training required to use them than to superior effectiveness.

The story of the *Mary Rose*'s excavation and 'lifting' in 1982, its study and display between 1984 and the opening of the present museum in 2013 is well known. The Royal Armouries bows, however, were recovered in 1841, thanks to underwater salvage work carried out by the brothers John and Anthony Deane, using a suit and helmet of their own invention. In the process they raised an inscribed bronze cannon enabling them to identify the wreck as the *Mary Rose*. Amongst many other items, they recovered eight bows, two of which were bought by the Board of Ordnance and added to their collections at the Tower of London (XI.1 and XI.2): this example, bought presumably by a private individual, was presented by H. Langley Esq to the Royal United Service Institute, where it was displayed alongside a cannon and wooden carriage. It joined the Royal Armouries in 1963, making the Armouries' collection the richest in early war bows until the *Mary Rose* surrendered her treasures twenty years later.

[128]

43

Armour (*mogami haramaki*)

Japan, 16th century · XXVIA.2

By the 9th century the Japanese archipelago was nominally under the rule of an emperor, but from the late 12th until the mid 19th century, real power lay with successive *shoguns*, with the emperor's role purely ceremonial. The society over which they presided had some similarities with that of medieval Europe (notably a military aristocracy and a mounted 'knightly' class, the *samurai*), although for centuries a primary weapon was the Japanese longbow or *yumi*, which their armour developed to counter. Their other equipment, swords, spears, armour, latterly guns, and their heraldry, whilst fundamentally different in construction and appearance, also had loose European parallels.

At the beginning of the 17th century, the Tokugawa Shogunate brought Japan under rigorous unified control. For the previous 150 years it had endured endemic violence in the *Sengoku Jidai*, or 'age of the country at war': the old social order was broken up as powerful landowning lords (*daimyo*) and their retainers fought amongst themselves, and ambitious minor nobles raised personal armies drawn from outside the traditional military class. Whilst medieval Japanese warfare had been dominated by horse archers, bodies of infantry equipped with spears were now the main combatants. This reliance on foot soldiers gained momentum from the 1540s with the introduction of firearms, driving Japanese armour to attain a pinnacle of practicality and efficiency. This plain but enormously significant item belongs to the end of this period, in which, as indicated by what may be battle damage, it saw service.

The armour is of *haramaki* or 'belly wrapper' form, in which the main cuirass wraps around the torso to fasten at the back. The thigh guards have multiple divisions to facilitate walking and running. Accompanied by shortened shoulder guards, the *haramaki* became popular as fighting on foot with swords and staff weapons increased: formerly, armours overlapped on the right side and had much larger shoulder defences, which limited arm movement. In contrast to the densely laced rows of innumerable small lamellae used in older styles, its larger plates of lacquered iron and rawhide were quicker to make, required less lacing, and offered better protection against musket fire. Utilitarian as it may look, the armour is also of superior quality, and the *mon* (crest) included in the decoration suggests it belonged to a member of the Shimazu family, governors of Satsuma province. Overall, it provides an excellent illustration of how such Japanese armour evolved in response to the changing forms of warfare.

Its later history, only recently elucidated, is of great interest in itself, as it was among the armours taken to Europe in the late 16th century by the Tensho Mission, a party of Japanese Christians sent to Spain by several prominent *daimyo* and Jesuit missionaries, who had themselves arrived in Japan in the 1540s. It was probably given to the king, Philip II (r.1556–98) when he granted them an audience in 1584, and an explicit description of it in a royal context occurs in a document of 1603. Later, it was almost certainly one of three armours passed to the Duke of the Infantado by Philip III (r.1598–1621). In 1841 it appeared as 'Lot 440, A suit of Moorish Armour' at Oxenham's in London, and as illustrated in the catalogue, was displayed entirely incorrectly and in poor condition. Despite this, it was purchased by the Tower Armouries, quickly recognised as Japanese, and displayed alongside one of the two armours given to James I by Tokugawa Ieyasu (r.1600–16) in 1614.

[130]

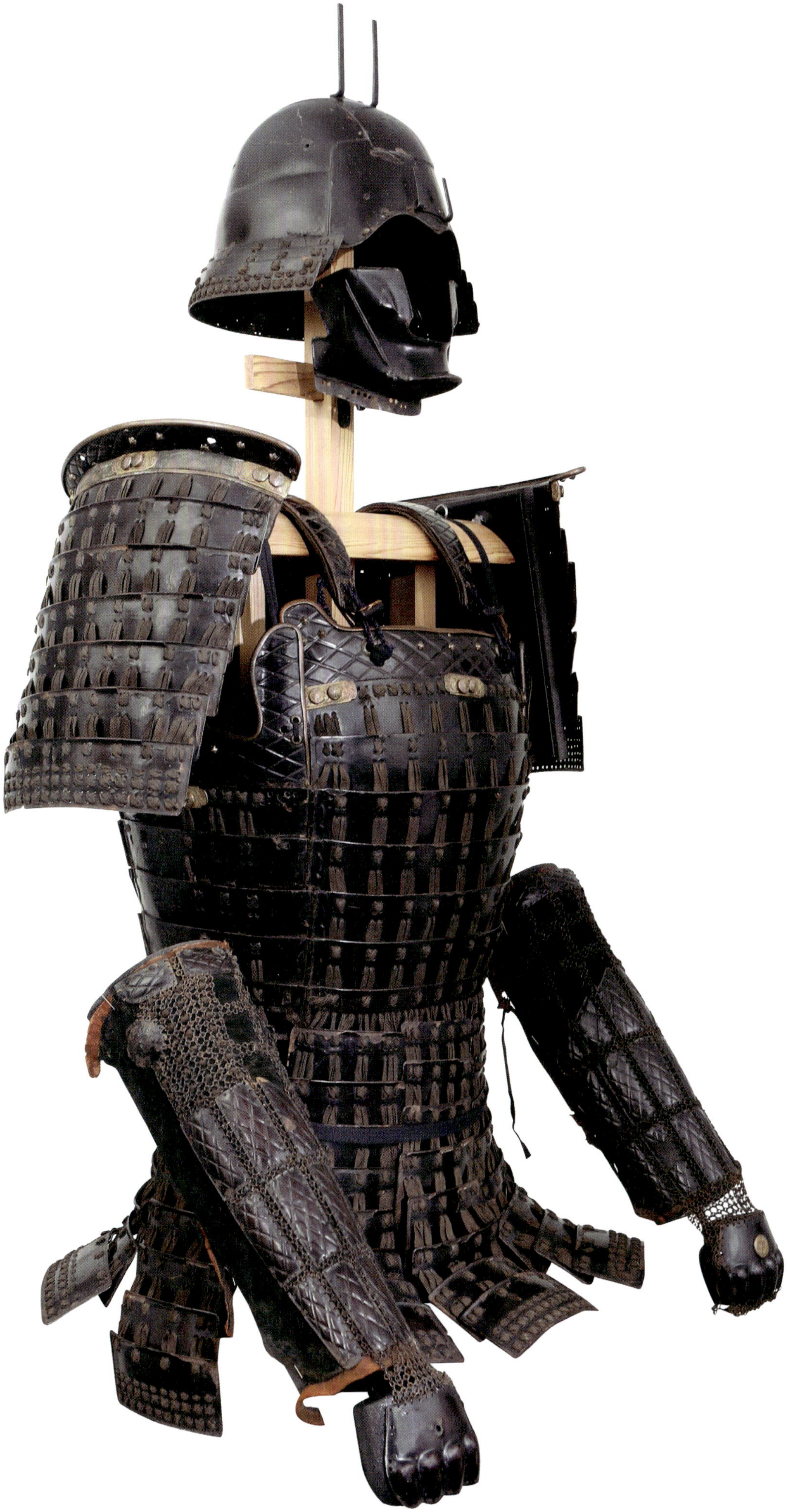

44
The 'Lion Armour'
France or Italy, 1545–50 · 11.89

The origins and results of decorating armour with three-dimensional embossing have been mentioned in in the context of the Negroli *buffe* [38], made for one of the grandest of the Italian territorial nobility in *c*.1490. By the middle of the 16th century the Negroli's patrons included European monarchs, not least the Emperor Charles V, who commissioned a parade armour in 1545. The kings of France were particularly interested in embossed armours, and Francis I probably owned the '*Armure aux Lions*', attributed to the German Benedict Clesze, displayed with numerous other French royal armours in the Musée de l'Armée in Paris; while certainly inspired by Italian examples, it is unknown if this was actually made in Paris or Milan, as the Valois kings employed their own accomplished armourers. The Royal Armouries' 'lion' armour is generally thought to have belonged to Francis' son and successor, Henry II (r.1547–1559), who certainly commissioned one related item, at least part-embossed, before he came to the throne. This cannot be attributed with certainty, although the Negroli of Milan were the dominant makers of this type and quality by the mid 16th century, and both Filippo Negroli and Giovanni Paolo Negroli have been proposed as possible makers.

The armour itself comprises a close helmet for field use, two associated gorgets, a breast and backplate, a fauld with tassets, pauldrons, vambraces, gauntlets, cuisses, poleyns, greaves and toe-defences, and could be assembled for wearing on foot or on horseback: reinforcing plates show that it could have been used in the *mélée*, although not in battle. As with Francis I's example, the 'lion' armour takes its name from the lion masks (flattened and stylised lion's faces) which appear abundantly on its most prominent surfaces, the lion having been a symbol of courage, power and sovereignty for millennia. In this case lion masks appear on the pauldrons, couters, top of the breastplate and backplate, gauntlet-cuffs, knees and toe-caps, with menacing expressions throughout. To crown it all, the helmet is fashioned to frame the face with the lion's open jaws, a favourite 16th-century conceit, in the manner of a Roman parade outfit using a real lion's head and skin.

The later history of the armour, as with its origin, is something of puzzle. At some stage after 1620 it has been rather crudely altered, notably by the shortening and widening of the breast and back plates and the enlargement of the face-opening of the helmet, implying that an unknown owner intended to wear it. The armour appears to have been in England from at least the mid 1620s when it was depicted in a portrait of *c*.1620–5 now in Bucharest, entitled 'Man wearing Lion Armour'. In about 1640 it appears in a portrait of Edward Montagu, 2nd Earl of Manchester, in a miniature of Charles II by Samuel Cooper, in 1669 in one of Cosimo de Medici (painted when in England) and in 1668 in a portrait by John Michael Wright of General Monck, Duke of Albermarle. This suggests that the armour was successively in the possession of the painters, somebody associated with the royal court, or perhaps the Stuart kings.

Nevertheless, we know that by the later 18th century it belonged to the Board of Ordnance armourer, John Cooper, who apparently lent it to the Ordnance Office at the Tower of London. It was then presented as the armour of Charles II in the display of mounted figures commonly referred to as the 'Line of Kings', and was later displayed as that of Edward VI and then Charles I.

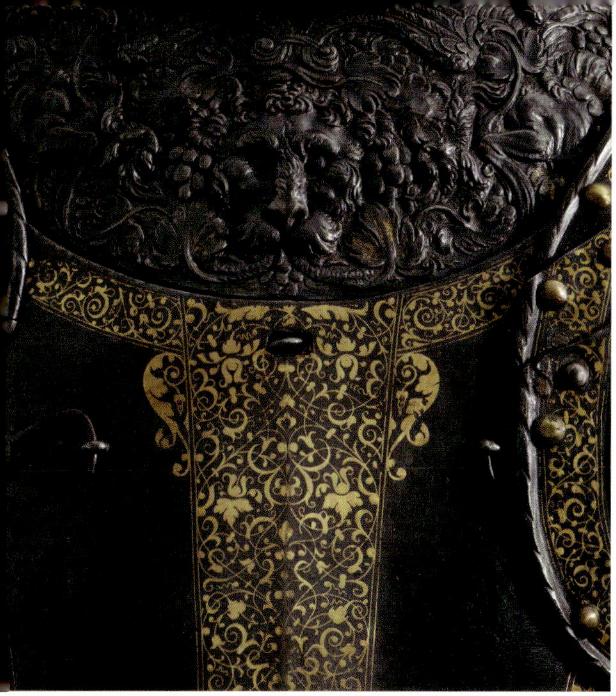
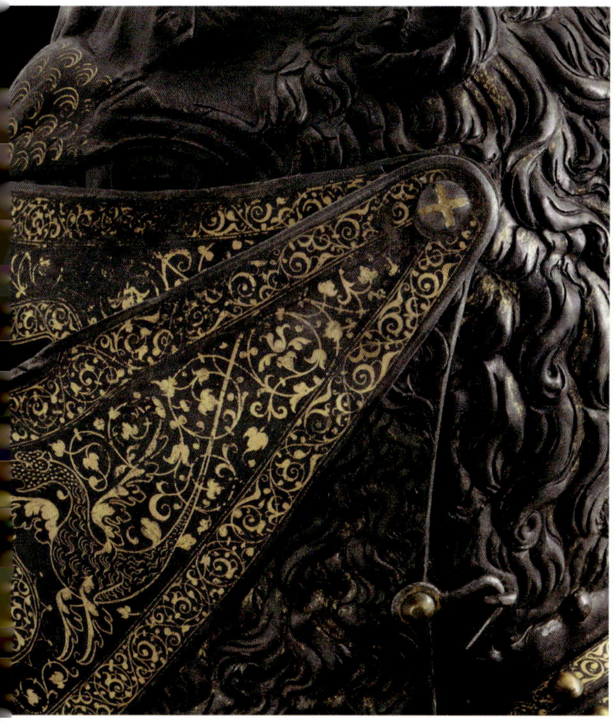
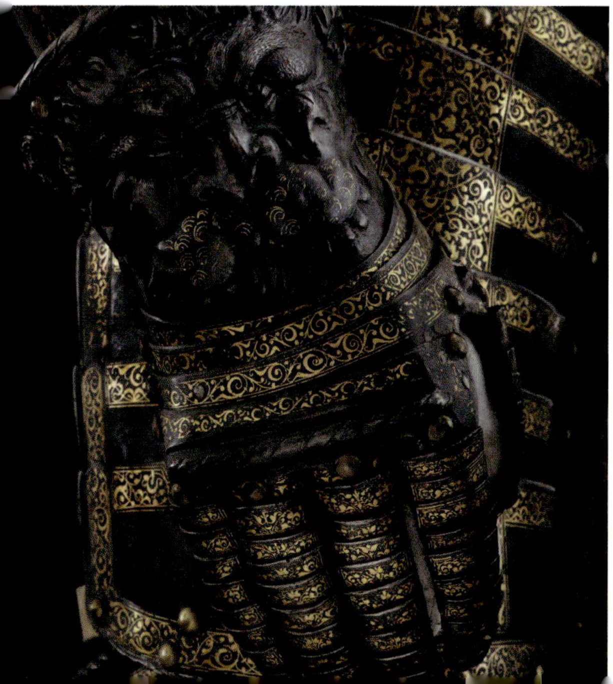
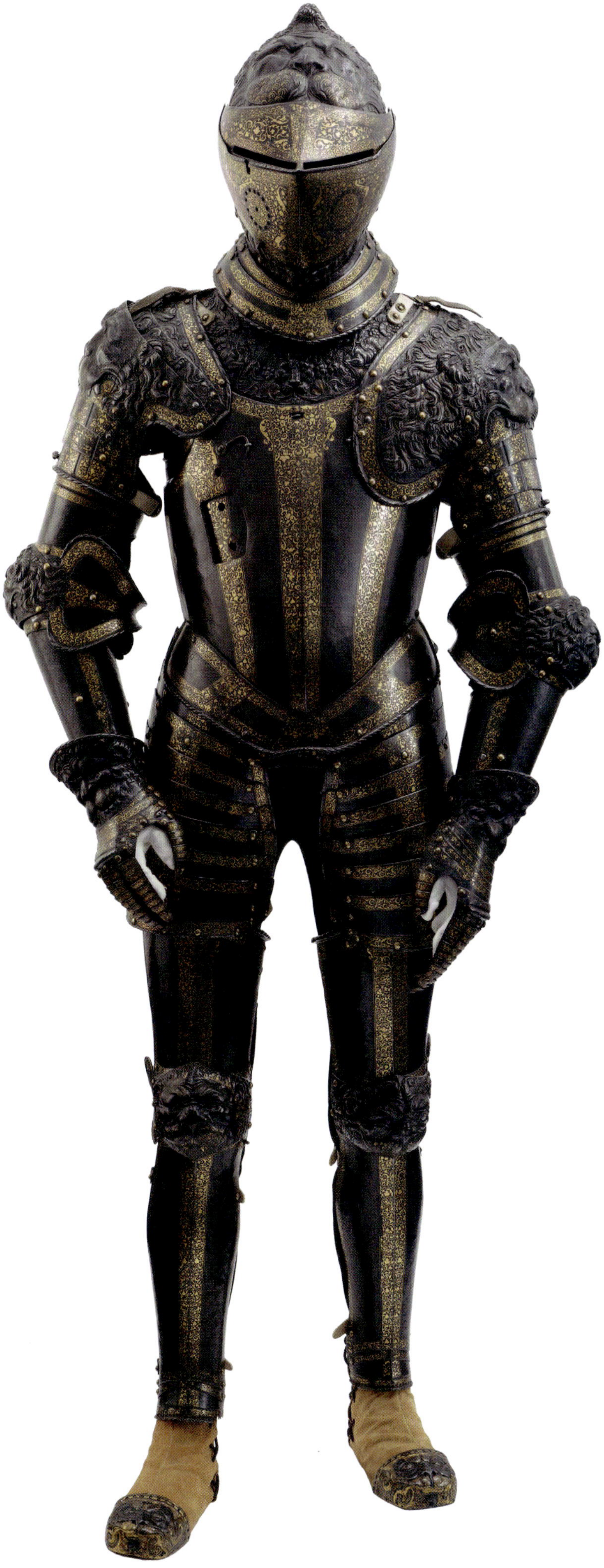

45

Boar sword

Probably Germany, *c.*1550 · IX.5391

Swords were carried for hunting purposes in prehistory, but it was probably not until the Renaissance, as hunting became more formalised, that they became routinely distinct from those used in war. This weapon, with its cruciform hilt, looks similar at first to most swords of the eleventh to the fifteenth century: more specifically, its long thrusting blade and two-handed grip are also features of the *estoc*, a weapon developed in the 14th century to offset the increasing effectiveness of plate armour, and which was also used in hunting. Nevertheless, this sword was something altogether different, specifically designed for killing wild boar.

In medieval and Renaissance Europe, boar – extinct in the British Isles by *c.*1450, although now reintroduced – were hunted in numerous ways, usually involving hounds and beaters, and the huntsman could dispatch the animals from the saddle or on foot. As boar are fast, aggressive, courageous, strong, thick-skinned and generally hard to kill, the sport was (and remains) a dangerous one, and of all its forms, hunting with the sword was the most challenging and prestigious: the great 14th-century sportsman and writer Gaston Phoebus (1331–91), a Burgundian nobleman, described its use as 'fairer thing and more noble' than hunting (in particular) with the spear, and at least one manuscript copy of his work shows this happening. In his *Livre de Chasse* ('Book of the Hunt') of the 1380s Phoebus also suggested that a sword for boar hunting should have a 4 ft (1,219 mm) blade with the top half left blunt, but it was not until the late 15th century that a specific and weapon evolved along these lines. As they were only intended for thrusting, boar-sword blades are, as Phoebus recommended, blunt for the majority of their length, enabling them to be thick and strong enough to withstand the force of a charging boar, and also meant that the sportsman could comfortably grasp the blade, to shorten his grip, for greater control of the point, or to drive the weapon deeper in. A shallow fuller, a groove which can lighten a blade but maintain its stiffness (rather as in an 'I' girder), runs the length of the thick, blunt section of the blade. But then, instead of tapering to an acute point of the *estoc*, the blade becomes abruptly both wider and thinner, taking the shape of a flattened diamond over its final third. This broad, edged portion could cause a much wider, debilitating and deadly wound, causing haemorrhaging during penetration, exacerbated by the animal's struggles against the blade. In addition, by making a broad wound, as opposed to the deep

[134]

piercing of an *estoc* blade, it kept the hunter at a safer distance from the boar. To ensure safety, boar swords could also be equipped with a bar or stop below the widened part of the blade – as in a boar spear to prevent the wounded animal 'running up' the blade and savaging the huntsman at close quarters. This object features a modern replacement 'stop' bar; originals were usually detachable, so that the sword could be scabbarded. This refinement was felt by some to be unsporting: certainly, in the *Triumph of Maximilian* (1526), a series of woodcuts glorifying the hunt-loving Holy Roman Emperor, only one of the five hunters in the procession has a 'stop' bar on his boar-sword. By the end of the century boar-swords of this type were falling out of use. They were superseded by firearms, shorter swords and the changing hunting practices of the 17th century.

46

Field and tilt armour of Robert Dudley, Earl of Leicester

England, *c.*1575 · II.81, VI.49

Robert Dudley (1532/3–88) was the 5th son of John Dudley, Earl of Warwick, who from 1531 was duke of Northumberland, briefly Lord Protector, and was executed in 1554 for attempting to enthrone Lady Jane Grey instead of Henry VIII's elder daughter, Mary. Implicated in this, Robert was imprisoned at the Tower, where he *may* have met his fellow prisoner, the future Queen Elizabeth I, to whom he later owed his rehabilitation, riches, and place in history. Her long dependence on and love for Dudley, driven partly by his startling abilities and certainly by his good looks, began before her accession in 1558, and lasted until his death; he was a crucial factor, both as a candidate and a secret pretext for refusing others, in managing the endless question of her marriage. Once queen, Elizabeth could reward him, immediately making him Master of the Horse and then Earl of Leicester in 1563, and by granting him the magnificent castle at Kenilworth (Warwickshire). Such a man at the Elizabethan court needed armour, for practical reasons and as an essential and powerful badge of rank – soldier (which he was), or not. During his lifetime Dudley possessed many personal armours, but he certainly owned three suits made by the elite royal workshop at Greenwich. This is one example, made under the Master Workman John Kelte or his successor Jacob Halder, and consists, as a 'garniture', of a field armour, accompanied by extra 'reinforces' for jousting (shown fitted here), a shaffron for his horse and steels for the saddles. Technically innovative and of the finest manufacture and design, the armour is also lavishly decorated, and when the etched areas were still gilded and the rest still of dark, blued steel, the effect would have been dazzling. In general form it owes something to contemporary clothes, hence, in particular, the rather bulbous tassets: by way of detail, the dominant motif is the 'Ragged Staff', part of the badge of the prestigious medieval earls of Warwick, adopted by the Dudleys, as is the muzzled bear (breastplate, backplate and left pauldron). Dudley's exalted status as a Knight of the Garter and of the French Order of St Michael is signalled too, while at the top of the central vertical band on the breastplate is a figure of Justice and the initials 'RD'. For stylistic reasons the armour can be dated to the mid 1570s, suggesting that it was made for the fabulous three-week 'entertainment unto the Queen's majesty', held at Kenilworth in July 1575 – laden with references to marriage, although whether to press his prospects or set him free is unclear. But certainly, the association is made by the appearance of this armour in the painting by Federico Zucarro (1539–1609, and in England only in 1574–5) 'of my lord in whole proporcion [that is, full length] ... in armor'), inventoried at the castle in 1578.

Exhibited by the Royal Armouries and its precursors since 1660, the garniture is a splendid representative of the Greenwich workshop's prowess. As an item respectively seen and worn by the protagonists, it also links us to the political and personal dynamic of 'Elizabeth and Leicester', the glamour of her court, a heady era of English history, and probably of one of the greatest parties of all time.

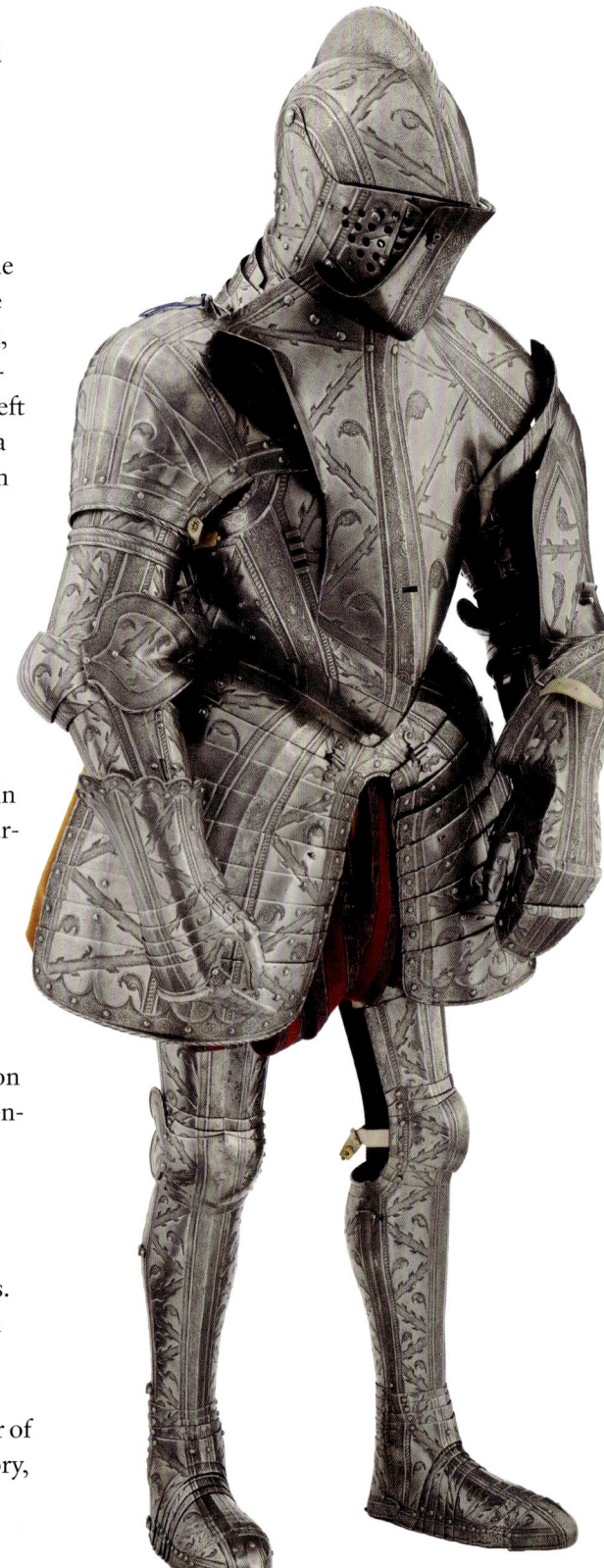

[136]

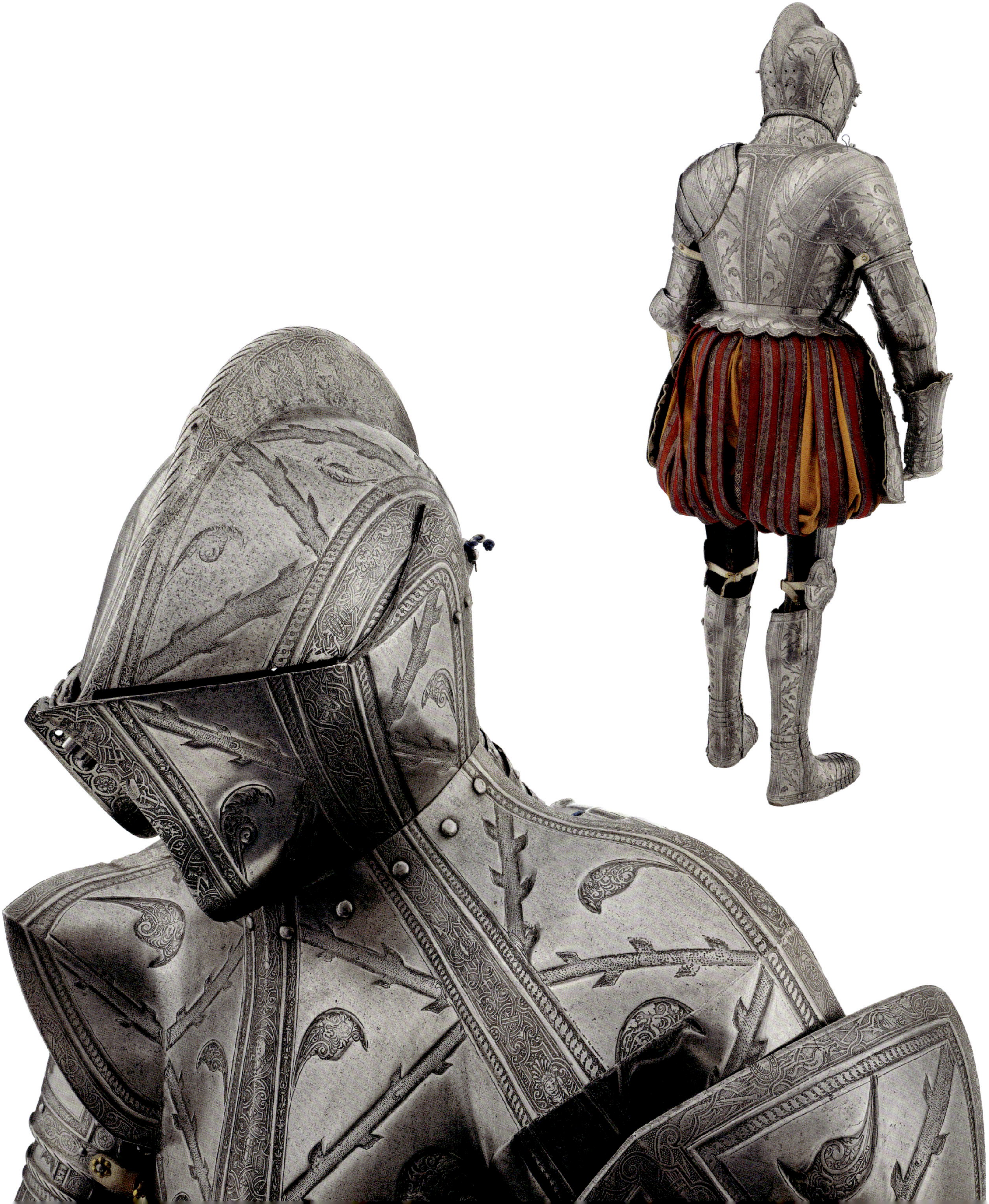

47

Jack of plate with plate sleeves

England, *c*.1580 · III.1884–5

The jack of plate is a –perhaps *the* – characteristic English body defence of the middle and later years of the 16th century. It was developed from the earlier, quilted textile jack which is first recorded in the late 14th century, and provided the mainstay of armour for the English infantry in the 15th century. Made in the form of a doublet, jacks of plate are composed of small square iron plates with central holes and cropped corners ranging between 24 and 37 mm square, between two layers of coarse canvas with a layer of fine linen, secured by a net or trellis pattern of cords through the central holes on an approximately one-inch grid forming a quilted pattern. The plates within the rows usually overlap towards the centre, while the rows usually overlap upwards, though there are examples where the rows overlap downwards and others where the columns overlap. The cords are knotted where they pass though the fabric and plates, each knot being covered by a tuft of green silk. Inside the jacks are lined with a layer of fine canvas.

Some jacks, such as Royal Armouries II.26–7, are of the deep-bellied form associated with civilian doublets of the 1550s and 1560s, while others such as Royal Armouries III.1277–8 and III.1884 (and probably III.44–6) have the deep peascods of the 1570s and 1580s. The former jacks open at the front, where they are fastened by laces through eyelet holes. Two of the peascod group have overlapping sections at the front, and are fastened by hooks and eyes, in the manner of buff coats in the 17th century. They have extensions over the shoulders, divided at the centres, where there is a single row of plates allowing articulation, and a low standing collar either formed of a single row of plates or two rows, and a short skirt divided into four trapezoid panels, between three and six rows of plates deep. The plates are usually of exceedingly rough manufacture and irregular in shape, but sometimes neatly made and of equal size. The plates from Rothwell church (West Yorkshire) do not have cropped corners, but seem unique in this, and all the others do (Royal Armouries III.1917). Recycled plates from brigandines seem quite often to have been used in their manufacture, seen in the example excavated from Beeston Castle in Cheshire and Royal Armouries III.44, 45 and 1045.

A few jacks were preserved elsewhere in England. This particular example was part of a group of three preserved at Worden Hall near Preston in Lancashire, part of a collection formed by Sir William Farington in the eighteenth century. Two of them retained their plate sleeves, the only surviving examples of such defences. The Farington collection was sold at auction in 1946. This jack with its sleeves was purchased in 1985 from a private collector in Amityville, Long Island, New York, while others of the group were kept on loan at Rufford Old Hall until 2016, when they were again sold at auction, the Victoria & Albert Museum securing one more for the nation.

These relatively light defences provided protection against *melée* weapons while providing the flexibility needed to handle bows and other missile weapons effectively. They provided little or no protection against firearms, but the increasing power of these weapons was causing armourers to increase the weight of plate armour in order to retain its effectiveness. Ultimately this was a battle the guns would win, less than a century after jacks of plate ceased to be used.

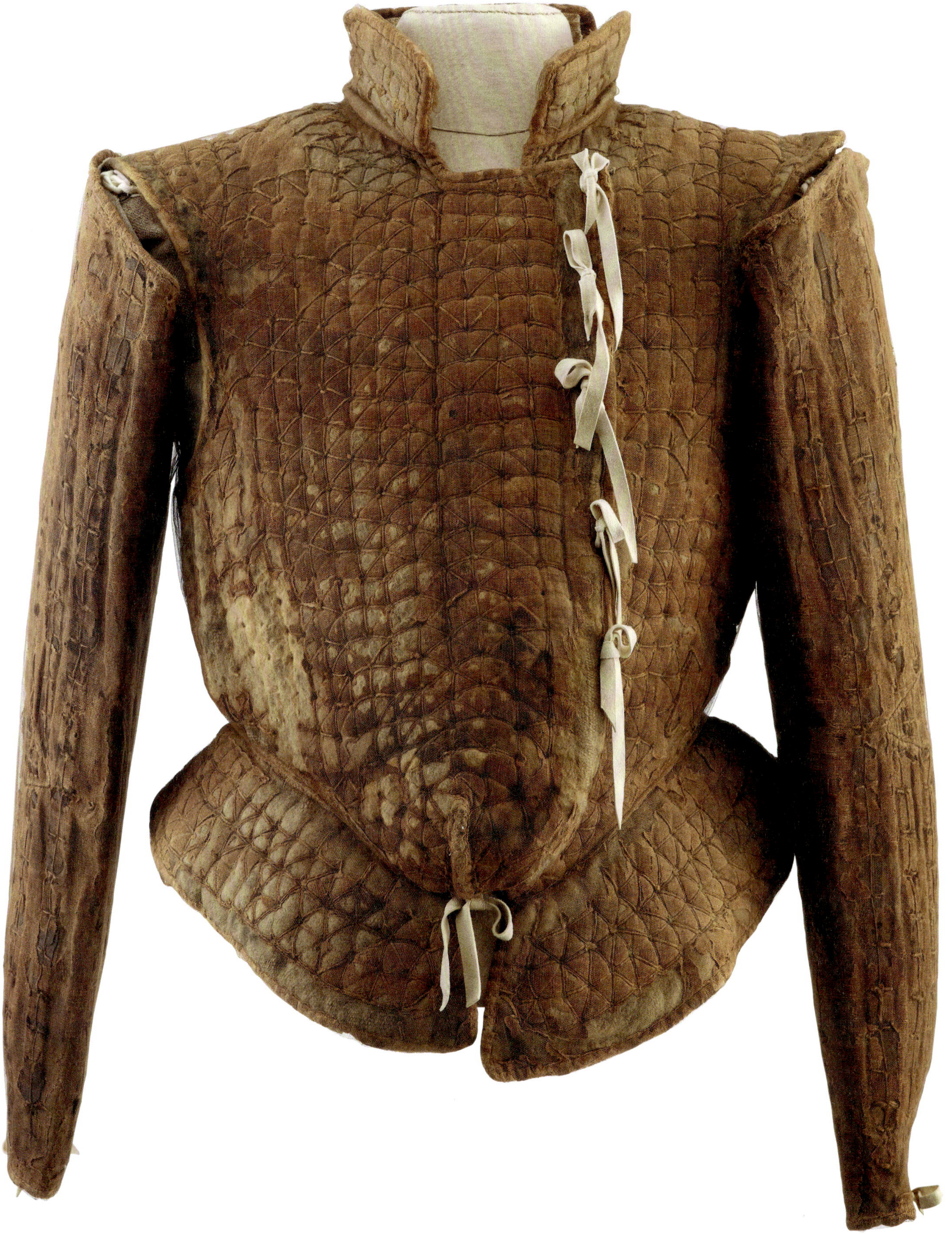

48

Armour of Sir John Smythe

England and Germany, 1580–90 · II.84

Sir John Smythe (1533/4–1607), from an Essex gentry family, was a soldier, courtier, diplomat and military theorist. After a spell at Oxford, he left England in the early 1550s and served as a volunteer in France, the Low Countries and, in 1566, in Hungary against the Ottomans. Ten years later he was appointed ambassador to Spain to negotiate for the better treatment of English residents and as an intermediary with their rebellious protestant subjects in the Low Countries. He was recalled with honours in 1577, and at the outbreak of war with Spain in 1585 proposed as ambassador to the Spanish commander; the embassy was cancelled, and his final commission, to train troops in 1587–8 was terminated ended by the Earl of Leicester, by now a bitter enemy. In 1590 he published *Certain Discourses* on military matters (advocating the use of the longbow), but again managed to insult the powers that be and was imprisoned for seventeen months in the Tower.

War with Spain, meanwhile, had prompted several courtiers and soldiers to look to Greenwich for field armours in readiness for an expected Spanish invasion, and Smythe was among them. His was designed and made by Master Jacob Halder, author of some of the finest examples produced at Greenwich in the late 16th century. First recorded in the 1558 list of the Almain armourers, Halder became Master Workman in October 1576 following the death of Master John Kelte. Of German descent, he is said to have come from either Augsburg or Landshut, both major centres of production. Not only did he make a major contribution to the development of English armour, he left a visual record of the armours he produce, including Smythe's, which helps us understand it. Known as the 'Jacobe' or 'Almain Album' and dating to *c*.1557–87, the twenty-nine armour designs it relates to the most favoured and powerful men in Elizabethan England. Illustrated with the use of stencils for the main outlines, and coloured washes to indicate the armours' finish, the designs were probably produced for pre-approval by the client.

Comprising a three-quarter length light cavalry armour composed of a cuirass, mail sleeves, burgonet and buffe, collar, gauntlets, tassets and saddle-steels, Smythe's field garniture also includes a morion and circular shield, known as a 'rondache' (now in the New York Metropolitan Museum of Art), for fighting on foot. Ornamented with broad recessed bands etched and gilt with strapwork decoration and classical figures, the scheme also features the motto FUTURA PRAETERITIS (roughly 'understanding the future by the past') encircling the head of the Roman god Janus, frequently depicted during the Renaissance as an allegory of time. Other figures, including Justice, Mars, Fame and Victory, reflect Smythe's knowledge of Roman military treatises. Some of its components, including the rondache, were made in Augsburg before being decorated at Greenwich.

A practical no-nonsense soldier with a disdain for the frivolities of fashion, especially when it came to soldier's apparel, Smythe's armour reflects his appreciation of the latest military developments and especially the role of the light cavalryman: tactically more versatile than the heavily armoured lancer, by the eve of the Armada in 1588 the proportion of light cavalry, armed with short-barrelled firearms and light lances, had greatly increased. Whether Smythe wore the armour is unclear, but he bequeathed it to James I. It was at Greenwich by 1611, at the Tower of London by 1649, and after a spell at Windsor returned to the Tower in 1914.

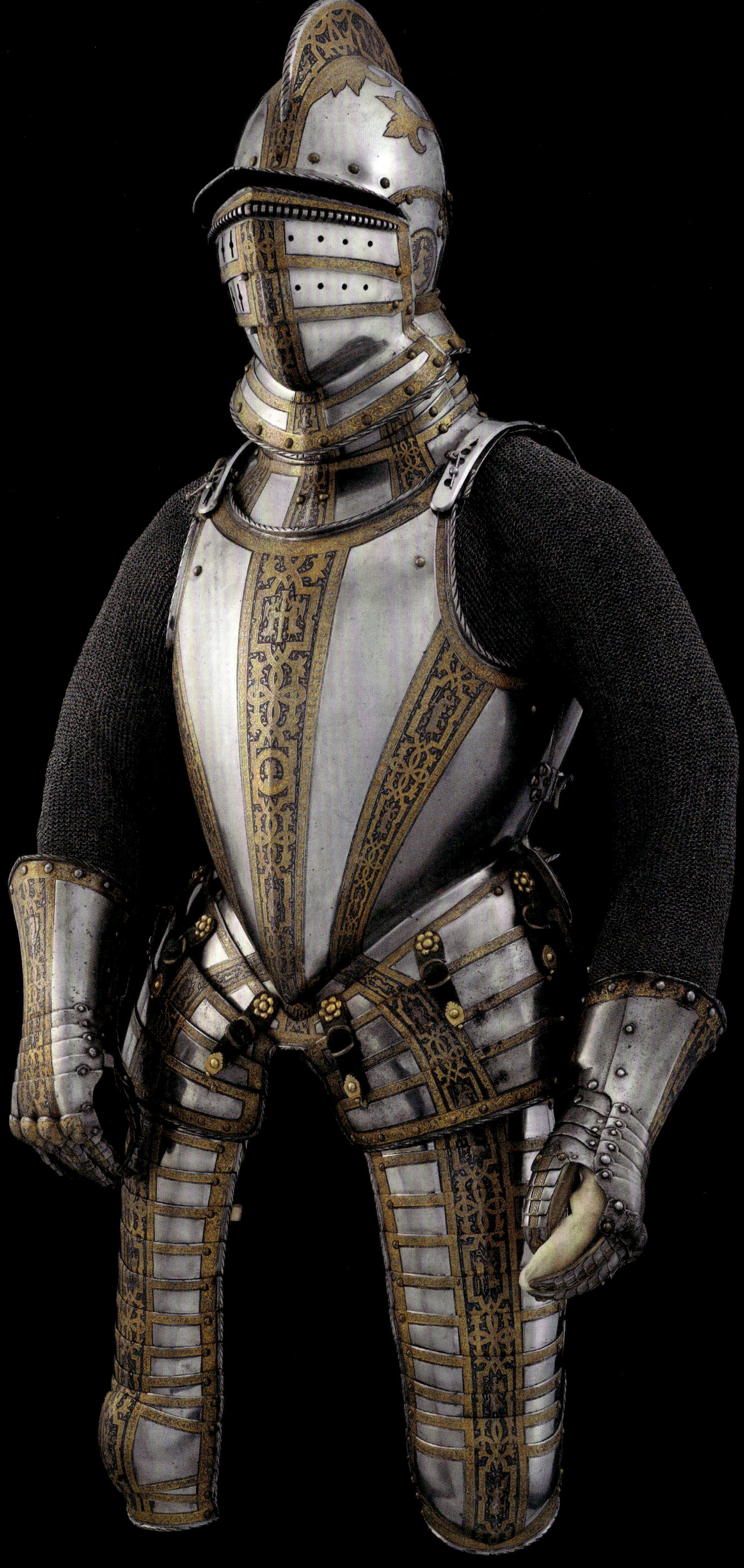

49

The 'Forget me not' gun

Probably France, *c*.1590 · XII.1764

In his work on the treatment of gunshot wounds, published in 1545, the famous French surgeon Ambroise Paré (1510–90) noted that 'those muskets called *poitrinals* … are of large calibre but short … and shot from the chest'. His words both describe the key characteristics of these weapons, but also reveal the origin of the term 'petronel', from *poitrine*, the French for chest. These guns, a sort of hybrid between a pistol and a carbine, but with a short butt designed to be pressed to the body, not the ear or the shoulder, and of questionable practicality, were never made in large numbers and then only from mid 16th to the early 17th century: primarily a military weapon, they were also used, as were pistols, in the chase, notably for delivering the coup de grâce to large game from the saddle. Technically, as is typical of these items, the Royal Armouries' example is a wheellock, in this case with a 90-bore smooth-bore barrel – and so in fact small enough, although of petronel form, to have been fired like a pistol. It is, however, as lavishly and certainly as enigmatically decorated as almost any other historic gun of any type. The most prominent ornament is the bone inlay to the stock and fore-end, featuring heads and animals, intertwined with plant stems and leaves of green–stained antler. These are drawn from a standard Renaissance 'grotesque' repertoire, as are the figurative elements, although these are surprisingly risqué: on the bone butt-plate, Venus and Cupid disport with unusual intimacy, while the vaguely phallic trigger sprouts suggestively from a second naked female. Grotesque decoration is also applied to the metal parts, the gilded barrel bearing chiselled motifs, including a hound's head at the muzzle and figures in unusual headdresses, and the lock plate a range of creatures, some half human, half beast. Most remarkable, however, in both material and subject matter, are the four plaques, two of which are effectively tiny mirrors with images painted on the reverse before the reflective foil was applied. These are set into either side of the butt, and both bear the date 1581, and the inscription VER GIS MEIN NIT (in modern German '*Vergiss mein nicht*'; 'Forget me not'); below the words, sprigs of the flower appear on a cartouche, along with a heart bearing the Christogram IHS. The other plaques are good-quality painted portrait miniatures, set below glass, of bearded but clearly different men. Whether the plaques were made for the gun is unclear, but seems probable: if so, we have a dated piece, and while the inscription and the lock might suggest German manufacture, the decoration points to a French origin. Otherwise, the gun poses more questions than answers – in particular, who is pressed not to forget whom? One of the men depicted in miniature who received this as a present? We can only guess. But we can be pretty sure that this beautiful (if questionably practical) object was much prized by its first owner, as it has been by the Armouries since its purchase in 1961 for £2,100, then the world record for a historic pistol, and more than the cost of an E-type Jaguar.

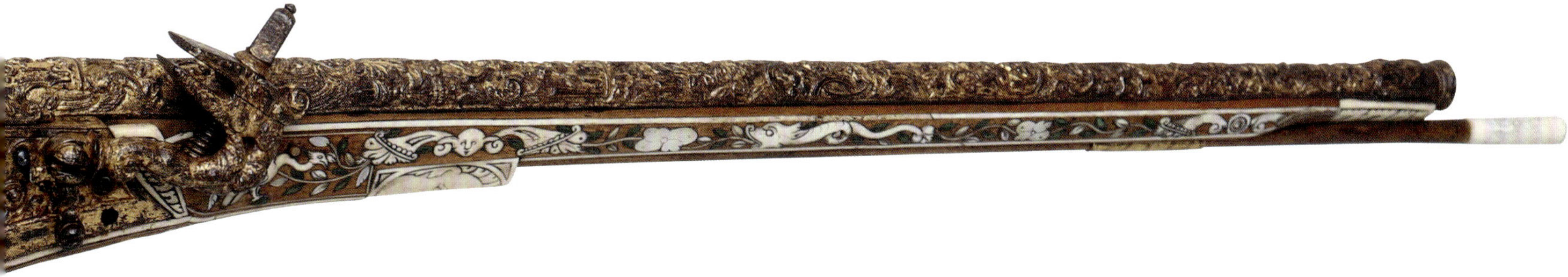

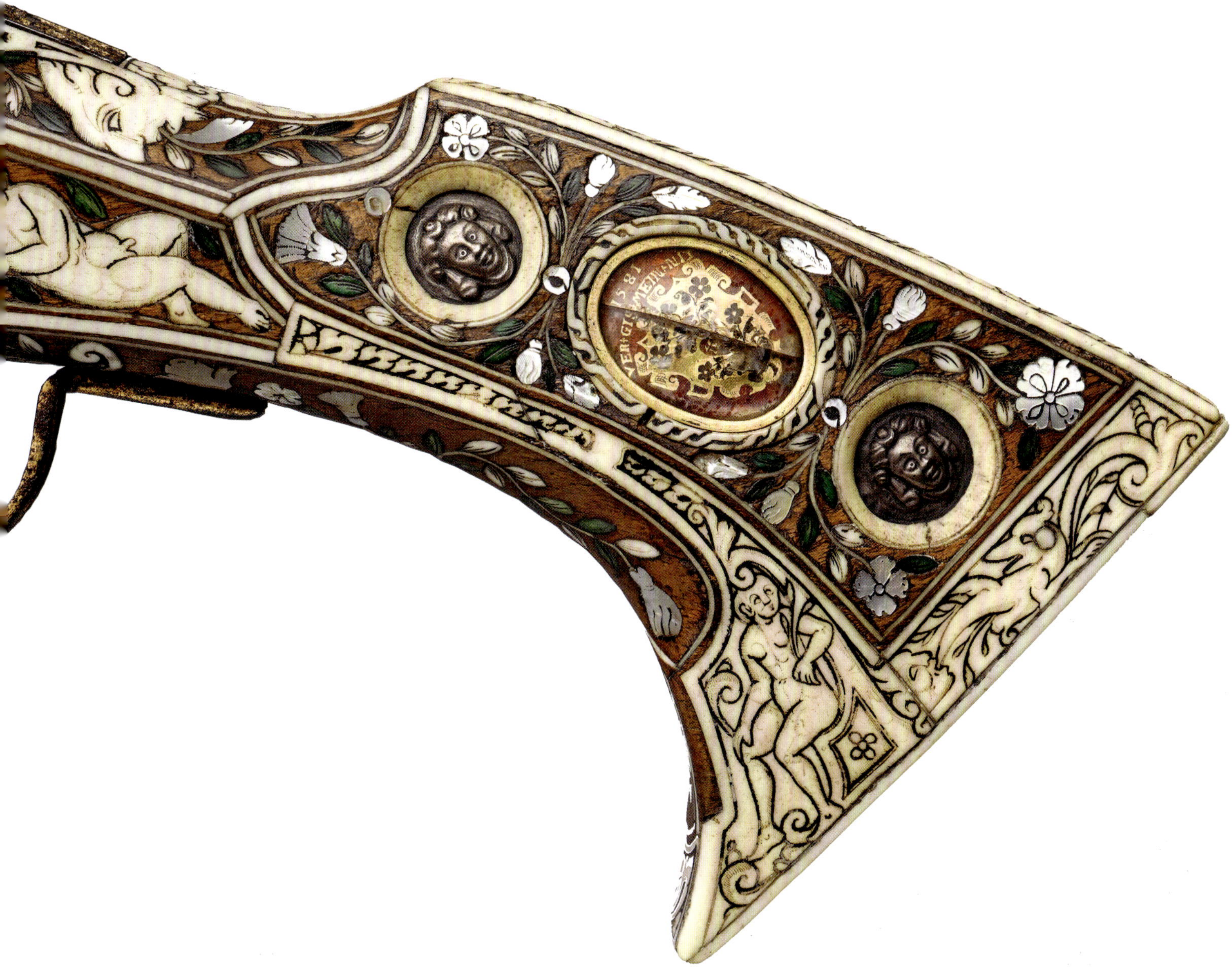
1581

50

Extending rapier

Germany, *c.*1590–1610 · IX.861

During the 16th century the term 'rapier', thought to derive from the Spanish *espada ropera* or 'robe sword' – that is, a sword worn with civilian dress – came to be applied to the long slender form it denotes today. By the end of that century, the greater the reach of blade the better it was held to be, giving an advantage both in thrusting with the point and parrying in defence.

This example has a complex form of bright steel hilt known commonly by later 19th century collectors as a 'swept hilt', thanks to its construction of sweepingly elegantly steel bars. It has a pommel with a pronounced tang-button, a grip bound with fine steel wire, terminating in upper and lower 'Turk's Head' knots. The guard is made up of fore and rear quillons of the cross, which are straight and of round cross-section, thickening towards each end.

The blade, however – at first sight of unremarkable length – has the astonishing capacity of instant extension by 216 mm: when in the un-extended position, its upper part, of flattened diamond section, slides into a slotted steel sleeve, which is part of the grip, and is locked into place by a stud towards the hilt. When released the blade is secured in the extended position by the stud locking into a pierced hole further down the sliding sleeve: the mechanism is similar to the spring studs found on a shooting stick or a Zimmer frame. When in extended use the 'sleeve' of the grip of this unusual rapier becomes, in effect, the lower unbound part of a longer grip.

Although cumbersome to handle at full length, the shock, surprise and confusion caused by the sword's sudden extension, and the reality of its extra reach, could have been a decisive factor in a duel. The ingenuity of the design would have been attractive in its own right, but its main purpose may have been to get around state or civic laws limiting the length of blades. These were prompted by what could be described as an 'epidemic' of duelling fatalities in the second half of the 16th century, resulting from aristocratic enthusiasm for duels as signs of courage, honour and distinction. In England, regulation included a decree by Queen Mary I in 1557 that no sword or rapier should be more than 'a yarde and a halfe quarter in the blade at most'. Under her successor and half-sister, Elizabeth I, a proclamation of 1562 also limited the lengths of swords and other weapons, and another in 1566 ordered the Cutlers' Company to break or cut off the points of swords seized for being too long. By way of enforcement, the watchmen stationed at London's city gates were supposed to check the weapons of those entering the city. However, then as now, such rules were often ignored: a servant of the powerful Howard family, for instance, passed through London's Aldersgate on 8 March 1580 with 'a sword of forbidden length and carrying it with the point upwards'; his response to the challenge was to use it on his accusers. In 1589 members of the Cutlers' Company were still searching for what were described as 'naughty and deceitful sword blades'. Not surprisingly, though, extending swords were never common: only four other surviving examples are known, along with mention of '*Une espée … dont la lame s'advance avec un resort*' in an inventory made for the Duke of Lorraine at Nancy (Meurthe et Moselle) in 1614.

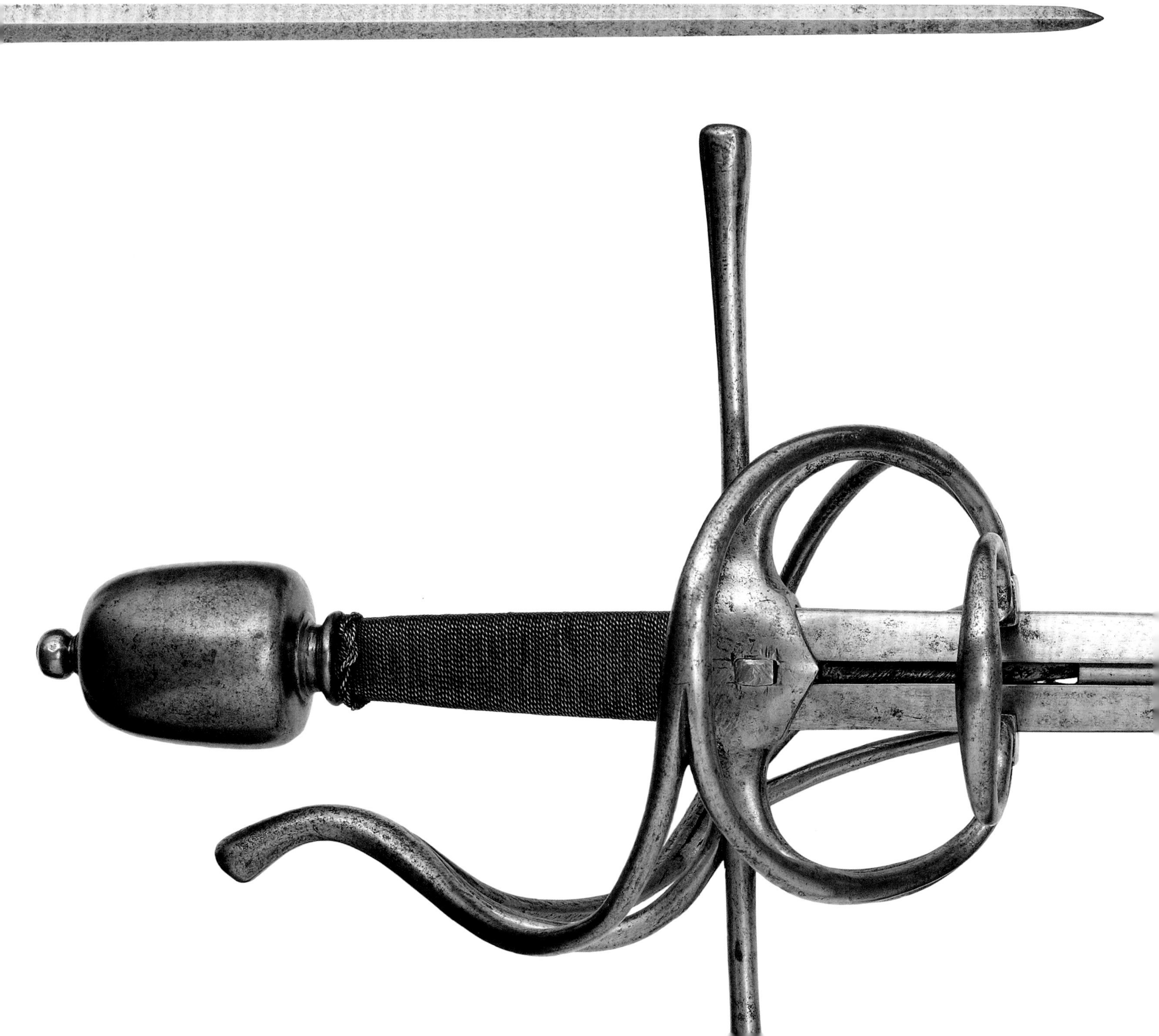

51

Foot combat armour of Christian of Saxony

Germany, 1591 · 11.186

In 1547 the Dresden-based dukes of Saxony, rulers of a semi-independent state within the Holy Roman Empire, joined the group of electors who appointed the emperor and had a role in his government. The throne was usually occupied by a member of the Hapsburg dynasty from 1438 until the dissolution of the empire in 1806, but the status of elector conferred immense prestige upon the princes and prelates involved. Among these, Saxony was one of the wealthiest and most powerful. As a result the Dresden armoury, now held by the Rüstkammer, Staatliche Kunstsammlungen Dresden, contains one of the greatest collections of Renaissance armour in the world and amply reflects the wealth and grandeur of the Saxon court.

Christian I (1560–91) inherited the duchy in 1586 and ruled until his early death in 1591. Although he had little interest in state affairs, he was an enthusiast for the chase, a lavish entertainer, and a keen and an active participant in tournaments from his youth. Fittingly, in 1591 Christian's wife Sophia ordered him a Christmas present of twelve very similar armours, although as it happened he died in September that year before their completion. One of these was to be worn by Christian himself and the rest by guests invited specifically to participate in the 'foot combat', a form of tournament historically considered a lesser sport than the joust (and merely a prelude to it). In the mid 16th century, however, a new form evolved, known as 'The Barriers', more closely reflecting the evolving style of infantry warfare beginning to dominate European battlefields. The combatants were separated by a waist-high barrier and fought with short wooden pikes or swords. By 1600 this had almost entirely replaced the older forms of foot combat, and was frequently part-choreographed and set to music, leading some contemporaries to complain that it was so far removed from real fighting as to be ludicrous, and a game for women and children. Several sword cuts to the helmet suggest, however, that someone did indeed compete in it after Christian's death.

The armours were made by Anton Peffenhauser of Augsburg (1525–1603), one of the foremost German armourers of the time. After becoming a master in 1545, by 1550 he had already established enough of a reputation to commissioned to produce armours for the court of the Holy Roman Emperor Charles v and King Sebastian of Portugal. Indeed, such was his reputation that he apparently never set a price until an armour was complete, knowing that whatever he charged his name alone would ensure its payment. The armours consist of a close helm, peascod breast and back, tassets, pauldrons, vambraces and gauntlets, all of which are blued with etched and gilt floral scrolls. The helmet also features a circular arrangement of heart-shaped breaths. The overall style of the armour closely imitates men's fashion of the time, and shows a distinct preference for overall decoration rather than the narrow bands of detail previously favour by the fashionable elite. Of particular note is the exaggerated, pointed stomach similar to that of the fashionable peascod doublet of the period. After delivery to Dresden, the armour and its companions began to be dispersed in 1610, and now only three remain there, possessions from 1806 of the kings of Saxony, and from 1919 the 'Free State of Saxony' within the Weimar Republic. Others of the set survive in Detroit, New York, Nuremberg, St Petersburg and Warsaw.

[146]

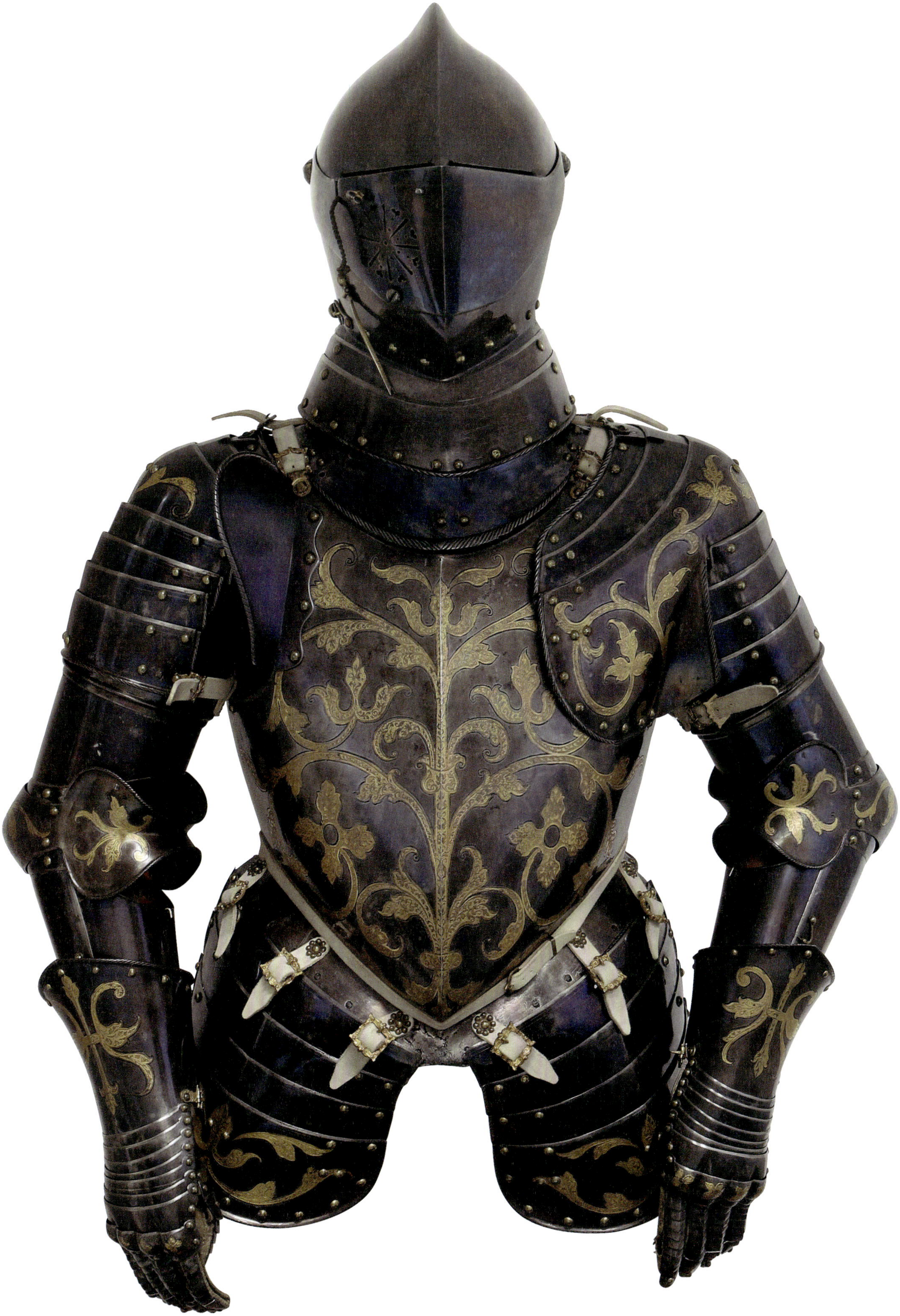

52

Portrait of Robert Radcliffe, Viscount Fitzwalter and 5th Earl of Sussex

Belgium, c.1593 · 1.36

From the middle of the 16th century it was fashionable for noblemen and other high-ranking individuals to commission their portraits in martial attire to reinforce their status and military credentials. Traditionally attributed to the Flemish artist, Marcus Gheeraerts the Younger (1561–1636), this painting of Robert Radcliffe does just that, and clearly expresses the expectations and promise of a young man about to embark on an active service.

By the 1590s portraiture had also developed its own conventions and language, understandable to the viewers of the time, if sometimes less so today. Sitters could be easily identified through heraldry, or in writing, as here, where a marble floor tile is inscribed 'Radclif Earl of Sussex'. More ambiguous messages could also be used, such as the Italian inscription here at top right, '*Armando et Fidando Troppo, son rovinato*' ('Loving and trusting overmuch I am ruined'), perhaps an oblique reference to the financial problems and debts he inherited on succeeding in 1593.

The painting's main messages, however, are to do with chivalry and military accomplishment. Radcliffe, at this time in his mid-twenties, is shown standing full length, bareheaded, facing half left, his armour configured for the foot tourney over the barriers (hence the absence of leg armour): it consists a cuirass, gorget, pauldrons, vambraces and gauntlets of bare polished steel ('white armour'). On the table is his helmet, fitted with a tourney visor. He also wears richly embroidered and jewelled silver-grey paned trunks along with hose and shoes, and at his side is a swept-hilted rapier of a type common from the mid 16th to the mid 17th century, suspended from a belt and hanger. He holds a pike in his right hand. This may well be the armour and costume which he wore in the Accession Day tilts of November 1593, spectacular annual events held from the 1580s to 1602 at Whitehall, intended to exalt the queen and secure the loyalty of the participants. The whole sumptuous ensemble would have sent out clear and flattering messages about the wearer, while the recognisably Greenwich armour, obtainable only with royal or high-level sanction, would itself have been a mark of the queen's favour. Other symbols are present in the careful positioning of items and even in colours: upon the orange-covered table, for example, rests the field close-helmet of the armour, surmounted by a high crest of jewel-studded silver feathers reminiscent of a peacock's display, and ostrich plumes in silver, grey and orange. Ostrich plumes were recognised symbols of noble passions, bravery and valour, while the orange colour of the cloth is traditionally associated with courage, endurance and strength.

How the picture left Radcliffe's possession is unknown, but by 1593 it had been acquired by one of the greatest English collector-patrons of the period, John, Lord Lumley (c.1533–1609). The Lumley collection, much of it held or displayed at Lumley Castle, County Durham, included paintings, books, sculpture and many other objects, and this picture appears in an inventory of that year. The portrait remained in the Lumleys' hands until 1785, and it was acquired by the Royal Armouries in the middle of the 20th century.

Amando et Fidando Troppo, son rouinato.

Radclif
Earl of Sussex

53

Powder flask bearing the arms of the Worshipful Company of Goldsmiths of London

England, *c.*1580 · XIII.149

Almost all hand-held guns until the mid 19th century were muzzle-loaders. They were charged by pouring powder and shot down the barrel and pressing it home, along with a wad, using a ram-rod. Amongst other accoutrements, the process therefore required some form of container or flask to hold a supply of loose powder. These were usually accompanied by smaller ones of similar shape and decoration to hold finely ground priming powder, poured into the priming pan after the main charge had been loaded.

Many materials, including iron, wood, ivory, bone, antler and horn were used to make powder flasks, and in a wide variety of shapes, but a form popular throughout much of Western Europe by the end of the 16th century, both for military and sporting purposes, had a triangular body with concave sides. These were made from thin panels of wood, necessarily reinforced by metal mounts and bindings. While military versions usually had very plain metalwork, those made for use alongside fine sporting firearms were often highly decorated, mirroring that of the gun with which they were made to be used.

Flasks of the type shown here had a nozzle designed to measure out an exact charge of powder suitable for the gun to which it belonged. The user placed a forefinger over the end of the nozzle, inverted the flask to fill the nozzle with enough powder for one charge of a musket barrel, whilst at the same time using the thumb to pivot a shutter at the nozzle's base: with this closed, the contents of the nozzle were then poured down the barrel.

In the case of this flask the wooden body is covered in velvet, originally dark red but now much faded, and has an outer casing of gilded sheet brass, held in place by three transverse screws with heads in the form of lion masks. The nozzle's shutter is operated by a sculpted lever in the form of a wyvern, a mythological fire-breathing beast – hence, presumably, its presence here. On the front of the flask the brass is pierced to create an elegant scrolled 'strap-work' pattern, mirroring contemporary graphic and architectural design; at its centre is an oval panel, within which, surrounded by further scrolling, are the arms of the Goldsmith's Company – one of the oldest and greatest of the Livery Companies of London and still flourishing today. As shown here, and as displayed when the flask was hung at the belt, the shield is upside-down, but would have been correctly presented and seen as such by the user when up-ended to charge the barrel. The arms are of medieval origin, and the leopards' heads shown in the first and fourth quarters, borrowed from the royal arms, recall the first ever English hallmark, instituted by Edward I. The flask was probably made for the use of a member of a body of musketeers raised by the Company after the creation of the London Trained Bands, militia units for the defence of the city, in 1572: lists of their members show that in 1588 two brothers, Richard and John Martin, both goldsmiths, were also captains of companies of soldiers. Richard Martin was elected Lord Major of London in 1593 and in 1599 was still recorded as a captain of a Trained Band company. Conceivably this flask was Martin's own.

The flask represents an essential part of the musketeer's and sportsman's equipment from the 16th to the 19th century. It is a fine object in its own right and a reminder of the role of the Companies in London's militia. As such, however, it is also a unique survival: while two muskets survive in the hands of the Haberdashers and the Stationers, this is the only known powder flask with any such association.

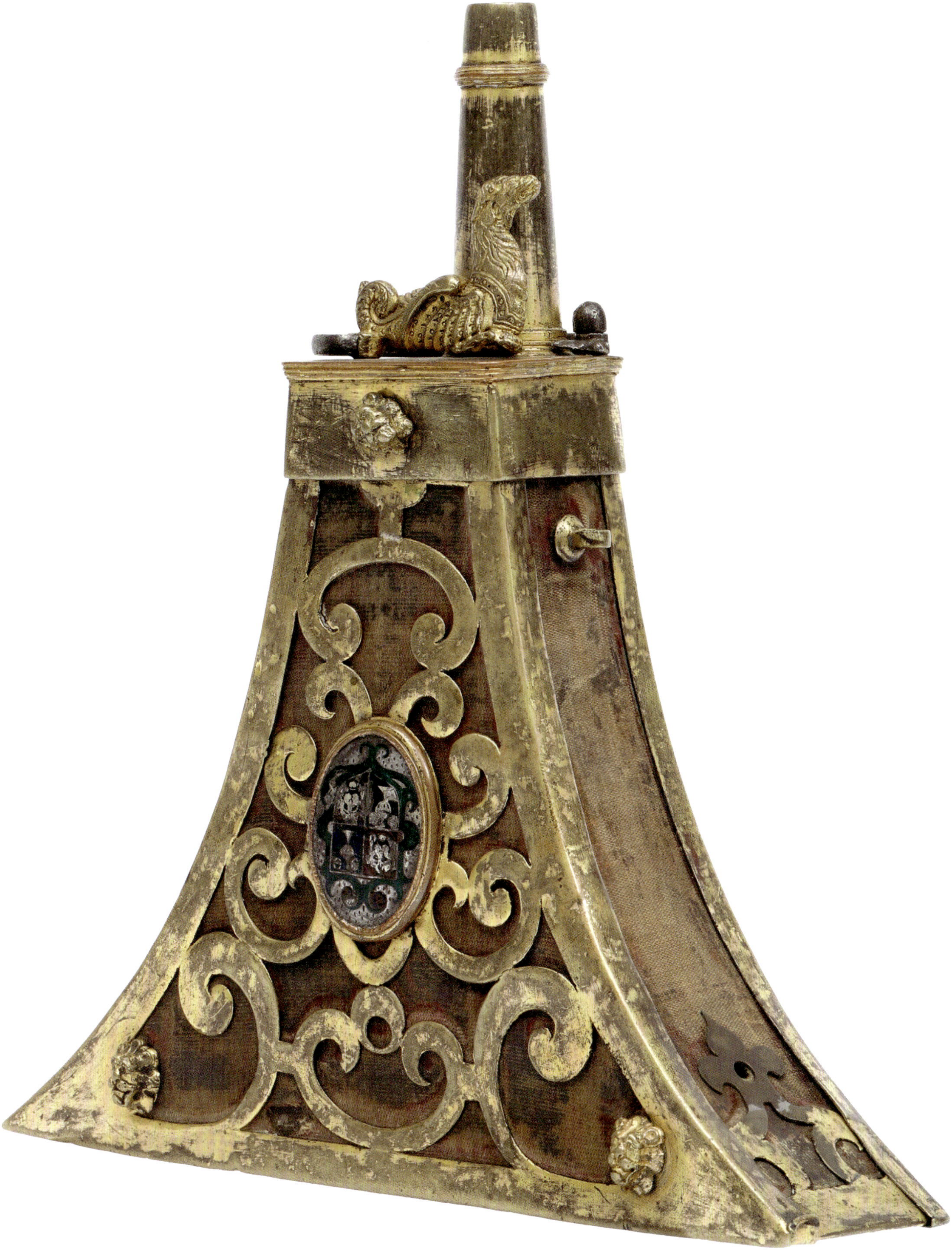

54

English crossbow

England, c.1600 · XI.295

As the word 'cross' suggests, the bow stave or 'prod' of a crossbow is not held vertically, as in an archer's bow, but fixed horizontally at right-angles to the end of a stock, allowing the bowstring to be spanned (drawn) mechanically and notched onto a release mechanism: the user holds the stock to the shoulder, as with a gun (or in this period, the cheek), and pulls a trigger to release the nut and the short, stiff bolt or 'quarrel'. The weapon seems to have originated in China in the middle of the first millennium BC. It was known to the Romans, occurs in the 10th century and was abundant by 1100. Among its advantages, the crossbow could be loaded and held ready for a steady aim, requiring neither the strength nor the training needed for archery; following the introduction of steel prods, it could also out-range most 'self' bows. Together with the longbow it was the most important hand-held projectile weapon of the Middle Ages.

Crossbows were used for hunting, from game birds – usually sitting – to deer, as well as in war: they were handled on foot or from the saddle, and the quarry was stalked, driven (in the field or in an arena), or shot and then brought down by hounds. There were endless other variations. As guns became increasingly effective on the battlefield in the early 16th century, the crossbow survived primarily as a sporting weapon. This was largely due to its silence, reliability and economy: not only was no powder involved, but the bolt or quarrel could be retrieved by specially trained hounds. By the end of the century, however, with the exception of the 'stone-bow' (designed to fire stones), it had been relegated to specialist or eccentric use, although crossbows have remained in production in small numbers ever since.

This example dates from about 1600, and has the long straight slender stock and long trigger lever favoured by English, French and Spanish sportsmen at the time. These could be spanned using a simple 'goat's foot' lever, a device pivoted on two iron pegs fitted to the stock, rather than the clumsy windlasses or cranequins needed for heavier versions. The English origin of this example – a very rare survivor – is suggested by similarities to others of known provenance, including one given by James I of England to Philip III of Spain in 1604, now in the Real Armería in Madrid. As with the Madrid example, it is profusely decorated with inlaid plaques of mother-of-pearl depicting flowers, petals and birds, interspersed bands and panels of engraved bone. The powerful steel prod is etched with strapwork and foliate scrolls, while the trigger lever and other steel parts bear traces of fine-quality gold damascened scroll decoration. As such it resembles one shown in the foreground of a painting, *The Carlile family with Sir Justinian Isham in Richmond Park* (1650), by Joan Carlile (1600–79), showing the closing moments of a stag hunt. A similar example survives in the Scott Collection in Glasgow. The combination of gilding, etching and mother-of-pearl inlays, used by London gunsmiths at the time, suggests a metropolitan origin: until this period, gunsmiths often made crossbows, and sometimes combined both in one weapon. In a variation on the theme, however, the maker in this case was perhaps the London sword cutler John Cradocke (working 1598–1623), who supplied many of the weapons for the Spanish royal gift in 1604, made to cement the end of the Anglo-Spanish war. Perhaps this crossbow was the swansong, at least in England, of the prestigious sporting crossbow and of a decorative and functional quality later applied largely to firearms.

[152]

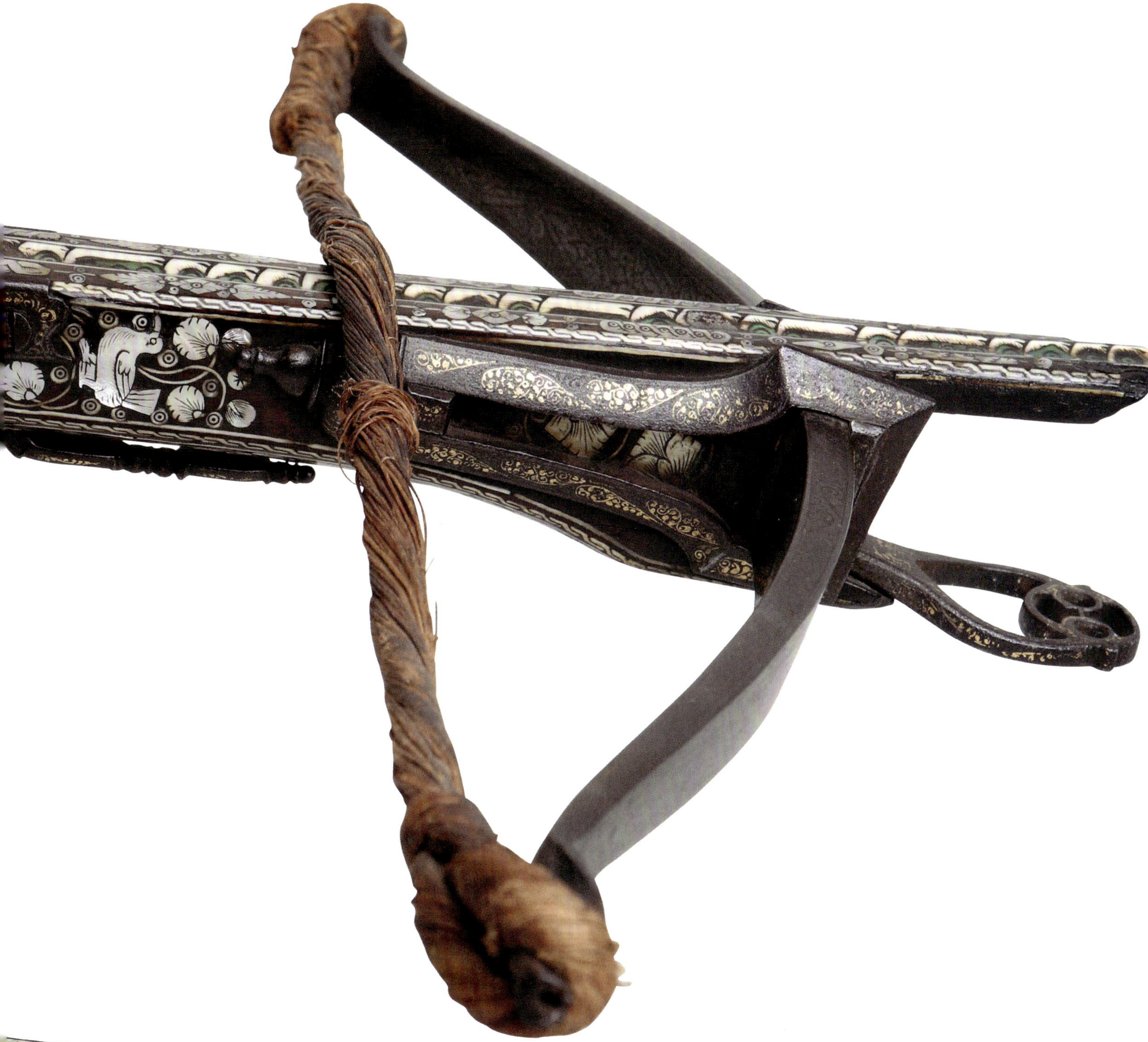

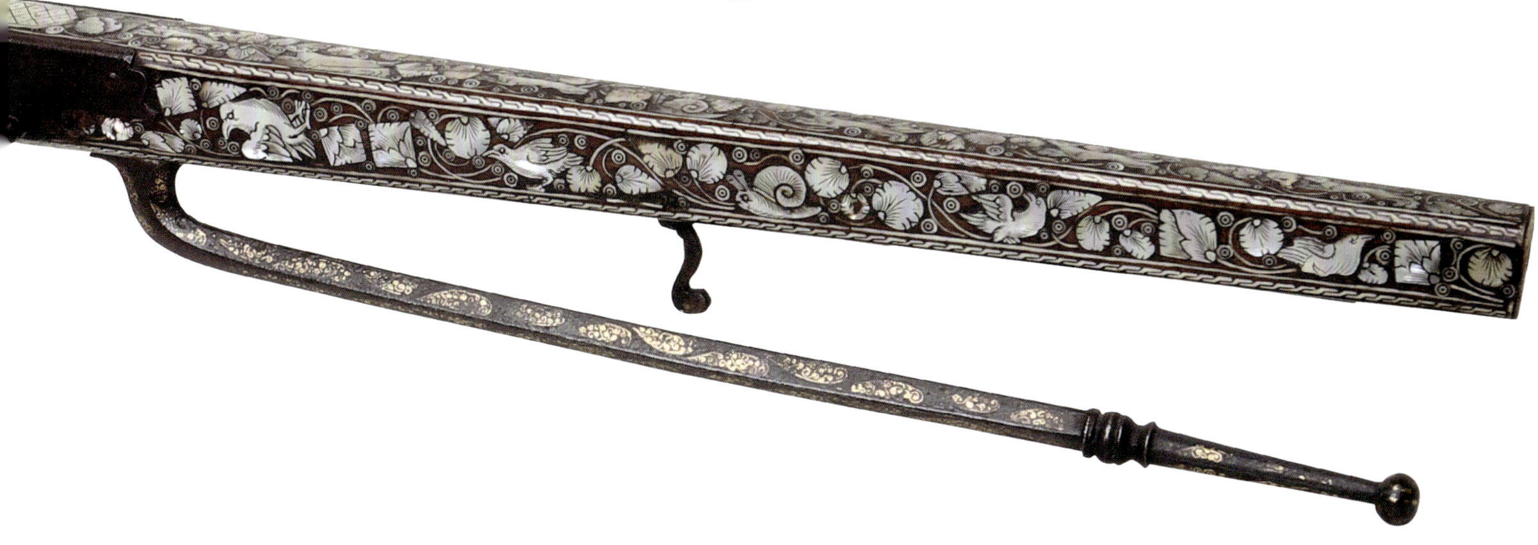

55

A parade burgonet from Augsburg, Germany

Germany, *c.*1600 · IV.154

The burgonet, described by Claude Blair as 'the headpiece par excellence of the infantry and light cavalry throughout the 16th century', derived from the sallet, and was initially known in French as the *salade à la bourgogne* ('Burgundian sallet'), and by a similar term in Italian. It took the form of a close-fitting open helmet with a combed skull and peak, with cheek pieces, pivoted at the sides, and from *c.*1550 it was often worn with a *buffe* to protect the face. Providing both lightness and unrestricted vision, in appearance the burgonet also consciously resembled helmets of antiquity.

This magnificent example, once part of a complete armour, is exceptional for its lavish, three-dimensional ornamentation. The main surfaces are of black steel embossed with bunches of fruit and flowers interspersed with birds and insects, to which have been applied fire-gilded cast copper panels and foliate borders to the neck, crest and peak. As such, incorporating such delicate decoration, the helmet would have been a liability in battle, but was abundantly suited for parade and ceremonial, where its beauty and elaboration trumpeted the power, wealth, culture and social aspirations of the wearer.

The helmet is a reminder of the importance accorded to fine armours by the great figures of the time, and its status as a branch of applied art. The attention paid to it owed not only (as with much art) to the flattering messages it projected about the owner, but – at a time when actual noble participation in battles was on the decline – demonstrated a continued link with a venerated chivalric past. The Holy Roman Emperor Charles V paid more for an armour (made by his armourer Desiderius Helmschmied) than for a painting by Titian, the most famous painter of the age; similarly, on receipt of a gift of armour from the Gonzaga Duke Federico II, Charles went so far to say that he 'valued it more than a city'. Consequently, 16th-century goldsmiths, long employed to decorate armour, began to make it themselves: among them was Eliseus Libaerts of Antwerp, who produced an exceptionally fine armour for Erik XIV of Sweden (r.1560–9). Not surprisingly, although such armours were occasionally worn, their permanent display and (by many princes) their systematic collection – was equally prevalent.

Taking a lead from the emperor, many of the greatest patrons of decorative armour were the princes of the Empire, of whom the electors of Saxony were among the most important. Deriving their wealth from local sources of silver, tin, copper, iron and semi-precious stones, they established themselves as leading patrons of the arts. In Dresden the Elector and Duke August of Saxony (1553–86) enlarged his collection of armour tenfold, whilst under his grandson Christian II (r.1591–1611), the collection was further enhanced with numerous jewel-encrusted weapons and extravagantly decorated parade armours, mostly from the famed workshops at Augsburg. One such high-quality armour, dated 1599, was purchased in 1602 from an unidentified Augsburg armourer and bears striking similarity to the Royal Armouries' burgonet. They may be by same hand.

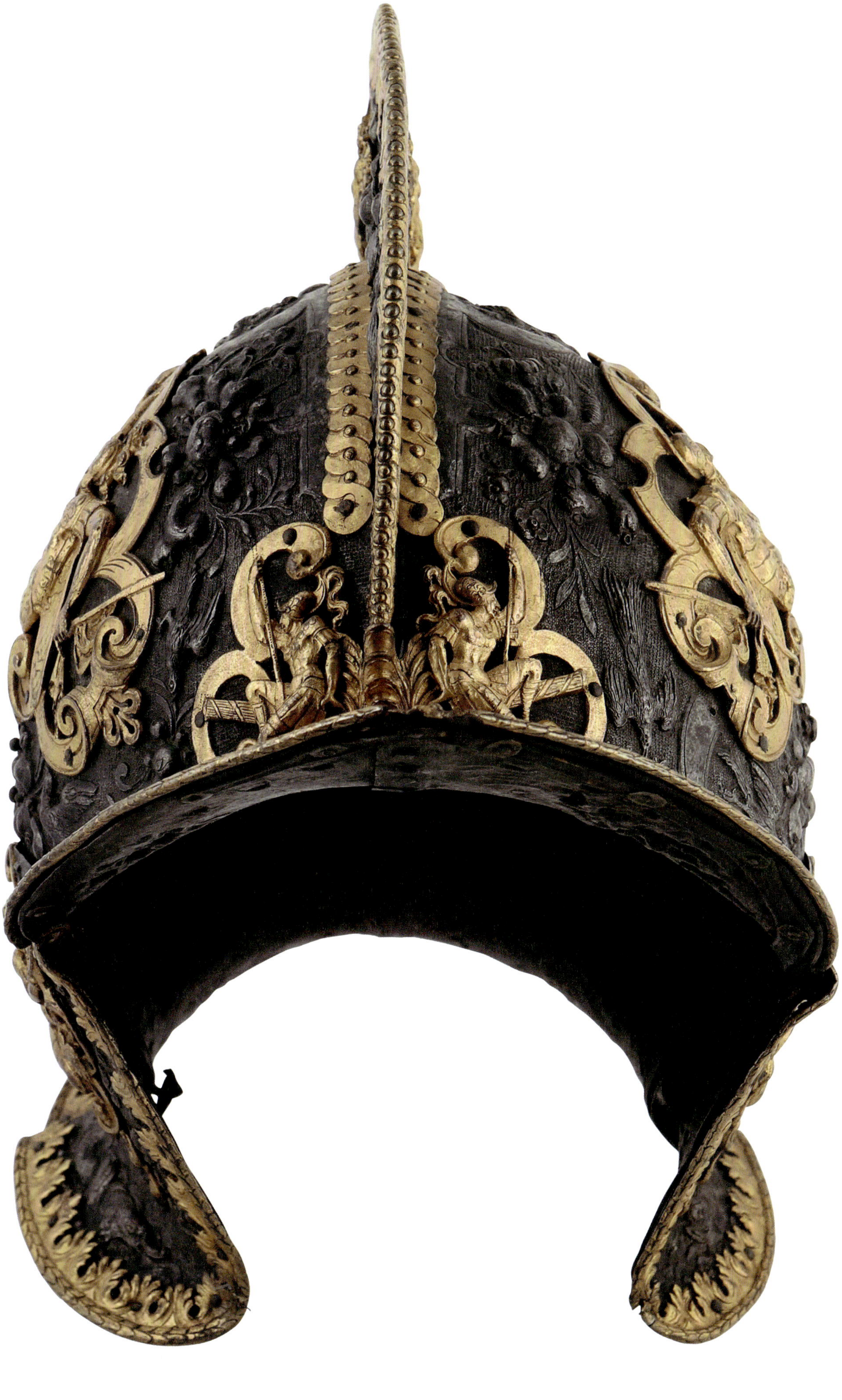

56

'The Emperor Charles v holding a drawn sword': portrait by Peter Paul Rubens, after Titian

Spain, 1603 · I.1661

The Royal Armouries most important acquisition of recent years is a portrait of the Emperor Charles v by Peter Paul Rubens (1577–1640), copied from an original by the equally famous Venetian artist Tiziano Vecello (1490–1576), in English called Titian. The original was probably painted in 1529–30, either when Federico Gonzaga, Duke of Mantua invited the artist to meet the Emperor in Parma, or a few months later in Bologna, where, eleven years into his reign, he was formally crowned by the Pope. The picture – now lost – was given to the Emperor, and he clearly cherished it, as it accompanied him to his place of retirement in 1557.

Artistically, the three-quarter length format and pose draws on a Low Countries convention, used in depictions of Charles's Burgundian ancestors. The unsheathed sword is a standard symbol of secular and royal power, but in Charles's case vividly recalled depictions of his namesake and ancestor Charlemagne, founder of the Empire, giving it an additional religious significance. The armour itself had been ordered by Charles from Kolman Helmschmied, the Imperial armourer at Augsburg, and was delivered to the Emperor in 1521: unlike the Titian, it survives (in the Real Armeria in Madrid) and is now usually known as the 'fleur-de-lys scroll armour' portrait. Its key characteristics include the etched and gilt decoration in bands containing both floral and scroll-like motifs, and flowers and radiating lines on the bands surrounding the central bosses of the besagews (rondels protecting the armpits). Elsewhere, including on the pauldrons and the neckline of the breastplate, the vertical bands contained a scroll-like decoration.

Rubens, born a year after Titian's death, studied and copied the work of many artists, but his exposure to Titian's work, firstly in Venice, then in Mantua and finally in Spain was the most influential. This copy was painted at the court of Philip II, Charles v's successor as king of Spain, whilst on a diplomatic mission on behalf of the Duke of Mantua: his initiative was presumably prompted by his admiration for Titian, but also for Charles v, in whose reign his homeland had been united under Hapsburg rule, an era he looked back on with regret: these suppositions tally with his retention of the picture, found in studio at his death in 1640. How much of it is Rubens's own work, rather than his assistants', is not yet clear.

The subsequent history of the picture reflects the status of the sitter and the skill of two great masters. By the mid 17th century the painting was in the possession of the princes of Orange-Nassau, the Dutch Stadholders, starting with Prince Frederick Henry, and from them descended to the Stadtholder William, who in 1689 was crowned William III of England and Scotland. William displayed it at Het Loo, his rural palace near Apeldoorn, and from him it descended to his great-nephew Prince Johan William Friso, and was recorded in the sale of his widow's possessions in Amsterdam in July 1713. It was bought for James Brydges, 1st Duke of Chandos (1673–1744) and hung to command the grand staircase of his magnificent but short-lived house at Cannons, Middlesex. After his death the portrait passed through various hands until inherited by Henry Edmund Skeffington, 13th Viscount Mountgarret (1816–1900), great-grandfather of Richard, 17th Viscount Mountgarret (d.2004) from whose estate it was generously gifted, with the aid of the Acceptance in Lieu scheme, to the Royal Armouries. Here it joins pictures of two of the Emperor's great-nephews, Archduke Matthias of Austria, later Emperor (r.1612–19), and Archduke Albert, Governor-General of the Netherlands (in post 1596–8) and is one of our most prized possessions.

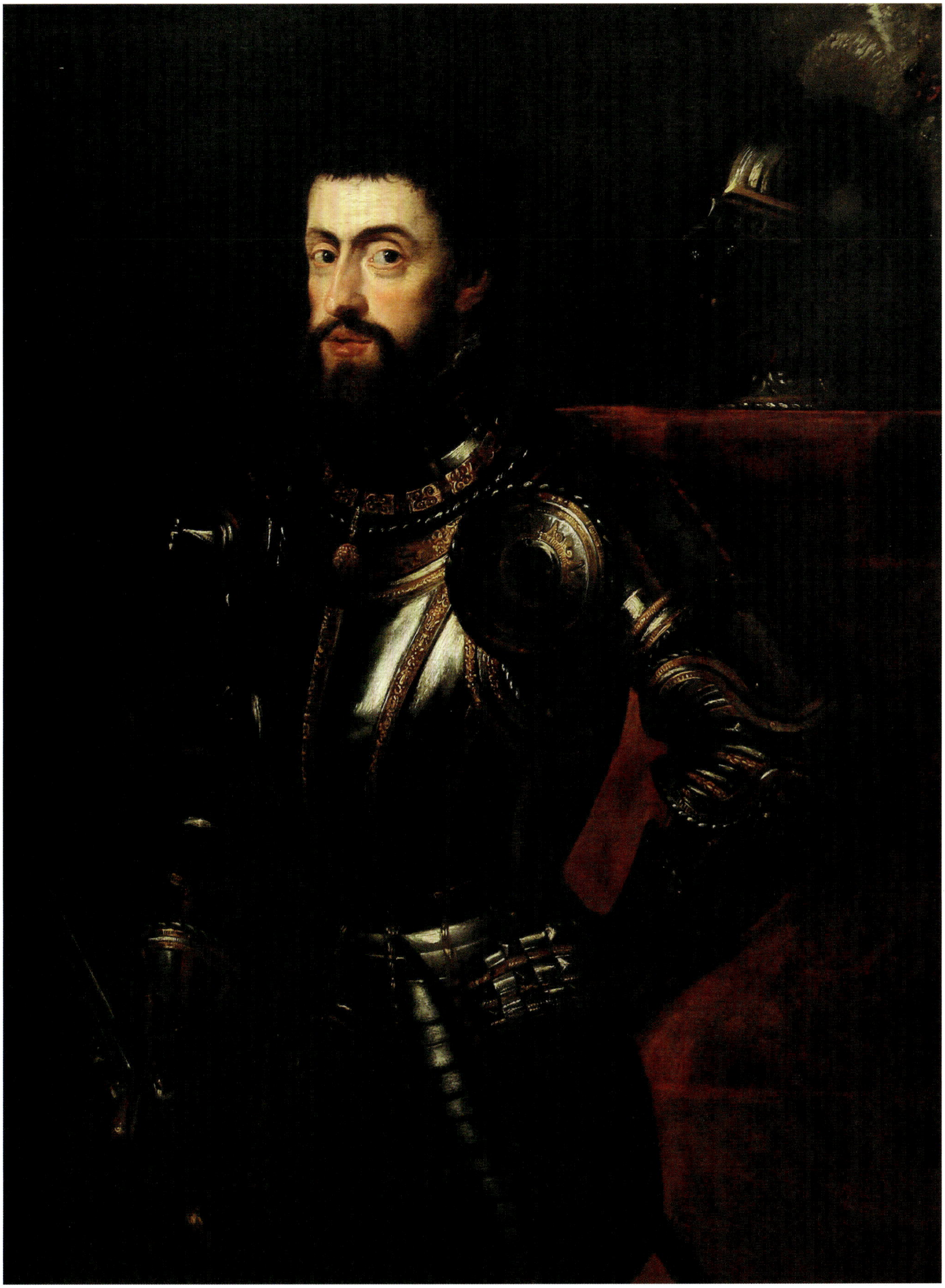

57

The 'Alexander' armour of Prince Henry Stuart

The Netherlands, 1607–8 · II.88

Prince Frederick Henry Stuart (1594–1612) was the gifted eldest son of King James I. He died, aged 18, leaving his brother Charles as heir to the throne. During his brief life Henry received several gift armours, as princes tended to, for in addition to their practical value they helped legitimise political and dynastic claims and strengthen diplomatic and personal connections. This example, decorated with the story of Alexander the Great, was formally presented to Henry in 1608 by Sir Francis Vere, who, along with his brother Horace, was then serving James I and the Dutch House of Nassau in the Netherlands: in 1605 Horace had become the leading English commander and was well respected by Prince Maurice and his brother, Count Frederick Henry, and it was probably he who placed the commission with Dutch armourers. The Veres' motives undoubtedly included gaining the support of the heir to the throne for their enrichment and military careers, and certainly in the case of Sir Horace (who by 1610 had become part of the prince's inner circle) they were successful.

Alexander the Great, king of Macedon and conqueror of the Middle East and India, was regarded by many in the 17th century as the greatest military hero of antiquity. No surprise then, as Henry approached adulthood, that contemporaries began to draw flattering and optimistic comparisons between the two men. For the Veres the choice of theme projected the importance of a strong, successful Stuart monarchy, able to play a leading role on the international stage.

The form of decoration owes a large debt to the gilt borders and strapwork on armours seen in contemporary portraits of members of the House of Nassau and leading European aristocrats, which itself often came from Italian pattern books. The models for the drawings, meanwhile, were probably the cartoons (full-scale designs) for a set of tapestries depicting the 'Life of Alexander' known to have been circulating amongst Flemish and Dutch workshops at exactly the same time. Following the tale (relayed in over 200 vignettes) is hard work, but it can be read as a continuous narrative from sabaton to helmet, flowing round the body as Alexander and his army move through Palestine, the Middle East, Asia Minor and the Indian subcontinent, before his eventual return to Babylon and death. To name a random selection, a vignette on the helmet shows the king on a lion hunt in Sogdia (Uzbekistan and Tajikistan), confronting the beast on foot with sword and shield, and nearby is the scene of him dashing to the ground the helmet full of water brought to him by a soldier in the Bactrian desert. The backplate shows Alexander's marriage to Roxane, and the couple embracing in a tented pavilion, and the left vambrace his victory at Hydaspes. over against King Porus (Punjab) and his elephants.

There is every reason to believe that Prince Henry wore this armour at some point, and almost as many to think that it prompted him to think admiringly about Alexander's campaigns and conduct. In doing so he would have encountered situations he might face as king, including the siege and destruction of cities, victory in battle, diplomacy and negotiation, the submission of vanquished rulers, and examples of the personal prowess of a warrior king. In the event, the armour was all too soon inherited by his younger brother, Charles, on whom such lessons were largely lost.

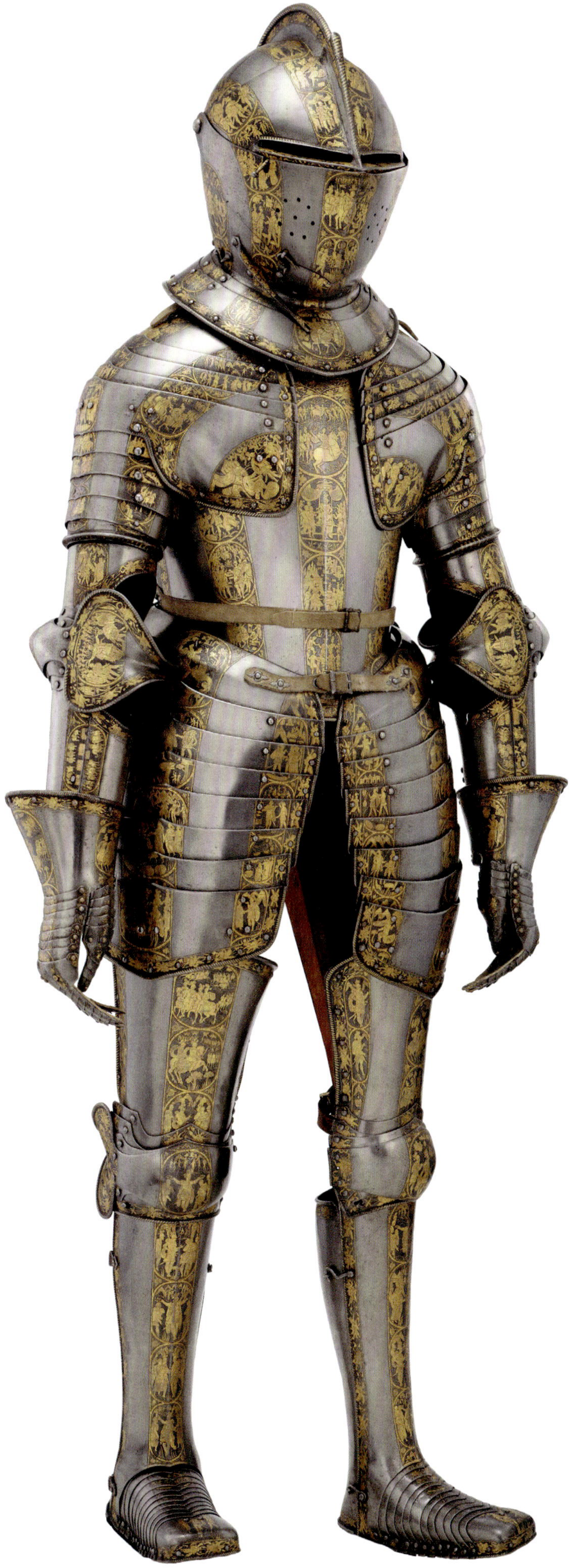

58
A Japanese armour presented to James I
Japan, *c.*1610 · XXVIA.1

Japan had had no direct contact with Europeans until 1543, when a Chinese ship carrying three merchants from Portugal, then Europe's most ambitious maritime nation, took shelter at Tanegashima, off Kyushu. The Portuguese swiftly established trading rights with the Japanese, founding a major base at Nagasaki in 1571, and traded very profitably between China and Japan. The Dutch arrived next, in 1600, with the English navigator William Adams on board, and despite the protestations of the Portuguese – jealous of their monopoly, and (having been absorbed by Spain) now at war with the Dutch – were well received and formally permitted to trade by Tokugawa Ieyasu in 1605.

The English meanwhile had founded the East India Company in 1600, and in 1611 despatched three ships under Captain John Saris, primarily to trade in the Spice Islands, but with discretion to sail north to Japan. This Saris did, anchoring the *Clove* off Hirado, at the very south of the archipelago. He was greeted by the local lord, Matsura Shigenobu, also known as Hoin, who he mistakenly took to be the 'King' of Japan, made him lavish gifts, and received a Japanese armour in return – the first one to be owned by an Englishman. Shigenobu sent word of Saris's arrival to Ieyasu, who although now retired in favour of his son, Tokugawa Hidetada, remained influential, and who ordered the (now expatriate) William Adams to accompany Saris to meet the Shogun. Saris's gifts to Hidetada included a telescope, now sadly lost but the first ever seen in Japan, and invented only a few years earlier. He wrote in his diary that 'towards evening the King sent 2 varnished Armours, a present to his Majesty the King of England', accompanied by the offer to set up a trading post at the capital, Edo (now Tokyo). In the event the English foothold remained in Hirado, although it was to be abandoned in 1623. Saris got back to England in September 1614, and the armours entered royal ownership as planned, one being housed at the Tower, where it was on display in 1660. By then, however, its true origin had been forgotten, and it was billed as 'Armour of the Great Moghul', that is, along with most far eastern items at the time, as Indian: it was not until the 1854 3rd edition of *The Tower, its History, Armouries and Antiques* by John Hewitt that the armour was correctly identified as Japanese.

In more recent times armour has been studied in more detail. Although signed by the acclaimed Iwai Yozaemon, the personal armourer of Ieyasu himself, it is of 15th-century *domaru* form, whereby the armour wraps around the body, fastened on the right hand side, and is made up of iron and rawhide plates, lacquered black and laced together with silk. As time was short, it is unlikely that Ieyasu ordered the armour specifically for Saris, and it was probably an existing item refurbished by Yozaemon to make it fit for presentation: this is further suggested by the *mon*, or family crest displayed on the armour, belonging to Takeda Katsuyori, defeated by Ieyasu and Nobunaga at Nagashino in 1575 and Tenmokuzan in 1582, after which he committed suicide and his property was acquired by Ieyasu. As a result, it is quite likely that this was one of his personal armours repurposed for presentation to the far side of the world by the Tokugawa.

What James I made of the armour is unknown, but the telescope created something of a stir, and contemporary Japanese descriptions exist. In 2013 these were used to create an approximate replica, and a reception was held at the Tower at which it was displayed, along with James's armour, in the presence of Mr Akira Matsura, Hoin's descendant.

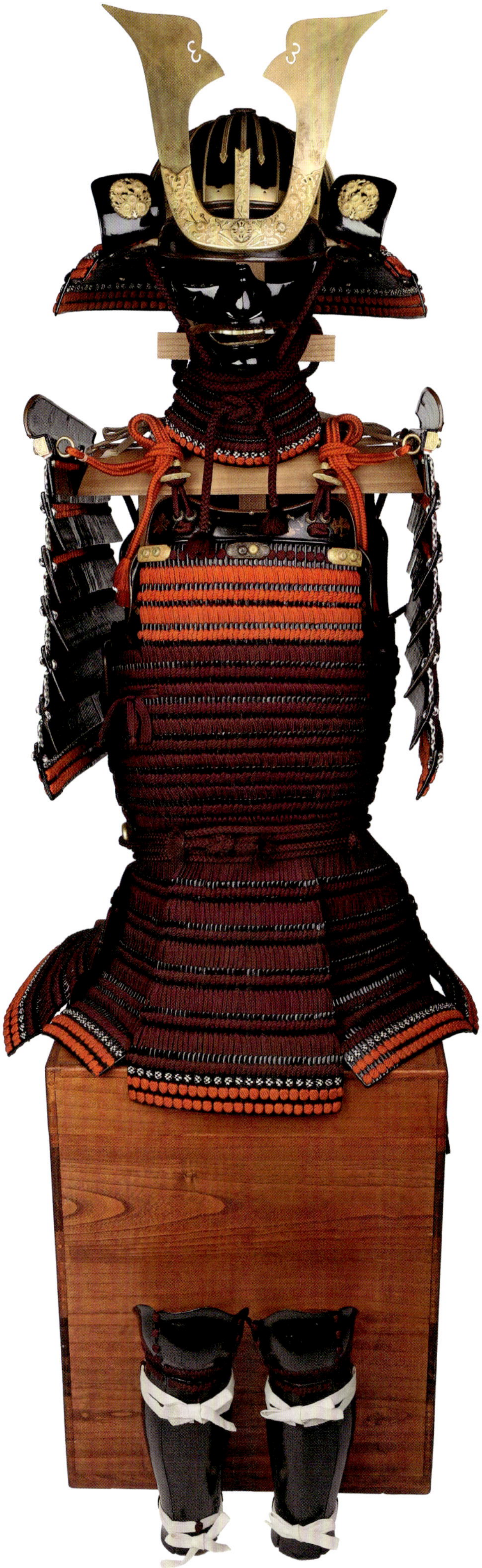

59
Gilt armour owned by Charles I
The Netherlands, *c.*1612 · 11.91

Gilding was widely used to decorate the finest arms and armours, particularly after the re-invention of 'fire' or mercury gilding in about 1490, whereby an extremely thin layer of gold was chemically fused to the underlying steel. Not only could gilding create a literally dazzling effect, but as a bonus it also protected ferrous metal from corrosion. Not surprisingly, its use on armours was much favoured by wealthy patrons, and in some cases (as here) the entire outer surface was gilded: examples include one made for Henry VIII, now in the Metropolitan Museum in New York, and others for Louis XIII of France and the Dutch Stadtholder Maurice of Nassau. Nevertheless, wholly gilded armours belonging to British royalty are a rarity, and this is probably the finest, not least as the surface of the armour is also engraved with a fluid, repeating pattern of foliage and flowers. Regrettably the surface has oxidised over time, but the original brightness achievable is illustrated, for example, in a portrait of Louis XIII [66]. It was originally accompanied by a chaffron and saddle steels decorated in the same way.

Although traditionally and popularly associated with Charles I, the armour was made, like the 'Alexander' harness, for his elder brother Henry. Its commission was perhaps prompted by the example of a gilded armour worn by Maurice of Nassau in a portrait of 1607 by Michiel Janszoon van Miereveldt (1566–1641) commemorating his defeat of the Spanish at Nieuwpoort in 1600: the suggestion is based on Henry's known admiration for Maurice and the fact that he had a copy made of the painting for his own collection in 1610. This would also be consistent with the presence of Maurice's armourer at Henry's court in 1611, where the Prince's requirements could have been discussed and his measurements taken. In any case, the actual procurement is likely to have been the initiative of Sir Edward Cecil, a former cavalry commander in the Netherlands and confidante of Henry, recently appointed by James I to command the British contingent of an international force dispatched to the protestant Rhineland duchies of Jülich and Cleve: certainly it was he who paid £450 for the finished armour in March 1613. Alas, by then the Prince was dead, among other things denying Cecil a powerful patron.

Various historians have suggested that Charles I wore the armour at the battle of Naseby (1645), but this is, alas, untrue, although he did wear 'bright armour' in the field a few days before. In reality, it remained at Greenwich Palace along with other royal armours displayed in the Green Gallery, from where it was sent to the Tower in 1644, where it probably remained for the rest of the war. After the king's execution in 1649 the armour had a narrow escape after his possessions had been dispersed and sold off, when it was rescued by an unknown connoisseur, who noted the 'Armor of great vallew of his late Majesties made last for his owne person put to sale at Somerset House ye which I procured of one Willet to prevent ye loss of it'. By 1660 it was at the Tower, and soon exhibited as the armour of Charles I in the line of mounted equestrian figures in the Horse Armoury, today often referred to as the 'Line of Kings'. Its royal provenance and spectacular appearance have ensured its almost continuous display ever since.

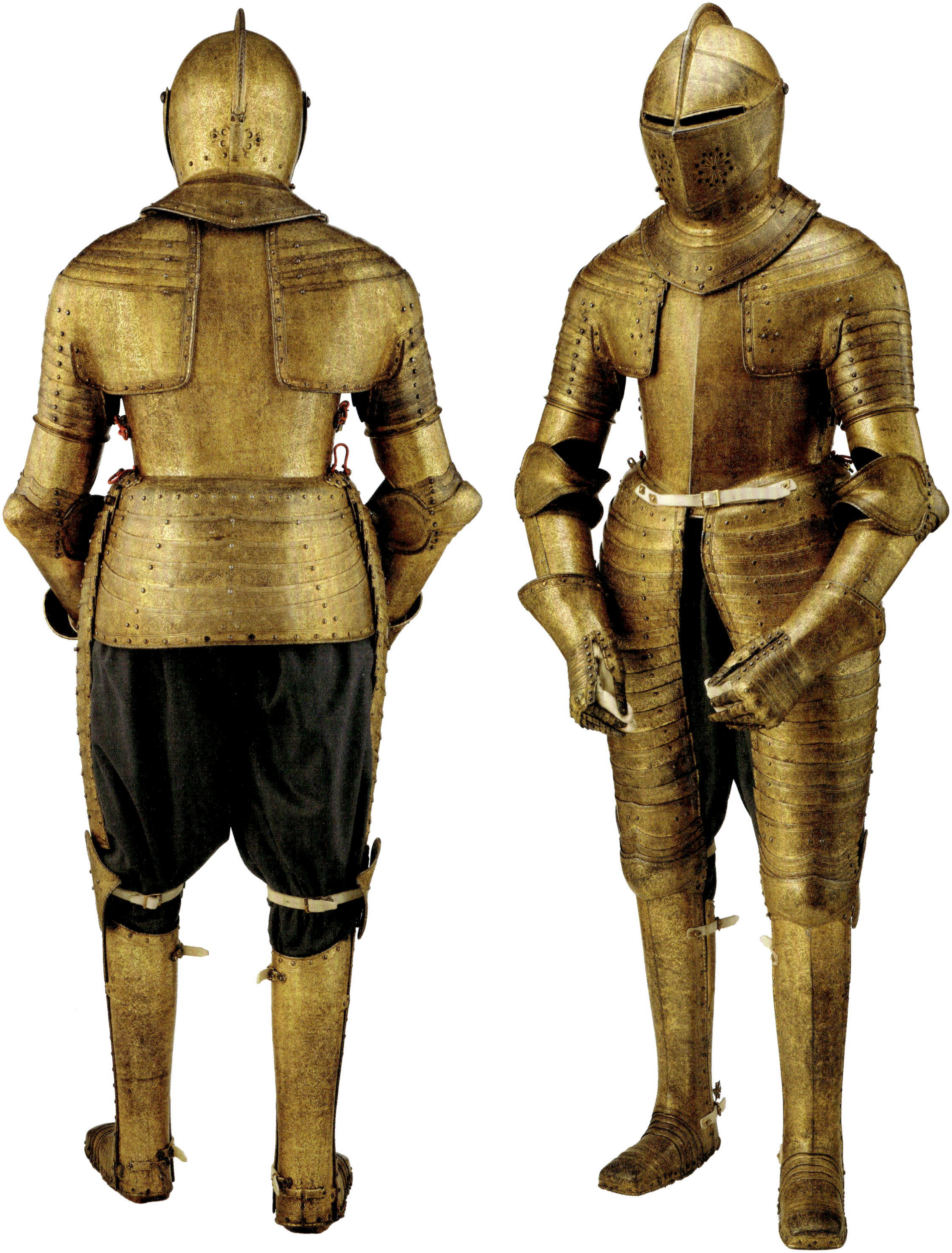

60

A rare Scottish flintlock long gun and a 'Fish-tail' butt pistol

Long gun: Scotland, *c.*1610–19 (lock about 1700); pistol: Scotland, 1619 · XII.737, XII.1786

Gun making developed at different rates and on varying scales in Europe in the 16th and 17th centuries: roughly speaking, in the early 16th century the great gun-making centres of Germany were the most productive, but in the 17th century the most innovative and artistic products were French and the most numerous Dutch. Scotland, although never a volume producer, was relatively precocious, establishing a mature industry by at least 1535, ten years before Henry VIII first appointed a Royal Gunmaker. In fact the earliest known reference to pistols in English comes from a Scottish record of 9 May 1549, relating to the prosecution in Stirling of two men for wounding and the 'schoting of his pistolate'. Scottish guns of the 16th and 17th centuries, including the two illustrated here, tend to display a number of idiosyncrasies, including a taste for all-metal construction and, frankly inexplicably, the omission of a trigger guard. They are also comparatively rare, particularly long guns (as opposed to pistols), of which only twenty-eight survive, five of them in the Royal Armouries collection.

The pistol is of a type known from the 'fish-tail' shape of the butt, used in England in the late 16th century, but particularly favoured in Scotland until the 1640s. This particular form seems to date from 1598–1645. The ignition system employed is the 'snaphance', a name derived from the Dutch *snaphaan*, meaning 'pecking cockerel', which it may be said to resemble, and first appeared in the 1550s. Its main parts were the cock – the pecking bit – which on pulling the trigger sprung forward and struck sparks off a steel plate, igniting the priming powder and thence the main charge: the mechanism was one of various related successors to the wheellock [49], and precursor to the true flintlock, simpler and more reliable, and the commonest ignition system used by Europeans until the 1840s. In this case the lock is on the left side looking down the barrel, implying that the pistol was one of a pair, as this is normally on the right. The lock plate is of brass, engraved with the initials CA, possibly a member of the Alison family of gun makers of Dundee – which would be in keeping with the abundant use of brass – and the date 1619 is engraved on the fence of the pan. All the metal surfaces, including the cock and steel, are engraved with foliage. In 1916 it was described by Charles ffoulkes, Curator of the Armouries, as a 'Pistol of Prince Charles (Charles I)', if perhaps only thanks to its suggestively 'royal' quality, and to his ownership of another gun made by the Alisons.

The long gun, originally using a snaphance, has subsequently been fitted with a flintlock: towards the breech, slightly puzzlingly, is a blank shield beneath a crowned helmet, and the base of the breech is engraved '161', the missing digit necessarily denoting a date between 1610 and 1619; the barrel is engraved with panels of scrolling foliage, including back-to-back 'C' scrolls. Most importantly the stock is entirely, and unusually, of brass, originally gilded, and its length is ingeniously adjustable for use by men of differing height. Similarities to the only other all-brass Scottish long-gun, also adjustable, made by James Low of Dundee and dated 1624, suggest that this may be his work. Meanwhile, the 'C's on the barrel are found on objects associated with King Charles I, just hinting, as with the pistol, that that this piece may have belonged to him.

[164]

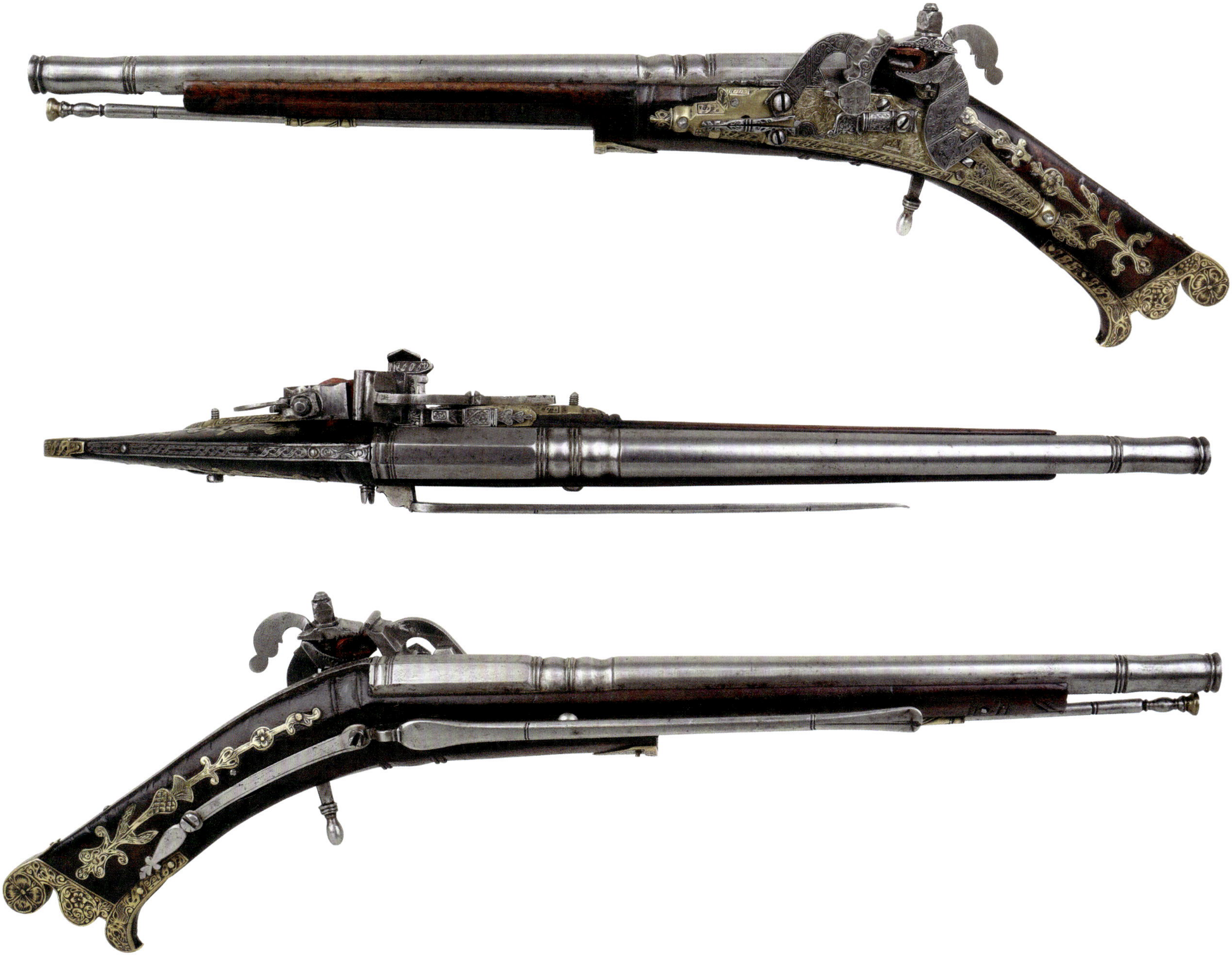

# 61

'Assassin's' crossbow

Italy, 17th century · XI.286

The rarest form of crossbow, of which only eighteen are known from before the 18th century, is a miniaturised version, often referred to as an 'assassin's' crossbow, or in Italy, where this was probably made, as the *balestrino* ('little crossbow'). The earliest known example, in Venice, dates from the late 15th or early 16th century. The Royal Armouries example, made entirely of steel, has a screw-jack spanning mechanism, a top thumb trigger to release the bolt, and a bow with a possible draw weight of about 100 kg. It is usually dated to the 17th century, although, in the absence of decorative detail, this is largely a guess. Experiments with another of similar form suggest that it may have a range of 300 m, equivalent – astonishingly – to that of a full-size crossbow, and sent a 14 cm-long bolt at close range right through a sheep carcase. These tiny weapons were therefore capable of use for game or target shooting, and 19th-century versions were certainly used for both. Their small size, however, particularly suited them for self-defence, and as the popular name suggests, for assassination.

As with small pistols, they were therefore frowned upon by national and municipal authorities, such as in Venice, where they were banned in perpetuity in 1545. In 1561 *balestrini* headed the list of small-scale arms banned by the city's governing Council of Ten, accompanied by savage penalties for contravention: possession brought a year's imprisonment in irons, followed by a fine and banishment; possession discovered after the eight-day amnesty following the decree meant two years as a galley slave, and if the culprit was masked, both hands were to be cut off followed by six years in prison – tantamount to a death sentence. In the 17th century, mere possession carried the death penalty, suggesting that the earlier deterrents had not worked, and clearly the authorities meant business, as in 1664 a Venetian called Zammaria Zerbinelli was convicted and executed for carrying a *balestrino*. The offending weapon was deposited in the armoury of the Doge's palace, and may be one of two remaining there today.

While no successful assassination with a *balestrino* is recorded, in at least two known instances this seems to have been the intention. The first, in Vienna in 1591, involved a catholic priest caught concealing one with intent to murder the Holy Roman Emperor Rudolf II, prompted by his alleged apostasy. The second was in the planning of an attempt in England on the life of Queen Elizabeth I, one of a number hatched in 1593–4 by the disaffected soldier, Catholic and Spanish spy, Sir William Stanley. In this case the two conspirators, Richard Williams and Edmond Yorke were arrested and examined on 20 August 1594, in the presence of the Attorney General Sir Edward Coke, Francis Bacon and William Waad, later Lieutenant of the Tower of London. They learned that the conspirators had discussed 'divers devices how to kill her Majesty. Some spake of a little cross-bow of steel, that should carry a little arrow level, a great way: and if the same did with a small arrow draw blood, being poisoned, she should not escape it.' In the end however, it had been decided that, in April 1594, Williams should shoot the Queen with a small pistol, backed up by Yorke armed with a poisoned rapier. The plot was foiled, and Williams and Yorke were imprisoned in the Tower of London, the former leaving his name ('RIC[H]ARD WI[LLI]AMS') carved into the wall of the Salt Tower, before being publicly executed at Tyburn.

Small and miniature crossbows have been made in numerous forms since the 17th century and many types are manufactured today, notably in the USA, advertised as suitable for hunting, fishing and target shooting.

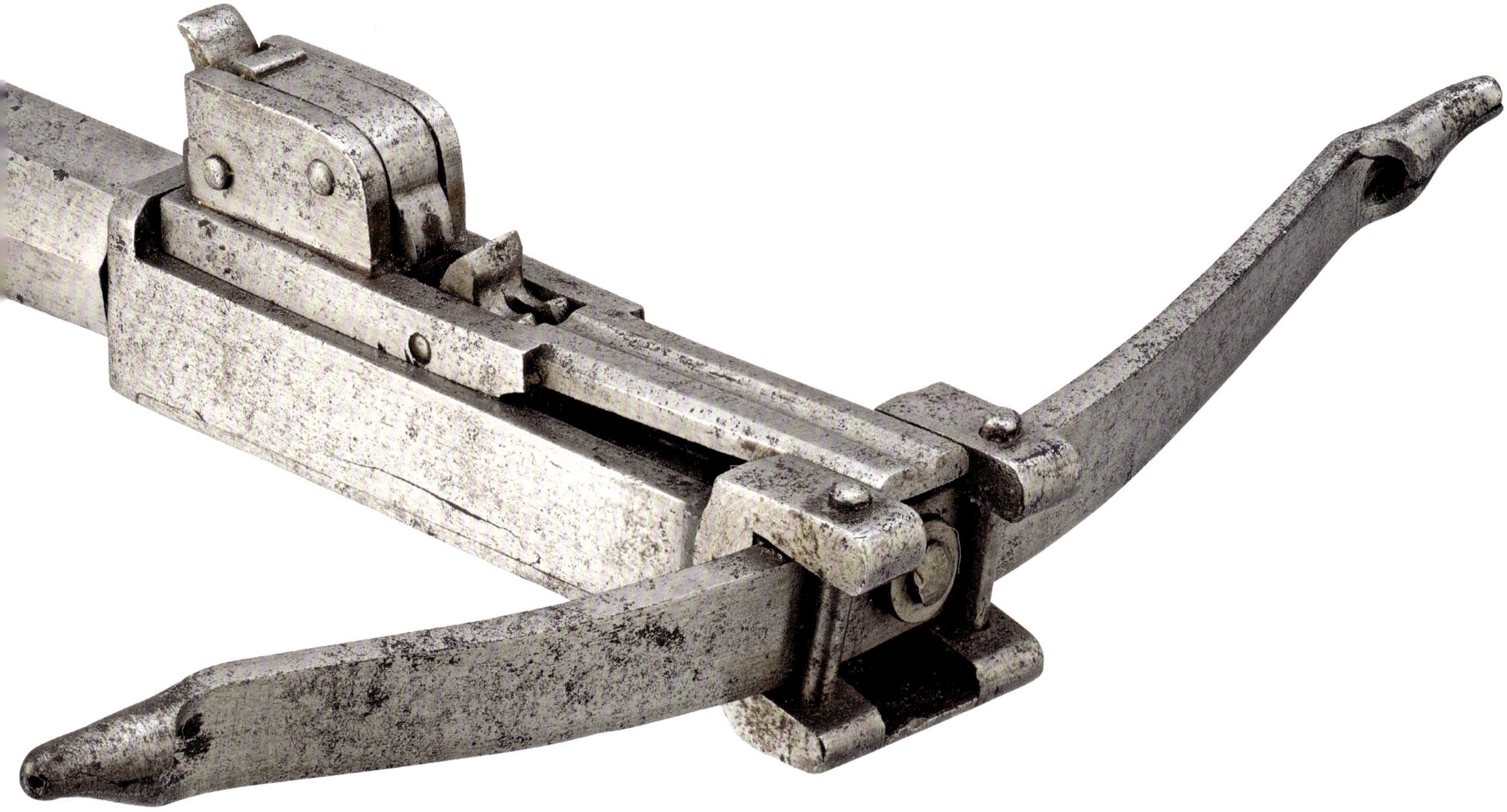

62

South Asian horse armour (*bargustavan*)

South Asia, 16th-18th century · XXVIH.18

At its greatest extent in the early 18th century, the Islamic Mughal Empire covered almost the whole of the Indian subcontinent, including what are now Pakistan, Bangladesh and Afghanistan. It had been founded by Babur (r.1526–30), a descendant of Timur (or Tamerlaine, 1336–1405) and Genghis Khan (1162–1227), and was consolidated and expanded by his most prominent successors, the emperors Akbar (r.1556–1605) and Aurangzeb (r.1658–1707). Under the Mughals India saw a major economic and artistic renaissance, although aspects of their material culture, arms and armour included, continued to reflect their nomadic origins.

The success of Mughal conquests owed largely to their cavalry, an elite corps throughout their history. In the heavier units both horse and rider wore armour. This was made of mail, of solid, hammer-welded and riveted links, and steel plates, together providing a good defence against arrows, swords, lances, maces and saddle axes, whilst also allowing ease of movement. Although surviving components of horse armour are rare, full suits appear in large numbers in contemporary illustrations, often covered in rich textile caparisons.

This South Asian horse armour dates to the time of Mughal rule, and is the most complete remaining example known. It also has a remarkably lengthy provenance as a museum object. Before arriving at the Tower, it had featured in numerous displays across London. It seems to have been acquired and matched with a mail and plate coat and helmet for a rider (also South Asian in origin, but not those currently displayed with the horse armour) by the dealer and showman, William Bullock, as first mention of this assemblage occurs in the guide to Bullock's 'Liverpool Museum' when it was transferred to London in 1809. The grouping was acquired by a similar character, Thomas Gwennapp, and displayed at his succession of shows at the 'Oplotheca' in Bond Street in 1816 (billed as the 'finest collection of antient armour in Europe'), the Gothic Hall, Pall Mall in 1820 and at the 'Royal Armoury' show at Haymarket around 1821. As they travelled between these displays, the coat, helmet and horse armour were repeatedly presented as the equipment of a European knight from the time of the Crusades. This mistaken attribution was probably encouraged by fables attached to the coat and helmet, which had previously been part of Dr Richard Greene's 'Museum of Curiosities' in Lichfield (sold 1793), and were reputedly obtained from Tong Castle in Shropshire, where family legend had associated them with their late-14th century ancestor, the soldier and crusader Sir Fulk Pembridge. Scholarship of arms and armour was still in its infancy in Britain, and this fanciful connection was not disproved; the mail and plate structure of the armour accommodated popular ideas about the attire of a crusader, and thus plugged a gap in display narratives. Following the dispersal of Gwennapp's collection in 1833 the horse armour and accompanying pieces for the rider were bought by the Board of Ordnance and displayed at the Tower of London. The objects' eastern origins, however, continued to go unrecognised, and in a Tower guidebook of 1834 the exhibit was described as 'A Norman Crusader, arrayed in a rich suit of chain mail on his barbed [sic] horse'. It was not until the 1840s that the armours were described as Asian, thanks to observations from, amongst others, the pioneer arms and armour scholar Samuel Meyrick, and the ordnance storekeeper, John Hewitt. Even then, the horse armour was generally thought to be Persian until the 20th century, when its similarities to other Indian mail and plate defences led to its re-attribution. Today, we recognise that this horse armour was amongst the earliest Asian material to enter the Armouries at the Tower, and it occupies its rightful position as a central figure in the Royal Armouries' displays of South Asian arms and armour in Leeds.

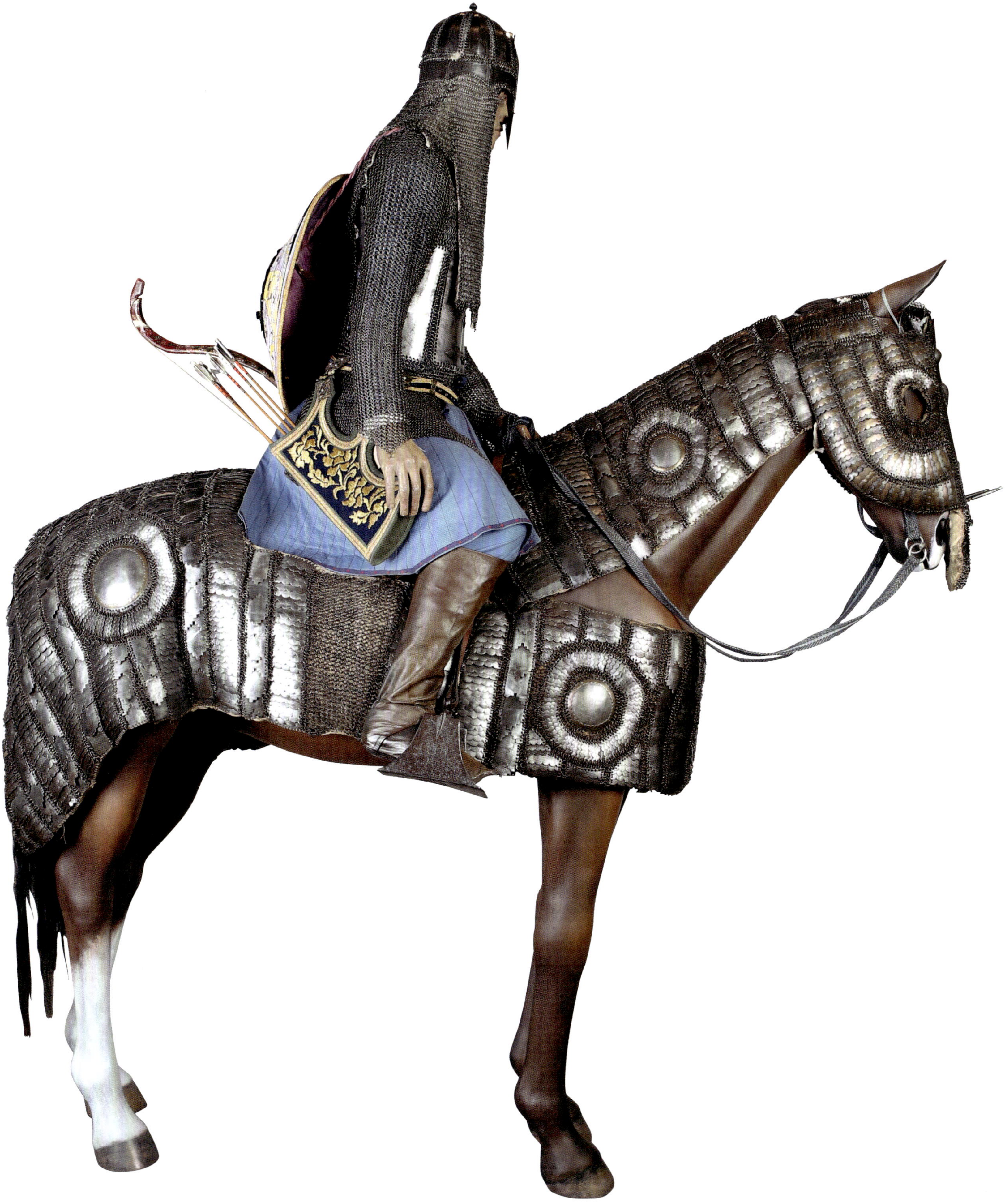

63

Japanese dagger (*aikuchi*) with a German blade

Japan, early 17th century · XXVID.190

Although the Japanese name for the European traders living and working in their country, from 1543 until all but the Dutch were expelled in 1641 was *namban* (loosely, 'southern barbarians'), they had a good deal of respect for their guests' technical prowess and for some of their customs. In the 1580s and 1590s the court at Kyoto briefly adopted Portuguese dress, made in Nagasaki, and the fashion extended to consumables, including wine, and glassware and other manufactured items, among both the mercantile and warrior classes. Most surprisingly, from the middle of the 16th century *namban* helmets and cuirasses, imitated or re-using European originals, began to appear in Japanese suits of armour: an excellent example is one associated with Tokugawa Ieyasu himself, preserved at the Nikko Toshogu Shrine, which includes a reused European cuirass of distinctive 'peascod' shape and a repurposed Spanish cabasset helmet bowl. European swords and other edged weapons, however, were regarded as crude in comparison to their own: the centuries-old process of combining different grades of steel and differential heat techniques produced blades with soft metal in the main body, providing resilient, flexible support for the extremely hard, sharp cutting edge – a product in many ways superior to the European equivalent.

In light of this, the dagger shown here is something of a surprise, for despite the obviously Japanese workmanship to the hilt and other features, the blade is unmistakably European. It bears the stamped inscription 'F(or P) …?S KEISSER ANNO' on one side and 'ME FECIT SOLINGEN 16??', showing it to be the work of Keisser family of swordsmiths at Solingen in the 17th century: the punched maker's mark close to the tang – a sceptre in an oval – is also one used by the family. The scabbard is covered with gilded and painted leather, then popular in Europe for wall covering and upholstery, with a raised texture particularly associated with Dutch leathers (*goudleer*). Nevertheless the blade is not in its original state, but has been reshaped, hardened and polished by a Japanese smith, and the scabbard embellished with a gilded *mon* (crest) associated with the powerful Matsura clan, governors of Hirado. The general form arrived at was that of the *aikuchi*, literally 'meeting mouths', as there is no guard between the hilt and blade.

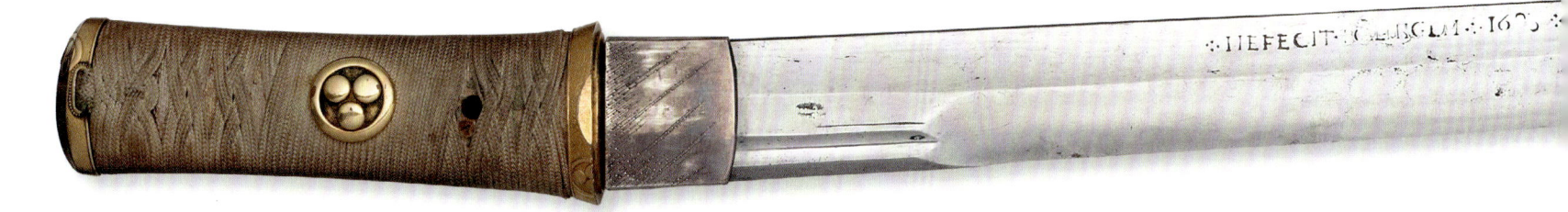

Why and when this adaptation came about is uncertain but there are some important clues. First, we know that high-quality blades from Solingen were popular trade items, regularly exported to Asia and more widely, including by the Dutch East India Company (Verenigde Oost-Indische Compagnie or VOC), founded in imitation of its English equivalent in 1606: its appearance in this part of the world, regardless of the Japanese opinion of western blades, can therefore be explained. Second, the fact that the original trading station of the VOC was on the island of Hirado, combined with the presence of the Matsura *mon*, suggests that the blade was imported by the company and came into the possession of the local ruling family: possibly they bought it, but it seems more likely that it was offered to the family by Dutch traders seeking their goodwill. The adaptation of the blade, meanwhile, could have been carried out by a Japanese craftsman before the gift was made, or later under the Matsura's instructions. As for when they acquired it, this is likely to have been before 1641, when the VOC were expelled from Hirado (although unlike other Europeans allowed to keep a foothold on the island of Dejima). In any case, this unique dagger is a special and astonishing hybrid, combining two very different traditions in one object.

64

Early modern hunting spear

France or Italy, early 17th century · VII.81

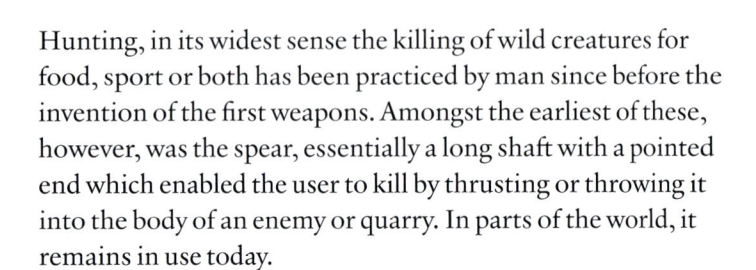

Hunting, in its widest sense the killing of wild creatures for food, sport or both has been practiced by man since before the invention of the first weapons. Amongst the earliest of these, however, was the spear, essentially a long shaft with a pointed end which enabled the user to kill by thrusting or throwing it into the body of an enemy or quarry. In parts of the world, it remains in use today.

Specialist spears for hunting appeared during the European Bronze Age, thereafter taking various forms depending on quarry and technique. One of these, to which loose class this example belongs, was designed to be used on foot and in dispatching dangerous and aggressive animals, which in Europe (including Britain until the 15th century), included bear and wild pigs (*sus scrofa*), usually called wild boar. Male boar in particular are fast, highly aggressive and armed with razor-sharp tusks, enabling them to bring down both men and horses. Boar were (and are) hunted in numerous ways, but heavy, short spears such as this one were used on foot – either against an animal driven towards the hunter, with or without the aid of hounds or nets, or by the pursuing horsemen dismounting for the *coup de grâce*. Keeping the boar at a distance was therefore essential, and a feature of such spears, as in boar swords [45], is a cross-bar to prevent the impaled but still-living animal continuing the attack by 'running up the shaft'. Examples of cross-bars survive from as early as the Bronze Age, and the Greek historian and soldier Xenophon (431–354 BC) described the value of the barred spear in that, once wounded, 'the enraged beast will come on and, but for the teeth of the blade, would shove himself along the shaft far enough to reach the man holding the spear'. 'Bar' or not, the skill and strength required to handle a spear in this way are almost unimaginable. Spears with sockets equipped with 'wings' or 'lugs' were also used by *bestiarii*, Roman gladiators who fought animals.

In the Middle Ages, spear development continued, and by the late 15th century the earlier triangular blade had given way to a more rounded leaf-like form: spears of the type are carried by a group of bear hunters in series of woodcuts forming *The Triumph of Maximilian I* by Hans Burgkmair, first published in 1526. Here the spear heads are mounted on stout rusticated shafts, spirally bound with strips of leather to improve the grip, and the cross-bars are bound to the sockets of the heads with leather thongs.

Later in the 16th century the antler tines or boar tusks so far used to make the cross-bars gave way to the use of a swivelling iron bar mounted on an iron staple, as in this example. The socket and bar, and the lower part of the blade, are decorated in low relief with silver lines, gold stars and other motifs, and the head has crossed palm fronds and four military trophies in gold. Similar decoration is found on other contemporary pieces which include some wheellock pistols built in the French manner. It has been suggested that these pieces, including this spear head, although French in style, were made in Florence by the goldsmith and medallist Gasparo Mola (1567–1640), who for much of his life worked for the Medici family.

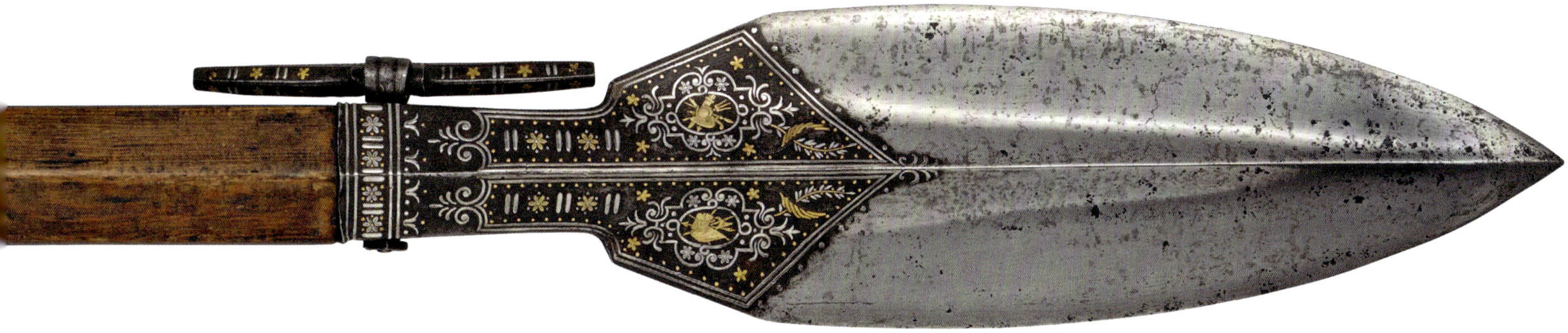

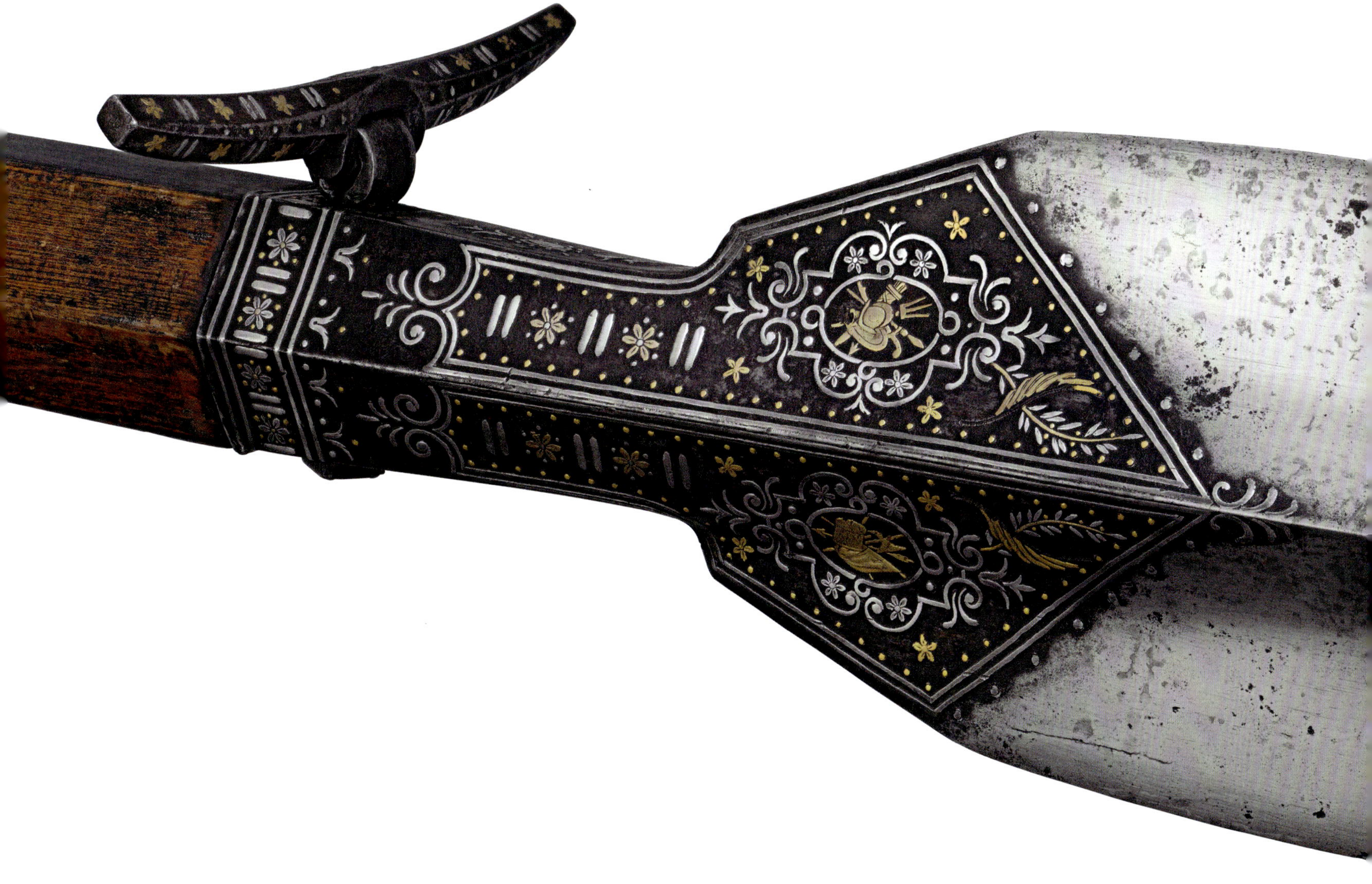

65

Elephant armour (*bargustavan-i-pil*) and tusk swords

South Asia, 17th-18th century · XXVIA.102 (a-f), XXVIM.40 (a-b)

To many people the war elephant brings to mind the Carthaginian general Hannibal, who used them against the Romans in the Second Punic War. At various times they have also appeared in Asia Minor, North Africa, the Levant, the Middle East and elsewhere, but it was in South Asia that their use was most widespread and prolonged, from the first millennium BC until the 19th century. The animals in question were Asian or 'Indian' elephants, weighing up to 5.5 tons, courageous, highly intelligent and tractable. In battle, their noise, enormous size and terrifying appearance could scatter an enemy on their own, but they were capable of throwing men and horses with their trunks and tusks, to which fearsome swords such as these could be attached. Meanwhile, from the security of their backs, especially if mounted in howdahs, crews of several men could rain down missiles on the enemy.

Nevertheless, elephants were as vulnerable as their riders to blades and arrows, and harder to miss, and a wounded animal could inflict more damage in its own ranks than on the enemy. The answer, as with horses, was to protect them, and elephant armour is recorded throughout the Indian subcontinent from at least the 11th century AD, including by the Ghaznavid dynasty, the Delhi sultanate, the Vijayanagara Kingdom, the courts of the Deccan and the Mughal Empire. The variety of armours worn included padded fabric, mail and metal plate structures, and images often show metal armour partly covered in colourful textile caparisons. Even armoured elephants, however, were vulnerable to artillery and firearms, and as the use of these became widespread in the 16th century, the military value of elephants declined: as a result, although still garbed in decorated armour, in warfare they served more as elevated command posts than in actual combat, although their presence and prestige ensured their continued use in processions and ceremonies.

The armour is made up of small metal plates joined by riveted mail to form large panels, and was originally lined with cloth. It originally comprised eight main sections – one defending the head, one covering the throat and three at either side of the body, two of which are missing. When complete the armour weighed nearly 160 kg and incorporated 8,440 plates.

The plate and mail structure of the armour was most widely used in northern and central India, in the 17th century, particularly in Muslim states. However, the peacock, lotus bloom and fish motifs embossed on the larger panels point to its use in a principality which maintained at least elements of Hindu beliefs. As it happens its known history also hints at a southern Indian provenance, as it was acquired by Henrietta, Lady Clive, whilst her husband, Edward, 2nd Lord Clive, was Governor of Madras. After three years in India she returned to England in 1801, bringing a vast array of artefacts and specimens of minerals, flora and fauna and the armour, which she displayed at Powis Castle (Powys). Lady Clive also obtained the tusk swords, recording them in her inventory (*c*.1801), alongside the armour, as '2 swords for the Tooth'. These are of immense interest in their own right as tusk swords are extremely rare, and unlike most surviving examples, these were clearly intended for practical use. Today, the armour appears to be the only surviving example of a near-complete mail and plate elephant armour from the Mughal era in any public collection in the world, a rare reminder of one of the most fearsome combinations of man, beast and weaponry ever known.

[174]

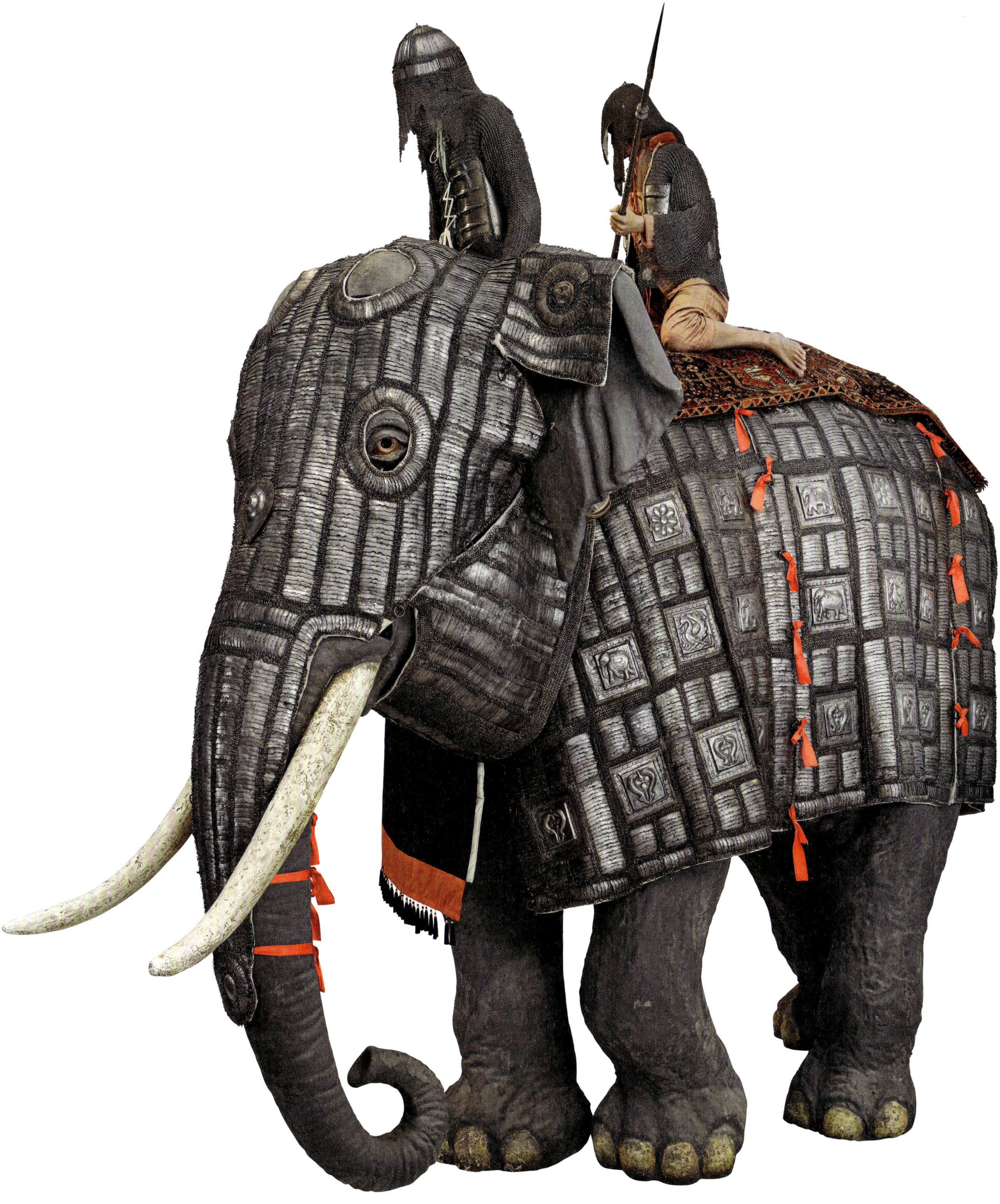

66

'Louis XIII being crowned by Victory', from the school of Peter Paul Rubens

France/Belgium, early 17th century · I.41

Modesty was not a common trait of 17th-century monarchs, and Louis XIII's cult of himself was second only to that of his son, Louis XIV ('the Sun King'). He is shown here in a nonchalant pose, hand on hip, holding a marshal's baton, about to be crowned with a wreath by the winged goddess of Victory. While she appears to part sit and part hover, the king is seated on a pile of arms and armour, both features derived from classical precedent.

The sitter's identity is clear from his face, well-known from numerous portraits, and from his *Ordre du Saint-Esprit* (Order of the Holy Ghost) hung on a green sash. If the painting refers to any particular victory, it must have been to one or more of those over his mother, Marie de Medici, in her last years as Regent, a result of Louis's wish to take power and Marie's to hold on to it. The main candidates are the siege of Caen in 1620 and the battle of Les Ponts-de-Cé (also called Drôlerie des Ponts-de-Cé), near Angers, in the same year. Another picture of the king being crowned by Victory was later painted by Phillipe de Champaigne (1602–74), following the fall of the rebellious Protestant city of La Rochelle in 1628, which shows the city in the background.

The picture is in a close imitation of the style of Peter Paul Rubens (1577–1640) and the allegorical theme is one invented by him: his *Victory crowning a Hero*, in this case a Roman one, painted *c.*1614 for the Gilde van de Oude Voetboog in Antwerp and now at Kassel, is a variant of the subject and has a loosely similar composition, while the winged figure is clearly the model for the picture here. A later version of the Kassel picture, by Rubens but perhaps reworked, exists in Vienna, and sketches of the same *Victory* figure are in Darnstadt. The Royal Armouries picture is now considered to be the work of two Flemish artists who had worked with Rubens, Justus van Egmont (1601–74), who produced other portraits of Louis XIII, and Simon de Vos (1603–76), who, it has been suggested, concentrated upon the armour and weapons. The likeness of the king was not painted from life but from another portrait in Antwerp. His youthful appearance places the picture in the early 1620s.

From the Royal Armouries' perspective, much of the painting's interest lies in the king's armour, and – to a lesser extent – the assorted equipment in the foreground. The former is essentially a cuirassier armour protecting only the upper body, although the solid one-piece tassets imply that it was set up for use on foot. Whether the artist was depicting an actual harness or a well-informed fiction of his imagination is unknown. Its most striking feature is that it is wholly gilded, a feature found in royal armours since at least the middle of the 16th century [59]. Closest to the viewer are two small wheellock pistols, probably of German origin, behind which are a larger ball or 'lemon-butt' pistol (French) and two carbines, all dating from the period *c.*1600–20. To the right foreground, the helmet, cuirass and pauldron belong to a good-quality Flemish pikeman's armour, and a Pappenheimer sword. Both the gilded armour and other equipment proclaim the young king's status and martial valour, but also reflect his lifelong fascination with fine arms and armour that earned him the nickname 'Louis l'Arquebusier'.

Neither the person who commissioned the painting nor its provenance before the 1930s is known, but it was acquired by the Royal Armouries in 1953. Today it is on loan to the Musée de l'Armée, its closest French equivalent, housed in the great military hospital built for Louis XIV.

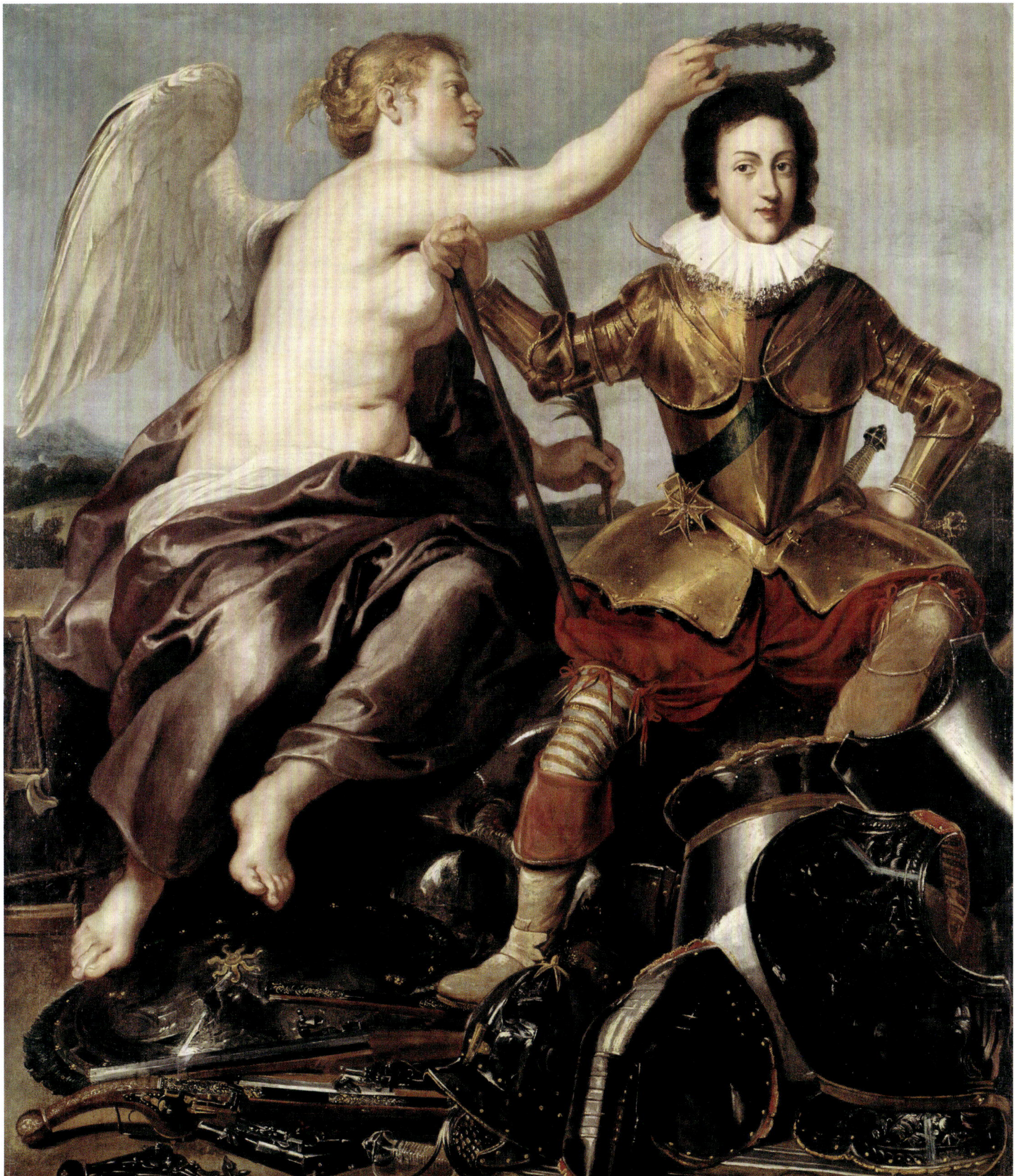

67

Harquebusier armour of Colonel Alexander Popham

England, *c.*1630 · III.1956–8, IX.2785/3624

Alexander Popham (1604–69), Member for Bath in the Short Parliament of 1640 and the Long Parliament of 1640–60, took the rebel side at the outbreak of the First English Civil War in 1642. He served in the West Country and was promoted to Colonel, but, as with many moderates, eventually backed the restoration of the monarchy in 1660. In the present context his importance lies in the armoury he assembled at Littlecote House in Wiltshire, the largest and most important survivor from the era of the English Civil Wars (*c.*1638–53); having remained there ever since, the armoury was saved from dispersal in 1985 by Nick Norman, Master of the Armouries, following a major publicity and fundraising campaign which involved marching to London dressed in armour of the period. The armoury includes a highly significant group of firearms and cavalry armours, probably made available as surplus to the needs of the army in Scotland and Ireland between 1649 and 1652, and bought to equip members of the local militia – part-time troops with territorially limited duties. In addition, and importantly, the assemblage also contains this very rare pre-Civil War cuirass and buff coat dating to *c.*1630, probably worn by Popham himself.

For more than a decade before the Civil Wars many countries had been dispensing with the fully armoured cavalryman or 'cuirassier', due to the cost and cumbersome nature of their equipment and associated changes in battlefield technique, in favour of the relatively lightly armoured 'harquebusier'. Taking their name from the 'harquebus' (a short-barrelled musket) they more typically carried a pair of pistols, a sword and less often the eponymous weapon itself. The metal parts of a harquebusier's armour, meanwhile, consisted only of a backplate, breastplate and helmet, frequently made pistol-proof, either by making the plates thicker or by overlaying two pre-existing breastplates together to create a 'duplex' construction. The armour was tested or 'proofed' with a pistol, leaving a distinctive dent, although this was easily faked.

For general protection, however, the harquebusier relied on the buff coat, highly resistant to sword cuts and spent bullets whilst permitting speed, mobility and tactical flexibility on the battlefield. It was therefore ideal for an offensive role. The first examples used in England, in the 16th century, were made from European buffalo hide (hence the name) but by the mid 17th century were largely from English cattle and deer hides, cheaper and more readily available. In their most basic form, coats were usually made from two skins, made up into a sleeved jacket with mid-thigh or knee-length skirts, although more elaborate versions used more pieces of carefully varied thickness: Popham's rather superior and fashionably tailored coat has the refinement of short elbow-length outer sleeves, doubly protecting the upper arms, with the addition of a stiff leather collar fastened by a series of wooden buttons, providing the perfect support for a stylish lace falling-band. The elegance of Popham's coat concurs with the abundant paintings of Dutch civic guards, the best overall source for the design of buff coats (as so few survive), showing that they could be as much a statement of fashion and prosperity as a practical defensive garment.

Although not the most eye-catching of pieces, Popham's equipment illustrates an important stage in the development of armour, towards the very end of its use, and its interest is enhanced by its known provenance and history. The buff coat is also a rare survivor of the most widely worn protective garment of the later 17th century.

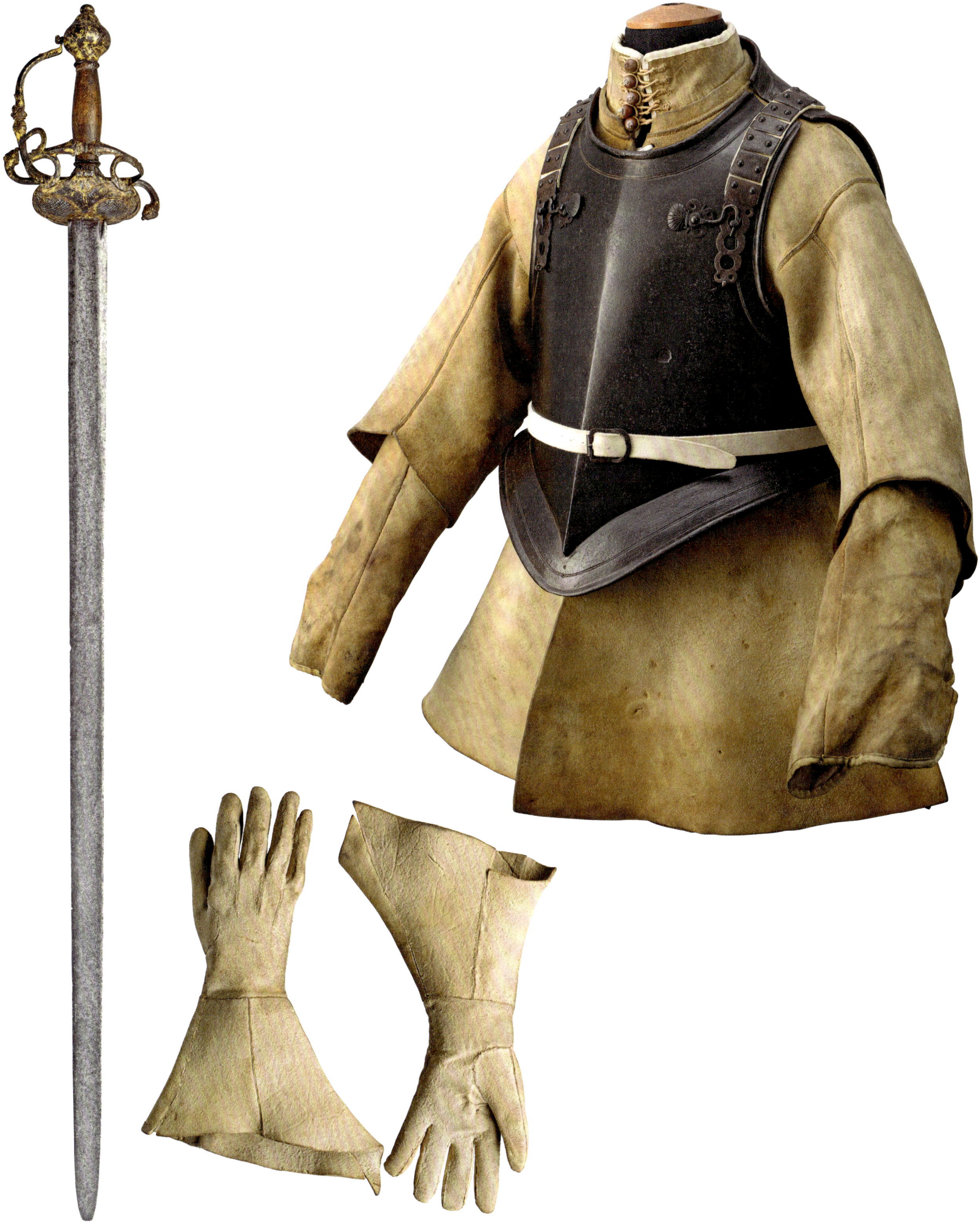

68

'Mortuary' sword, reputedly Oliver Cromwell's

England, *c*.1640 · IX.1096

Oliver Cromwell rose to prominence as a politician and soldier in the British Civil Wars, was instrumental in the defeat, trial and execution of Charles I and ruled the short-lived republic as Lord Protector from 1653 until his death in 1658. Surviving personal effects are few and far between, making this sword of interest as one of ten traditionally associated with him, in addition to representing a particular moment in the development of the weapon itself. The link with Cromwell – historically, its greatest claim to fame – is tenuous but not impossible. The sword was first noted in 1848 in the Naval and Military Museum, founded by the Duke of Wellington in 1831 (and later to become the Royal United Services Institute, or RUSI) in an article written under the pen-name 'Bosquecillo' in *Colburn's United Service Magazine*. The author's identity is still unknown, although he was clearly a member of RUSI and a soldier. He wrote that:

Crossing over to the case next to where Napoleon's relics are, we find some very extraordinary articles. Among them is Cromwell's sword, which he used at the siege of Drogheda, 10th September, 1649, and which bears the marks of two musket balls and several hacks on the blade. Twice his troops mounted the breach, and each time repulsed, until he led them himself, and carried it. He put the whole garrison to death, including the governor.

It was then noted in 1850 in a popular London guidebook (and in many successors), and in the same year in the *Illustrated London News*, as 'the ... sword of Oliver Cromwell', and in 1896 it was illustrated and confidently captioned as such in R.R. Holmes's *Naval and Military Trophies, and Personal Relics of British Heroes*. The story is repeated in the Institute's first published catalogue of 1908, and in subsequent editions. Given the Institute's policy of acquiring objects associated with great men and great moments, the Cromwell provenance presumably dates from its acceptance: according to a chance reference in a work of local history in 1851, we know that the donor was a 'Joshua S. Simmons Smith Esq, as a collateral descendant of the Protector'. Simmons' identity is uncertain, but he was probably the Major of that name, gazetted in December 1831, who appears in the Army List of 1836.

Independent of any Cromwellian association, however, the sword and hilt are of an important period-specific British form known since the 19th century as the 'mortuary sword'. Favoured by cavalry, it was in use between about 1630 and 1670. The term, still current, seems to be a 19th-century invention based on the male head with a 'van Dyke' beard which appears on some examples and was presumably thought to represent Charles I, although in reality swords of this type were used by both Royalists and Parliamentarians, and most examples do not carry it at all. Practically, however, the guard provided good protection, and these weapons are invariably decorated, albeit quite simply, and generally fitted with fairly broad cut-and-thrust blades, usually of a length suitable for cavalry use. In this case the blade bears marks of possible use, with thirteen nicks to the edge (seven toward the tip), but whether these were made during the working life of the sword, let alone at Drogheda, is impossible to tell. The hilt meanwhile has at some later date been japanned in black and painted with gold foliate patterns and trophies of arms of including axes, cannon, cannon balls and a Union Flag, the use of which was restricted to the navy until 1707; possibly this was done, however misguidedly, to support the Cromwell association. As such it belongs to a category of object, well represented in the Royal Armouries collection, fondly associated in the popular mind (and, at the Tower, by the Yeoman Warders of the time) with celebrated historical figures, thereby enhancing their appeal to collectors, visitors and purchasers.

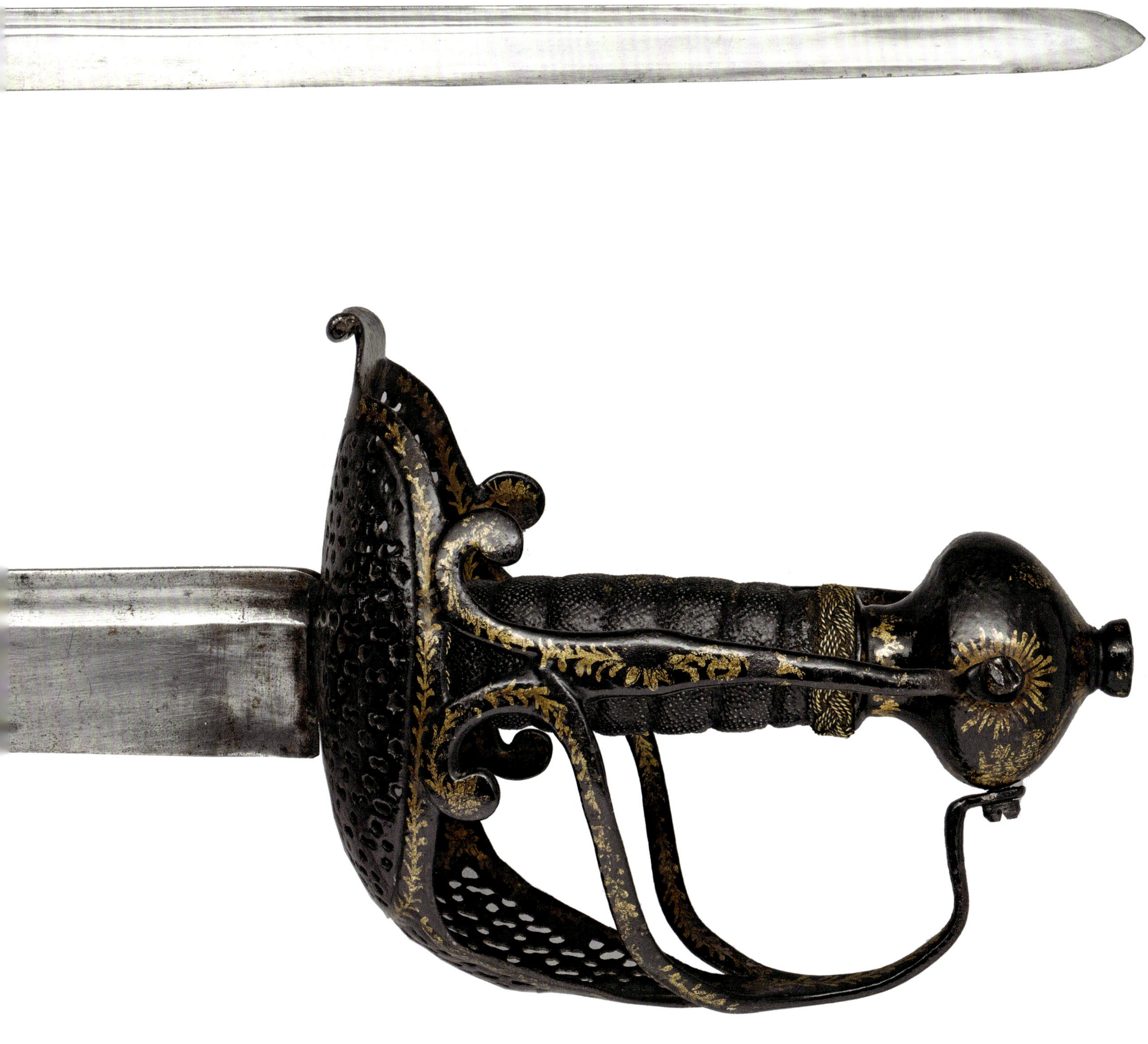

69

Flintlock sporting gun with stock by Jean Conrad Tornier

France, 1646 · XII.154

The study of firearms and gun makers has tended to concentrate on their working parts and technical prowess rather than their decoration, and even less on the subsidiary trades required to make a complete piece. In the case of this gun, a single-barrel 78-bore flintlock sporting gun, the plain octagonal barrel, dated 1646, carries the initials 'IS' of its otherwise unknown maker, while the lock was made by a certain Franz Kruter, of whom little is known other than that he worked in Solothurn in Switzerland. That two craftsmen were involved is a reminder of the fact that in German-speaking lands, the making of locks, stocks and barrels was tightly controlled by exclusive craft guilds, forbidden to stray into each other's territory. In keeping with this, the stock of this gun was made by yet another craftsman. It is its most remarkable feature, and recalls the importance of the relatively unsung (and usually anonymous) 'stocker' and the level of artistic skill they could achieve. Many stockers were also, or mainly, cabinet makers; here, the craftsman was Jean Conrad Tornier, working in the small town of Massmünster (Masevaux) in Alsace. His cabinet-making skills are exemplified by a coffer or box, now in the Wallace Collection in London, which happens to have panels inlaid with exactly the same motifs and designs as found on this gun: it is inscribed '*Fait en Massevaux par Jean Conrad Tornier Monsteur d'harquebisses L'en 1630*' ('Made in Masevaux by Jean Conrad Tornier maker of arquebuses in the year 1630'), showing that Tornier thought of himself primarily as a stocker. This is also the sole source of his identity, along with another signed coffer – now lost – sold in Cologne in 1886.

Tornier's work is particularly distinctive in his use of plain, green and yellow-stained stag horn amongst the plethora of small and large inlays, whether on firearms or caskets. The designs he favoured, well displayed on this gun, usually involve a central inlay depicting a cluster of green or yellow fruit and foliage from which radiate curving branches and tendrils. Among these are disposed occasional birds, such as a parrot and hoopoe (seen here and on the Wallace casket). Around the base of the butt are further inlays depicting huntsmen pursuing stags with spears and hounds, and a little humour creeps in on the left side in a depiction of a bear with a spear threatening a prone hunter. Stylistically, working as he did on the Franco-German border, Tornier reflects the traditions of both countries. He is also known to have stocked at least two other guns in a similar manner, including a wheellock rifle of 1645 in the Wallace Collection; others may exist, but the fact that he was working during the Thirty Years War (1618–48) probably reduced demand.

The Royal Armouries acquired the gun in 1953 from William Randolph Hearst's collection at St Donat's Castle in Wales, which he had purchased in 1922 and subsequently spent a fortune filling with works of art from all over Europe. Hearst's agent bought this gun for the collection at Sotheby's in 1936.

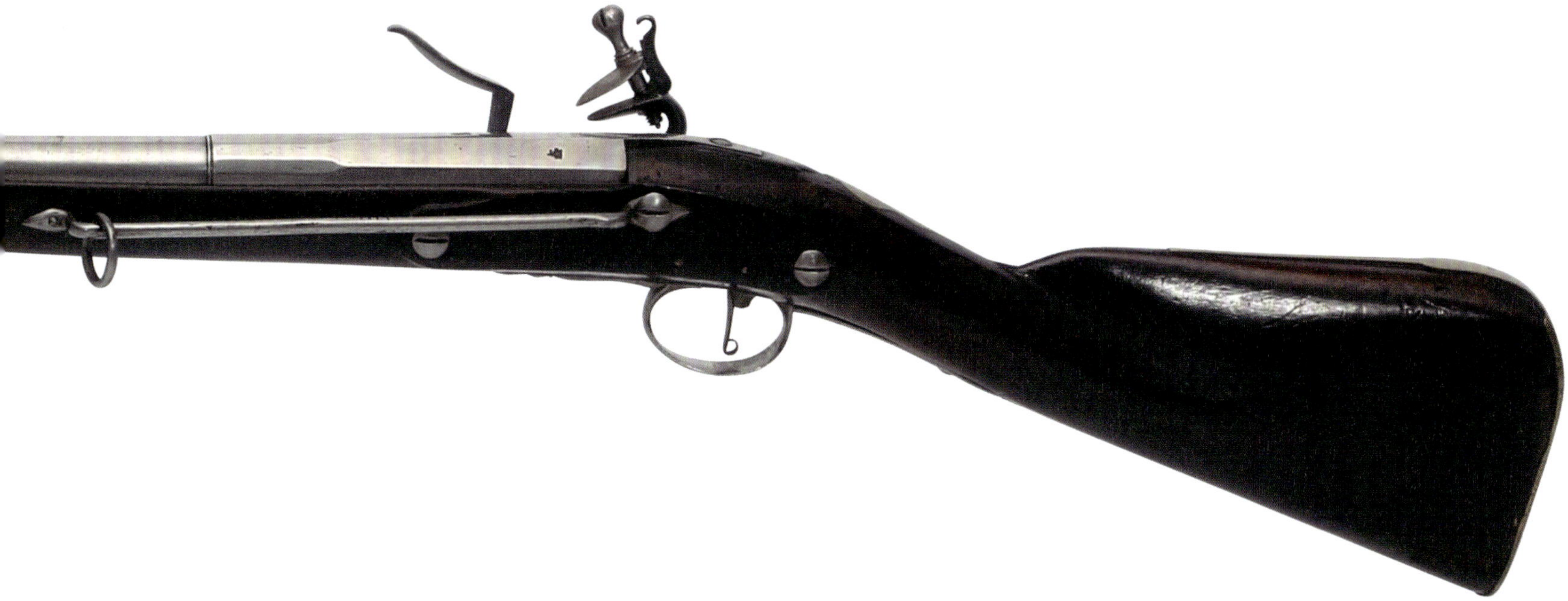

70

Snaphance revolver that inspired Samuel Colt

England, *c.*1680 · XII.1780

Since the dawn of their craft, gun-makers have striven to improve their products' range, accuracy and rate of fire. Advances in propellants and the introduction of rifling were crucial to the first two, and the first major aid to rate of fire, almost as old as the gun itself, was breech-loading. However, apart from the many-barrelled medieval *ribauldequin*, its later variants, multi-barrel handguns and superimposed charges, the earliest and most enduring repeating mechanism – allowing the user to fire successive shots at will – was based on the 'revolving' principle.

As first attempted in the first half of the 16th century, clusters of barrels were designed to rotate against a fixed stock, loosely akin to the familiar 'pepperbox' pistol of later centuries: the earliest survival is a three-barrelled matchlock pistol in the Palazzo Ducale in Venice, dated *c.*1540. By the end of the century snaphances were being fitted, but further development then seemed to lapse until the 1680s. In the revived versions, however, the cluster of barrels was replaced by a 'cylinder' of chambers which rotated behind a single fixed barrel – the basic principle of the modern revolver.

This example has a smoothbore barrel, relatively short and small in calibre at 241 mm and 38 bore (12.6 mm), although the large cylinder still makes for an extremely heavy pistol at 2.8 kg. The cylinder is brass, as is most of the metalwork, and the stock of burr walnut: the lock is technically of the by-then archaic snaphance type, but deliberately so, to allow the cylinder to rotate. The most remarkable feature of the gun, however, is that whereas in most cases the cylinder was turned by hand, this is the first known example of one that that rotated automatically whenever the piece was cocked: to fire it, once all chambers were loaded and their pans primed, required no more than pulling back the cock, pivoting back the steel (from which the spark was struck), and pulling the trigger. As such it is a landmark in firearms technology, preceding any attempt until the 1730s and Samuel Colt's famous 'single-action' design by some 155 years. Certainty as to the inventor, alas, eludes us, although technical similarities to signed guns suggests it may have been the London gunmaker John Dafte (d.1697).

Given the key features shared between this 17th-century gun and Colt's 1836 patent, it is interesting to know that Colt saw it, then in the collection of the United Services Institute, during his well-publicised visit to London in 1851. However, although Colt was indeed (wrongly) accused in 1852 of stealing a revolving arm from the Tower of London, and of plagiarising other people's ideas – particularly the Wheeler-Collier model of 1818 – the mismatch in dates rules this one out as his source. He was, however, highly sensitive to any slur on the utter originality of his invention, and although admitted knowledge 'since 1835 of the existence of ancient examples of repeating fire-arms', was quick to emphasise their impracticality. In a lecture at the Institute of Civil Engineers in London in 1851, he cited this one specifically:

In the collection at the United Service Museum, London, is a brass model pistol, with six chambers, said to have been constructed in the time of Charles the First. This specimen displays more ingenuity and greater skill in its design, than any of the early weapons hitherto discovered; but …had it been used, it would have been blown to pieces by the first discharge.

Whether his last statement is correct is unclear but Colt's defensive damning with faint praise hints at a grudging respect, and only emphasises what an ingenious and precocious weapon this is.

[185]

71

Scythe blades captured from the rebel army at Sedgemoor (1685)

England, before 1685 · VII.960–1

Among the Royal Armouries more unusual possessions are two worn and battered scythe blades, mounted on straight hafts to form the business ends of improvised weapons, picked up on the battlefield of Sedgemoor in 1685. The story of James, Duke of Monmouth and his rebellion has been told many times, but suffice it to say, he was the illegitimate but Protestant son of Charles II: whilst in exile in Holland, he was persuaded in the spring of 1685 to rebel against his newly succeeded uncle, James II, whose highly politicised Roman Catholic agenda was causing widespread discontent. Monmouth anchored off Lyme Regis (Dorset) on 11 June, and his eighty men were swiftly joined by local recruits. After some minor successes, however, he was crushingly defeated at Sedgemoor (near Bridgewater, Somerset) on 6 July and beheaded on the 15th on Tower Hill. The notorious Bloody Assizes then dispatched over 300 of his followers and hundreds more were transported.

Monmouth had brought armour and some equipment for about 3000, half for cavalry which, as so few horsemen joined his cause, went unused. His men – at their greatest numbers some 7000 – were therefore hopelessly ill-armed, as contemporaries observed, with the occasional old sword, halberd or fowling piece, but otherwise with clubs, slashers and 'prongs' (pitchforks). But it was the re-hafted scythe which was to be the most important of Monmouth's improvised weapons, and certainly the one for which the rebellion is best remembered. In working form the scythe is used with both hands, upright, for reaping hay and cereals, and has a long, light, rough blade at right angles to the haft. A few minutes of blacksmith's work, however, can bend the tang round to be in line with the blade, ready to be fitted to a six – to eight-foot pole. The resulting weapon was used across Europe, at least from the 1490s, in countless insurrections and resistance movements, right up to the defence of Pomerania against the Wehrmacht in 1939.

These weapons won few battles and no wars, but, as described by a Sedgemoor eyewitness, were 'desperat' (that is, frightening and effective), their reach and carving-knife sharpness easily killing and mutilating both men and horses, while their psychological impact on regular troops, new to such things, incited terror and panic. Huge numbers survive in museums across Europe, especially in the East, although in England, perhaps only the present two and the twelve examples in the church at Horncastle (Lincs), possibly associated with the Pilgrimage of Grace and related risings of 1536.

Monmouth himself had faced re-hafted scythes in 1679 at the battle of Bothwell Bridge (Lanarkshire), and, ironically, it was perhaps this experience that prompted him on 19 June, at Taunton (Somerset), to commandeer 'all such scythes as can be found' from neighbouring villages, for speedy re-hafting. As contemporaries record, 'sithemen' played an active part in skirmishes before Sedgemoor, and up to about 500 in the battle itself, where they seem to have been deployed as elite shock troops in the manner of grenadiers.

Having seen the carnage of the battlefield on the day after, an eyewitness later wrote that 'these Sithes …were brought up to London and laid up in the Armoury of the Tower of London'. There they were duly inventoried in September 1686, and from at least 1693 visitors were regaled with lurid tales about their performance. They remained on display, in decreasing numbers – finally only these two – until the 1990s. In the future they will be displayed again, as a telling memento not only of Monmouth and his doomed rebellion, but of countless others across the centuries facing forces they could rarely hope to beat, and as representatives of a weapon largely ignored by the mainstream study of arms and armour.

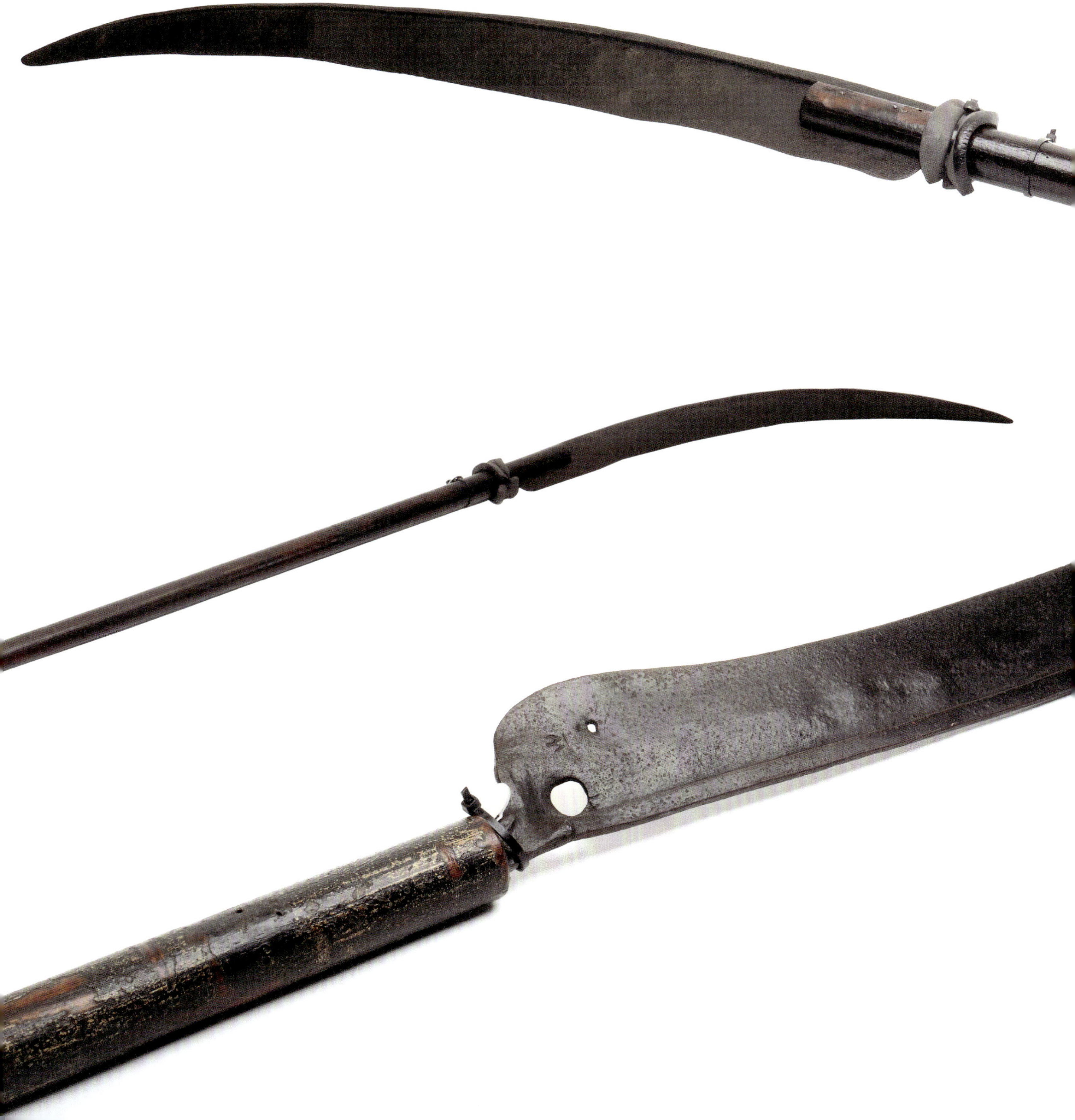

72

Armour of King James II

England, 1686 · II.123

James II, son of Charles I and younger brother of Charles II, was king of England and James VII of Scotland from February 1685 to December 1688. Thanks to his attempts to bring back Catholicism he was driven from the throne by William of Orange, his Protestant son in law, ruler of the United Provinces of Holland, and subsequently William III. The key role of parliament in these events permanently increased its authority over the crown, an important episode in constitutional history swiftly called the 'Glorious Revolution'. In earlier years, however, James had distinguished himself both as a soldier and sailor, and had worn many and varied armours in the field. As king, in 1686 he took delivery of the 'Harquebus Armour' illustrated here, embellished with 'white parcel gilt & chased and lined with Crimson sattin', comprising 'a Breast carbine Proof, Back Pistoll Proofe, Potte Pistoll Proofe' and a 'Long Elbow Gauntlett'. Although following the format prescribed for cavalrymen since 1663, and wholly practical, as shown by the 'Proofe' (the test of its efficacy against bullets) the harness was of exceptional quality, costing £100 rather than the £2 required for ordinary 'munition' equivalents. Armours of this type were named after the 'harquebus' [67], the heavy handgun used by earlier forms of cavalry: in James's time the horsemen carried a sword, carbine and pistols, wielded in the right hand, while the left, protected by the gauntlet, managed the reins; the 'potte' was the helmet. In this case all components are decorated with trophies of arms, formalised clusters of weapons, banners and standards, punched and engraved into the surface. Originally silvered and gilded (the 'parcel gilt'), these are arranged in vertical bands on the back and breast, around the brim and crown of the helmet, and along the upper surface of the gauntlet. In addition, at the neck of the breastplate is a crown above crossed sceptres, flanked by the letters I and R, for *Iacobus Rex*, ('James the King'). A number '2', differentiating him from his grandfather James I, appears above. Most strikingly, the faceguard – normally consisting of plain vertical bars – takes the form of the royal coat of arms flanked by its 'supporters', the lion and the unicorn, cut out of sheet steel and finely engraved. Signs of wear and repair show that the armour saw hard use, although (given its date) not in battle but during hard-riding military reviews, in which James took great interest. Under the armour, as was normal at the time, the king wore a 'buff coat' of thick leather, and the example shown here, although not his, is of the period.

This harness occupies a special place in the history of armour. First, it was the last example commissioned for field service by an English monarch, as by the 1680s the use of armour was waning fast. Second, it is the only English armour known to have been made for a king of England by a named London craftsman (as opposed to the elite Greenwich armoury [31]) and showed, if at the eleventh hour, what they were capable of. Finally, Holden himself was the last of the London armourers and his death in 1709 brought centuries of tradition to an end.

[188]

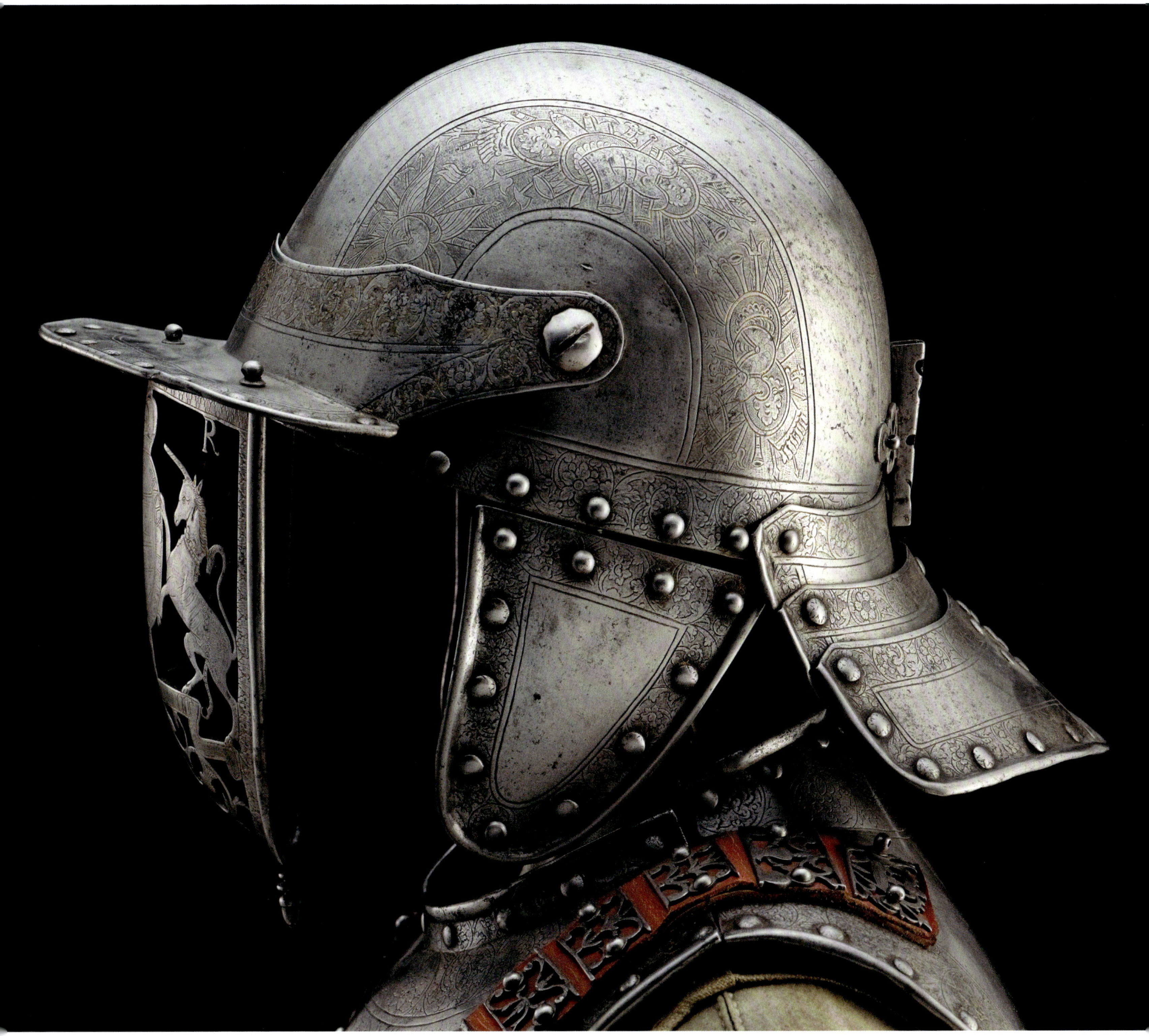
R

73

Flintlock sporting gun by Bertrand Piraube

France, *c.*1685 · XII.1690

This volume features many highly decorated items of arms and armour used as diplomatic gifts, acknowledging and enhancing the status of both donor and recipient. The gun depicted here is among them. It was made for Louis XIV of France and was, according to his descendants, given by the king to Charles Lennox (1672–1723), first Duke of Richmond, natural son of Charles II and his mistress, Louise de Kéroualle. It remained in the family's possession until acquired by the Tower Armouries in 1958.

Technically speaking, the gun is a flintlock 20-bore smoothbore sporting gun with a single 42-inch barrel, octagonal at the breech and round for the remainder: probably the piece's most astonishing feature is that this is not steel but solid silver, as found in a few late-18th century pistols but probably unique in a long-gun. The use of silver might appear impractical, but a gun that was unusable or dangerous to its user would have been pointless and a poor gift, and the fact that two of the known silver pistols have Tower proof marks shows that such things were useable.

Precious metal apart, the gun is remarkable for its lavish decoration. The barrel is chased with trophies of arms, foliate scrolls and at the breech, a figure of the god Mars standing on a pedestal under a canopy. The lock plate (also silver) and other steel fittings are chiselled with classical imagery. The butt plate bears the figure of a victorious general in Roman armour, the screw plate is chased and pierced with an image of Apollo in his chariot, and the silver escutcheon plate has a portrait of Louis XIV as a Roman emperor. The walnut stock is inlaid with scrollwork in silver wire. On either side of the butt is an oval medallion depicting a camp scene with the sun god – an allusion to the king – in a four-horse chariot with a sceptre topped with a fleur-de-lys. The lock plate is inscribed '*piraube aux galeries*', identifying its maker as the Frenchman Bertrand Piraube (d.1725), barely known before 1670, but described in that year as '*maitre armurier*', and given lodgings and a workshop by the king in the 'Galeries du Louvre': this was the ground floor of the gallery linking the Louvre to the Tuileries Palace, occupied by craftsmen under royal patronage. However skilled, Piraube drew on the services of others when it came to the overall design of its decoration, in this case probably Jean Bérain the Elder (1637–1711), a chief designer to the king from 1674, who published editions of his *Diverses Pièces très utiles pour les Arquebuziers* in 1659 and 1669. The chiselled decoration to the lock, probably carried out by a medal maker (such as Jérôme Roussel) is based on designs published in 1660 by Adrien Reynier (called Le Hollandois), also a gun maker, who was to succeed Piraube as *Arquebusier Ordinaire du Roi* in 1723.

The story of Louis' benefaction derives from little more than family tradition, but is perfectly plausible: Lennox and his French mother were both used for diplomatic ends by both kings, and he certainly visited Paris in 1681–2, was enthusiastically received there by Louis there in 1685, and again in 1688 when he joined a wolf-hunt with the king at Versailles on 23 March. Alternatively it may have been a gift to Charles II, who passed it on to his son. Either way it would have made a more than fitting present: as stated in the Christie's catalogue of 1958, 'This is probably the finest firearm ever offered for public sale in this country'.

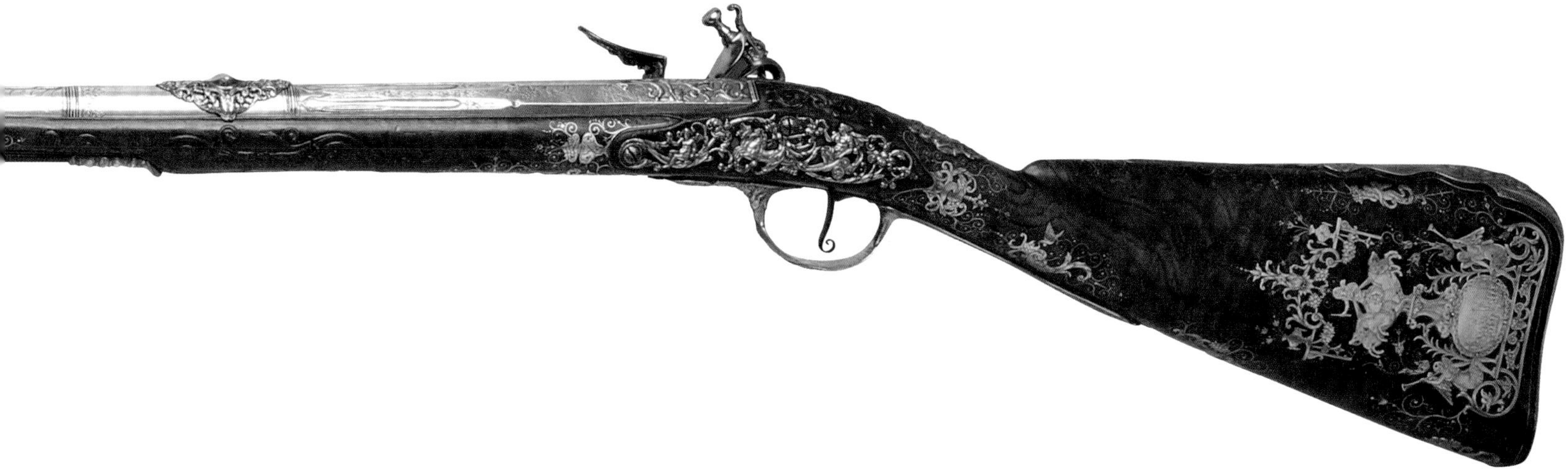

74

Grinling Gibbons' wooden horse

England, *c.*1686 · XVII.18

A life-sized sculpture of a horse, this 'Treasure' is remarkable as a component of one of the earliest and most enduring arms and armour displays at the Tower of London – the Horse Armoury, now often called the 'Line of Kings'. It is also a work of art in its own right and occupies an interesting place in the development of mounted statues in England.

The origins of the 'Line of Kings' date from before the English Civil Wars, but in approximately the form that survived (if much changed) into the 20th century, it consisted of a row of sculpted horses carrying armoured figures representing English kings and noblemen. Its purpose was essentially propagandist, underlining the ancestry and legitimacy of the monarchy, restored, after the vulgar blip of the Interregnum, in the person of Charles II in 1660. This sculpture, however, was made a little later, thanks to James II's enhancements in replacing the existing figure of his father Charles I and adding a new one (now lost) for his late brother, Charles II. The horses were made by the leading sculptors and carvers in Restoration England: Thomas Quellins, Marmaduke Towson, William Morgan, William Emmett, John Nost and Grinling Gibbons (1648–1721), who made the two new ones. Gibbons, though English, had been born and trained in the Netherlands, moved to England in 1667, was introduced to Charles II by John Evelyn in 1671, and was employed at Windsor Castle between 1676 and 1682. He was appointed Master Carver in Wood to the Crown, and went on to carry out many famous commissions – both statues and decorative carving. The choice of Gibbons in 1685 is therefore not surprising, and Ordnance Office records show that in 1685 he had been paid £40 for supplying the horse for Charles II and 'ye sd late Kings face to be placed in ye said armour', although those for Charles I's figure, delivered in 1687, are lost: the identification of this horse as Charles I's depends, reasonably securely, on its early association with the monarch.

The horse's body is of hollow, box-like construction, using four thick elm planks, with legs, and neck made up of separate pieces with a solid head. The tail is modern. Originally painted off-white, with a black mane, tail and hooves, it has since been eight times re-painted. The pose is that of a spirited beast, highly animated and lifelike, and the detail, notably the head and mane, is superbly carved. A stallion of fourteen hands, he probably represents a '*ginete*', a relatively small, fast and part-Arab breed originating in Andalusia, suitable for use by light cavalry: highly prestigious, these horses had been bred at the royal studs since the reign of Elizabeth I, and Gibbons' choice of model for Charles I would have been entirely appropriate.

Whilst the armours made sculpting the riders' bodies unnecessary, makers and patrons considered their creations as equestrian statues. Although, deriving from Roman tradition, these were known in Renaissance Italy, they were latecomers to England – the earliest may be the 'Lumley Horseman' of the 1580s currently on loan to the Armouries. Italian (small-scale) bronzes of horses were, however, brought to England in the early 17th century, notably those by Giovanni Bologna (1529–1608) given to Henry Prince of Wales in 1612. Others were owned by James I and Charles I: the full-size statues of Charles I by Hubert Le Sueur (*c.*1580–1658), Giovanni's pupil, was commissioned in the 1630s, but none then appeared until after the Civil War. As Jeremy Warren has pointed out, the pose and detailing of the Tower horse derives firmly from these models, and can be attributed to a personal admiration of the Italian originals by Gibbons and his fellow sculptors.

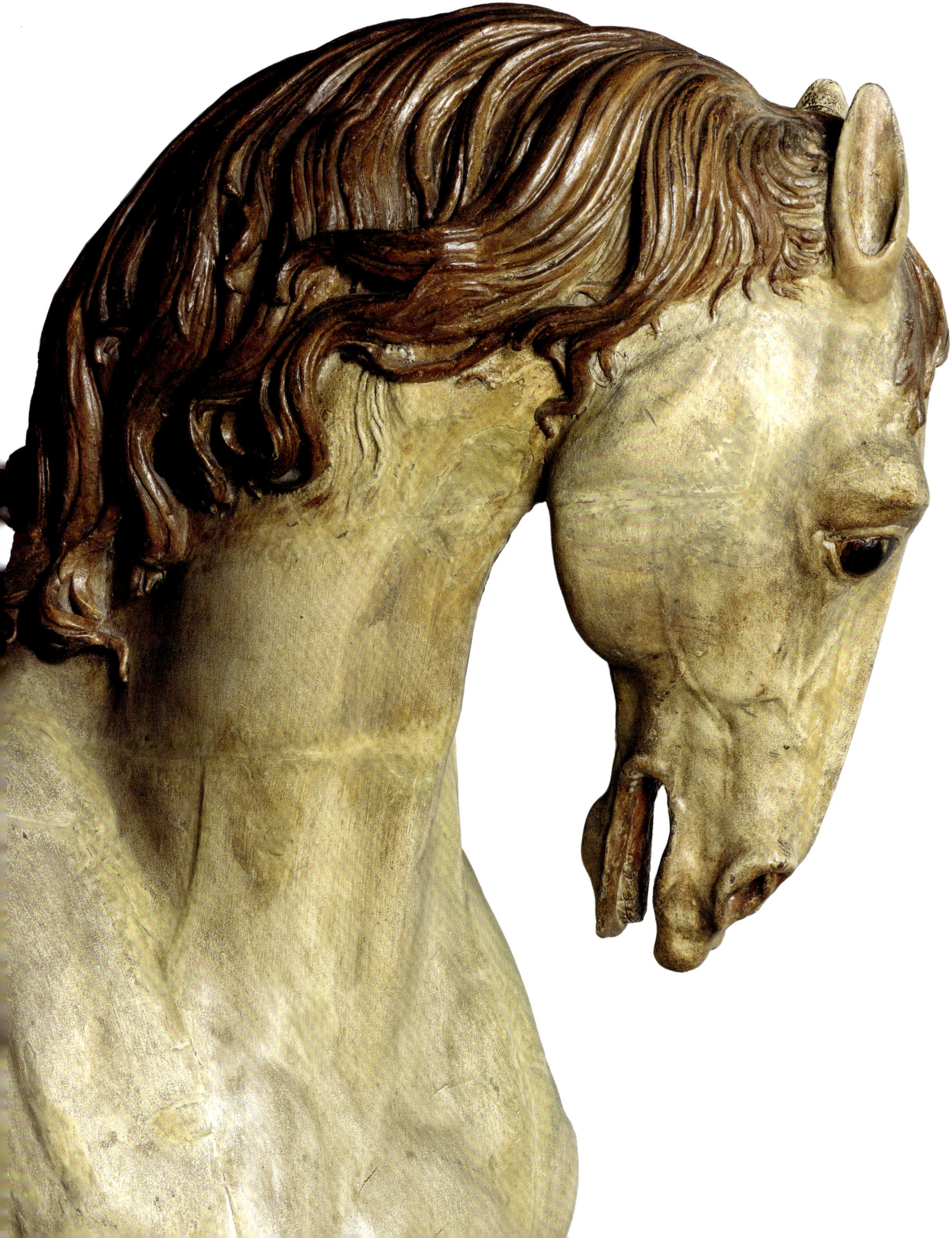

75

Flintlock sporting gun for George Legge, 1st Baron Dartmouth

England, 1688 · XII.11769

The decades after the restoration of the English monarchy in 1660 saw a rapid expansion of the Board of Ordnance's activities at the Tower of London, including the making, assembling and storage of small arms. This example is distinguished for being one of only two known sporting guns made at the Tower, by its quality, its well-known maker, the identity of the client, and the intriguing inscriptions on the butt plate. The first of these reads:

THE BARRELL MADE BY MOORE OR TURK | CRISP MADE Ye REST ALL ENGLISH WORK | Ye SILVER TRIED WITHOUT DECEIT | 1688

As claimed, the barrel is Turkish, of the late 16th century, with inlaid silver floral motifs and an Arabic inscription meaning 'God Protects'; these barrels were much prized in the 17th century, and this one was conceivably given by Louis XIV, who had several similar ones, to James II or possibly to Dartmouth himself. The second line then identifies the maker as (Henry) Crisp (otherwise Crispe or Crips), Gunmaker to the Ordnance and Furbisher in the Tower of London from 1680 to 1707, who lived and worked in the castle. The third line proclaims the quality of the silver used in furnishing the gun, and the fourth (to scan, read out as 'Sixteen Hundred and Eighty-eight'), the date of its completion. The gun is stocked in burr walnut and lavishly decorated with inlaid silver wire, following designs published in 1684 by the French court gun maker, Claude Simonin (c.1635–93), and applied solid silver mounts bearing by

[194]

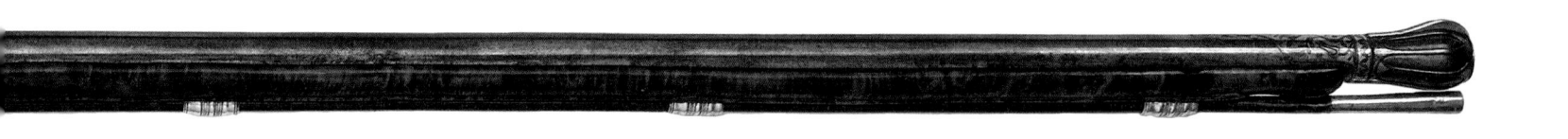

the London silversmith William Knight (better known as sword hilt maker), and an Assay Office mark dating it to 1686–7. As such it has the distinction of being earliest-known English sporting gun with silver furniture.

Underneath Crisp's is a second inscription in an elegant cursive hand, which reads: '*Ex Dono Georgy Baronis Dartmouth Apud Spithead*' ('By the gift of George, Baron Dartmouth, at Spithead'). The man in question was George Legge (1647–91), 1st Baron Dartmouth since 1682, who in 1688 was simultaneously Master General of the Ordnance, Admiral of the Fleet, and Constable of the Tower of London. His rather chequered career, however, began and ended in the navy, first seeing service under Charles II in 1666 and then rapid promotion under his brother and successor, James II. In 1688 Legge's task was, of course, to prevent William of Orange and his forces from landing, but unfavourable winds drove his fleet into Portsmouth harbour, and the Dutch landed unmolested in Torbay (Devon) on 5 November. What followed was a near-bloodless coup which saw James's deposition and the joint coronation of William III and Mary II in April 1689. Legge was personally shattered by his failure, and (while not dismissed by James) in January 1689 William stripped him of his offices. In 1691 he was imprisoned and died at the Tower, aged forty-three.

What happened to the gun, however, is less clear. The inscription tells us no more than that it was owned by Legge in or by 1688, and that it was to be presented to an unidentified recipient on board ship at Spithead, the navy's favoured anchorage outside Portsmouth harbour. Perhaps it was, but all we do know is that it belonged to the Wyndham family – with whom there is no known connection to the Legges – at Orchard Wyndham (Somerset) in the 1960s.

[195]

76

Partizan for Louis XIV's *Gardes du Corps*

France, *c.*1680–90 · VII.1358

The partizan derives from the broad-bladed infantry spear of the late Middle Ages, distinguished by its wide double-edged blade, with upward – and outward-curving wings at the base to help parry sword cuts, and its relatively short haft (rarely more than 2 m). In the 16th century it was widely adopted and adapted by personal guards and retainers of noblemen and monarchs, in part because the wide blade provided an excellent field for decoration and the display of heraldry and insignia. Their use lives on today in the case of the Papal Swiss Guard, founded in 1506, whose members, in full dress, carry partizans or halberds. On ceremonial occasions, the British monarch's bodyguard of the Yeomen of the Guard and the Yeomen Warders of the Tower of London also bear partizans, emblazoned with the royal cypher. In a military context they were carried as a badge of rank from the 17th century, and its derivative, the 'spontoon', was carried by non-commissioned officers in the British army until 1830.

This example, dating from the late 17th century, is a rare survival from the court of Louis XIV, the longest-reigning, most powerful and flamboyant monarch of the age. During most of his reign he had two large groups of guards, one serving 'outside' ('*dehors*') and the other for 'within' ('*dedans*'). The latter group came into being in his reign, remained in existence until the end of the Ancien Régime, and comprised four companies: the bodyguards, the 'Swiss Guards' (or '*Cent Suisses*'), the provost-guards (or '*hoquetons*') and the guards of the door. The bodyguards were further divided into four companies, three French and the other Scottish, the oldest and the most prestigious, among whom twenty-five men had the status of 'Archers of the body', known as the '*gardes de la manche*' ('guards of the sleeve'), always at the sovereign's side. Their main weapon was the partizan.

In this case the blade is profusely decorated from top to bottom on both sides, in gold counterfeit damascening, bearing the motto NEC PLURIBUS IMPAR ('Equalled by few'), the sun in splendour, a trophy of arms surrounded by four fleur-de-lis, the arms of France and Navarre surmounted by a crown, including the initial 'H', and surrounded by the collars of the Orders of the Holy Spirit and Saint Michael; the 'H' refers to Henry III of France, founder the Order of the Holy Spirit in 1578. The top of the octagonal socket is chiselled with acanthus foliage, the remainder is blued and counterfeit-damascened in gold with fleur-de-lis. The haft is a modern replacement.

The solar symbolism reflected Louis XIV's self-image and adulation as the 'Sun King' – the bright, illuminating centre of all things, a conceit first thought to have appeared at the great *Carousel* of 1662, a spectacular event which celebrated the birth of his son and heir, the Dauphin Louis. Overall, the quality of the decoration suggests the partizan may be the work of Jean Bérain the Elder, who worked for the king from 1675 and as principal designer after 1690, working on everything from stage sets to the decoration of his ships: partizans to his designs survive in other collections including the Wallace Collection, London. Along with the guards' uniforms and other equipment, these weapons had an important role in projecting the power, image and splendour of the monarch, but they and their bearers were also for real: Henry III and Louis' grandfather Henry IV were both assassinated (in 1589 and 1610 respectively), and at the end of his reign Louis' guards numbered nearly 3000.

[196]

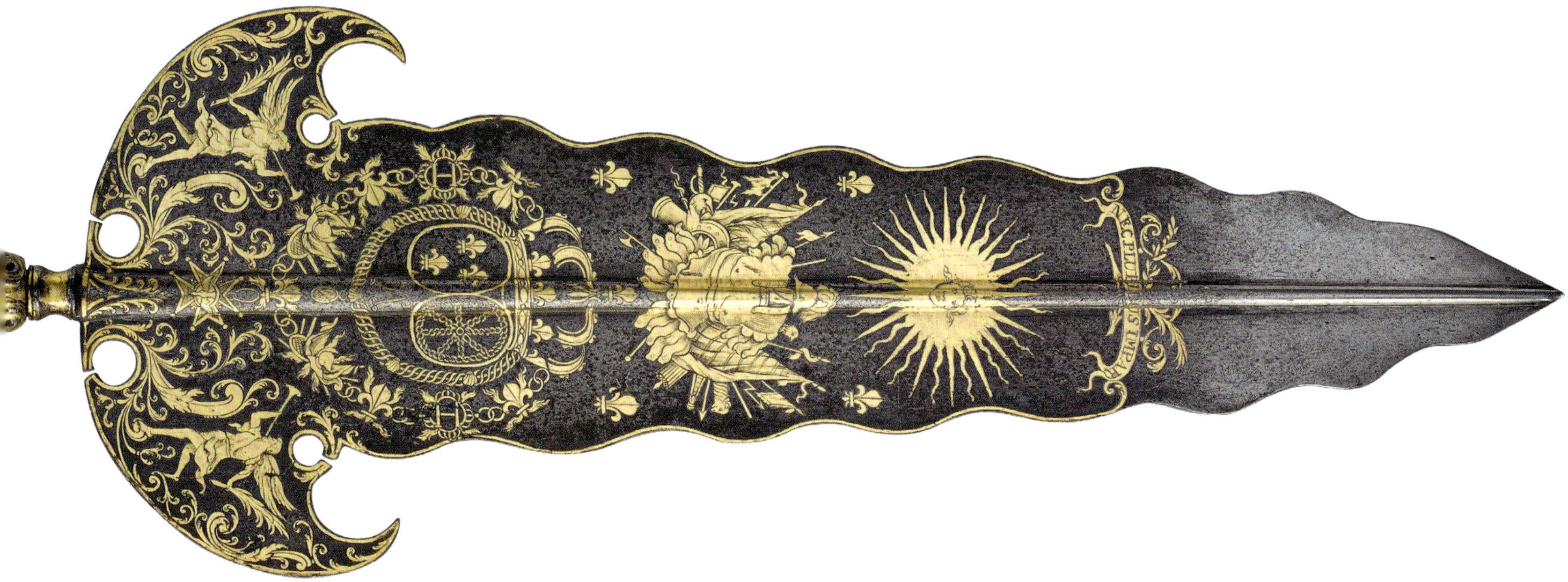

77

Pocket set of tools for maintaining firearms

England, *c*.1690 · XIII.192

Until the introduction of smokeless propellants in the late 19th century all firearms used black powder for their main charge and priming, which after firing fouled both the barrel and the lock mechanism with an obstructive and corrosive residue. This made it necessary, after use, to clean not only the barrel, as with a modern rifle or shotgun, but to regularly take out and clean the lock and its moving parts. In the case of a sporting weapon this was normally done in the gunroom, but this rare 'pocket' set of tools allowed its owner to do so while travelling or in the field.

The tools are contained in a flattish iron case, rectangular in section but with sloped corners and a hinged lid at the top, not unlike a cigarette packet.

This in itself is an exquisite and highly decorated artefact, each surface engraved with classical military motifs: on the front, a human figure, perhaps Victory, wears an extravagant open helmet, a flowing cloth garment and calf-length boots, and sits on a drum, one hand clasping a marshal's baton and the other an oval shield; in the background is an elaborate trophy of arms, comprising two quivers full of arrows, two trumpets, two cannon, a sword, a large barbed dart, and a grotesque mask. Above, on the lid, is a trophy made up of a scale cuirass, two cannon, powder barrels, shot, and equipment for loading and firing. On the back, a bound male captive sits awkwardly on a shield with a quiver at his feet and, alongside a cannon, banners, an axe, spears and sword forming a trophy. Importantly, the hinge to the lid, bears the signature DOLEP. A rectangular socket on the lower edge of the box is occupied by a short tongue attached to an iron disc engraved with the distinctive grand ducal 'Roman' crown of the Medici, below which is a monogram: the letters FM, the F repeated and arranged back-to-back.

Each housed in its own socket, the tools consist of three spring clamps, a threaded rod with a hook, a vent pricker, a hammer head, a screwdriver blade and a spiral spring. A small screw in the hammer head can be used to secure it to the tang of the screwdriver blade, enabling the blade to form a handle, while a similar arrangement is found in the socket on the underside of the box. Removing the disc bearing the Medici monogram enables the screwdriver blade to be inserted into the socket, the box thus becoming the screwdriver's handle.

As the signature shows, the set was made by the distinguished gunmaker Andrew Dolep (*c*.1648–1713), who had arrived in England from the Low Countries in 1681, anglicising 'Andreas' to Andrew. Already highly skilled, he swiftly secured the patronage of Sir Philip Howard, Colonel of the Queen's Troop of Horse Guards, and then, better still, of George Legge, 1st Baron Dartmouth [75]. It was probably this connection that led to Dolep's selection by James II, after his flight to France in 1688 and subsequent exile at the French court, as the maker of prestigious diplomatic gifts. As suggested by the initials, the recipient in this case was probably Ferdinando III de'Medici, Grand Prince of Tuscany (r.1670–1713), a keen sportsman, patron of the arts, and of the most famous Italian gunmakers of the time. It is possible that this set of tools was supplied by Dolep for a fine superimposed-load sporting gun, now in the Armeria Reale, Turin, which bears the same monogram inlaid in iron wire into both sides of its butt. As with the powder flask described earlier [53], the tool set exhibits the technical and artistic attention that could be paid, in the context of prestigious firearms, not only to the gun itself but the complex array of equipment needed to keep it working.

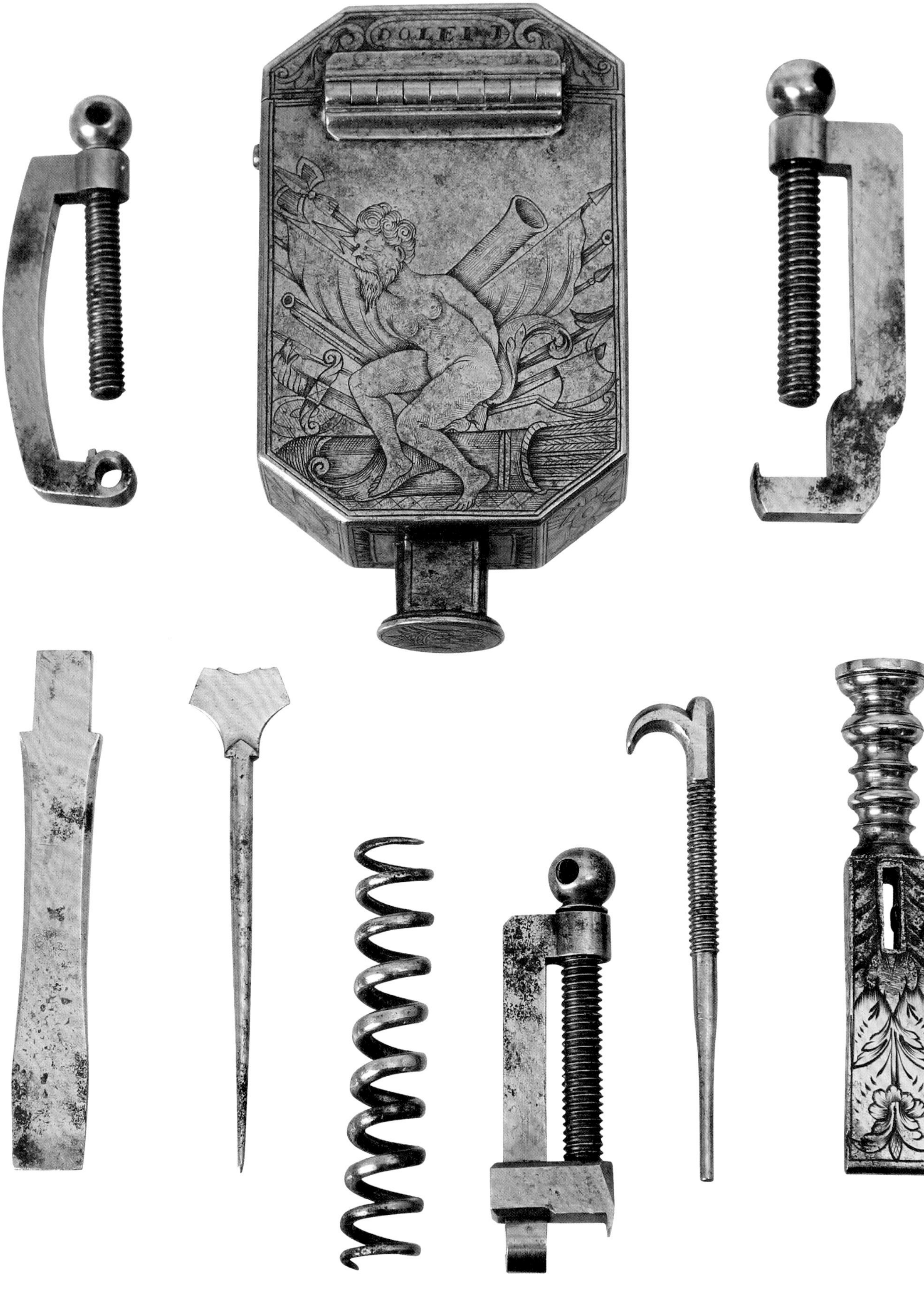
DOLEP I

78

Japanese helmet (*harikake kabuto*)

Japan, late 17th century · XXVIA.89a

The years from 1603 to 1867, during which the *shoguns* of Japan were successive members of the Tokugawa family, is known after its capital, Edo, the old name for Tokyo. Under their firm rule, the country was peaceful and prosperous, although largely cut off from western influence until the 1850s, when forcible American and European intrusion brought the era to an end.

To support their drive for peace, the shogunate demilitarised and disarmed the majority of the population, and while the warrior class (*buke*) retained their rank and emphasis on martial skill and honour, the likelihood of actual warfare diminished. Despite this the armour industry remained active, and much surviving Japanese armour across the world dates from this period. Its nature was changing, however: by the later 17th century armourers concentrated more on the visual effect and artistic qualities of their product than practicality, increasingly seeking to exalt the status of the wearer in parades rather than to protect him in battle. This development was encouraged by the policy of *sankin kotai* or 'alternate attendance' which required all *daimyō* to split their time between their domains and their mansions in the capital: travel between them was undertaken on a grand scale, the *daimyō gyoretsu* or procession of a lord and large numbers of retainers in full pomp and splendour offering excellent opportunities for *daimyō* and their ranks of samurai to show off their wealth and prestige.

This helmet, part of an associated suit of armour, is typical of those manufactured in Kaga province, probably in the later 17th century, by then one of most significant centres of production in the country. The governing Maeda family encouraged artisans to move there, while trade with the Dutch and Chinese of Nagasaki provided the decorated leather, woollen cloth and ivory which became characteristic features of their armours. At the probable time of the helmet's manufacture, the industry had helped to make the Kaga *daimyō* among the wealthiest in Japan, and the extravagance of their own processions to Edo was legendary.

In form and construction the helmet neatly demonstrates how the role and design of armour responded to these social and political circumstances. The underlying metal bowl is a simple structure fashioned from large plates and coated in russet lacquer, providing the wearer with very real protection, and is of a type originating in the *sengoku jidai* [43], when large numbers of troops needed to be equipped quickly, effectively and economically. The plainness and practicality of this core component, however, is almost entirely obscured by its elaborate superstructure: this consists of a moulded scallop shell lacquered in silver grey, surmounted by a carved and gilded hare, positioned affronté to perch above the brow of the wearer, its detachable ears (modern replacements) extending high into the air. Descending from the underside of the shell is a thick fringe of red and white silk streamers which covers the majority of the neckguard (*shikoro*). The peak and lowest lame of the *shikoro* are faced with gilded leather and sport applied metalwork decoration. Such additions, made from wood, paper, leather and textile, became very popular in the Edo period, making armours distinctive and personal to individual *samurai* whilst adding little extra weight, with a showiness perfectly suited to what was now their main purpose.

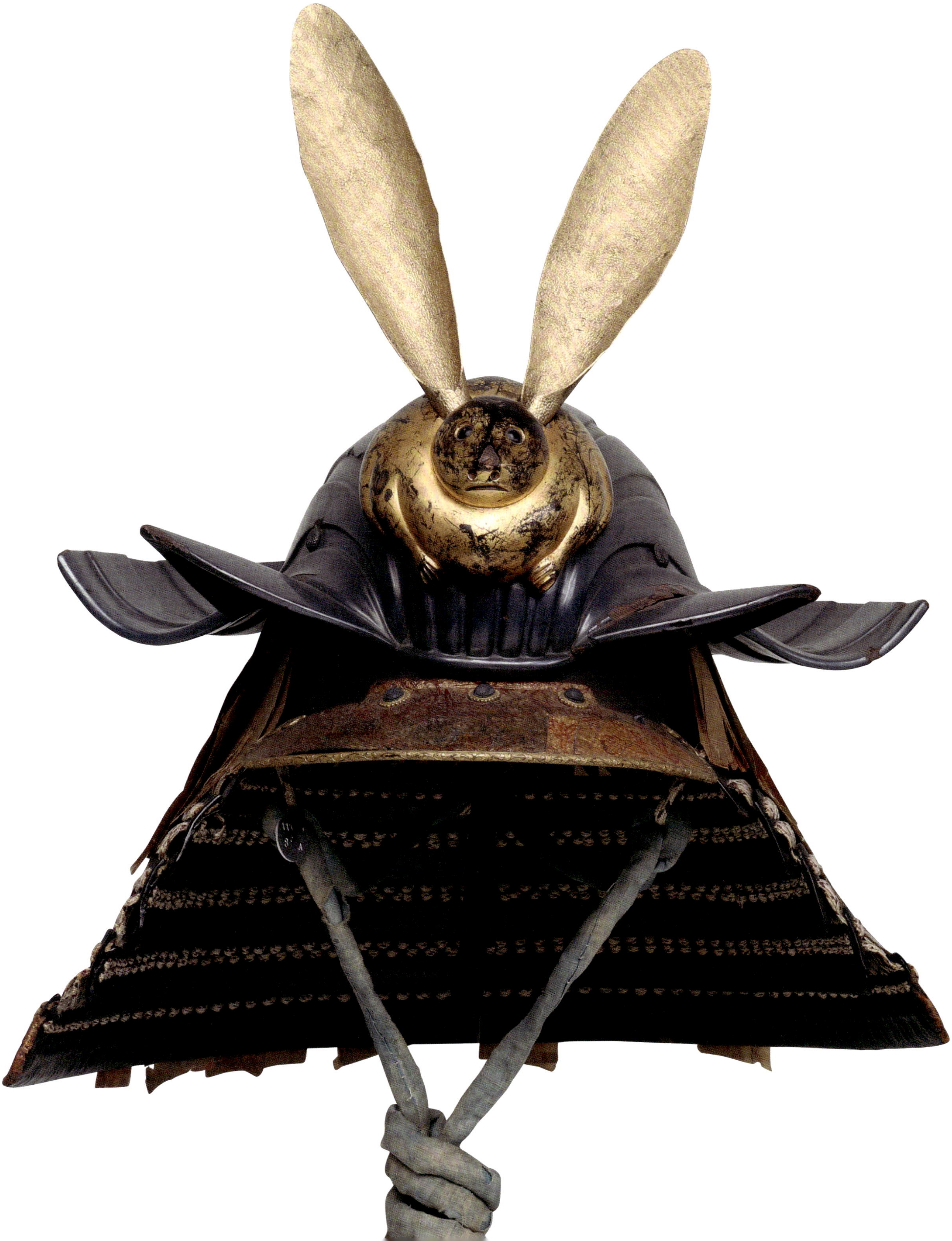

79

Flintlock breech-loading magazine gun by John Cookson

England, 1690 · XII.10597

Guns signed by John Cookson were made from the 1680s to the 1750s, the explanation being that there may have been two men of the same name, perhaps related: one certainly worked in London, and the other was active in Boston, Massachusetts between 1701 and 1762. Very few examples of their work, however, survive.

This example, perhaps the older of the two, was made in London about 1690, and is inscribed IOHN COOKSON FECIT. It takes the form of a single-barrel smoothbore flintlock (14 mm; a 28-bore), intended for sporting use, and is abundantly decorated: chiselled in high relief on sections of the barrel, breech and trigger-guard are fronds of foliage and grotesque masks, whilst deeply chiselled foliate scrollwork and animal faces feature on the remainder of the iron furniture. Stocked in burr-walnut, the butt is carved in the manner of a creature's top jaw clamping down on the wrist of the gun: there is no fore-end, and so the barrel is of naked steel, and has a curious foresight shaped like the upturned blade of a battle axe.

On the whole, however, the gun's appearance is most unusual, even ungainly, thanks to its most remarkable feature – the incorporation of a breech-loading repeating magazine system. The inventor of the system has long been identified as the Sienese gunmaker Michele Lorenzoni (c.1650–1735) between 1660 and 1670: the system itself, gradually improved, remained in use until the 19th century. Lorenzoni worked mostly in Florence where his patrons included Cosimo III de' Medici, Grand Duke of Tuscany, whilst his work equalled that of the best Italian gun makers of the time, such as Matteo Cecchi (known as Acquafresca) and Giacomo Berselli. In the provision of multiple shots, the system was the commonest alternative to the revolving principle until abandoned in the mid 19th century.

Too complex to describe in detail here, the astonishingly ingenious mechanism was operated essentially as follows. First, powder and ball, enough for nine shots, were loaded into separate compartments of the main magazine in the wrist, through a hinged gate above and to the left of the trigger guard. The steel lever on the left-hand side, parallel to the barrel, was then rotated 180 degrees, in succession filling the priming pan, closing the frizzen, cocking the gun, and lining up the internal rotor system with the powder and ball compartments. The user then had to tip the muzzle forward towards the ground, which allowed enough powder for one shot and a single ball to fall into separate dials in the rotor. The lever was then rotated in the opposite direction, which carried the ammunition and powder into the barrel, and returned the priming pan to its upright position, hidden by the now-closed frizzen. The gun was now ready to fire, and repeating the process, allowed it to be fired again.

A drawback of the system is the danger of the main magazine exploding if reached by burning gas from the exploding charge: damage to several known examples of Lorenzoni-system guns shows that this certainly occurred, and would have seriously injured or killed the user. However, as this weapon seems to have been used, its intact condition is a testament to Cookson's skills as a craftsman and engineer of the highest calibre. Their inherent risk, however, together with their enormous cost, explains why Lorenzoni-system guns were never made in large numbers.

[202]

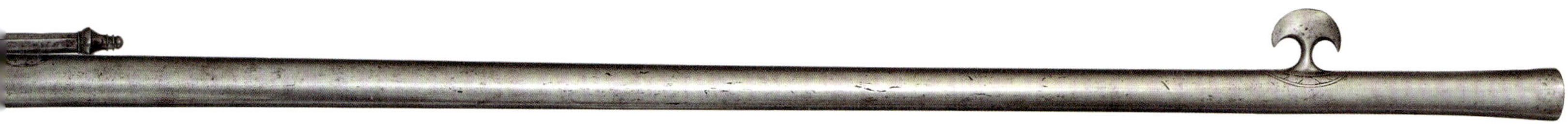

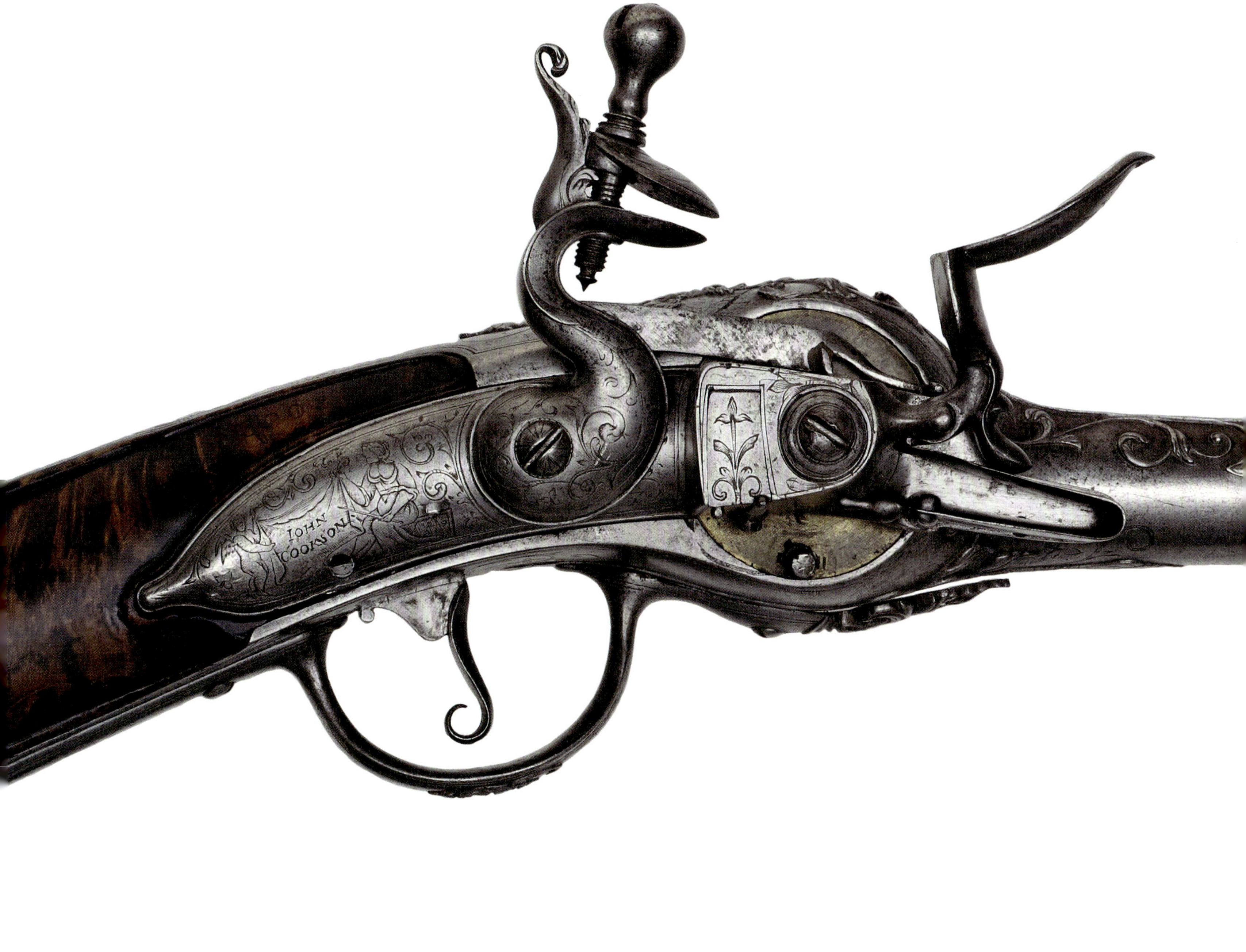
IOHN
COOKSON

80

Tympanum sculpture from the Grand Storehouse at the Tower of London

England, 1691 (salvaged in 1841) · XVII.119

The Office of Ordnance, itself born of the medieval Great Wardrobe, was the government department responsible for supplying the English armed forces, and for their premises and fortifications, at home and overseas, from the early 15th until the early 19th century: it was also, incidentally, the institutional ancestor of the Royal Armouries. For most of that period the Office's headquarters and largest stores were at the Tower of London, and from 1547 concentrated in a vast timber structure stretching across the whole width of the castle to the north of the White Tower. By 1686, however, this was in a 'crazy condicon', and early in 1688 George Legge, 1st Baron Dartmouth and Master General of the Ordnance, signed off drawings and an estimate (1 March 1688) for a new building, ordered its 'speedy going in hand' (5 April), and work had started four days later. The designer is unknown, but was probably an Ordnance engineer, although the contractor is known to have been John Fitch (1642–1706), with whom the Office had had a longstanding relationship. The work was overseen by Robert Barker and finished in 1691. By then, James II, however, was king no more, and while his initials appeared on the keystones of the lower windows, those above were of his successor, William III. At 109 m long and 18 m wide, towering over the medieval curtain wall to the north, it was an impressive building, with a showy if slightly dated façade overlooking Tower Green and the White Tower. Mostly of red brick, it had Portland stone dressings, an elaborately treated central bay, above which a pediment framed the tympanum, carved in 1691 by John Young, who had worked on many important London buildings. Architecturally the sculpture belonged to a long European tradition of adorning fortifications and public buildings with great trophies of arms, proclaiming the martial might of sovereign or state, although first evident in England only in the 1660s. Stylistically Young's work is boldly baroque, in deep relief, although various claims that it was painted and gilded seem to be unfounded. Flanking the royal arms at the centre, in carefully arranged disorder, are an abundance of weapons and equipment, most British and contemporary, but lent flattering associations with antiquity and empire by the addition of two shields and a bow and quiver of 'Roman' form, and – befitting a monument to British prowess – two swords which may be French. To the left appears a mortar on its carriage, with

[204]

its bombs and equipment, along with flags, swords, a pair of kettle drums and an oboe – instruments used in ceremony and signalling. To the right, a cannon and field carriage are accompanied by a powder keg, case-shot, a cavalry helmet, a drum, musket ammunition, more flags and another oboe. The showy carving and its subject aptly heralded the building's content and purpose, for whilst intended as a working storehouse, by 1696 its contents had been deliberately arranged in fantastic patterns and compositions to impress and delight the Tower's visitors. The artist was a gun maker working for the king, John Harris, and the result, as described in 1741, 'one of the greatest, curiosities, in its kind, ever formed by the art of man'. Tragically, the building was burnt and most of its contents destroyed in 1841, to be replaced in 1845–50 by the Waterloo Barracks. The tympanum, however, recognised as a work of art and a functioning symbol of the nation's might, was re-erected outdoors in about 1870 near the Martin Tower. In 1975 it was placed out of the weather, fittingly enough, in the New Armouries, which had been built as an ordnance store by James II's brother and precursor, Charles II.

81

Pair of flintlock holster pistols by Pierre Monlong

England, late 17th century · XII.3829–30

In the mid 17th century France led the world in the technological development of firearms and their decoration: it was there in about 1610–15 that the true flintlock was developed, and gun makers were able to copy and collaborate with some of the greatest designers of the time. One of these was Pierre Monlong, who began his career at Angers (Maine et Loire) in about 1660, and in 1664 was appointed one of the *Arquebusiers de la Maison du Roi* (Gunmakers to the Royal Household). He moved to Paris and went into a productive partnership with the gunsmith Pierre Frappier; many of their creations, bearing their joint signature, still exist in royal collections today. Monlong, however, was a Huguenot – a Calvinist Protestant: while, in this overwhelmingly Catholic country, they had been protected from persecution from 1598 by the Edict of Nantes, in the early 1680s Louis XIV reversed the policy, and Monlong was one of those who fled abroad, followed by many more after the edict's formal revocation in 1685. Along with many others, he settled in London, with his wife and four children, and established a gun-making business near Charing Cross, close to the court at Whitehall and Westminster and in an area favoured by foreign artists. There, although technically outside the city and its jurisdiction, the Wardens of the Gunmakers Company of London carried out inspections and fined Monlong for not having the appropriate proof marks on his barrels. It was not long, however, before his talent was recognised and rewarded by a grant of denization in 1688, and the following year he was appointed as a 'Gentleman Armourer to his Majesty-in-Ordinary', roughly equivalent to his Parisian position.

It was in London that he made this pair of 32-bore flintlock holster pistols, designed to be carried on horseback, one on each side of the saddle. They are not dated, but the absence of proof marks, permissible only under royal patronage, points to manufacture after 1664, while if the portrait bust on the lock is of William III, as it seems to be, the pistols must postdate his accession in 1688: if so, they may have been made for the king himself. Certainly they are of more than fitting quality. However, whilst proudly marked MONLONG LONDINI ('Monlong of London'), they are completely French in design. The decoration is based on the famous pattern books of Claude and Jacques Simonin of 1685 and 1693, although no detail has been copied directly, suggesting that the designs were adapted by Monlong or provided anew by Simonin, conceivably before he left Paris. The walnut stocks are inlaid with silver filigree and with various figures, such as Apollo driving the sun chariot in front of the trigger guard and of Fortitude near the fore end. All steel parts are ornately decorated, chiselled with intricate scrollwork and lions' masks, the cocks are engraved with demi-figures and foliate scrolls, and damascened gold is abundantly used against a blued background.

Monlong died in 1699 and was buried without ceremony in the parish church of St Martin-in-the-Fields, London. His business died with him, but his work survives in a number of great European collections. These two pistols are widely considered, whilst French in design and by a Frenchman, to be the most highly furnished and exquisite pistols ever made in Britain.

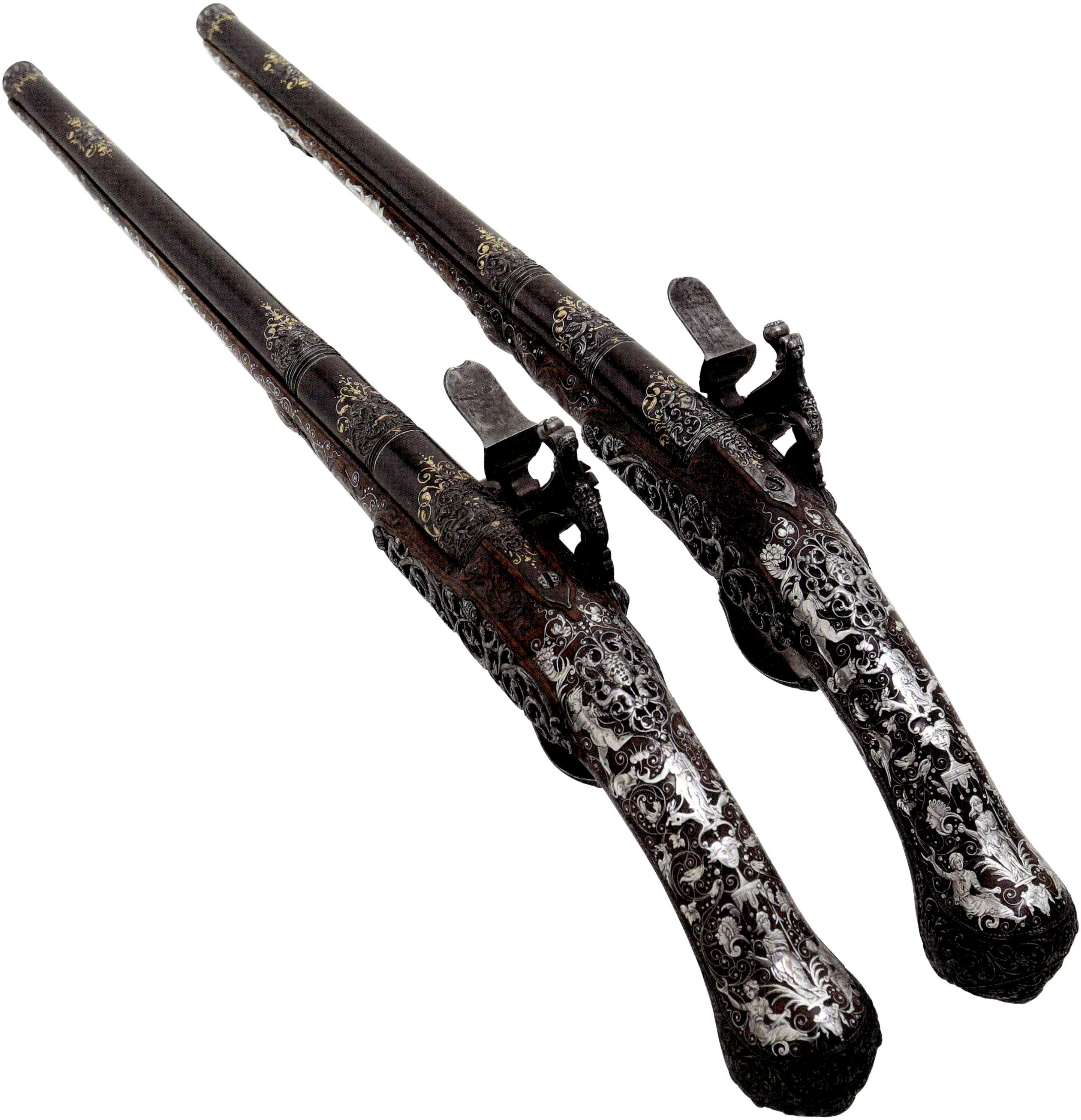

82

Dagger (*khanjar*) from the Mughal empire

India, late 17th century · XXVID.145

The magnificence of the Mughal emperors and their courts, by 1600 rulers of most of South Asia, attracted skilled artists and craftsmen from far and wide to their courts at Agra and (old) Delhi. The imperial workshops had to meet a constant demand for luxury objects for distribution as diplomatic gifts, to individuals close to the rulers as symbols of high office and favour, and to ornament courtly activity. Gorgeously decorated weapons featured prominently among them, and contemporary paintings depict emperors and nobles carrying bejewelled and gilded swords, and daggers with elaborately shaped hilts set with precious and semi-precious stones. A variety of styles of dagger were worn, but the *khanjar* with its slender, double-edged blade was particularly favoured. Many had ivory, rock crystal or hardstone hilts carved into the shape of startlingly realistic animal heads.

Amongst these many represented horses, reflecting their paramount importance to most Asian powers at this time, whose swift, mobile cavalry forces, dominated by mounted archers armed with composite bows, had created their various empires. The Mughals were no exception: it was this model that allowed the first Mughal ruler Babur and his son Humayun to establish the footholds of their empire in north-west India, and by which his grandson Akbar extended control across much of the northern and central realms during his long reign (albeit with the aid of artillery and firearms). Once the regime was secured, the Mughals retained a special reverence for horses, which bestowed prestige on their owners and proclaimed their wealth, taste and status.

This beautiful dagger is a clear expression of the horse's status in Mughal society. Instead of the more common nephrite (a form of jade), the hilt has been fashioned from a block of striking, boldly flecked serpentine. The carving is very sensitive, drawing out the form of a fiery, spirited horse with an arched neck, flaring nostrils and ears laid back to show a touch of temper. The neck of the horse has been subtly sculpted to provide a comfortable grip for the fingers, and broadens into a lobed guard decorated with delicate floral motifs executed in relief. This flair for naturalism implies a 17th-century date, when Mughal artists were celebrated for making intensive studies of nature and achieved an astonishing level of realism.

The blade, meanwhile, is double-curved, and although not ostentatious, is wonderfully elegant and of superb technical quality. It is made from crucible steel (*wootz*) and exhibits a lovely rippling 'watered' effect on its surface, particularly in the grooves either side of the central rib. The sharp point of the blade is thickened and reinforced, which allowed it to pierce mail if used with enough force. This trait reminds us that this dagger was produced in an era when warfare was an ever-present reality, when prominent individuals were expected to be warriors, and military prowess was just as important as cultural sophistication. As a result, whilst this dagger is a work of art to delight the eye and to be prized by its owner, it is no less of a weapon for all that, capable of deadly effect as circumstance required.

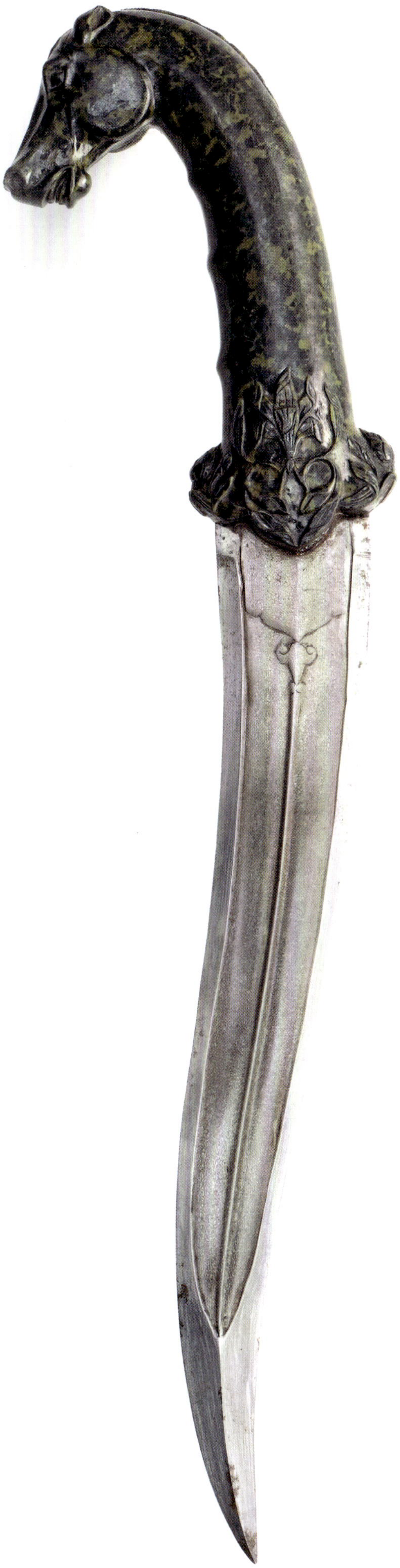

83

A Sikh quoit turban

India, 18th century · XXVIA.60

When the Sikh faith first emerged in India in the late 15th century, it faced hostility and religious intolerance from the Muslim Mughal empire. In response, an order of Sikh warriors called the *Akalis*, or Immortals, was established to defend their people and to secure the survival of their faith. The *Akalis* quickly proved themselves to be ferocious warriors, scoring major victories against far larger forces, as for example in December 1703 when 800 Sikh warriors successfully defended Anandpur against a besieging force of 10,000, or the Battle of Saragarhi (1897) at which twenty-one Sikhs made a heroic last stand against 10,000 Afghans.

The traditional attire of the *Akalis* had various components, most famously their vivid blue tunics, but more unusual and visually striking were their spectacular turbans, or *dastar bungga*, which translates quite appropriately as 'Towering Fortress'. The purpose of the turban was both spiritual and practical. For instance, the *gajgah*, the large crescent at the bottom of the turban represents superior strength, intellect and daring while the double-edged blade, known as a *khanda*, at the top of the arrangement, represents the balance between masculine and feminine power or energy. The structure is reinforced and held together with a wire wrapping cord, the *tora*, into which are thrust small daggers known as *kirpan*, symbolising the *Akalis*' duty to stand against oppression and tyranny. Hanging loose from the top of the turban is a trail of fabric called the *farla*, a mark of honour worn only by those of the highest rank of the *Akali*. The *farla* also serves as a miniature battle standard, a tradition started by the Tenth Guru, Gobind Singh (1660–1708). Following the annexation of the Punjab by the British in 1849, the traditional form of turban was adopted and modified for use in the Sikh regiments.

Arranged up the length of the turban are several steel quoits, known as *chakram* or *chakkar*, which are blunt along the inside edge but razor sharp on the outside. These were carried to war on the turban itself or sometimes, more practically, on the warrior's arm. As the *Akalis* approached the enemy a quoit was looped over the forefinger and spun at speed and then flung towards them, a projectile weapon capable of inflicting terrible wounds. There is a tradition amongst the *Akalis* of reciting verses from the Guru Granth Sahib as well as a composition known as Dumāllānāmā Pātashāhī Dasaviṅ ('The Epistle of the Conical Turban, by the Tenth Sovereign'). Part of this composition refers to the steel quoits: '*sir par mukaṭ, mukaṭ par chakkar*' ('on my head is the *chakkar* that is liberated and liberates').

The quoit turban was given to the Board of Ordnance in 1851 by the East India Company. This was a time when academic interest in the histories and cultures of East Asia was at its peak: entire galleries of the Great Exhibition (held the same year) were given over to the display of Indian arms, armour and craftsmanship, both new and old. It was also a time of increasing British military activity abroad, including the Anglo-Sikh wars (1845–6, 1848–9), which prompted a fresh wave of public interest in a feared and much-respected opponent.

[210]

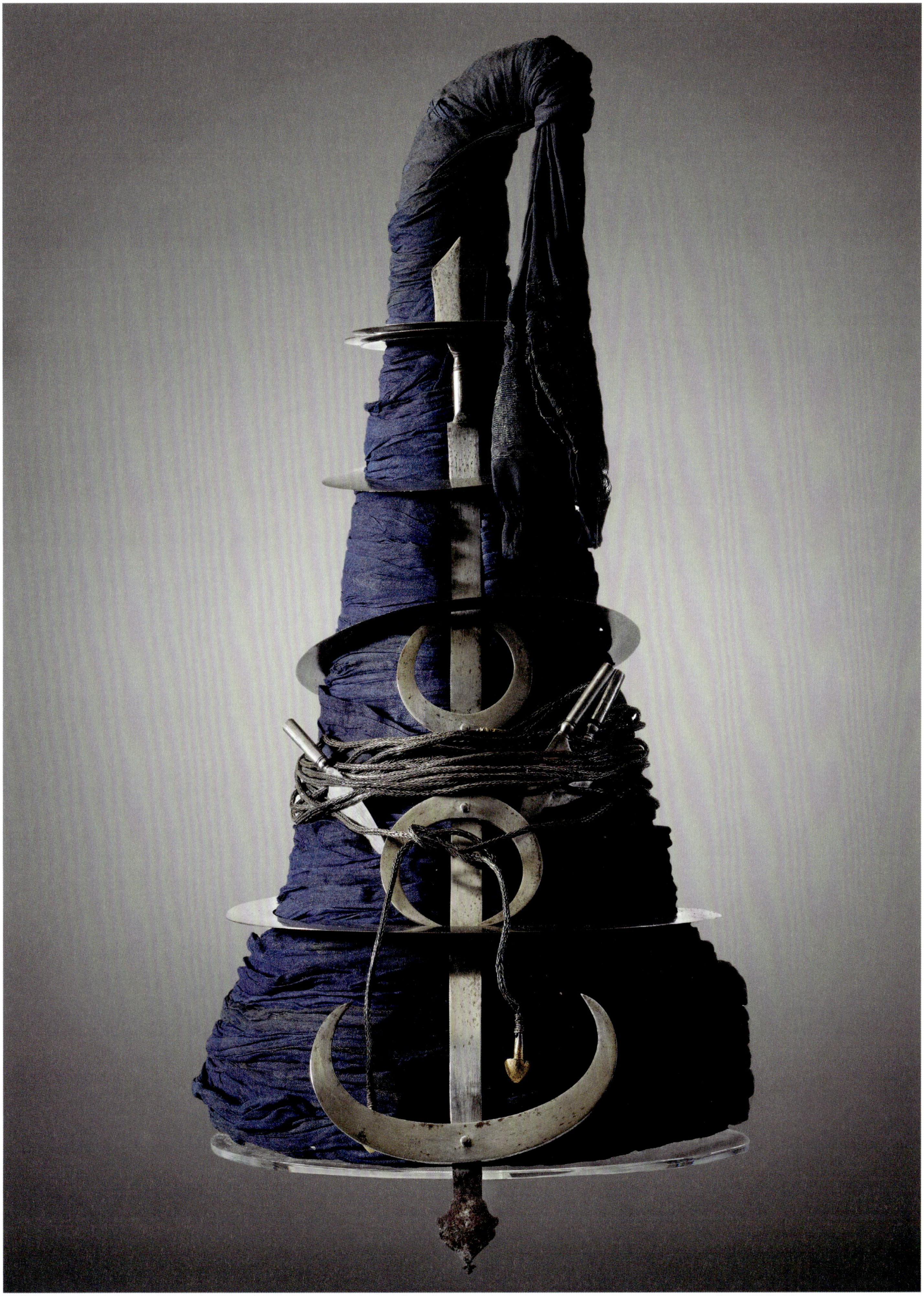

84

Bronze dragon cannon

Probably Thailand, late 17th or early 18th century · XIX.123

Artillery was widely adopted in south-east Asia in the 16th century. Major foundries were established at Ayutthaya (capital of the Siamese or Thai kingdom of the same name which held influence over much of the area of modern Thailand), which employed Chinese gun founders, and at Pegu (present-day Bago in Myanmar), which used the skills of Indian and Portuguese craftsmen. A series of wars between the Burmese Konbaung Dynasty and the Ayutthaya Kingdom in the 1760s culminated with the capture of the city of Ayutthaya in 1767. Stylistically it is most probable that the series to which this magnificent gun belongs is Thai, and that it was captured and removed by Burmese forces with a huge number of guns to the Konbaung centre of power in the Kingdom of Ava (now Myanmar) in 1767.

Despite setbacks in the east, the kingdom of Ava continued its expansion into Assam and Manipur, bringing it into conflict with the East India Company. British annexation of Burma was achieved by a series of wars, in 1824–6, 1852, and finally in the Third Anglo-Burmese (or Anglo-Myanmar) War which started on 14 November 1885, when Major-General (later Sir) Harry Prendergast's expedition was ordered to march on Mandalay with a force of 9,034 soldiers, twenty-four machine guns and a flotilla of fifty-five river boats and other craft, and ended a fortnight later on 28 November when the capital was taken. King Thibaw Min (r.1878–85), the last king of the Konbaung Dynasty, was deposed and Myanmar placed under British rule. Thibaw lived on in exile in India until 1916. Some of the choice trophies from Mandalay were cannon, and an illustration published in a London newspaper of 1886 illustrated the fascinating range of Burmese guns brought back to Britain and distributed among the royal family.

The gun is finely cast in the form of a magnificent dragon, the head forming the muzzle. The tail, from which a small piece at the end is missing, curves upwards above the cascabel. The concept is probably Chinese, where numerous *longshen pao* (な身炮 dragon-bodied cannon) are recorded. This along with three similar large dragon guns were taken from King Thibaw's Palace, Mandalay, on 28 November 1885. One was presented to Queen Victoria, one to the Prince of Wales, one to the Rotunda Museum, Woolwich (now the Royal Artillery Museum) and one to the Viceroy of India. The first was transferred from Windsor in July 1901 to the Tower of London, and thence to the Rotunda in October 1930. The Royal Artillery Museum thus has two of the guns. The present Royal Armouries gun is the one originally sent to the Prince of Wales, given by Queen Mary to the Victoria & Albert Museum, and transferred to the Tower Armouries in 1951. Other smaller swivel guns in the form of dragons were also made in the same style, and the Royal Armouries collection also includes one of these. Yet another of these guns is supposed to have been captured in China by a company of the Madras Foot Artillery (subsequently 111 (Dragon) Battery, Royal Artillery) at Guangdong during the First Opium War in 1840, perhaps a Qing trophy also from Ayutthaya. The Royal Armouries collection also includes the personal armour of General Maha Bandula (1782–1825), leader of the Burmese forces in the First Anglo-Burmese War of 1824–6, and a *shwei-zawa* lacquer box illustrating scenes from the Second Anglo-Burmese War of 1852.

[212]

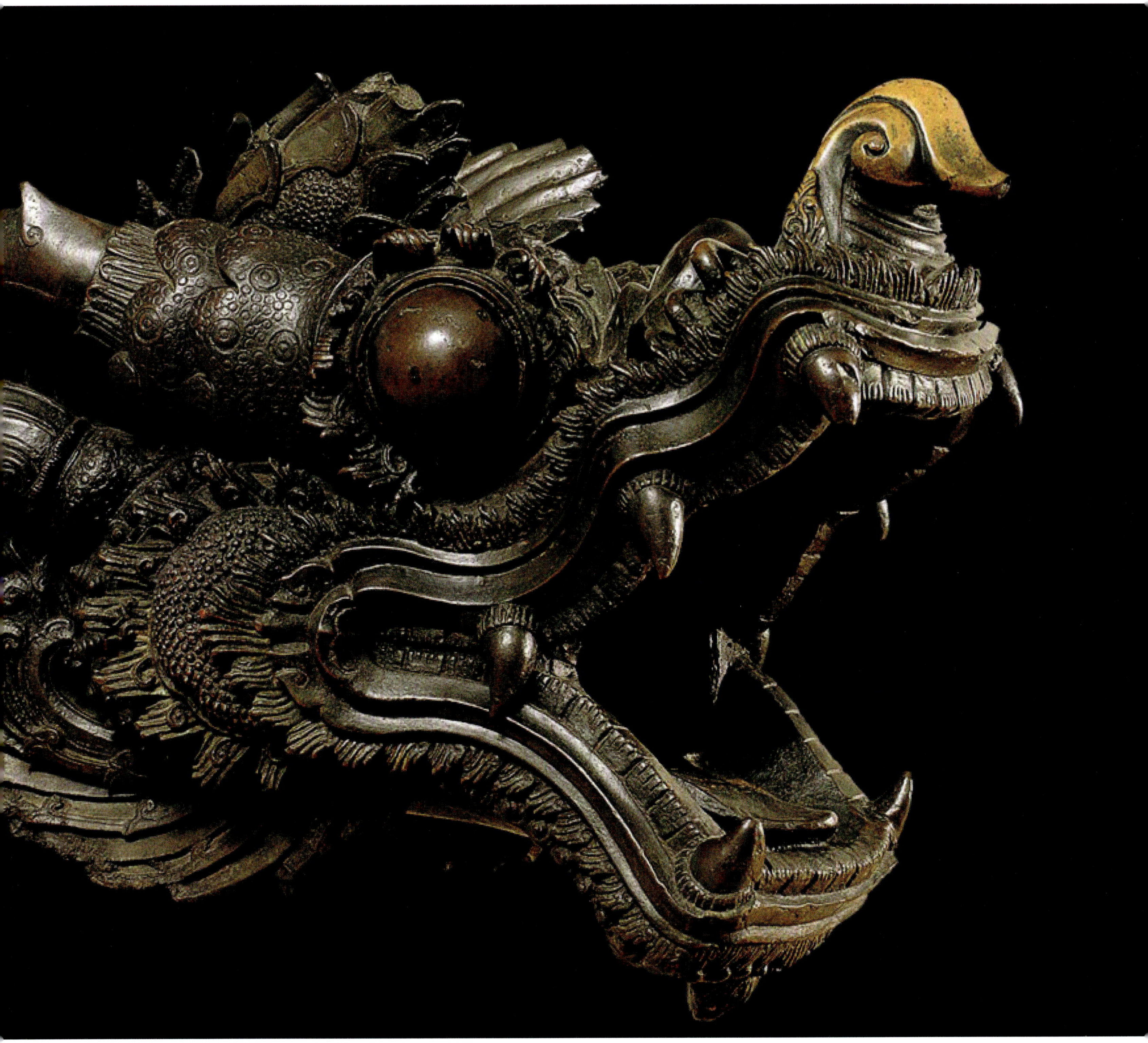

85

A sporting gun for a prisoner in the Tower

England, 1721 · XII.1789

This sporting gun has the triple distinction of being loosely a product of the disastrous 'South Sea Bubble' financial crash of 1720, a sporting gun of real quality made in early-18th century England, and one of the very few ever made at the Tower of London. It was made for Thomas, First Earl Coningsby (1656–1729), a politician and privy councillor imprisoned in the Tower between 27 February and 29 July 1721 for libel. A gold-inlayed inscription on the gun barrel tells its curious tale:

I in the Tower became a gun, In Seventeen hundred Twenty one
Earl Coningsby Prisoner there, Bespoke and took me to his care
And fit I am for Loyal Lords, Made of the Blades of Rebels Swords
Fit for ye noble Earl whose Crime, Was Speaking truth in South Sea time
Traytors beware Wn we are enlarg'd, When He or I shall be Discharg'd
For this my first and true Report, Pray use me well at Hampton Court.

These humourous lines, though hardly of the quality of Pope or Swift – both of whom poked fun at Coningsby, Pope later portraying him, after his death, as a villain in his 1733 work 'Epistle to Bathurst' – are probably by the owner. They are laden with meaning. Through reference to the 'Rebels' (the Scottish Jacobites of 1715), the owner proclaims his loyalty to the Crown, while the claim that the gun was made from their swords is at least plausible; the 'Crime' was libelling the Earl of Macclesfield, the Lord Chancellor, over the allegedly illegal appointment of Sir George Caswell, cashier of the South Sea Company, as a Justice of the Peace. 'South Sea time' refers to the company's disastrous attempt to invest in trade and fishing in the seas around South America. Although seen by the Bank of England as a way to consolidate and repay the national debt through joint investment with the private sector, the 'bubble' burst in 1720 and led to bankruptcies and suicides. The last two lines, with its two *double entendres* – 'Discharge', applicable both to Coningsby's release and the gun's going off, and 'Report', referencing the record set out here and noise of the gun's firing – looks forward to the return of man and gun to his country house, Hampton Court: still standing, near Leominster, Herefordshire, this was the seat of the Coningsby family until its purchase by Richard Arkwright, son of the inventor, in 1810.

The gun itself is an 11-bore flint-lock fowling piece, single-barrelled, with a silver-mounted half-stock and a browned barrel, and an escutcheon plate bearing Coningsby's arms. The plain lock is of an advanced design that includes a water drain, engraved with the maker's name w mills, that is William Mills, who was employed by the Board of Ordnance as a 'Barrel Forger and Frobisher within the Tower'; as such he worked for the government producing military equipment, but could occasionally take on private commissions. Though regarded as one of the twenty best qualified of the Board's gun makers, Mills' career had its ups and downs, and in 1718 he was dismissed briefly for corruption.

Coningsby presumably used his gun once back at home. Certainly he seems to have taken some perverse pride in his incarceration, as the White Tower appears in the background to his portrait of 1772 by Godfrey Kneller (1646–1723), also in the Royal Armouries collection. In this he clutches a rolled copy of the Magna Carta, expressing, no doubt, his righteous indignation about the episode which led to the creation of this gun.

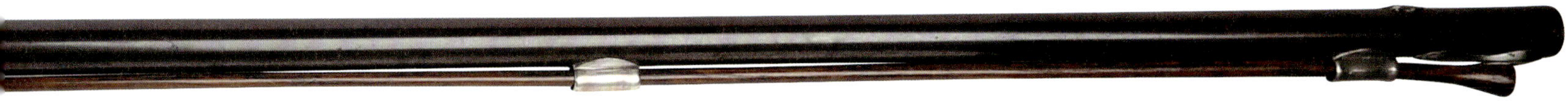

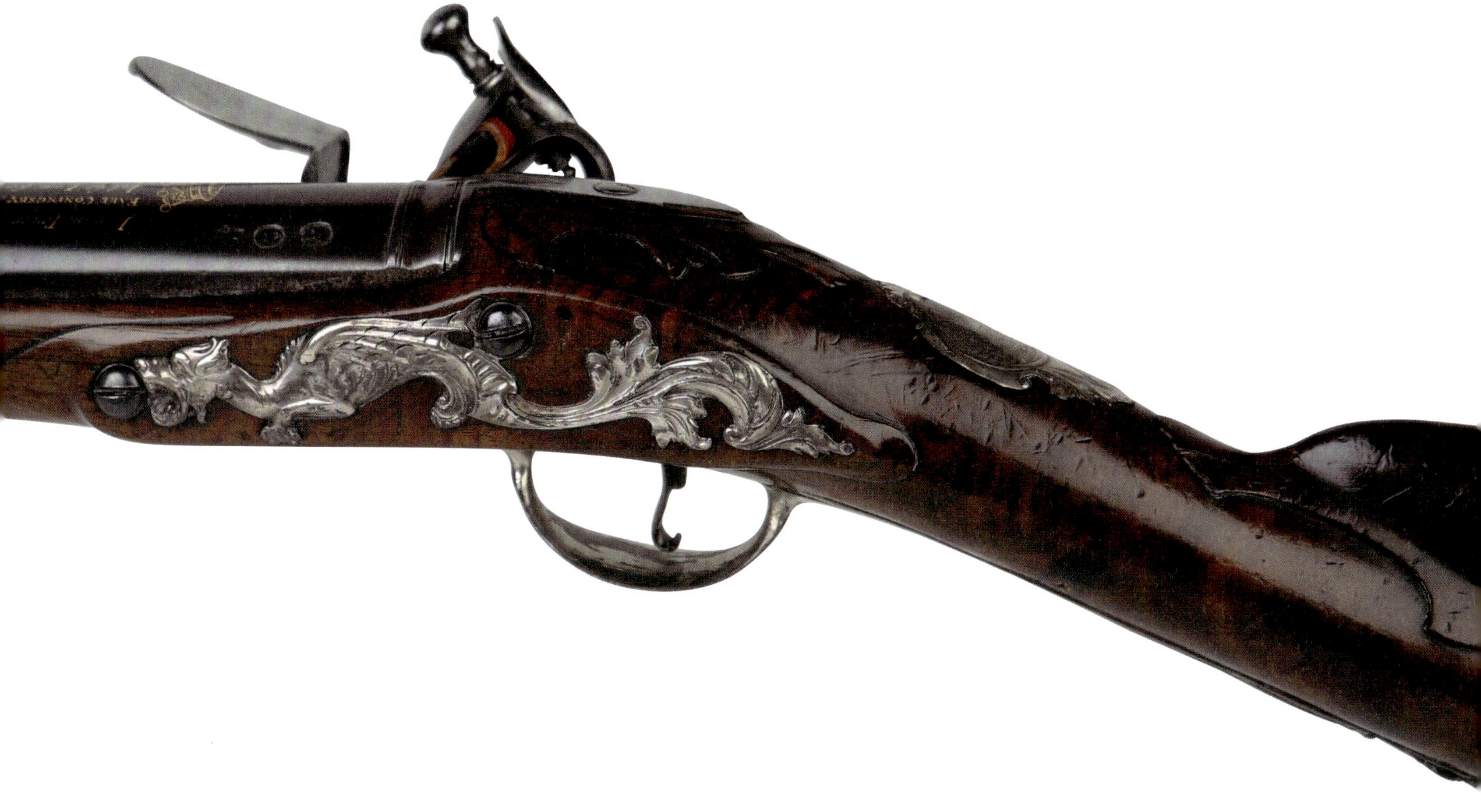

86

A sporting gun for a future king of France

Germany, 1723 · XII.4855

In the 17th and 18th centuries it was not unusual for boys to be given fully functional but child-sized firearms to train with, in preparation for warfare and sport. Those made for aristocratic children frequently matched their full-sized equivalents in quality and finish, and were often made by the best makers.

The Royal Armouries has a number of examples, among them five plain half-size military muskets, of both English India Pattern, three of them with accompanying bayonets. They were made in 1828, in what was then the Electorate of Hanover, at the Herzberg factory in Lower Saxony, owned and managed by Carl Philipp Crause (1778–1857). The recipient was George William (1819–1904), later Duke of Cambridge, a grandson of George III, then aged ten and living in Hanover, for practicing military tactics. Predictably he then pursued a military career, first in the Hanoverian army and from 1837 in the British, from 1856 until 1895 as Commander in Chief of the British army and from 1862 as a Field Marshal.

This piece, made a century earlier, is a splendidly decorated child-sized (only 110 cm in length) single-barrel smoothbore sporting gun made in 1723 by the court gunsmith to the Dukes of Brunswick, Johann Sebastian Hauschka (1695–1775), one of the greatest gun makers in Europe. In 1721, at the age of twenty-six, he was appointed court gunsmith to the then-Duke August-Wilhelm of Brunswick-Lüneburg (1662–1731), who subsequently from 1714 became the prince of Brunswick-Wolfenbüttel. Intended as a gift from the prince to the young king of France, Louis XV, who achieved his majority in 1723, it bears the French royal arms and Louis' monogram on the breech and an escutcheon plate inset into the wrist of the gun, both executed in gold. As with all the Bourbons, from his great-great grandfather Henry IV onwards, Louis was obsessed with hunting and shooting, and it is an interesting possibility that his skill was honed as a teenager by using this gun.

The rest of the piece, stocked in carved French figured walnut, is richly decorated in the rococo style advocated in the *Diverses Pièces d'Arquebuserie*, a pattern book by Frenchman Nicolas Guérard published in Paris in about 1720. During the 18th century gun makers across Europe used pattern books of decoration, such as those published by De Lacollombe (fl. c.1702–36) in 1706 and Guérard, as their inspiration and guide. The decoration is executed with inlaid silver wire and plaques on both sides of the stock. The plaques depict huntsmen, running boar and hounds. Both the lock and sideplate are also chiselled with scenes of stag hunting set within scrollwork.

Overall, the quality of this piece is superb, and matches those Hauschka made for his own patron as gifts for the Holy Roman Emperor, Charles VI and for the King of Prussia, Frederick William I. It is among Hauschka's earliest work and it is his only known creation for a child.

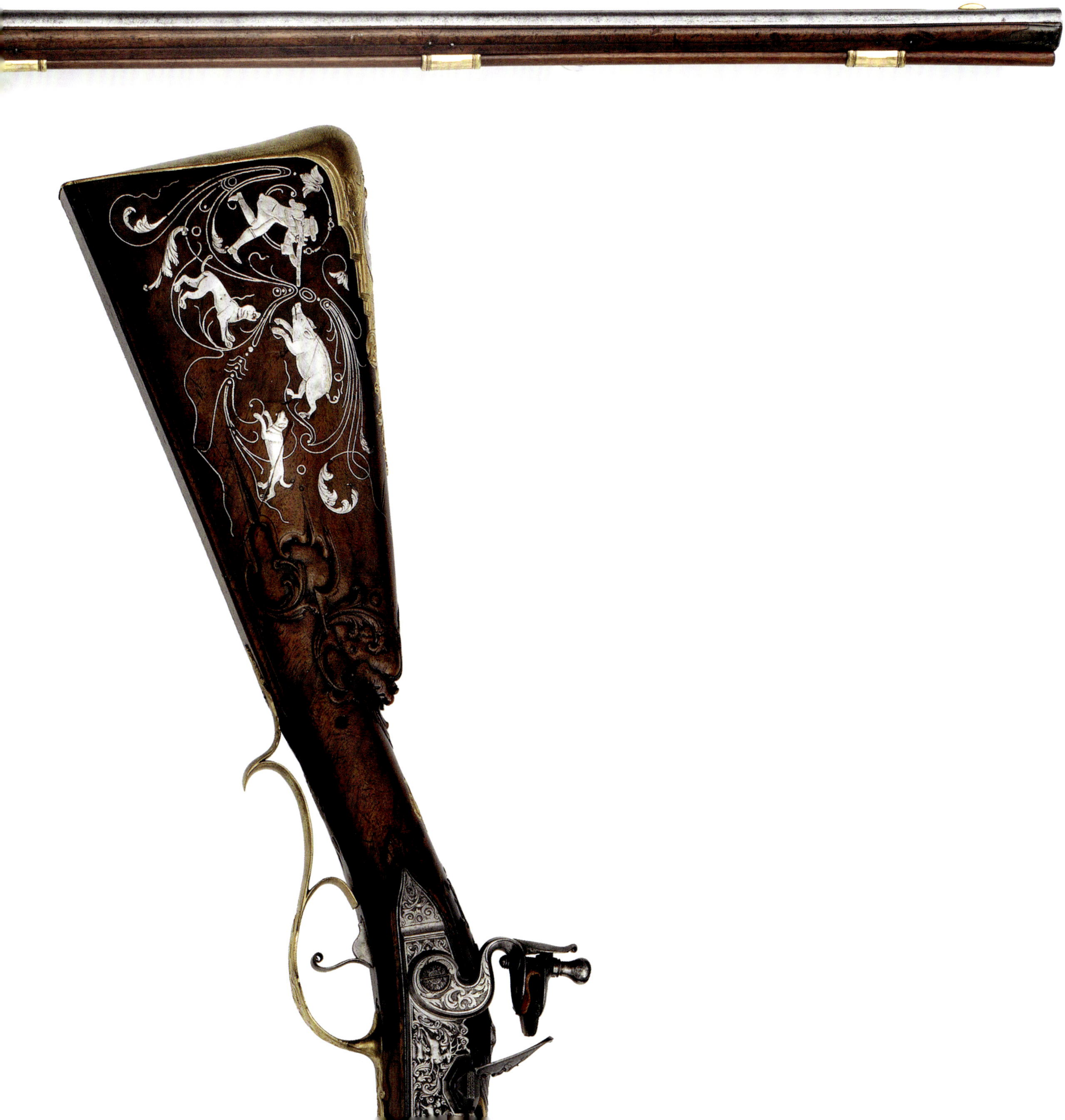

87

Celebrated sporting gun signed by William Simpson of York

England, 1738 · XII.5843

In 1975 the collector and scholar Keith Neal suggested that this gun, then in his collection, was the finest English example from the 18th century. The claim remains unchallenged on either technical or artistic grounds. It has the added distinction of being – at least ostensibly – a Yorkshire not a London product, of having puzzled historians for decades, and of having been made for a most unusual purpose.

A single-barrel, 14-bore flintlock sporting gun, it is of advanced design in discarding the usual cross-head screws in favour of square holes, thus long pre-dating the modern 'Allen Screw', as well as having an ingenious and reliable 'safety catch'. Its chief glory, though, is its decoration: the lock is chiselled in relief with rococo leaf scrolls and shell motifs, and the mounts with scrolls incorporating monstrous creatures, dolphins and fruit, while the browned barrel is chiselled in low relief at the breech with lively foliate scrolls on a gilt ground. The stock is exquisitely, abundantly and precisely inlaid with silver wire, the themes including floral scroll – and strap-work, silver dots, and with engraved silver plates of various sizes. These are delicately drawn and shaded, depicting flowers, leaves, bunches of grapes, snakes, snails, butterflies, shells, monsters, cherubs and angels, not to mention a lion (reclining on a cornucopia) and a unicorn beneath a palm tree, together with allegorical figures of Fame and Victory. The source and inspiration for this – except for the lion and unicorn – is largely Nicolas Guérard's *Diverses Pièces d'Arquebuserie* [86]. Crucially, the gun is also signed, the name SIMPSON appearing on the lock and SIMPSON YORK at the breech of the barrel. This was William Simpson, listed as a gun maker in York trade directories from 1738 to 1756, and who had previously worked for the Board of Ordnance in London.

Whilst a provincial origin might seem surprising, fine gun makers were not confined to London. Henry Ellis, working in Doncaster between 1690 and 1723, was another example from Yorkshire. However, the parts of many 18th-century guns were made by separate and highly specialised craftsmen, and the 'maker' did little more than put them together: in this case the barrel's London proof-marks imply a metropolitan origin, and the consensus is now that Simpson procured the components from the finest London craftsmen, although his own skills as a silversmith suggests that much of the decoration may have been his work.

Normally speaking such an outstanding item would have been commissioned and we would expect to know by whom: in this case it was long assumed that the patron was Cuthbert Constable or his son William (1721–91), of Burton Constable Hall near Hull, where the gun remained until after the Second World War. The absence of a bill in the family archive, however, left this unproven and the date of the gun unknown. However, in the early 2000s it was noticed that the *York Courant* of Tuesday 11 July 1738 contained the following notice:

To be raffled for by subscription at one Guinea a lot A New Gun, valued at fifty Guineas, design'd for a Fowling-Piece … with more Variety in the Ornamental Part, better executed, than any thing of the kind that has yet been shewn … to be seen at WILLIAM SIMPSON's, *the maker, at the corner of Castlegate, York.*

This can be little other than Royal Armouries' gun – made, it seems, as a publicity and marketing stunt to announce to the Yorkshire market that a London gun maker of exceptional skill was now amongst them. How far this worked is questionable, as no other gun bearing Simpson's name is known, but his extravagant claims about this object were certainly justified.

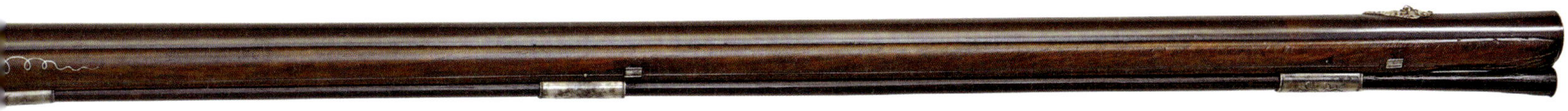

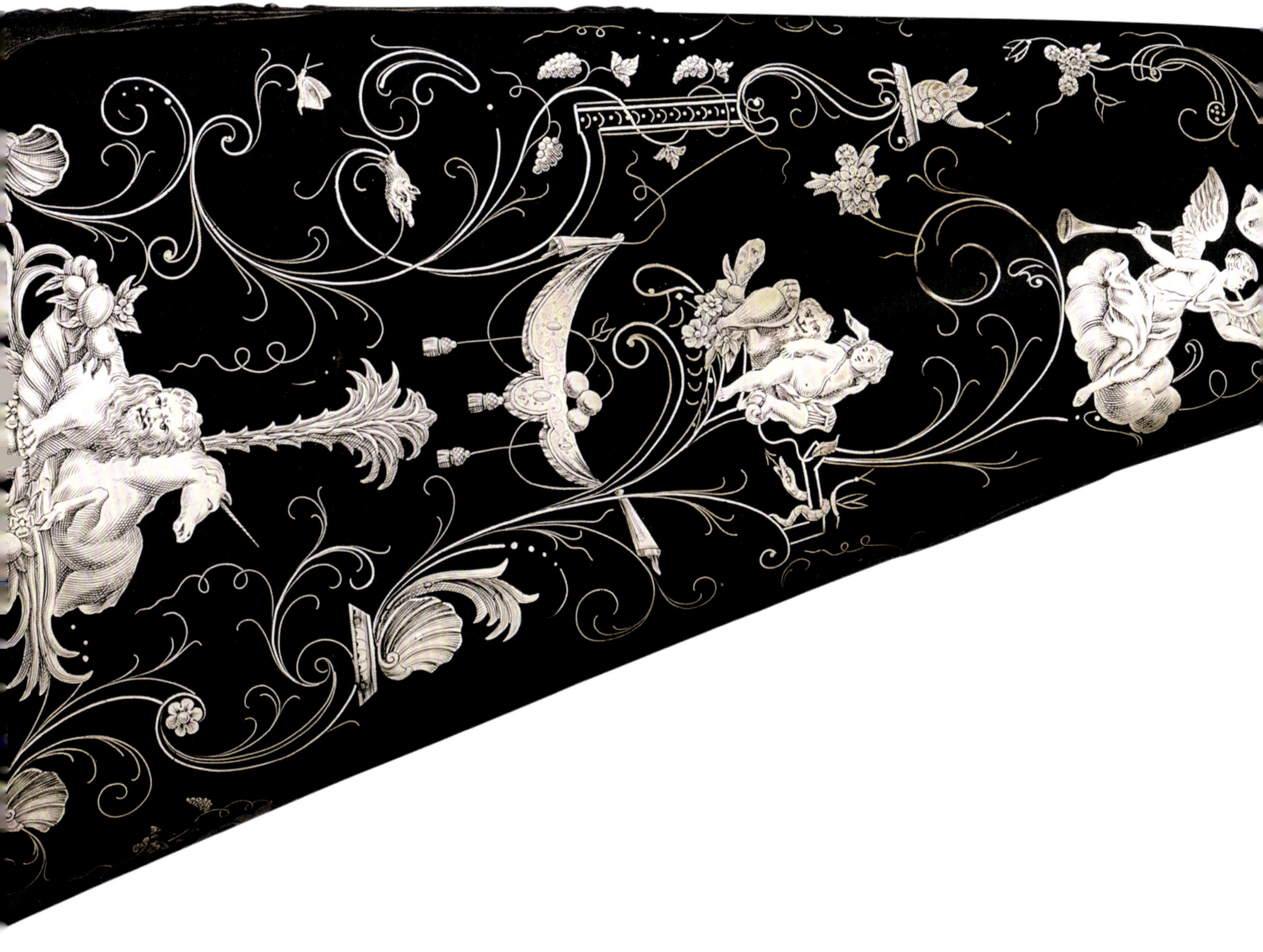

88

The 'Tula garniture' for Elizabeth, Empress of Russia

Russia, 1752 · XII.1504–6, XIII.150, XIII.998, VI.356–7

From the 17th century, and more so in the next, high-quality guns and related sporting equipment were made in sets or 'garnitures', a word used to describe the many pieces that made up multi-purpose armours that were particularly suitable as prestigious gifts. This garniture was made for the Empress Elizabeth of Russia (r.1741–1762), daughter of Peter the Great (r.1682–1725) and Catherine I, who seized the throne by *coup d'état* in 1741 and became the country's third female ruler. She was a keen and skilful sportswoman and appreciated art, design and craftsmanship, as this garniture demonstrates. It is a product of the Tula arsenal, about 200 km south of Moscow, where arms had been made from the 16th century. Tula was the site of an Imperial factory established by Peter the Great, initially to produce military weapons, but whose craftsmen, with government support, later also made fine, presentation-quality specimens such as these. Known since the Soviet era as the Tula Arms Plant, it still makes military and sporting guns today.

In this case the garniture consists of a single-barrelled flintlock shotgun, a pair of pistols (used in the hunting field in the 18th century, including from the saddle), all dated 1752. As with many Russian sporting arms of the period, these are decorated in the French style, closely associated with the designs of De Lacollombe and Nicolas Guérard [86, 87]: the inlaid silver decoration showing a boar attacked by hounds, whilst also being aimed at by a lady archer and a man with a gun, is firmly based on of one of Guérard's engravings. The motifs on the other side – rather incoherently assembled – include a Roman-looking horseman, a Roman trophy of arms, a cannon barrel and a figure of Victory in a chariot, again taken from Guérard. The mixture of sporting and loosely military themes was meant no doubt in reference to Elizabeth's enthusiasm for hunting and Russia's military prowess during her reign. The lock and sideplates have chiselled decoration on a gold ground, a primary characteristic of mid-18th century Tula products, and the wrists have silver gilt escutcheons displaying the Imperial Russian eagle, while the barrel is decorated along its entire length with Rococo ornaments, flowering bushes and military trophies on a gilded background. It also bears the empress's monogram and the inscription 'Tula 1752'. The pistols are similarly decorated. The stirrups accompanying the guns, also from Tula, seem to have been added in the late 18th century, and the powder flask after the garniture's acquisition by the Tower Armouries in 1950.

Complementing their decoration, both shotgun and pistols also incorporate advanced safety features. Housed in the steels are additional pan covers operated by a spring catch, accompanied by sliding safety-catches to the rear of the cocks. After loading the firearms via the muzzle, one primes the pan, by pushing the main part of the frizzen back and away from the cock, leaving the priming powder covered and held in place, but with the steel striking surface of the frizzen safely out of the way. On closing the frizzen a spring catch within it engages with the separate pan cover so that when the lock is fired the pan cover opens with it to expose the priming powder.

The subsequent history of the firearms is also of interest. Letters dating from 1814 held in the Royal Armouries' archive suggest that they may have been brought back from Moscow by a certain Chevalier Louis Guérin de Bruslart, shortly after Napoleon invaded Russia in 1812. Bruslart, a man of colourful character and by all accounts a Bourbon agent, had been entrusted by a Russian nobleman to deliver them to a French aristocrat, but instead Bruslart deposited the group with William Vardon, an ironmonger of Gracechurch Street, possibly as security for a loan. Bruslart, however, never retrieved the garniture and it remained in the possession of Vardon's descendants until its sale in 1950.

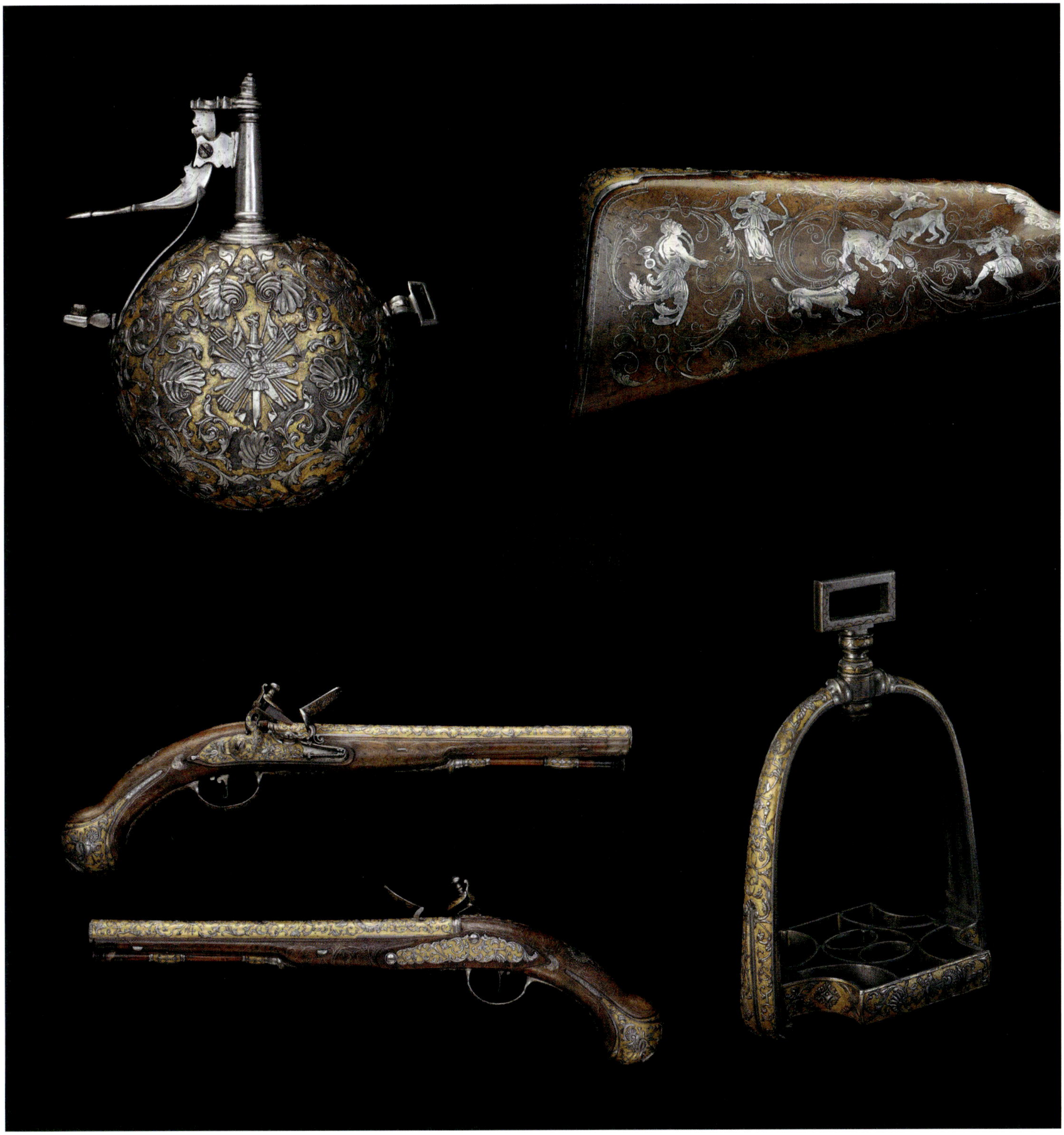

89

An Ottoman flintlock pistol (*kubur*) from Algiers

Algeria, 18th century · XXVIF.114

This pistol belongs to a large group of coral-mounted pistols, long guns, powder flasks and other firearms accessories, as well as swords (Turkish: *yataghans*) hilted with semi-precious stones, all presented as diplomatic gifts to the royal houses of Europe in the early 19th century by the Deys of Algiers. Well might the Deys have required such artistic diplomacy, for the Regency of Algiers, a vassal state virtually independent of the Ottoman government in Istanbul, was the home of the Barbary corsairs, whose depredations on European shipping, in particular the capture of Christian slaves for the Ottoman fleet's galleys, had been a significant obstacle to European trade since the 16th century. Two Barbary Wars (1801–5 and 1815), prosecuted mainly by America and Sweden, failed to suppress them, and it was only a bombardment by the British fleet under Lord Exmouth in 1816 that brought Algiers under control, the abolition of Christian slavery forming the principal item in the negotiation.

Coral was a popular form of decoration across the Ottoman Empire, the main centre being Trabzon, on the Black Sea. Algiers, however, had its own source of coral, and produced coral-mounted items in a distinctive style: where the Trabzon corals were generally grooved or striated, the Algerian corals were generally cut with flat faces and polished. Gifts of arms including long guns and pairs of pistols were given to the Prince Regent, the future George IV, by the Dey of Algiers in 1810 and 1819, now preserved as two pairs and a single pistol in the Royal Collection, Windsor Castle (the latter the pair to this pistol). Others formed parts of diplomatic gifts to the royal houses of Europe, including a pair in the Livrustkammaren, Stockholm, three pairs in the Real Armería, Madrid, and one in the Hermitage, St Petersburg. Others have lost their provenances, such as one in the Metropolitan Museum of Art, New York, a pair sold at Christie's, one formerly in the Rick Wagner collection in Massachusetts and one in the Tareq Rajab Museum, Kuwait. Though many of the pistols are of Algerian manufacture, they are all fitted with 'French' flintlocks, which have internal mainsprings, unlike the long guns of the whole group which have the Ottoman miquelet lock with external mainsprings. Most of these are Algerian in manufacture while a few, like the pair in the Wallace Collection, London, have French barrels and locks. While most of the long guns are signed and dated by their makers, few of the pistols are signed; two of those in the Royal Collection presented in 1810 are signed '*amal Mustafa* and dated 1152, making them seventy years old at the time of presentation. A pair of pistols in the Museum of Islamic Art, Doha also retains its coral-decorated holsters designed to be strapped to the pommel of a saddle, the only surviving example of the type; it is likely that other pistols in the presentation group were presented with holsters, along with the saddles and other horse furniture which formed part of the diplomatic gifts.

[222]

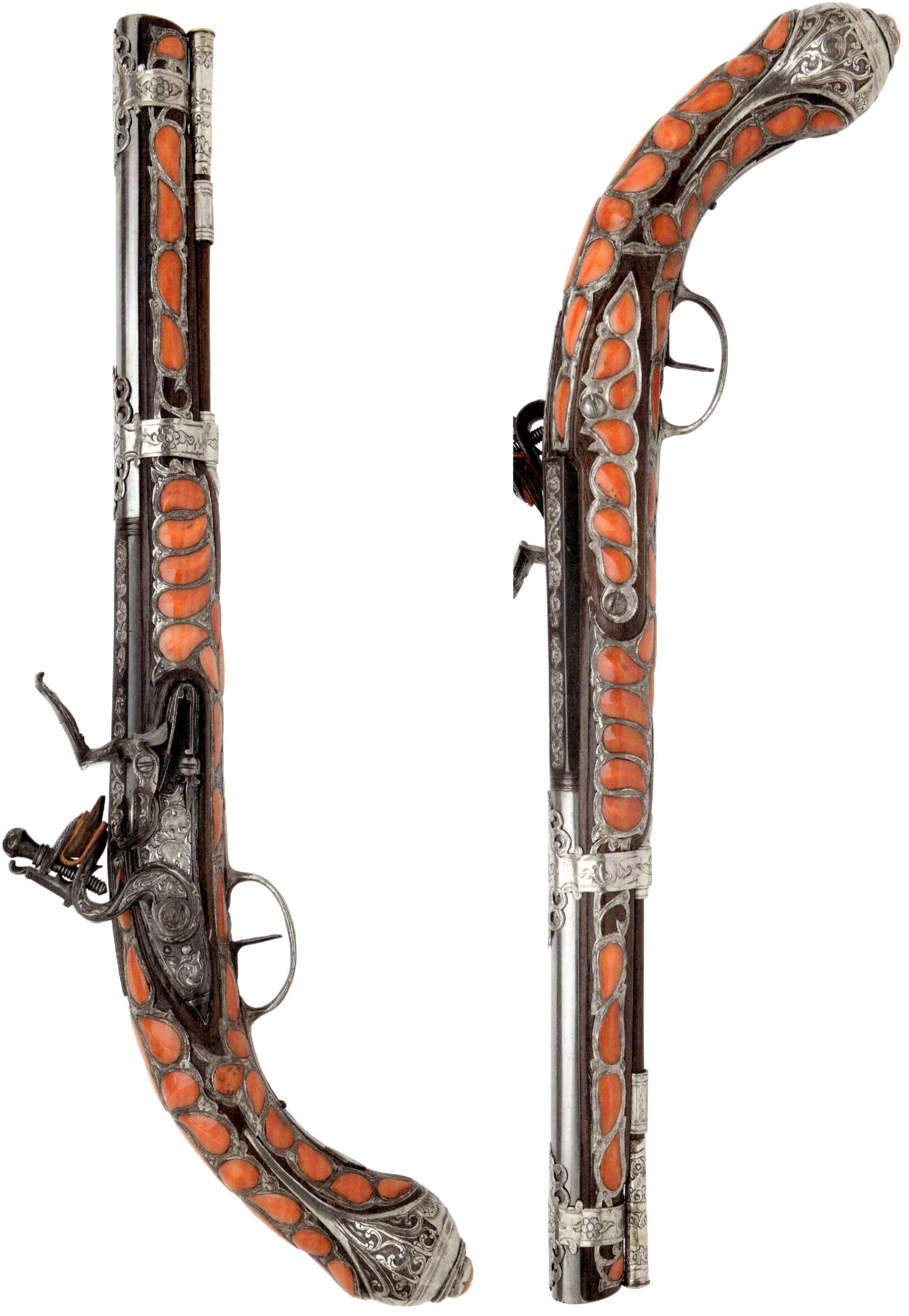

90

First English edition of Domenico Angelo's *The School of Fencing*

England, 1765 · RAL 27206

By the eighteenth century fencing was viewed not just as an art of war but as an essential gentlemanly accomplishment. Domenico Angelo was one of the most influential fencing masters of the mid-eighteenth century, and this book was his great work. Born in Livorno (Leghorn) in 1717, Angelo probably began his training as a fencer in Italy, but in about 1744 was sent to Paris by his father to hone his business skills. Instead, he was drawn into the world of horsemanship and dancing, and fencing under the master Monsieur Teillagory. Thanks to his relationship with an Irish-born actress, Margaret Woffington, Angelo moved to London and briefly to Dublin. When their liaison ended, he returned to London in 1755, where his existing reputation as a horseman gained him the position of Master of Horse to Henry, 10th Earl of Pembroke. In about 1758 he was appointed by Augusta, Dowager Princess of Wales as riding and fencing master to her sons, George, Prince of Wales (from 1760, King George III), and Edward, Duke of York. By now well established, well connected and well-heeled, in 1761 Angelo bought a large house in Soho Square, which he opened as his own School of Arms. This quickly became London's foremost academy of horsemanship, swordsmanship and gentlemanly behaviour.

Angelo then turned his hand to codifying his teaching in a book, *L'Ecole des armes, avec l'explication générale des principales attitudes et positions concernant l'escrime*, which was published in London in 1763. The publication was financed by subscriptions from over 200 of his clients, and the forty-seven engravings were made after drawings by the artist James Gwyn RA (1700–69). The drawings were taken from life, and Angelo himself was the principal model.

The English translation, *The School of Fencing*, appeared in several editions, though none were as lavish as the first of 1765. Dedicated to Princes William Henry and Henry Frederic (younger brothers to George and Edward), both of whom were Angelo's pupils, it is the only edition in which Gwyn's engravings were hand-coloured. It is also the only one to have parallel English and French text on each page. It is thought that Angelo was assisted in translating the text into English by his friend the famous French-English diplomat, spy and transvestite, the Chevalier d'Eon, another former pupil of Teillagory.

The School of Fencing primarily teaches the use of the small-sword and fencing foil, with brief sections on the use of weapons for the off-hand, including dagger, cloak and lantern (for dazzling an opponent during night-time attacks). There is also a section on the use of the small-sword against the military sabre (or broad sword, as Angelo terms it). In its day the book was recognized as a clear, concise and useful guide to fencing, and the author was praised for his appreciation of fencing as gentlemanly exercise and accomplishment, not just a means of self-defence. Tellingly, Angelo's text was used in its entirety in Denis Diderot's *Encyclopédie* (1751–65), accompanied by redrawn and scaled-down engravings. Today, Angelo's book is viewed as one of the first works on modern fencing, and to have been hugely influential in the development of the sport. Only seven other copies survive in public collections worldwide, a factor behind the Royal Armouries' recent decision to publish a facsimile edition.

The Royal Armouries' copy of this rare and beautiful book is in very good condition. The colours of the engravings are as bright as ever, although two of them (including plate 6, shown here) have been altered by the addition of pencil marks, presumably by a previous owner improving on the original. In the featured illustration, the fencer on the left is in the third guard or position, whilst his opponent is thrusting from the fourth position or guard. Note the added pencil mark repositioning the head of the fencer on the right so that he is watching the fencer on the left, not his sword tip.

Position pour la garde de tierce et le coup de quarte sur les Armes. Plate 6.

Publish'd according to Act of Parliament Feb. 1763.

91

The 'Furies Gun': a sculptural masterpiece cast by Horatio Alberghetti

Italy, 1773 · XIX.79

Usually known as the 'Furies' gun, thanks to the sculptures on the trail, this is undoubtedly the most lavishly decorated barrel and carriage in the Royal Armouries' collection. Its bore ranks it as a small field gun (2.5 in), firing a two-pound shot, roughly equivalent to the Falcon of earlier times. Its fabulous ornament and clear intent to impress notwithstanding, it is also a fully functioning weapon, as an inscription on the muzzle, ET POMPA ET USU ('both for display and service'), succinctly reminds us.

Although made in 1773, unusually and confusingly the gun bears two dates and the names of two makers: the base ring carries the Latin inscription HORATIUS ANTONIUS ALBERGHETTUS PUB(LICE).FUS(OR).VENETUS AN(NO) MDCLXXXIV ('Horatius Anthony Alberghetti, public gun founder in Venice, 1684'; or in Italian, 'Orazio Antonio'). The chase, meanwhile, is inscribed PHILIP(US) LATTARELLUS ROM(AE). DELIN(EAVIT) ET SCUL(PSIT) ('Philip Latarelli of Rome designed and sculpted [it]'), above which is a small scroll with the date 1773: Alberghetti was a member of a gun-founding dynasty based at the main arsenal of the Republic, in Venice, since the early 15th century. Of Laterelli, astonishingly, nothing else is known other than from this inscription. The best explanation is that Alberghetti made a gun in 1684 (now lost), that a cast was taken from it to which further decoration and inscriptions were added, and that a fresh mould was then made from which the existing one was cast in 1773. The carriage was made for it at the same time.

[226]

The recipient and owner of the gun was the Order of St John, or the Knights of Malta (originally the Knights Hospitaller), the 12th-century military order based in Jerusalem, which, after spells in Turkey, Rhodes and elsewhere, was established on the island in 1530: this is indicated by the arms of the Order on the second reinforce, accompanied by those of its Grand Master from 1773–5, Francisco Ximinez de Texada y Eslava. The initiator of its creation, meanwhile, is depicted in a shield supported by two cherubs and named on a pedestal below as LE C(HEVALIER). DE BOYER D'ARGENS COM(TE) ('The Chevalier de Boyer d'Argens, Earl'), otherwise Luc de Boyer d'Esguilles, a member of the Order since 1724 and Commander of the Artillery from 1767 to 1777. The pedestal with two male figures – one possibly in chains – is appropriately inscribed TERRENI FULMINA MARTIS ('The thunderbolts of earthly war'), supported by chained captives.

Other significant decoration includes the head of Medusa on the cascabel, a powerful symbol of warning and intimidation from the ancient world and inscribed SCINTILLA SVFFICIT VNA ('A single spark suffices'). The gun also carries extensive decoration in high relief of laurel branches, escutcheons and other figures over its entire length. Equally ornate and remarkable is the carriage and trail, also of 1773, carved with two torch-carrying Furies – the infernal goddesses of Greek mythology – and the wheel hubs representing Helios – the sun in Greek mythology – and the spokes depicting the rays.

Both gun and carriage remained at Malta until the capture of the island by Napoleon, en route for Egypt, in 1798, from where they were dispatched to France aboard the frigate *La Sensible*. In the Strait of Sicily, however, she was captured by the British frigate *Seahorse* under Edward Foote, Captain, and later in the year gun and carriage were deposited at the Tower of London. By 1800 they were in the Grand Storehouse among many other items trumpeting the success of British arms. Three years later a guidebook noted 'the carved figures of two furies, whose features are strongly expressive of rage', displayed along with other material from the same source.

92

Helmet and cuirass from South India

South India, late 18th century · XXVIA.139

During the second half of the eighteenth century, the kingdom of Mysore in southern India was one of the most loyal supporters of the French East India Company and opponents of the British company. From 1782 until 1799 it was ruled by Tipu Sultan, whose father, Haidar Ali, had deposed the House of Wadiyar in the 1750s. Together, father and son fought to secure and expand their realm at the expense of the Mahrattas and the interests of the East India Company. Three Mysore Wars between 1766 and 1799 culminated in the capture of Tipu Sultan's capital, Seringapatam, and the restoration of the Wadiyar dynasty as puppet rulers.

Whilst keen on new technology, Tipu also valued some of the traditional forms of south Indian arms and armour, of which this beautifully embroidered, vivid armour, reputedly from the royal arsenal in Seringapatam, is a striking example. Fabric armours like this were based on ancient forms, worn by warriors across the southern regions of the subcontinent for centuries. The helmet and cuirass (*peti* in Hindi) are made from multiple layers of quilted cotton overlaid with velvet, densely embroidered in gilt thread. Together, the layers of cloth provided a thick barrier capable of protecting vulnerable areas of the body and combined lightness and flexibility with effective defence, forming a type of armour which continued to rival the metal mail and plate armours used elsewhere. The helmet, secured around the head with a tough band of wound green silk, originally had a metal nasal lodged through the silk band which would probably have flared out to cover the lower face with an anchor-shaped plate.

After Tipu was killed during the British storming of his stronghold at Seringapatam on 4 May 1799, his palace and city, including the arsenals, were plundered and the booty distributed or auctioned off. A kind of 'Tipu mania' took hold in Britain, and objects held to be associated with him, however tenuously, became extremely fashionable. Lord Mornington, the Governor General, ordered that many of the most prestigious items held to be directly linked to Tipu himself should be retained for presentation to the king and other members of the royal family, including the duke of York, the recipient of this helmet and cuirass: when his collection was auctioned off after his death in 1827, these and several other pieces found their way to the Tower of London. The 1841 guide to the castle described the helmet and belt on show in the Eastern Vestibule of the Grand Storehouse [80] as the late property of the duke of York, but more importantly, as the former possessions of 'Tippoo Sahib', a name and a legend that the castle's visitors would have recognised and regarded with awe.

[228]

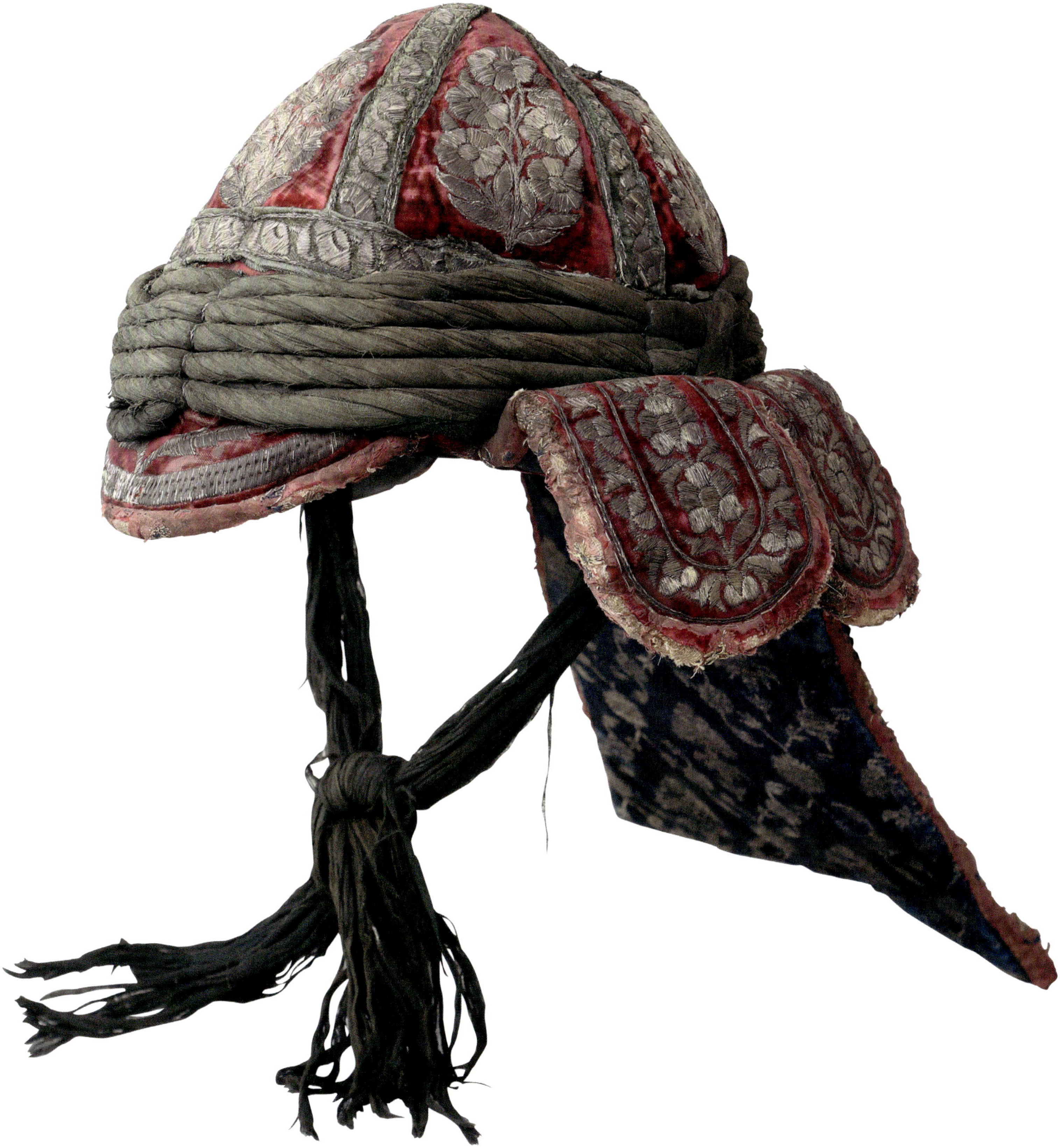

93

Bronze tiger mortar from Mysore

India, late 18th century · XIX.119

Tipu Sultan, ruler of Mysore, was a formidable leader and warrior [92]. Feared and admired by the British, he was proactive in modernising his armies through training and the development of weapons, and particularly interested in new forms of firearms: his gun makers at his capital Seringapatam achieved the highest standards, and at Bangalore, where he built a summer palace in 1791 using mechanisms based on the most modern European examples (thanks sometimes to the Sultan's direct involvement). Numerous products of these workshops survive at Powis Castle, in the Royal Collection at Osborne House, the Government Museum, Madras and in private collections. The guns are all characterised by European-esque form combined with the lavish use of Tipu's tiger stripes (*bubri*) in their decoration and the heart-shaped Haider talisman in honour of his father. The guns were very high quality, as noted by an English officer at the time: 'a degree of perfection has been attained in every stage of the process truly astonishing to those of our officers who visited the different workshops: he had even got the late European invention of boring guns perpendicularly, and also had his machinery kept in motion by water'. Of the 929 pieces of artillery in Seringapatam in 1799, over 200 were made by Tipu's gun founders, and the rest were European imports, mainly British. The majority were conventional cannon and howitzers, and only a very few in this highly unusual mortar form. One such signed and dated gun was cast by Ahmad Pali at the royal foundry at Seringapatam in 1790/1.

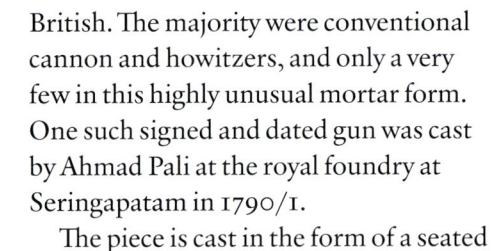

The piece is cast in the form of a seated tiger, the muzzle issuing from his open jaws, propped by his forelegs, while the whole surface is decorated with conventional *bubri*. This was in keeping with Tipu's celebrated appropriation of the great cat's mantle of strength and courage, and tiger motifs adorned not just his artillery but other weapons; the association remains today, upheld not least by a particularly famous object associated with him, 'Tipu's Tiger', an organ built into a moving model of a tiger mauling a uniformed European soldier, in the Victoria and Albert Museum. The mortar itself was never finished, since the vent is not drilled through to the chamber, and the bore was not cleaned after casting. In 1838 it was found concealed in the Konda Reddy Fort at Kurnool, Andhra Pradesh, on the northern border of the Mysore sultanate between Bangalore and Hyderabad, together with two similar mortars, one now in the collection of the Royal Artillery Museum and the other in private hands. A 24-pounder gun was also found, now in the Royal Armouries' collection, whose muzzle, trunnion ends and cascabel button are formed as tiger's heads with *bubri* appearing on the unfinished chase. Although clearly never used, if they had been completed these guns would have combined deadly firepower with appearances that would have recalled the ferocious reputation of Tipu himself, the self-styled 'Tiger of Mysore'.

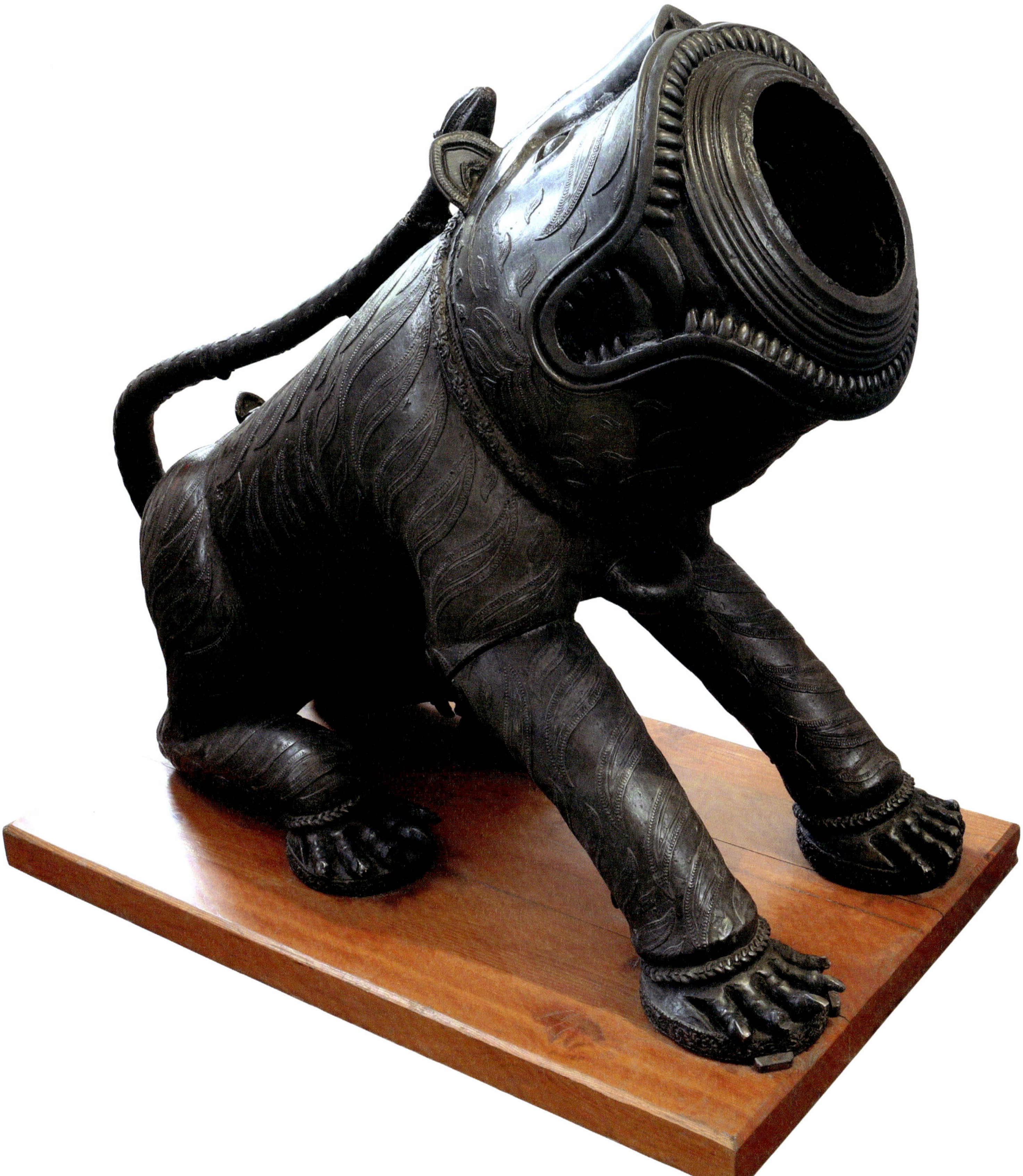

94

A present from Napoleon to the king of Spain

France, 1802 · XII.1278

In 1802 the king of Spain, Charles IV (r.1788–1808), received a wonderful gift of eleven guns from his more powerful ally Napoleon Bonaparte, then First Consul of France. Bonaparte's generosity, however, was not without purpose: in a tradition going back to antiquity, and exemplified elsewhere in this volume, fine weaponry was being exchanged for political ends, in this case to help cement the 3rd Treaty of San Ildefonso. The deal itself was wonderfully one-sided. France got the vast if ill-defined American province of Louisiana, and as a little extra, six mighty warships; Spain got the vague promise, never really fulfilled, of a made-up principality in Italy. All the more important, then, that there were no false economies with the guns, which cost, in today's terms, about five million pounds. The maker was Nicolas-Noël Boutet (1761–1833), one of the greatest gunsmiths of all time, and a consummate survivor who worked for successive royal, republican and imperial governments. In 1793 his *atelier*, later the *Manufacture Nationale d'armes à Versailles*, was established in the outbuildings of the former royal palace. Most of its output was for the military, but Boutet's speciality was fabulous *armes de luxe*, and his official brief no less than 'to surpass everything else ever made and reach a level of perfection that foreign countries will despair of'. His success lay partly in his dual role as director and – being a talented artist – as chief designer, earning him the unique title of *Directeur artiste*, as engraved on the lock-plate of this example.

Charles's gift consisted of two rifles of different and complex forms, two *pistolets de combat*, a *fusil double* (double-barrelled fowling piece) and six 18-bore *fusils simples* (single-barrelled smoothbores), of which the Armouries' piece is one. The decoration is largely in the obsessively classical *Directoire* style, its subject matter chosen to match the status of the recipient and the object's purpose: details include a relief figure (silver on a gold background) of the goddess Diana, with hound, bow and quiver on the finial, a lively boar hunt in Greco-Roman style on the left lock-plate, a Medusa's head and trophy of the Liberal Arts on the trigger guard, and a trophy of Roman arms on the butt-plate. In less solemn vein, a golden fox on the lock plate attacks a golden hound, a conceit borrowed from the famous animal painter, Jean Baptiste Oudry (1686–1755), while the contemporary mania for all things Egyptian left its mark in the three-dimensional ebony caryatid on the underside of the grip. Meanwhile the royal recipient is personally acknowledged by the escutcheon plate bearing a crowned 'C', and his portrait, framed by attributes of royalty, at the ramrod socket. The extent and quality of all this ornament is amply matched by the gun's beautiful balance and handling: in an age when royalty ate off gold plates, this was a practical piece, intended for use. But whilst as near to a work of art as a gun can get, Boutet's creation is, every bit as importantly, a reminder of the historical importance of arms and armour in oiling the wheels of international diplomacy.

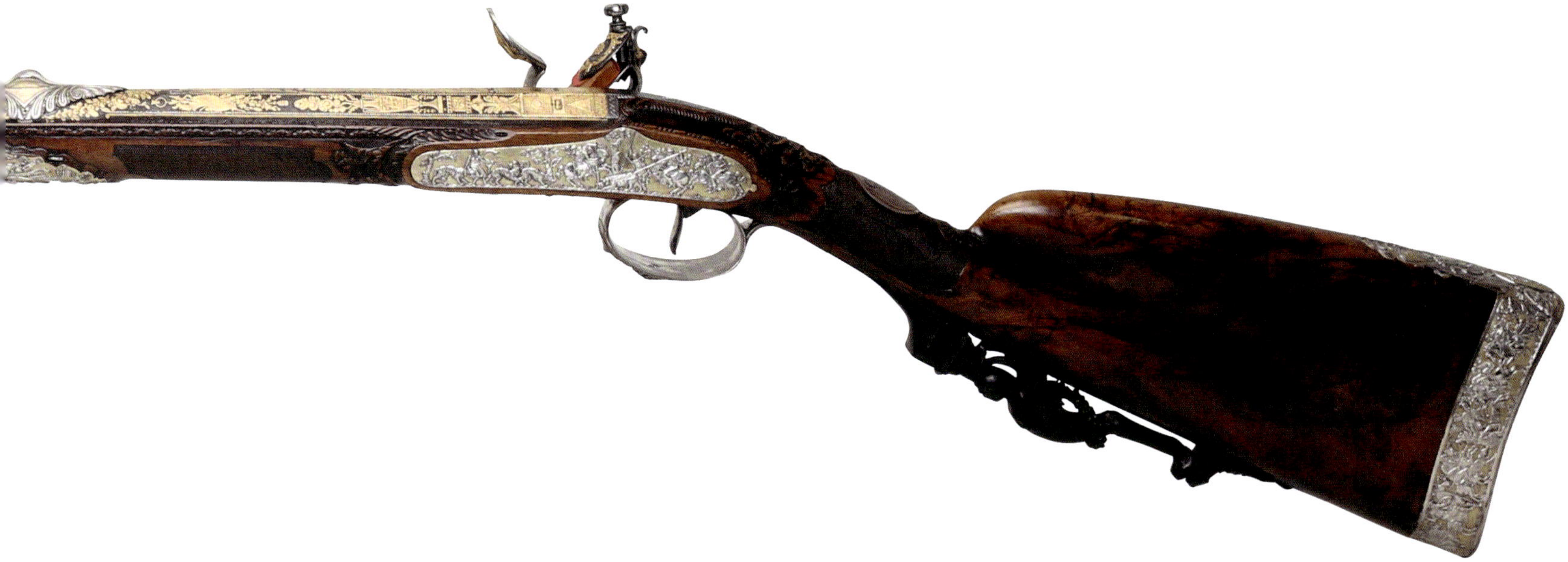

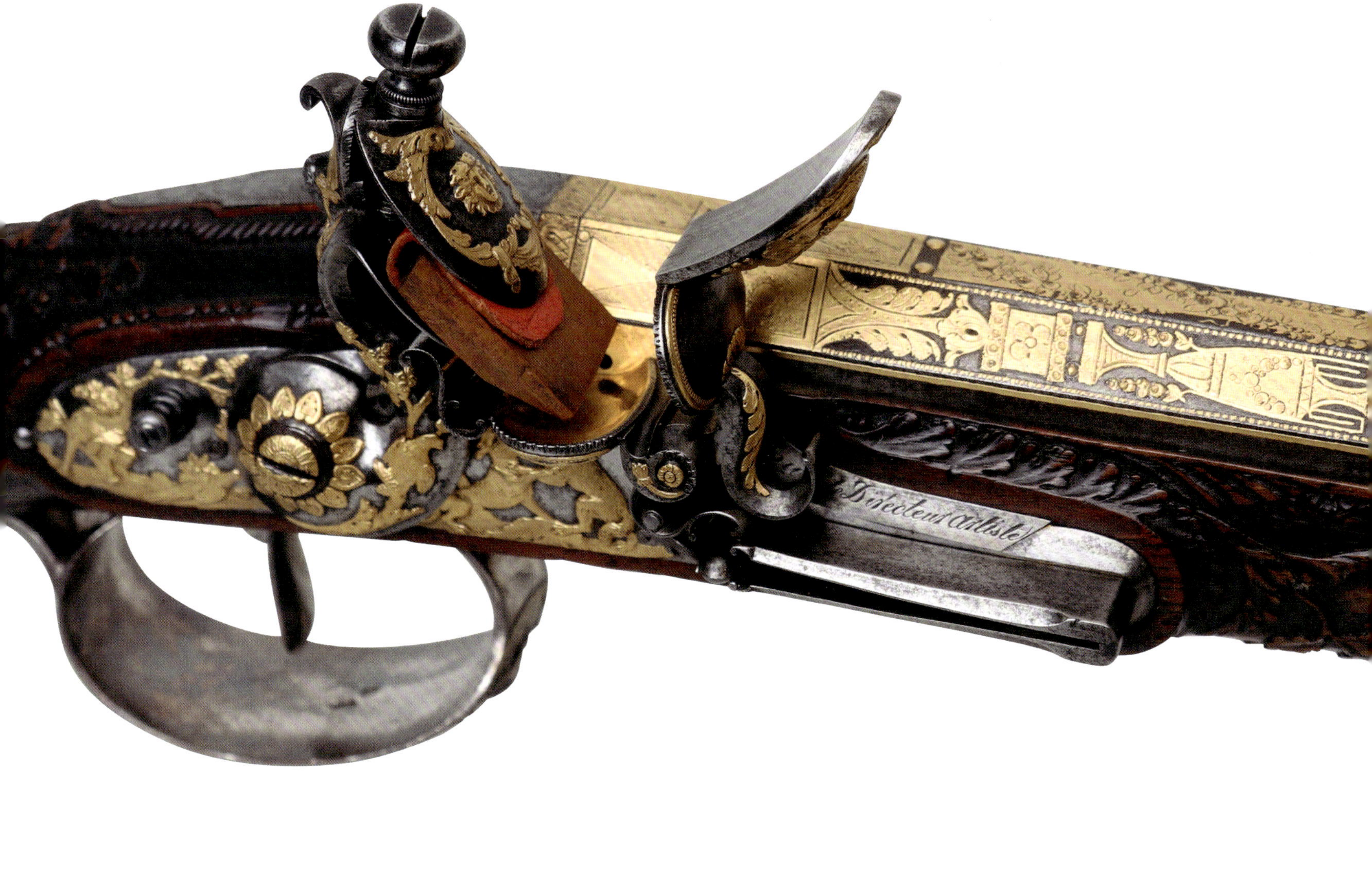

95

Heavy Cavalry Trooper's sword, variant of Pattern 1796

England, early 19th century · IX.968

Before 1786 swords used by the British army varied according to unit, personal choice and regimental resources. This plain-looking weapon is important as an example of the first centrally issued regulation British army pattern sword, and its introduction owed much to the efforts of one man in particular, Major-General John Gaspard le Marchant (1766–1812). Its inscription, meanwhile, associates it with a famous hero of Waterloo, Corporal John Shaw (1789–1815).

By the late eighteenth century, swords were only carried in the British infantry by officers, non-commissioned officers of sergeant rank and above, drummers and musicians; in the cavalry, meanwhile, they were still borne by all ranks, and the sword-wielding cavalry charge remained a potent battlefield reality. Divided into heavy and light units, the former smashed through enemy formations while the latter skirmished and generally harassed. Heavy cavalry swords tended to have straight blades; light cavalry, from about 1760, curved ones. The efficiency of the British cavalry, however, when it came to sword use, was compromised by poor drill and inadequate equipment, both of which Le Marchant was to transform. From an old Guernsey family he joined the regular army in 1783 and served in the cavalry as a brigade major against the French in Flanders in 1793–5, when he observed the superior weapons and swordsmanship of Britain's Austrian allies. A skilled practitioner himself, he prepared a manual which was adopted by the British army as *The Rules and Regulations for the Sword Exercise of Cavalry*, published in 1796. His obvious abilities compensating for lack of patronage, Le Marchant attracted the attention of George III and was promoted to Lieutenant Colonel in 1797, and then in 1810 successfully recommended the foundation of staff colleges, the forerunners of Sandhurst. Having returned to active service, he was killed in 1812 at Salamanca whilst leading a cavalry action. As the king told him in 1804, 'This country is greatly indebted to you'.

The inscription on this sword's stirrup guard meanwhile, introduces Shaw and another tale. It reads:

This sword belonged to SERGT SHAW OF THE LIFE GUARDS WHO KILLED 13 MEN AT THE BATTLE OF WATERLOO. *Presented by Col McVicar to E Young Esqr* MD WHO NOW GIVES IT TO HIS *G.son Henry Wiley Middleton January 1st 1864*

In contrast to Le Marchant, John Shaw, born in Wollaton, Nottinghamshire, was of humble origin and never commissioned, but nevertheless achieved greater popular fame. Although he joined the 2nd Dragoons in 1807, his first distinction was as a pugilist, and in 1812 and 1815 he was tipped as a future national champion. His impressive physique led to work as a model for the painters Benjamin Robert Haydon (1786–1846) and William Etty (1787–1849), important connections which brought Shaw to the attention of Walter Scott, who was to add greatly to his fame. At Waterloo, Shaw served as a corporal in the Life Guards and fought with celebrated distinction. He died of wounds the day following the battle, and was buried at La Haye Sainte. Scott, who visited the battlefield very shortly afterwards, heard the tales of Shaw's exploits and was much moved.

Whether the sword really *was* Shaw's is of course not clear, since the inscription dates from long after Waterloo, and at least in one version of his heroics his sword broke in his hand. But either way its existence perpetuates his memory, helping to ensure, as John Haskins put it in his poem 'The Battle of Waterloo' (1816):

Nor 'mongst her humble sons shall SHAW *e're die Immortal deeds defy mortality."*

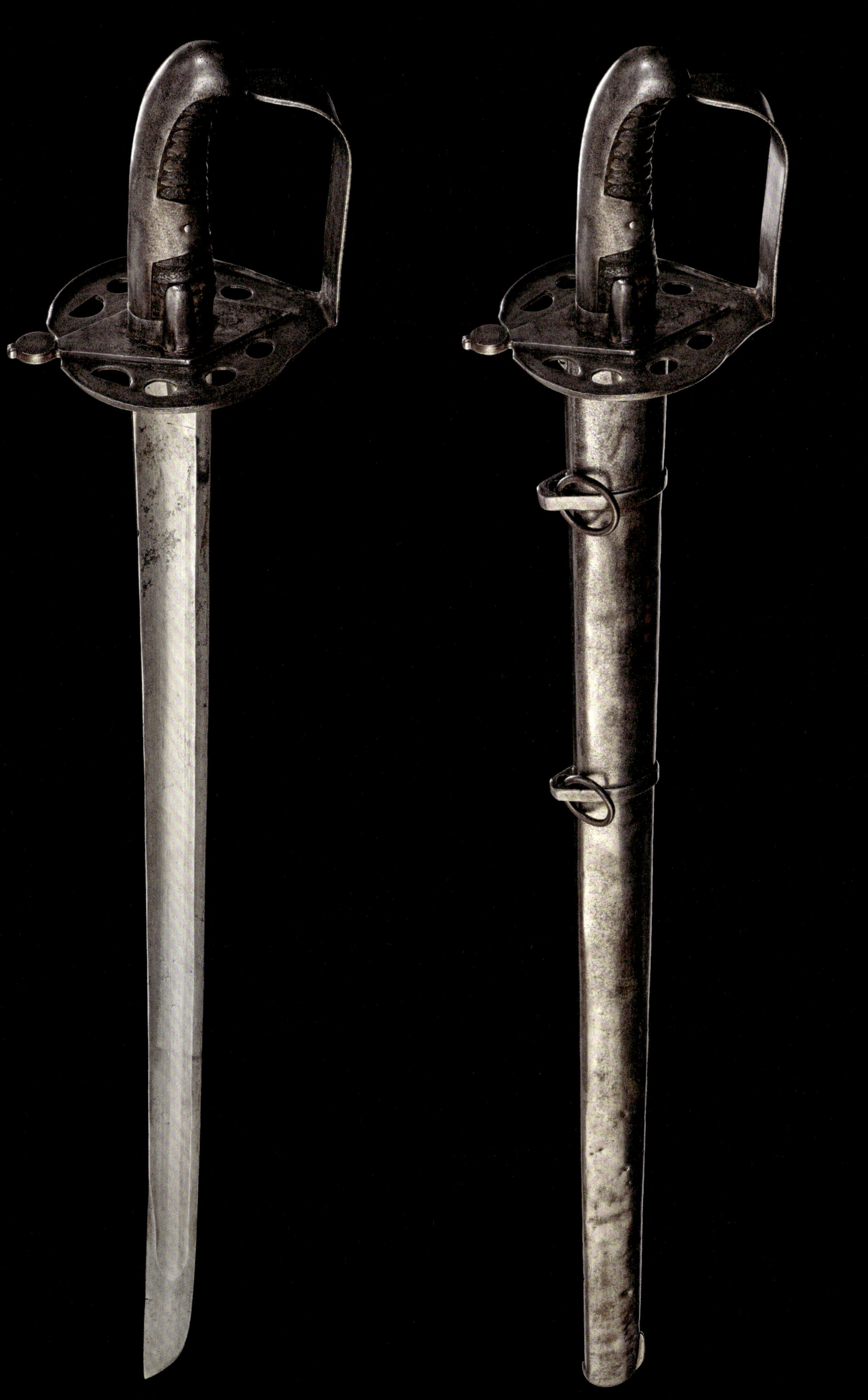

96
Jewelled presentation sword for Admiral Collingwood
England, 1806–7 · IX.909

From 1797 the Corporation of the City of London has accompanied its ancient award of the Freedom of the City, as applied to military men, with the gift of a sword. Since 1803 a similar scheme has been operated by the Lloyd's underwriters, the Patriotic Fund (after 1854 the Lloyd's Patriotic Fund) rewarding exceptional service with swords, of a quality depending on rank, and other offerings. In the case of the Corporation, the overall commander of an action or campaign received a sword and scabbard valued at 200 guineas, the second-in-command – or an officer distinguishing himself in a single action – 100 guineas. To date sixty-three such awards have been made, the last two in the 1982 Falklands War.

This example was awarded to Vice Admiral Lord Collingwood (1748–1810), an immensely important figure in naval and British history who was overshadowed in his lifetime and since by Horatio Nelson – a man who was his friend and ten years his junior, but from early on his senior officer. The sword therefore has a particular significance in marking official recognition of Collingwood's achievements, though still, it has to be said, through an association with Nelson.

The man himself, Cuthbert Collingwood, was the son of a Newcastle merchant and joined the navy as a midshipman in August 1761. Lacking patronage his promotion was slow, but he was finally made lieutenant for his services in a naval brigade at the Battle of Bunker Hill in June 1775, an early engagement in the American Revolutionary War. In 1779 he received his first ship – the brig *Badger*, previously Nelson's first command – and both men went on to earn Gold Medals for their conduct in battles of the Glorious First of June (1794) and Cape St Vincent (1797). In 1804 Collingwood became Vice Admiral, and his ship the *Royal Sovereign* was the first to engage the enemy at Trafalgar (21 October 1805), a victory which thwarted Napoleon's plans to invade England. Collingwood remained in service, as a highly successful Mediterranean commander-in-chief, but in 1808 asked to be recalled. Permission was finally granted in 1810 but he died at sea.

The Corporation of London, meanwhile, had voted in November 1805 to present him with a sword, making him the eleventh to receive one of the thirty-five swords awarded between 1797 and 1816, and the ninth naval officer so honoured. His citation is inscribed on the sword's shell:

for the brilliant & decisive Victory obtained by His Majesty's Fleet under his Command (upon whom it devolv'd upon the ever to be lamented Death of Vice Admiral Lord Viscount Nelson) over the combined Fleets of France & Spain, off Cape Trafalgar on 21st October 1805. Thereby affording to the World at large an additional & lasting proof of British Valour.

The weapon itself, made in 1806–7, is 'small sword' form, with a light hilt and shell, with a plain, hollow triangular-section blade, both elegant and deadly. Decoration is therefore concentrated on the 18-carat gold hilt, featuring martial trophies in relief, and exquisite enamel plaques bearing Collingwood's arms on one side and the Corporation's on the other, both surrounded by inset diamonds. The pommel too has plaques on each side, depicting naval trophies with flags, and the knuckle guard is inscribed 'ENGLAND EXPECTS EVERY MAN TO DO HIS DUTY' – Nelson's famous signal at Trafalgar – picked out in diamonds against a blue enamel background.

The sword was forwarded to Collingwood's widow, Sarah, and remained in the family until 1899. During the First World War it was bought by Sir Bernard Eckstein, who left it to the Royal Armouries in 1948.

[236]

Presented by the
Corporation of the City of London
pursuant to a Vote of Common Council
Pafsed the 26th Novr 1805
The Right Honble James Shaw Mayor
to VICE ADMIRAL
COLLINGWOOD
for the brilliant &
obtained by his
under his Command
lamented Death
Viscount Nelson
on the 21st October 1805

97

Wellington's telescope from Waterloo

England, *c.*1799–1805 · XVI.74

Sir Arthur Wellesley, victor of the Peninsula War and Waterloo, Duke of Wellington (1814) and Prime Minister (1828–30), is among the best-known figures of British and European history. As Constable of the Tower of London (1826–1852) and Master General of Ordnance (1819–27), he also plays a significant part in the history of the Royal Armouries and its precursors. The cult of Wellington, at its height in his own lifetime, survives today: items that belonged to him – his boots, his hat, his swords – have the status of relics, and this telescope is one of them.

Invented in Holland in 1608, the telescope's usefulness in warfare was immediately recognised. In that year, at the negotiations in The Hague which led to the first international recognition of the Dutch Republic, Maurice of Nassau showed one to Ambrogio Spinola, the Spanish commander: he presciently responded that 'I could no longer be safe, for you will see me from afar'. By the spring of 1609 spectacle-makers were selling small telescopes on the streets of Paris, and during the course of the century they became a standard piece of military equipment on land and sea. In 1780 the Dollond company (later Dollond and Aitchison) introduced the Army Telescope, or the 'improved achromatic telescope', the brass and mahogany form on which Wellington's is based.

The Duke's telescope is unusual for its period in having four 'draws', or brass tubes that slide inside each other, giving it up to 25 times greater magnification than achieved by the more common two or three-draw versions (compared to the average 12 times magnification of modern birdwatching binoculars). It is the work of Matthew Berge of London (d.1819), about whom little is known other than that he worked as a foreman to Jesse Ramsden (1735–1800), perhaps the greatest instrument maker of the time. When Ramsden died Berge took over his business and ran it until his death in 1819, trading from their premises at 199 Piccadilly in London. On Ramsden's death Berge's first task was to finish instruments already begun, and for a few years these were signed 'Berge, late Ramsden's', as is this one. This dates it to between the last years of Ramsden's life and 1805 when the double signature was dropped.

The telescope's provenance is proclaimed by a brass plaque screwed to the mahogany casing of the first draw which reads 'Telescope by Berge of London used by the Duke of Wellington at the Battle of Waterloo presented to Sir Robert Peel'. This is very believable, not least as Wellington is shown carrying it in several portraits, including one by Thomas Heaphy in the National Portrait Gallery and by William Robinson in the National Maritime Museum, at least the first of which dates from 1813, showing the Duke in Spain. Robert Peel, meanwhile, best known as the creator of the Metropolitan Police and later twice Prime Minister, was a friend and political ally of the Duke, notably in the government of 1828–30 which Wellington ran from the Lords as Prime Minister while Peel, as Home Secretary, led the Commons: it was perhaps in this context that Wellington gave Peel the telescope, a highly personal and moving gesture that Peel no doubt much appreciated. It later belonged to the businessman and collector Sir Bernard Eckstein, who very appropriately left it to the Tower Armouries at his death in 1948.

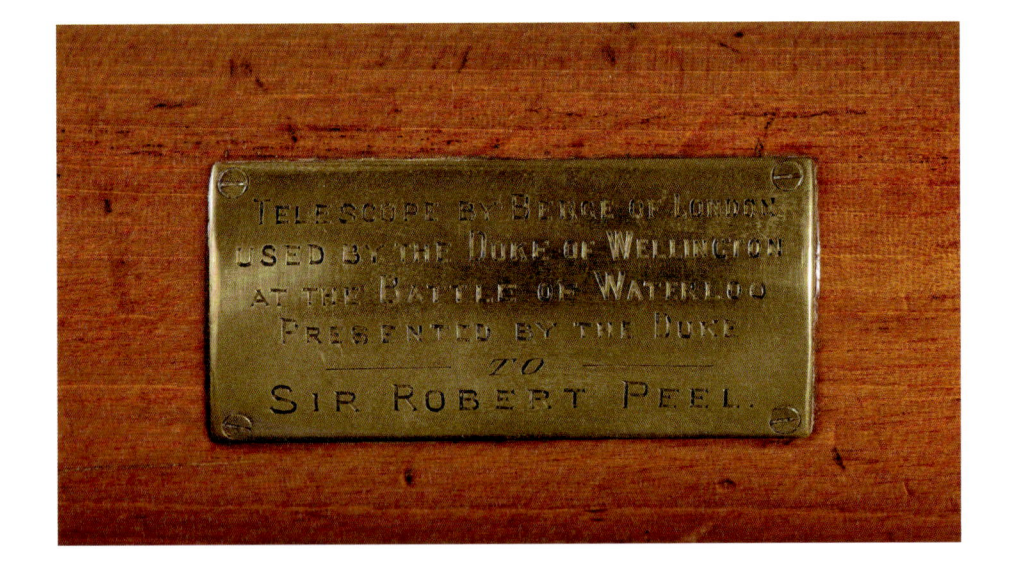

[238]

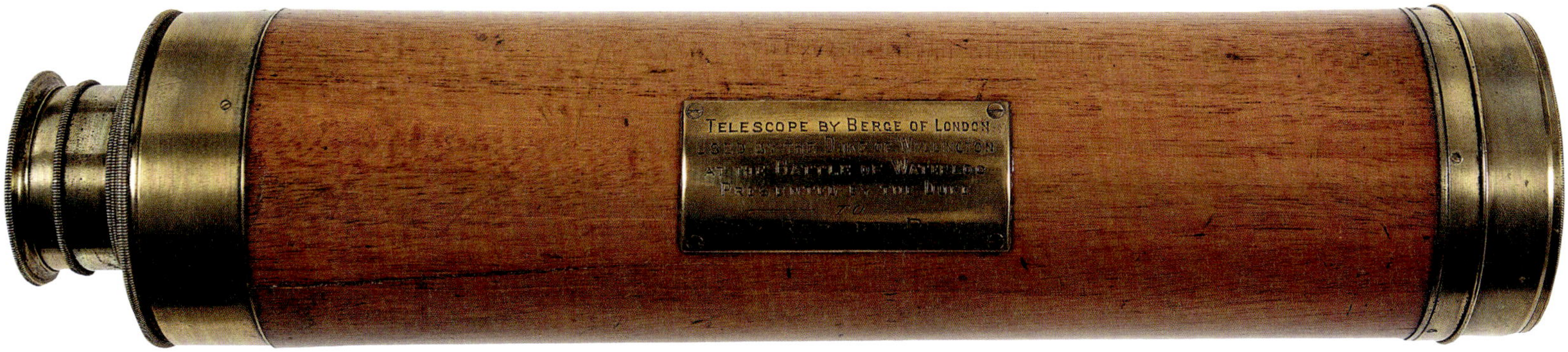
TELESCOPE BY BERGE OF LONDON
AT THE BATTLE OF WATERLOO

98

Pistols for the Prince Regent

England, 1811–20 · XII.5694–5

Ezekiel Baker (1758–1836) of Whitechapel, London was arguably the best English gun maker of his age. The Prince Regent, later George IV, was his most prestigious customer and a connoisseur of, amongst other things, fine guns. These pistols neatly illustrate both Ezekiel's skills and George's enthusiasms.

Baker had been apprenticed to Henry Nock, the leading gun maker of the previous generation, and like him was both technically inventive and a talented designer. In addition to making fine weapons, Baker was the creator of the Baker rifle, accepted in 1800 by the British military, and which remained in service for fifty years. Meanwhile the Prince of Wales's obsession with things martial began at an early age, and is captured in the painting *Queen Charlotte with her two eldest sons* (1765) by Johann Zoffany: attired in fancy dress, Frederick (later Duke of York) wears a classical Turkish costume, whilst George is dressed as Telemachus, in an approximation of classical arms and armour. As a young man it had been George's wish to serve in the field, but as heir to the throne this was forbidden by his father, George III, although he later allowed his son's appointment as Colonel of the 10th Light Dragoons on the condition that he would not serve abroad. An outlet for the resulting frustrations was, for example, to design uniforms for his Dragoons, but more importantly the development of his collection of arms and armour, originally displayed at his London residence, Carlton House. The majority survives as part of the Royal Collection and is housed at Windsor Castle. This was an interest which Baker must have felt he could turn to his advantage: in 1805, something of a showman himself, he invited the prince to try out a selection of pistols and rifles, probably with a view to encouraging his enthusiasm and securing his patronage. Whether it was this or subsequent meetings that did the trick is not clear, but the prince remained a customer until at least 1828, Baker providing him with newly made firearms in addition to maintaining and sometimes modifying items in his existing collection.

These pistols were commissioned by George as Prince Regent between 1811 and 1820, as revealed by a receipt in the Royal Archives dated to 1813 and indicating and cost of £63. In form they are double-barrelled, over and under, smoothbores with gold touchholes, swivel ramrods and browned barrels, on which the name 'E. Baker' is inlaid in gold. Situated prominently above the finely chequered grips are gold thumb plates in the form of the Prince of Wales's feathers. The quality of the pistols is found not only in the craftsmanship, but also in the ingenious single trigger mechanism, which fires the barrels in succession, a refinement which makes what are otherwise quite plain and utilitarian pistols of particular technical interest.

George was a profligate if generous man with an utter disregard for economy, and often commissioned firearms as gifts. These, however, he ordered and kept for himself, until he presented them to the Peninsular War veteran Sir J. H. Elphinstone. The Royal Armouries acquired them in 1987 at auction in Monaco.

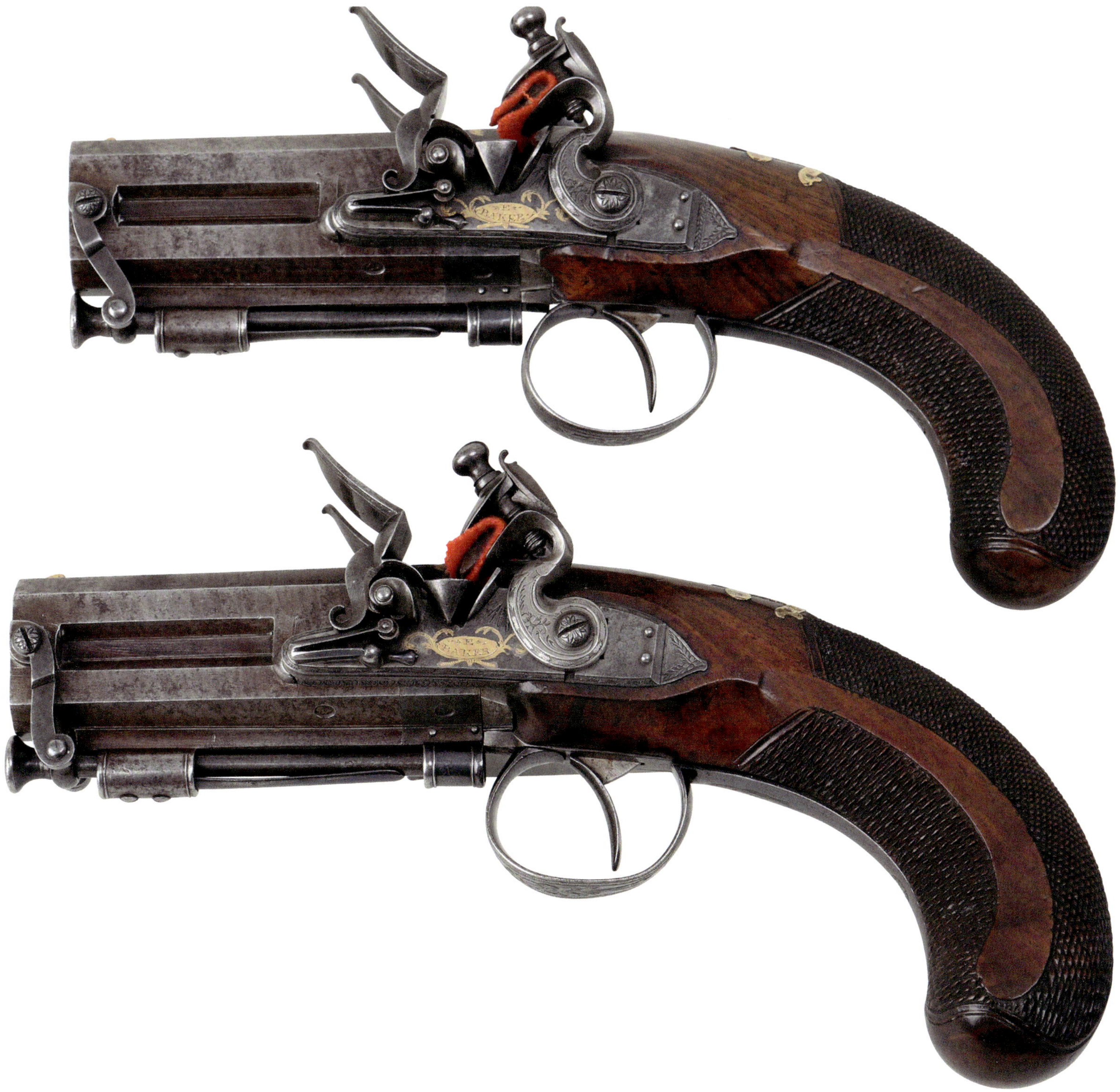

99

Pistols for Robert Fitzroy, Captain of HMS *Beagle*

England, 1831 · XII.1387–8

On Thursday 8 September 1831, the day of William IV's coronation, two men walked through the doors of 314½ Oxford Street. This was the premises of James Purdey & Sons, among London's best gun makers who stood on par with Nock, Manton or Egg. In their different ways both men were to make history. One was the twenty-two-year-old Charles Darwin, and the other the twenty-six-year-old Lieutenant Robert Fitzroy, the recently appointed captain of HMS *Beagle*, a meteorologist who was entrusted with the expedition which he had invited Darwin to join. His mission was to survey the coastline of Tierra del Fuego, Patagonia and the Southern Cone of South America.

The two men were at Purdey's to acquire equipment for the voyage. Fitzroy, a rich man, was a mighty spender and had an extensive shopping list, and on that day committed £400 to the purchase of firearms, ammunition and accessories. Darwin was sufficiently carried away to spend over £50 on a 'case of good strong pistols and an excellent rifle'.

Alongside Fitzroy's purchases of a double rifle, a double shotgun, a pair of pocket pistols, a pair of duelling or target pistols, were another pair of double-barrelled pistols of .700 calibre. These pistols, acquired by the Royal Armouries in 1947, are percussion models with back-action locks and half stocked in black stained walnut. The barrels are browned with a captive ramrod. The hammers and trigger guards are engraved with simple trophies of arms and the escutcheons with Fitzroy's initials. The butts have a cavity beneath spring-loaded butt caps to take spare percussion caps. These pistols were designed and purchased for personal protection, whether from man or beast, necessary despite the peaceable and scientific purposes of the expedition. Darwin, in *The Voyage of the Beagle* (1845) describes an occasion in Tierra del Fuego, in January 1833, when the point was proven: Fitzroy had to deploy his pistol, 'being very anxious from good reasons, to frighten away a small party [of Fuegians], he first flourished a cutlass near them, at which they only laughed: he then twice fired his pistol close to a native'. As it happened, the Fuegian was most unimpressed, and just looked puzzled at the unexpected sound.

As the expedition was expected to be a long one – rightly so, as the *Beagle* took five years to return – the quantity of gun supplies taken was immense. The following list from Purdey's own records gives a flavour: 20,000 caps, 24 lbs of wadding, 100 lb of powder, 6 cwt of shot and assorted flasks, and covers. These were put to good use upon reaching South America, as Fitzroy and Darwin regularly spent up to a month at a time away from the ship hunting for specimens.

After the *Beagle*'s return in October 1836 Fitzroy went on to become governor of New Zealand. He was also the founder of the Meteorological Office and invented the 'weather forecast', becoming a scientist of great distinction. Ironically, on the publication of *On the Origin of Species* in 1859, now a committed Christian, Fitzroy was appalled by his former shipmate's conclusions, which he had had such an important hand in facilitating. A troubled man and beset with depression, he took his own life in 1865 at the age of 59.

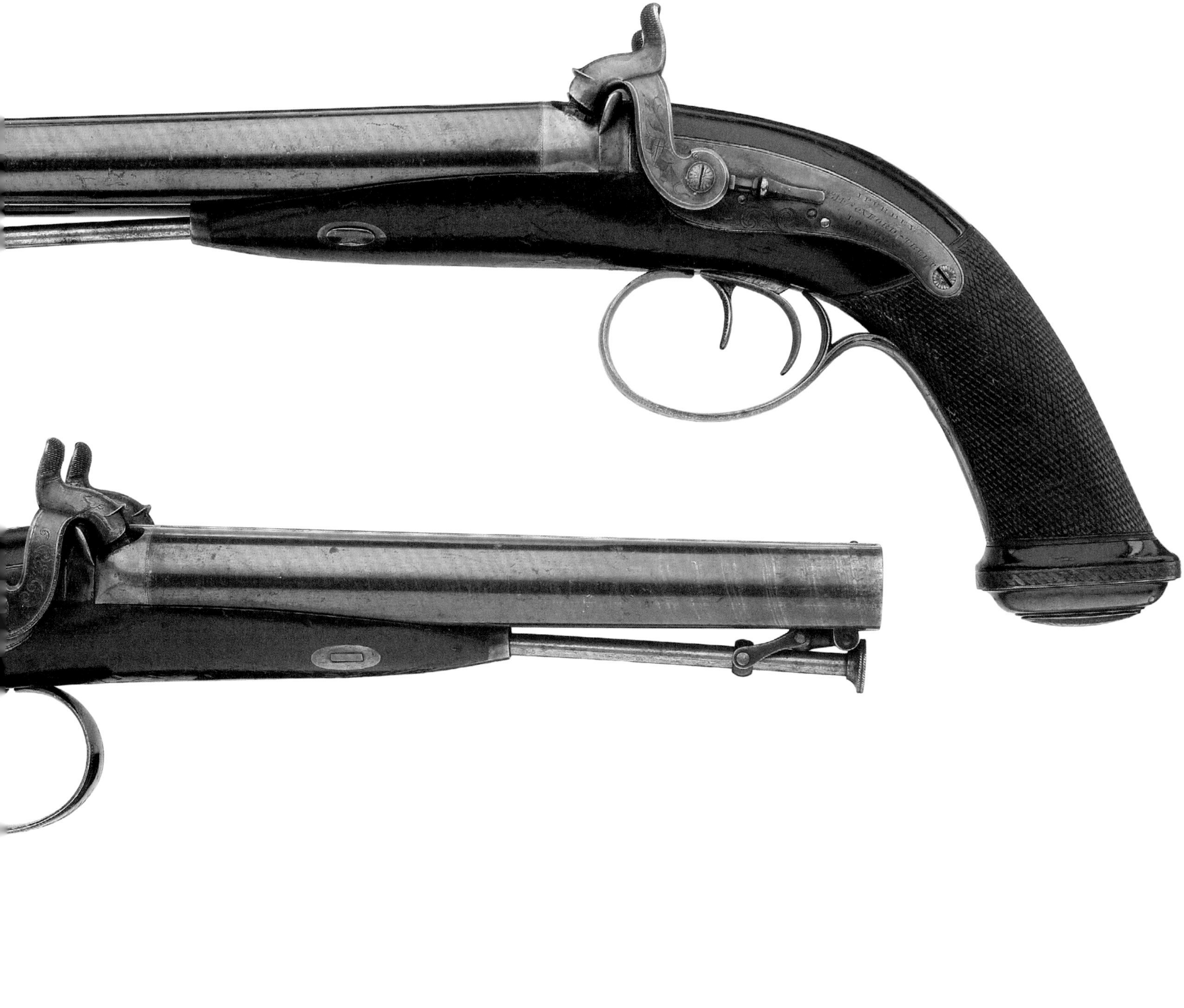

100

A monster weapon for the Crimean War

England, 1857 · XIX.286, XIX.305 and XXV.184

The war of 1853–56, between Britain, France and Turkey on one side and Russia on the other, was fought largely on the Crimean Peninsula, on the north coast of the Black Sea, in addition to decisive naval action in the Baltic. It was one of the most famously misconducted wars of all time, by all parties, and is best known today for the activities of Florence Nightingale and the Charge of the Light Brigade. It was also the first major war to be thoroughly reported: new technology enabled William Howard Russell to telegraph despatches to *The Times* and Roger Fenton to take photographs in the field, some of which were then engraved for the *Illustrated London News*, causing outrage at home and the eventual resignation of the Prime Minister, Lord Aberdeen.

Britain's entry into the war in 1854 was designed to counter Russian expansion in the Near East, seen as a threat to British India. Troops landed in September, their objective being the capture of the massively fortified Russian town and naval base at Sevastopol. The ensuing siege did not go well. British organisation was inefficient, maps were inadequate, communications unreliable, medical care haphazard and liaison with the French problematic. Until the civilian contractor Sir Morton Peto built a field railway from the chaotic harbour at Balaclava to the Sevastopol front, soldiers had to carry heavy ammunition up the long steep climb to the batteries. After terrible sufferings over the winter of 1854, the Allies had made little progress despite heavy artillery bombardments and assaults, repeatedly thrown back by General Todleben's resourceful defence.

Crucial to the offensive were mortars – short-barrelled weapons using an explosive shell, then known as a bomb, fired at high elevation to achieve range and to drop vertically onto the target, not possible with a siege gun; they could fire safely over friendly troops and massive ramparts, causing tremendous damage to both hard and soft targets within. At Sevastopol, however, the Russians managed to make repairs at night, negating their effect. Moreover, the two types of mortar used by the British had their limitations: in addition to being tremendously heavy (the land mortar weighed around 36 cwt [4,032 kg], the naval nearly five tons [4.75 tonnes]), they were laborious to load, and being iron castings could blow up without warning. Nevertheless, a similar type of weapon that was still seen as the way of breaking the stalemate – but this time of a wholly different scale and construction – was the innovative 'monster mortar', proposed by the eminent Irish civil engineer Robert Mallet (1810–81).

Mallet designed his 36-inch (914 mm) mortar of forty-two tons to hurl spherical cast-iron bombs filled with gunpowder, weighing over a ton, to a range of 2,500 yards (1,287 metres). The risk of blowing up, meanwhile, was averted by forging the powder chamber using layers of wrought iron, while the chase was of cast-iron rings secured by massive bars. It was mounted on a gigantic timber bed, and a crane was supplied to load it.

No ordnance official, however, dared to authorise such a revolutionary weapon, so the Prime Minister himself, Lord Palmerston, ordered two, from Mare & Co, Blackwall, London in May 1855. Manufacturing challenges delayed delivery until 1857, by which time Sevastopol had eventually fallen and the war was over. Nevertheless, Mortar No 1 was successfully test-fired, although No 2, mounted today at Fort Nelson on a concrete replica of the original bed, never fired a shot. Prominently sited in front of one of the forts famously associated with Palmerston, the mortar is a telling memorial of the war it was made for, and the bold and ingenious experiments it prompted.

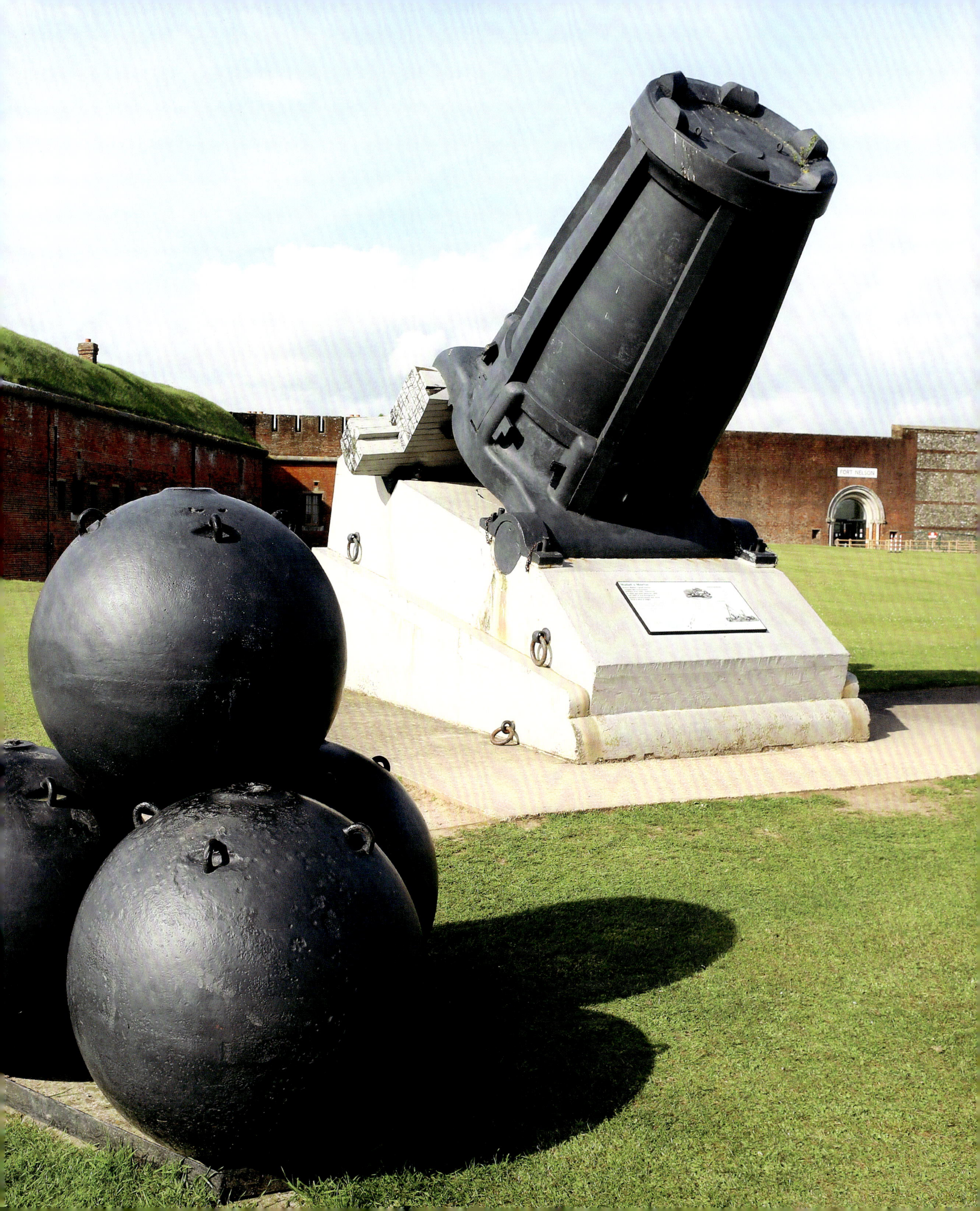
FORT NELSON

101

The first modern artillery – the 'Armstrong Gun' of 1862

England, 1862 · XIX.506

Inkerman, the third and last major battle in the Crimean War (5 November 1854), averted a Russian attempt to relieve Sevastopol (100). Victory was achieved, however, at the cost of over 4,000 Allied casualties, and in the end had hinged perilously on the bombardment of a strong Russian position by two 18-pounder cast-iron smoothbore muzzle-loading guns: massively heavy and only accurate at short range, they had taken over three hours to get in position. These deficiencies, which had almost led to defeat, caused dismay at home, prompting the lawyer-turned engineer and industrialist William Armstrong (1810–1900) to set about designing a replacement for the cast-iron smoothbore, little changed for 300 years, using technology developed during the Industrial Revolution.

Improvements were even more urgent thanks to the limited introduction of rifled muskets, used to good effect by the British at Inkerman, outranging enemy infantry and putting gun crews serving smoothbore artillery at their mercy. The answer lay in rifling artillery too, which brought other requirements and advantages. Key among these was the difficulty of muzzle-loading a rifled gun that called, if possible, for breech-loading, and – in order to cope with greater pressures and to cut weight – cast iron had to be replaced by steel and wrought-iron in layers. At first, Armstrong used a solid lead projectile like a giant rifle bullet, the lead being gripped by the rifling to spin the projectile: this worked, but his experimental gun was too small for military use, so for larger calibres he devised a cast-iron projectile coated with lead.

Armstrong presented his prototypes to the War Office – the post-Crimean successor to the Board of Ordnance – and unlike many other inventors, eminent and obscure, he obtained a hearing. The result was the creation in 1858 of a government committee to consider the question of rifled artillery for the army and navy. Other engineers were consulted, but the next year, hastened by fears that Prussia and France were on the same tack, Armstrong's proposal was taken up: it was so widely celebrated that one general officer remarked that 'there was nothing half so wonderful in the Arabian Nights'. Armstrong – now Sir William – was put in charge of gun production at the Royal Arsenal, Woolwich, although continued to make others at his own factory on the Tyne at Elswick (Tyne and Wear). His rifled breech-loading system (RBL) was rushed into service and applied to everything from field artillery to heavy calibres for the navy, but alas without sufficient testing and development, with unfortunate results: in the field, pieces of the lead jacket detached from the shell soon after leaving the muzzle, injuring friendly infantry, while the 7-inch naval gun suffered from problems with the breech and lack of power. The resulting reaction relegated the 7-inch guns to fortress artillery, where many lingered for the rest of the 19th century. Rifling, however, was here to stay, and a compromise was reached whereby rifled artillery of all sizes was once again, for about two decades, muzzle-loaded (RML).

Today, the disgraced 7-inch RBL guns are exceptionally rare: the Royal Armouries' example at Fort Nelson, mounted in the West Haxo Casemate where a similar one was originally emplaced, is probably the only survivor fit to fire blank, as it does on occasion, serviced by the Portsdown Artillery Volunteers; it was built in 1862 at the Royal Gun Factory, acquired in 'excavated condition' in 1988, conserved and provided with a replica breech mechanism and mounting. The failure of the 'wonder' weapon, however, and the curious backward step in technology that ensued, does nothing to diminish the truly revolutionary nature of Armstrong's invention and its status as the first modern gun.

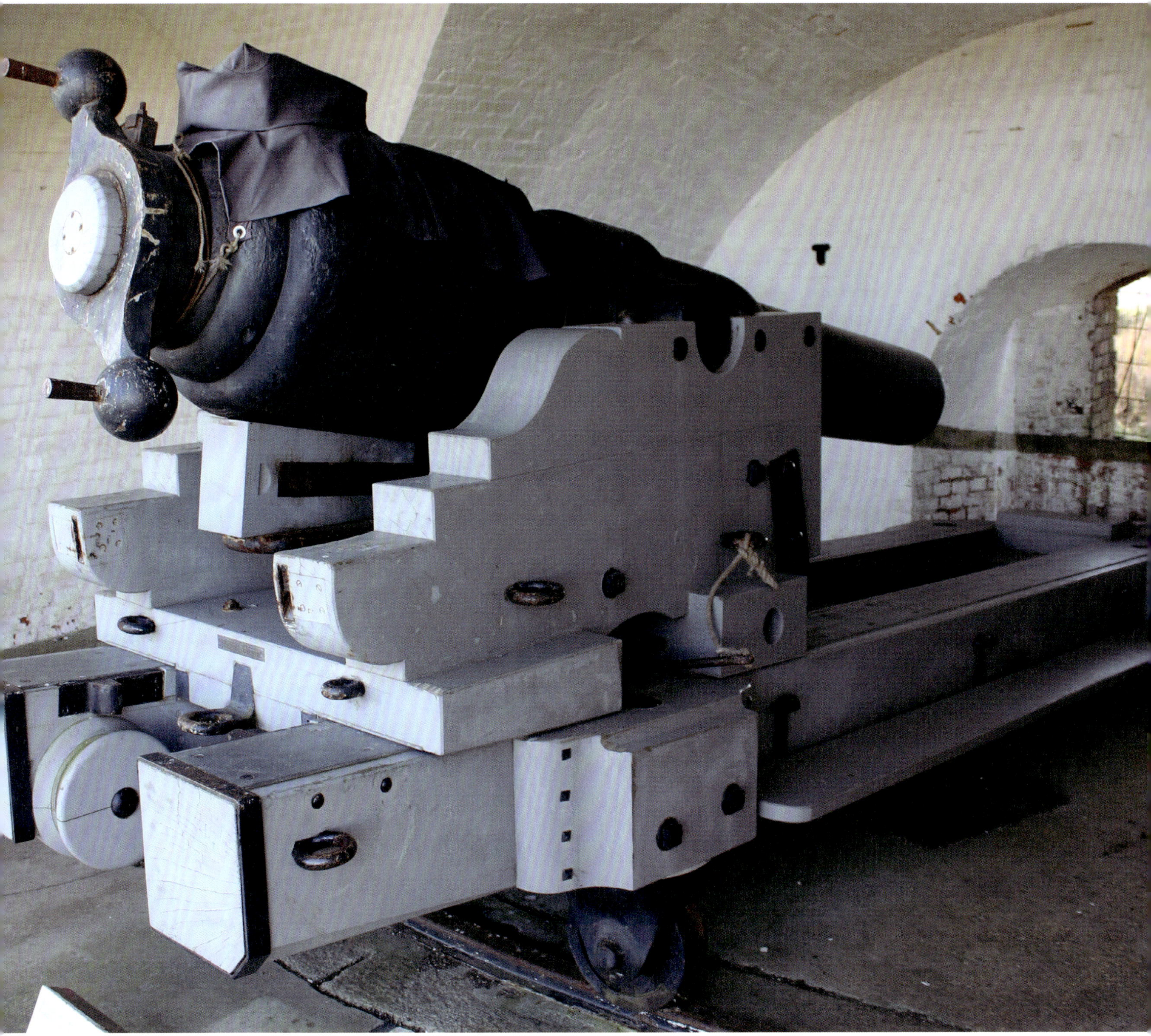

102
A masterpiece for the London World's Fair
France, *c.*1860 · XII.4751

Exhibitions showing off the prowess of a country's arts and manufacturing had been held in France in the first half of the 19th century, but it was the Great Exhibition of 1851 in London that spawned the later tradition of 'expositions', held in Paris, Manchester, Vienna and elsewhere. To some extent it lives on in the guise of the modern international EXPOs. The 1851 exhibition, initiated and supported by Queen Victoria's consort, Prince Albert, was conceived to show off the artistic and technical achievements of participating nations, providing an opportunity for manufacturers, designers, artists and inventors to display the best of their work to an increasingly discerning and affluent public. Among the results were some of the most lavishly decorated and finely made artefacts, and some of the most ornate weapons, ever created.

The Great London Exposition or World's Fair of 1862 offered similar opportunities, and – as in 1851 – gun makers were prominent exhibitors. Among them was Gilles Michel Louis LePage-Moutier (1810–1887) of Paris, whose business had been founded by his great uncle Pierre Le Page in 1743, at 8 rue de Richelieu. For the 1862 exhibition he produced a range of ornate and luxurious sporting arms decorated in the latest style, earning them a medal 'for the quality and beauty of his workmanship in his guns and pistols' awarded by the exhibition's sponsors, the Royal Society of Arts, Manufacturing and Trade.

One of these is this wonderful double-barrelled percussion shotgun, intended to astound and delight the observer with the complexity and virtuosity of its decoration. This is taken closely from the *Recueil d'ornements et de sujets pour être appliqués à l'ornementation des armes*, by Charles Claesen, published in Liège in 1857, in which he presents fantastical neo-gothic and romantic designs for firearms. The work itself was done by a series of the best craftsmen in Paris working in both wood and metal, although their names are unknown.

The two bright steel percussion locks are heavily chiselled with hunting scenes of hounds bringing down a roe deer on one lock face and a boar on the other, while a frightened wolf atop a tree stump forms the hammer. The half stock of dark polished walnut is deeply carved in low relief with floral scrolls. The bright steel butt plate is cast and chased with an allegorical scene of Diana, goddess of hunting, surrounded by hounds and female attendants preparing for the chase, and the trigger guard with a cherub blowing a hunting horn. The steel fore-end cap is wrought in the figure of a stag's head. The side-by-side barrels, by the renowned Parisian barrel maker Leopold Bernard (*c.*1832–70), are of bright steel and the breeches and muzzles carved with an intricate pattern of oak leaves and acorns. The rib is inscribed 'Le Page Moutier Arq[ebusi]er'. J. B. Waring, an architect involved in the exhibition, noted in his 1863 catalogue *Masterpieces of Industrial Art and Sculpture at the International Exhibition* that 'the gun of LePage-Moutier yielded in no respect to the rest'. Waring was right: the entire weapon is an intentional and highly successful *tour de force* of the arts involved. The runner-up among its near-contemporaries is perhaps another by LePage-Moutier – a similarly decorated gun presented in 1879 by the President of France, Jules Grévy, to Don Manuel Gonzales, then-Mexican Minister for War (and later President). This would have been a fitting use for the Royal Armouries gun, although its history prior to acquisition by the collector Keith Neal, and by the museum in 1979 is unknown.

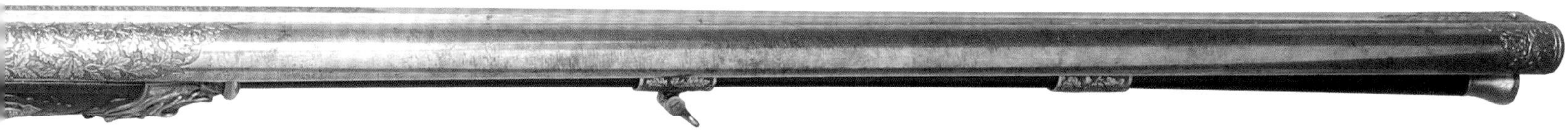
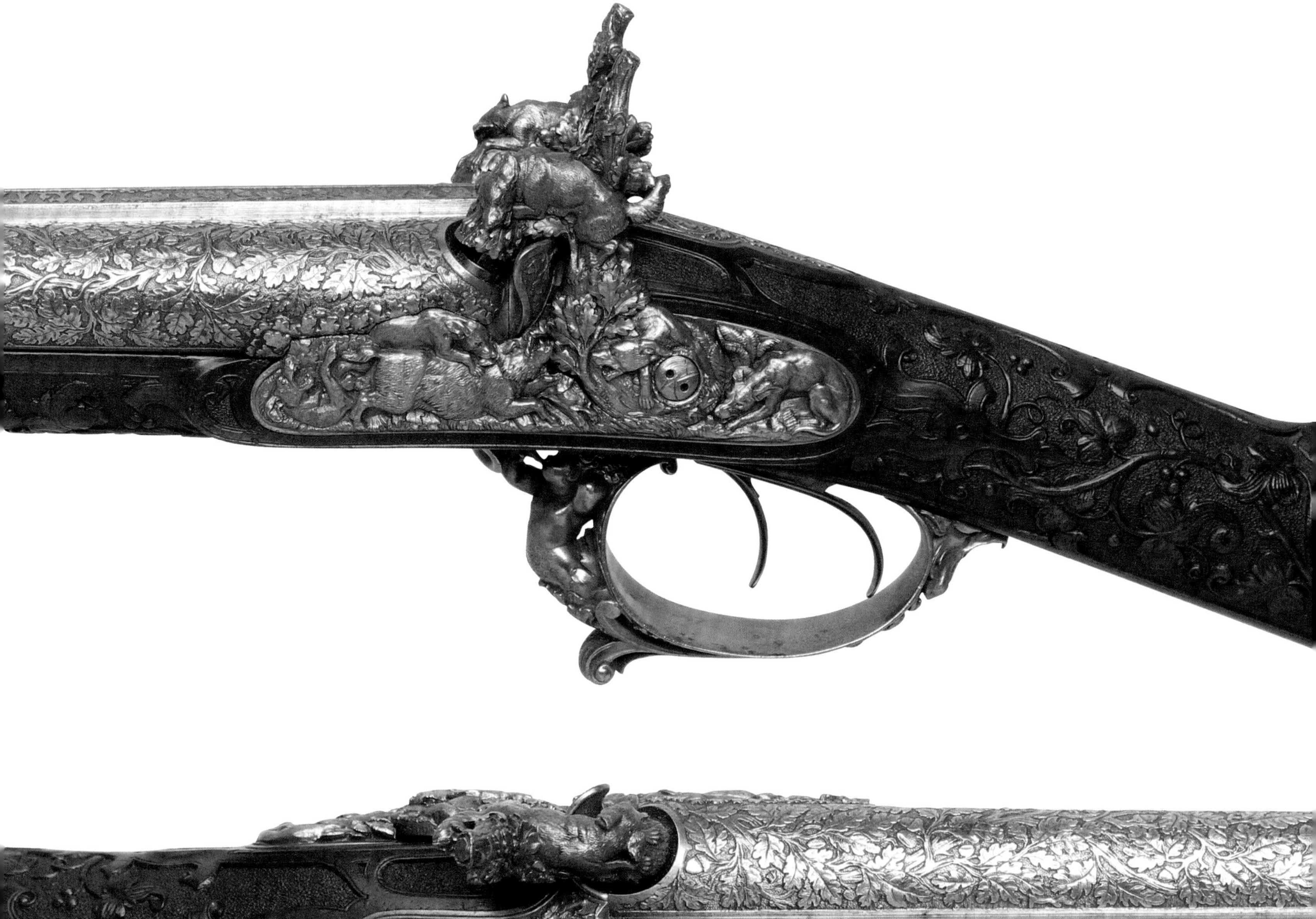
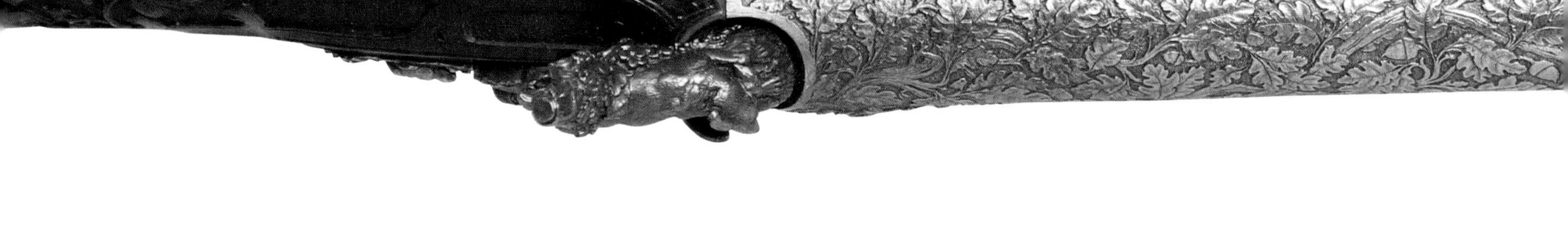

103

Presentation percussion revolvers by Samuel Colt

USA, 1863 · PR.3536–7

Samuel Colt (1814–62) was a brilliant inventor, but the fame, commercial success and importance of his weapons owed largely to innovative manufacturing methods, and, crucially, to ruthless sales strategies, which included selling weapons to both sides in various conflicts and the presentation of his products to powerful people. Colt patented his first revolver in Britain in 1835, presumably with the European market in mind, as lodging a patent in America first would have would have prevented this and opened the market to imitations. Although earlier self-rotating designs exist, notably Elisha Collier's flintlock version of *c.*1814, Colt's 1830s version used percussion ignition and was quite literally revolutionary. Conceived as a compact weapon for personal protection, it was the first really practical multi-shot handgun.

Both this weapon and its successors were intended to be plainly functional and affordable by ordinary people, whether soldiers, sailors or civilians, and was made possible by machine manufacture, mass production, and a minimum of hand fitting and finishing. The Colt 'Navy' model of 1851 and its improved 1861 successor were no exception: originally called the 'Revolving Belt Pistol of Naval Caliber', it was a .36 calibre development of Colt's earlier single-action designs, essentially an improved and more compact version of the huge and unwieldy Dragoon model of 1848. In its size, weight, and multi-shot capacity, it established the basic attributes of all modern pistols. The 'Navy' saw civilian and military use in the United States and elsewhere, including some 24,000 examples purchased for use in the Crimean War by the British army and Royal Navy. In 1861 its derivative the 'New Model Navy' pattern adopted an improved loading lever and a more aesthetically pleasing sculpted barrel assembly.

This important cased pair of 1861 'Navies' has all the durability of the standard model, but these are no mere

[250]

workhorses: although machine-made, they are finished by hand to the highest standards. The 'cylinder scene' depicting a naval battle, usually rolled onto the cylinder by a specialised machine, is here hand-engraved, and the barrel and cylinder are rust-blued to a mirror finish. The frame and loading lever are colour case-hardened, the trigger guard and backstrap are silver plated and the stocks are of the finest walnut.

Presentation-standard percussion Colts are rare, but this set is also of particular historical interest. As an inscription on the backstraps confirms, this set was presented to industrialist Mark Firth (1818–80) of the Sheffield steel firm Thomas Firth & Sons. Firth had established the company with his brother and father (the Thomas of the company name) in 1842. The gift of these pistols in 1862 marked a new phase in the company's history, as it began to manufacture armaments and their components, supplementing production at Colt's own English factory at Pimlico, London, opened in 1853. Thereafter Firth supplied most of the iron and steel used in Colt's weapons and probably machined cylinders for three of Colt's range of revolvers, the established 'Navy', the 1862 Pocket Navy, and the .44 calibre Army model of 1860. Colt himself died the same year that these pistols were presented, and it is not clear whether they were a personal or a corporate gift, but the business relationship was crucial for both parties and continued until after Firth's death in 1880.

Overall, these pieces are an interesting combination of modern industrial manufacture and artisanal craft production, and a reminder of a little-known but important instance of Anglo-American collaboration. They represent the ultimate muzzle-loading repeating firearm before the introduction of the self-contained metallic cartridge.

104

The first machine gun – the experimental Maxim 106 of 1884

England, 1884 · PR.10510

The centuries-old quest to fire hundreds of rounds fast and continuously ended with the invention of the 'machine gun', as he called it, by an American, Richard Gatling (1818–1903) in 1861. Early models had six barrels rotated by hand-crank, the ammunition dropping into place from a hopper, later versions being capable of 400 rounds per minute. The first automatic machine gun, however, was the work of the versatile and prolific inventor Hiram Stevens Maxim (1840–1916), an American who moved to London in 1881, became a British subject in 1899 and was knighted in 1901.

Neither a soldier nor initially – or ever primarily – a firearms designer, Maxim was an engineer and inventor who turned his hand to everything from hair-curling irons to flying machines, one of his earliest inventions being a 'self-powered mousetrap'. While visiting Vienna in 1882 he was supposedly inspired by an old American acquaintance to move into arms design: 'Hang your chemistry and electricity!' he said, 'if you want to make a pile of money, invent something that will enable these Europeans to cut each other's throats with greater facility.' Back in England, Maxim set out to do so, his revolutionary idea being to harness the recoil energy released by a fired cartridge to eject the empty cartridge and load the next, a concept he claimed came from feeling the recoil of a bolt-action rifle as a child.

Maxim registered his patent in London in 1883, and founded the Maxim Gun Company (with the backing of the Vickers family) in 1884. He produced a number of prototypes, but this one, of 1884, is thought to be the earliest of the three survivors and is probably the first complete and functioning example ever made. All were chambered for the .45-inch cartridge, originally designed for the Gatling gun.

By the beginning of the following year, he began refining his invention, culminating, in 1887, in a redesigned model known as the 'World Standard'. On the back of these successes, in 1888 Maxim merged his company with rival machine gun makers Nordenfelt to become the Maxim Nordenfelt Gun and Ammunition Company, in turn purchased by Vickers in 1897. This huge enterprise officially became Vickers, Sons & Maxim Ltd, and Maxim's guns were called the 'Vickers-Maxim' until his retirement in 1911, and the 'Vickers' thereafter.

The Maxim gun was adopted by the British army in 1888, and first used in colonial warfare, for which it is perhaps most famous, including in the First Matabele War of 1893–4, in what is now Zimbabwe. In Hilaire Belloc's *The Modern Traveller* (1898), African adventurer Captain Blood famously reassures his fellow villains:

'whatever happens we have got the Maxim Gun, and they have not'

By the start of the First World War in 1914, the British had replaced the Maxim with its close derivative, the Vickers Machine Gun, and it was used (as were the enemy equivalents, mostly of Maxim type), to famously devastating effect. The Vickers derivative, however, remained in use until the 1960s, and Maxim pattern guns over 100 years old have appeared on the battlefield as recently as the Russian invasion of the Crimea in 2014. Of his many inventions, Maxim's gun is the best known and had the greatest impact on arms design and world history.

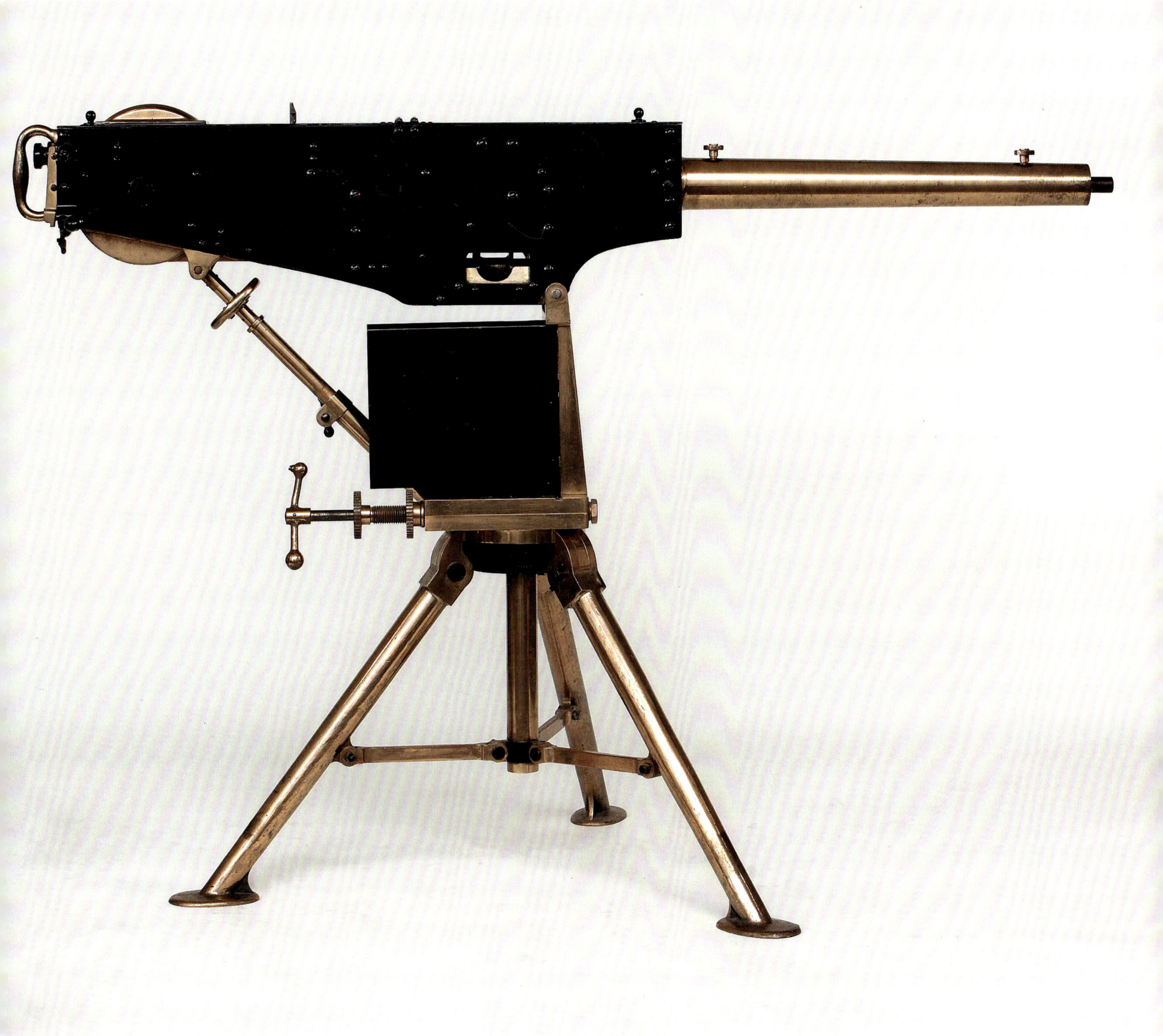

105

A giant rifle and an African adventure

England, 1884 · XII.3420

Big game hunting for sport – most famously in Africa, India and North America – had its heyday between 1880 and 1950, although it continues on a smaller scale today amidst a host of ethical and conservation arguments. The main quarry included elephants, rhinoceros, buffalo, lions and leopard, often referred to as the 'Big Five'. Its enthusiasts included the crowned heads and presidents of Europe, the American president Theodore Roosevelt, Indian princes, the writer Ernest Hemingway and many others who achieved near-heroic status at the time thanks to their skill and well-publicised exploits. Explorers and traders such as Sir Samuel Baker (1821–93) and Henry Morton Stanley (1841–1904), mapping and opening up the African interior to Europeans, also had to be well equipped and practiced shots. The defining weapon in this sphere from the mid 19th century was the large-bore rifle, of which the 4-bore, firing a quarter-pound projectile, was the largest useable type.

These were designed for short-range use – fifty yards at the most – using a 1.052-inch diameter bullet, weighing between 1,500 and 2,000 grains, and generating about 1,300 fps; to accommodate this power – necessary to bring down big game before the advent of more powerful nitro powders in the 1890s – they weighed over 20 lbs. The key English makers of such things – and there were few others – were Holland and Holland of London, established in 1835, who built this double-barrelled example in 1888.

Described in their order books as a 'Royal Model', this was sold in that year to a Mr H. C. W. Hunter, about whom little is known, but in 1897 it was re-sold (having been re-acquired by Holland & Holland) to the young Ewart Scott Grogan, one of the most swashbuckling and colourful figures of African colonial history. Born in 1874, one of the twenty-one children of William Grogan, Surveyor-General of the Duchy of Lancaster, by the age of 21 he was elected the youngest-ever member of the London-based Alpine Club, been sent down from his Cambridge college, walked out of the Slade School of Art, and had become a veteran of the 1896 Matabele War, in which he served in Cecil Rhodes' personal escort.

To recover from his war experiences and an illness later contracted in Mozambique, he set off on the long voyage from Britain to New Zealand, where he quickly met and fell in love with a beautiful heiress, Gertrude Watt. Her stepfather, however, was not impressed, and insisted that he prove himself a worthy suitor, to which he responded with characteristic flamboyance by declaring his intention to be the first man to trek the 6,500 miles from Cape Town to Cairo. Now aged 24, he set about equipping himself, and his fiancée's uncle, Arthur 'Harry' Sharp whom he had met in Africa and had agreed to accompany him, with appropriate equipment, guns and rifles: the 4-bore was among them, alongside his trusty double .303 rifle and a 10-bore double paradox, capable of firing both shot and bullets. In 1898 they set off, and after many adventures and near-death experiences, including an occasion on which Grogan used the 4-bore to dispatch a charging rhino, he returned to London in early 1900 as a popular hero.

Grogan duly married Gertrude in 1902, wrote up his experiences in *From the Cape to Cairo* (1902), and in 1904 they moved to Kenya. There he served in the First World War, built up a business empire alongside a reputation as a 'bad boy', and made a major contribution to the economic development of the country. He died aged ninety-two in 1967.

[254]

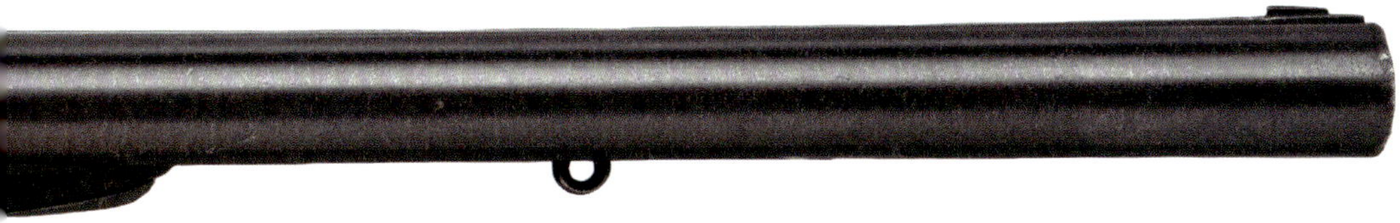

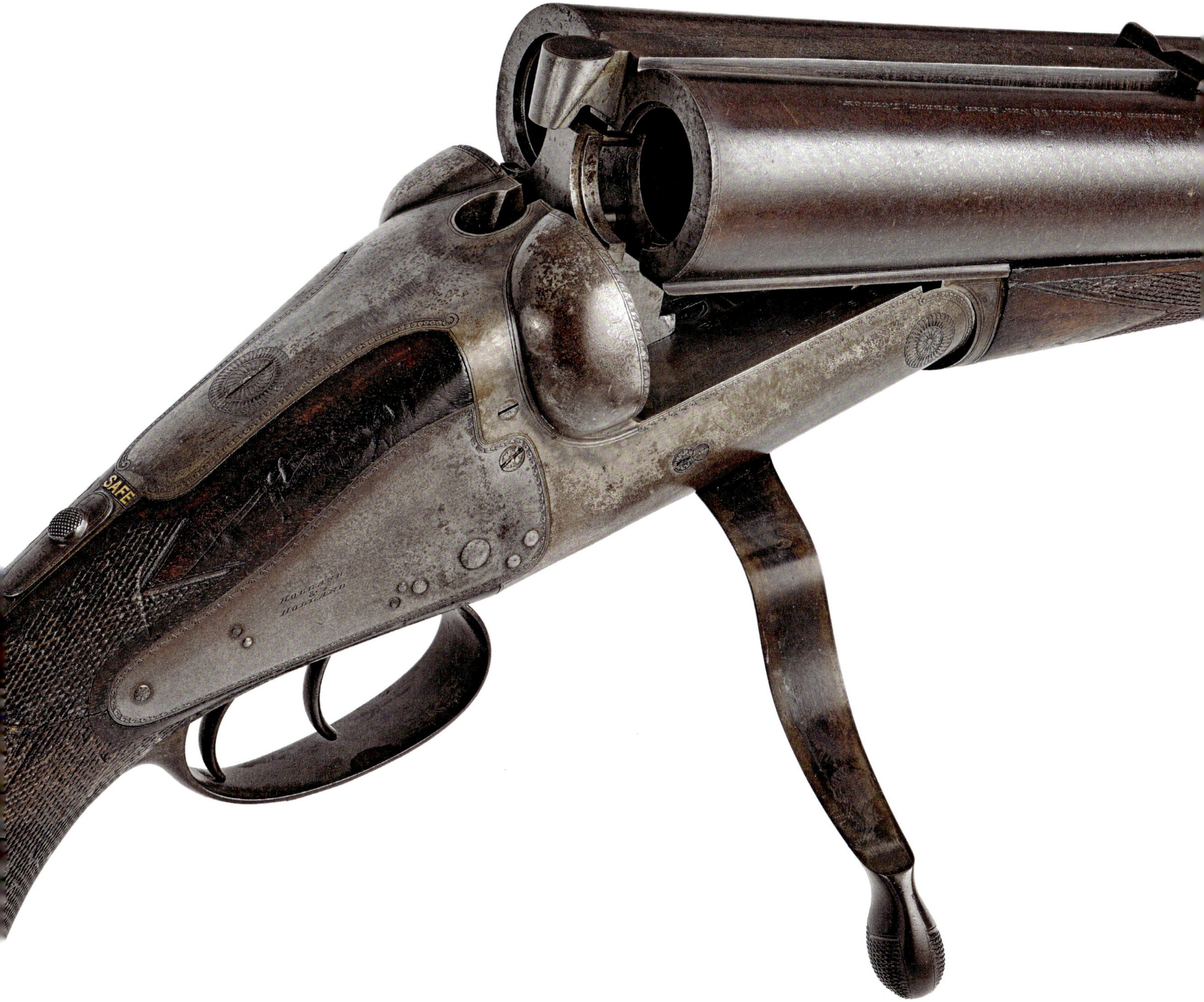
SAFE

106
The first modern field gun – the 'Soixante-Quinze'
France, 1918 · XIX.972

'J'Accuse …!', ran the headline to a letter on the front page of the Paris newspaper *L'Aurore* on 13 January 1898. Addressed to Félix Faure, President of France, the letter was written by the famous author Emile Zola (1840–1902) and condemned the conviction of Captain Alfred Dreyfus (1859–1935), who happened to be Jewish. The '*Affaire Dreyfus*' polarised French society, revealing a deep undercurrent of anti-Semitism. Public opinion was roused against him thanks to a memo found by a French spy in the wastepaper basket at the German embassy in Paris, touching on the development of a top-secret gun: alleged to be in Dreyfus's handwriting, it was in fact the work of a real traitor, Major Charles Esterhazy (1847–1923). Shamefully convicted of treason in 1894 and sentenced to life imprisonment, Dreyfus was sent to Devil's Island, and was only exonerated and returned to the army in 1906.

The actual quick-firing 75-mm gun, the root of all this sensitivity – often called the 'Soixante-Quinze' – turned out to be the first truly modern field gun. Designed by engineer officers Lieutenant Joseph-Albert Deport, Etienne Sainte-Claire-Deville and Emile Rimailho at the government's Puteaux Arsenal (Hauts-de-Seine) the new gun included major technical advances and was a masterpiece of precision engineering. It was the first to address the problem of controlling the recoil of a field gun, which previously required them to be laboriously manhandled back into position after every firing, preventing truly rapid and accurate fire. The '75, however, overcame this problem by virtue of a hydro-pneumatic system, in which the recoil was absorbed by two superimposed airtight cylinders forming a hydraulic buffer or 'air spring'. This allowed the barrel to run back on its slide, without disturbing the position of the carriage on the ground, and which then drove the barrel forward again, ready to fire. The details of this revolutionary system long remained a French state secret, not even fully divulged to the Americans – much to their frustration – who adopted the gun in 1917.

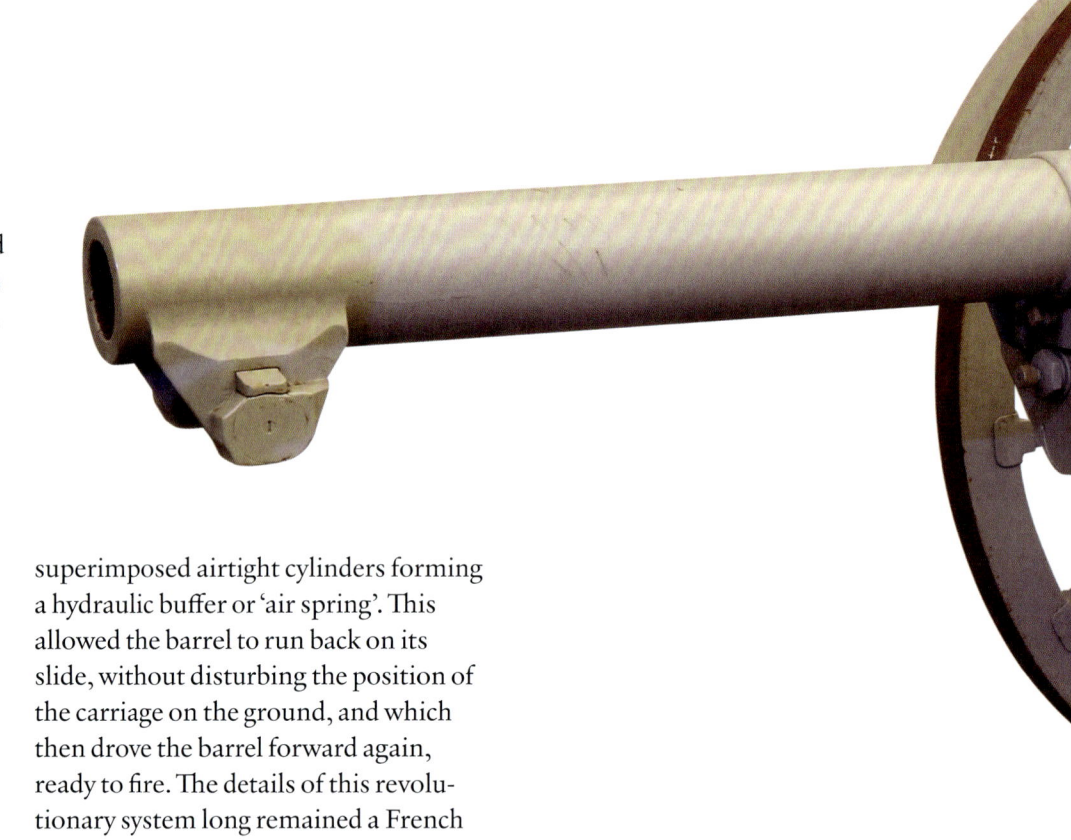

The eccentric screw breech designed by the Société Nordenfeldt, founded by the Swede Thorsten Nordenfeldt (1842–1920), was simple, strong and swift to operate. The ammunition was 'fixed', that is, consisting of projectile and time fuze attached to a brass cartridge case, fitted with a percussion primer, for quick loading, assisted by an automatic fuze-setter. The propellant was the latest smokeless powder, giving more power for its weight than black powder, and which avoided both blinding the gunners or giving away their position. The sighting system was easy to use and unaffected by the elevation of the barrel, providing for ranges up to 6,500 metres, although 8,500 metres could be achieved. Unlike many field guns of the time, it was fitted with a shield to protect the crew.

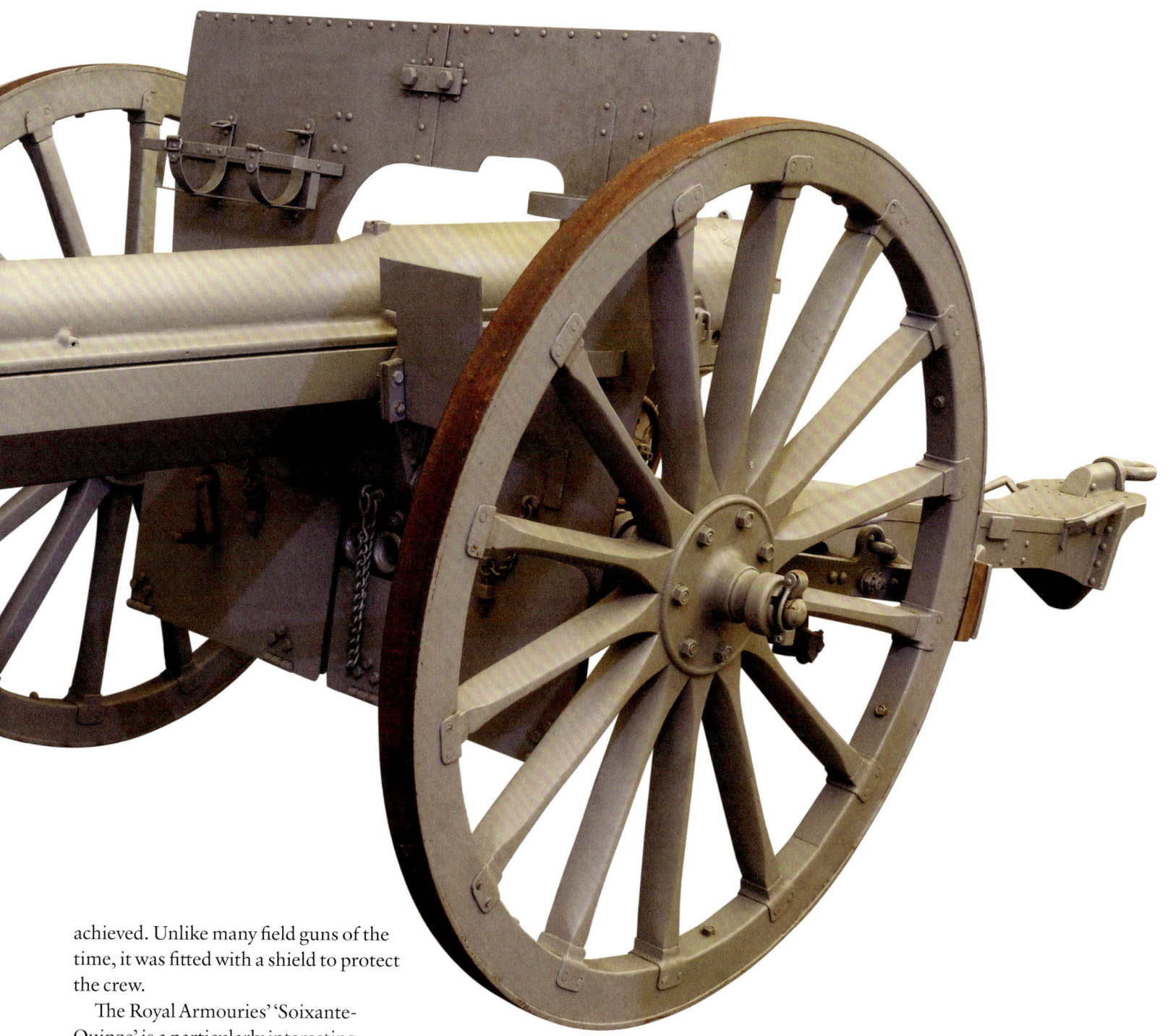

The Royal Armouries' 'Soixante-Quinze' is a particularly interesting example of the type, illustrating the pressures of wartime production and America's entry into the war in 1917: its barrel was made at the Arsenal in Bourges (Cher), but the shield and carriage by a Paris crane builder, Applevage, in 1916. In 1917 it was modified to fire at a higher elevation to gain range, and in the following year it was fitted with a new rifled tube by the renowned Bethlehem Steel Corporation Pennsylvania – proof of its American service.

The 'Soixante-Quinze' made all other field guns obsolete, to the shock of the major powers, especially the Germans, whose newly introduced 7.7-cm Fk 96 had to be swiftly modernised at great expense in 1904. It remained the mainstay of the French field artillery in both world wars.

107

The last British cavalry sword: Sealed Pattern 1908, MKI

England, 1908 · PR.6836

Standardisation of British army small arms (as opposed to artillery) began in earnest with the introduction of the 'sealed pattern', whereby a weapon design was given official status, and a seal applied to a perfect example from which others could be copied. The 'sealed patterns' were kept together at a succession of locations, both as a working collection and for historical reference, before they were gifted by the Ministry of Defence to the Royal Armouries in 2005.

In Britain, the standardisation of swords lagged behind that of firearms, and it was only in the late eighteenth century that centrally prescribed forms began to be issued to different arms. Despite rapid advances in firearms technology during the second half of the 19th century, cavalry remained an important part of most European armies, with the sword its primary weapon.

The British cavalry had used the 1899 pattern, designed for cutting and thrusting, but its weight and other problems led to extensive criticism during the Second South African War (1899–1902). As a result, committees to develop a new pattern were established; membership included the distinguished cavalry officers General Sir John French and Major General Douglas Haig in 1903, and the renowned fencer Alfred Hutton in 1906. Abandoning over fifty years of tradition, the 1903 committee determined that the new sword should have a straight, narrow, 'T'-sectioned blade for thrusting only, and 200 variants on this principle were issued to cavalry regiments for testing in 1904. The thrusting-cutting debate continued as further prototypes were tested, and it was not until 1908 that this version was chosen, when King Edward VII – who thought it 'hideous' – was persuaded to approve it by French and Haig.

The new weapon's ergonomically sculpted grip, weighted pommel and thick, stiff, spear-pointed blade succeeded in making it the perfect sword for delivering a thrust when mounted. Adjustments to the pattern were made in 1911, with the addition of serrations to the shoulder of the blade to retain the buff-leather washer (ensuring a good scabbard seal) followed in 1912 – as in this example – by replacing the serrations with a metal pin through the blade, to finally arrive at the Pattern 1908 MKI*.

The sword was such a departure from previous patterns that a new sword exercise was needed, incorporated in the new *Cavalry Training* manual. This neatly expressed the single purpose of the new sword that 'each man should ride at his opponent at full speed with the fixed determination or running him through and killing him'; in contrast to previous sword exercises which involved greater variety of motions, 'eliminating as much as possible the intricacies of the art [of swordsmanship]' was impressed upon instructors and pupils alike.

The Pattern 1908 sword saw service in the First World War, where in the opening stages cavalry with swords routinely made first contact with the enemy. Here the new pattern (and its officer variant the Pattern 1912) with accompanying drill performed well, even accounting for the first British 'kill' of the war, but as a war of stalemate replaced one of movement cavalry action became a rarity. Over the following decades horses and swords were traded for tanks, and although both were retained for ceremonial duties, the millennia-long presence of sword-armed cavalry on the battlefield came to an end. It is ironic perhaps that what was, arguably, the most perfect British cavalry sword of recent centuries (at least of the 'thrusting' form) was also the last.

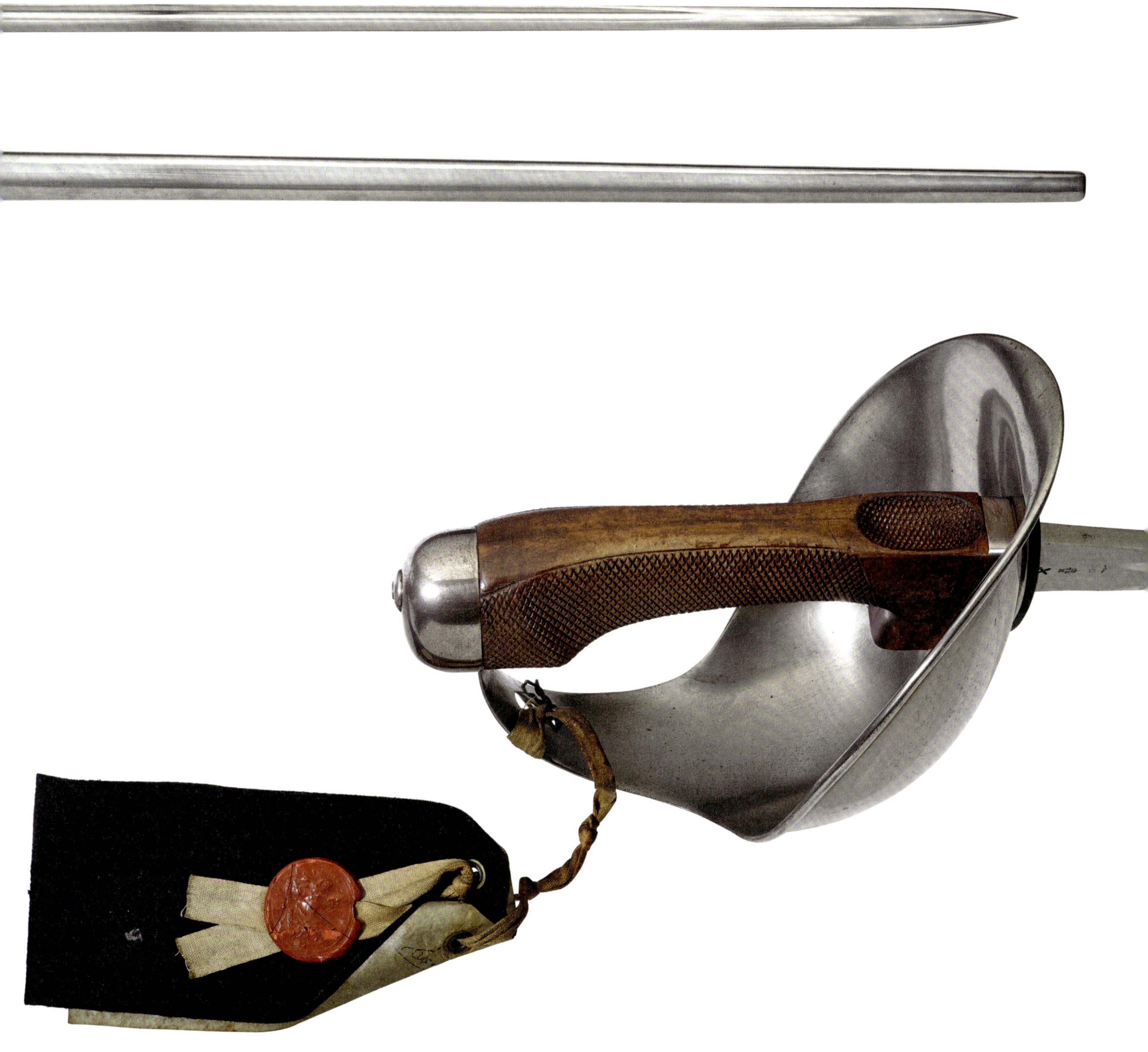

108

The quick-firing 18-pounder of 1903

England, 1918 · XIX.529

The 18-pounder was the British army's standard light field gun during the First World War. In August 1914 the Royal Field Artillery took 324 of them into the field, representing 60% of its artillery: by November 1918, 3,215 were in use, still representing 42% of an exponentially increased number of guns. In total, 18-pounders fired over 100 million rounds, playing a massive part in the artillery's crucial contribution to eventual Allied victory.

Concerns raised before the Second South African War (1899–1902) about the adequacy of British field artillery, and reports in 1897 of the revolutionary French 'Soixante-Quinze' (106), led the government to commission General Sir Henry Brackenbury (1837–1914) to advise on re-equipment. His recommendation was wholesale replacement within three years, but practical realities intervened, and a model designed by Heinrich Ehrhardt (1840–1928), made in Düsseldorf, was selected with eighteen batteries (108 guns) purchased as a temporary measure. In 1901, however, the government set up a committee under Major General Sir George Marshall (1843–1909), who had commanded the Royal Artillery in South Africa, to develop an improved British version. Various firms submitted prototypes, and the eventual product incorporated design components from Vickers, Armstrong and the Royal Ordnance Factory. These companies and others were contracted to produce them: this example, a Mark 11, was built by Vickers Ltd, probably in Sheffield, in 1918.

In production and in service from 1903, the 18-pounder had a 3.3 in (83.8 mm bore) wire-wound nickel steel barrel, a hydraulic buffer inside a case containing the running-out springs of the recuperator, mounted above the barrel to absorb recoil: the Mark 11 model matched the sophistication of the 'Soixante-Quinze', in that re-laying after firing was not needed. The 18-pounder was accompanied by a lighter 13-pounder version for the Royal Horse Artillery. Its range on flat ground was around 6,000 m (6,562 yds), which compared well with the German equivalent, the 7.7 cm Feldkanone 96, with an effective range of 5,500 m (6,000 yards). In use, it was served by six men, with six guns forming a battery. The ammunition limber, carrying twenty-four rounds, was towed with the gun and carriage by a team of six horses. A second team of six drew another limber and ammunition wagon carrying a further thirty-eight rounds each.

The First World War, however, presented very different conditions to those of South Africa, and what had appeared to be a robust, reliable and ballistically effective field gun was soon found wanting: firing at high elevations was now needed to provide plunging fire into enemy trenches, which the 18-pounder's single pole trail made difficult, while the recoil system springs broke under sustained fire. Initially there were also problems with volume production and only shrapnel, designed for destroying enemy forces in open country, was available. These difficulties were swiftly overcome thanks to improvements in supply and the introduction of the Mark II and Mark III model: along with smaller numbers of the higher-trajectory 4.5-inch howitzer, the 18-pounder was able to play a major part in the destruction of fixed fortifications, and their assault with aid of the 'creeping barrage', whereby shells fell ahead of infantry as they advanced on enemy positions.

The 18-pounder remained in service throughout the First World War and inter-war period and was used, now equipped for motorised traction, by Territorial Army units of the British Expeditionary Force in 1940. Nothing is known of this example's service history but a former curator of the Royal Armouries, Charles ffoulkes, is said to have personally selected it for the collection at the Tower of London after the war.

109

Thompson machine gun

USA, 1921 · PR.7704

The Thompson submachine gun, or 'Tommy gun', was designed by an American, General John T. Thompson (1860–1940), incorporating an action patented in 1915 by the naval officer John Blish. It was intended as a 'trench broom' – Thompson's term – for close-quarter action in an over-run trench, but by the time the prototype was ready in 1919, the First World War was over and the weapon's intended markets had evaporated. It was, however, used well into the 1960s by numerous armies across the world, most notoriously by police and gangsters in inter-war America. In a British context it is best known for its use in Ireland, and indeed its very genesis may have had Irish associations: the company set up by Thompson in 1916, Auto-Ordnance (headquartered in Hartford, Connecticut), was financed by the Irish-American Thomas Ryan, who may have had sympathies with the republican Easter Rising of that year.

The rising was crushed, but continued tensions led to the Irish War of Independence in 1919–21, ending with the Anglo-Irish Treaty and the establishment of the Irish Free State, whilst Ulster remained under British control. Many in Ireland, however, refused to accept the partition of the island. Most important among these were the first incarnation of the Irish Republican Army (IRA), formed in 1919, which was to fight the Irish Civil War with the Free State government in 1922–3. The IRA naturally needed weapons and were impressed by both the Thompson's firepower, and with the stock removed, its easy concealment. How the IRA made contact with Auto-Ordnance is unclear, as there were numerous informal American-Irish channels of communication: possibly the IRA simply spotted the first advertisements for Thompson guns that appeared in the Irish press in December 1920. In any case, the first guns were ordered in January 1921, and the ultimate order totalled 653. 495 guns were smuggled aboard the collier the *S.S. East Side*, at Hoboken, New Jersey, as 'engine room supplies', but the ship was raided in port by the FBI and the guns seized. The remaining 158, however, were eventually smuggled to Ireland, mainly after the Truce on 11 July, and were no doubt used in the Civil War.

Several factors show that this gun, PR ('Pattern Room') 7704 was one of the contraband weapons. As here, the serial numbers had been removed to prevent the guns being traced, but Colt – one of the three Thompson manufacturers – applied an extra serial number beneath the barrel, which can only be removed using special tools: examination by Mike Sterry of the Royal Armouries found one here (no. 212). This enabled the historian Patrick Jung and Thompson specialist Gordon Herigstad, using FBI records, to prove that PR.7704 was part of the *East Side*'s cargo; whether it is one of the undiscovered 158, though, is unclear, as the 495 confiscated in New Jersey were also eventually shipped to Ireland in 1925.

When or how PR.7704 was transferred to the Ministry of Defence Pattern Room – since 2005 part of the Royal Armouries' collection – is not documented, but it is believed to have been captured from the Provisional IRA, perhaps one of the hundred Thompsons and magazines discovered in County Mayo by the Irish Garda in 1942. A purely functional, battered, unornamented and modified weapon, deprived of its serial number, the importance of PR.7704, like so many Royal Armouries items, depends on its historical association. In this case they are firmly rooted in its part, as a type and as an item, in the struggles of the 1920s between Britain and Ireland, as a preferred weapon of the IRA until the 1980s, and its popular association with the history of both.

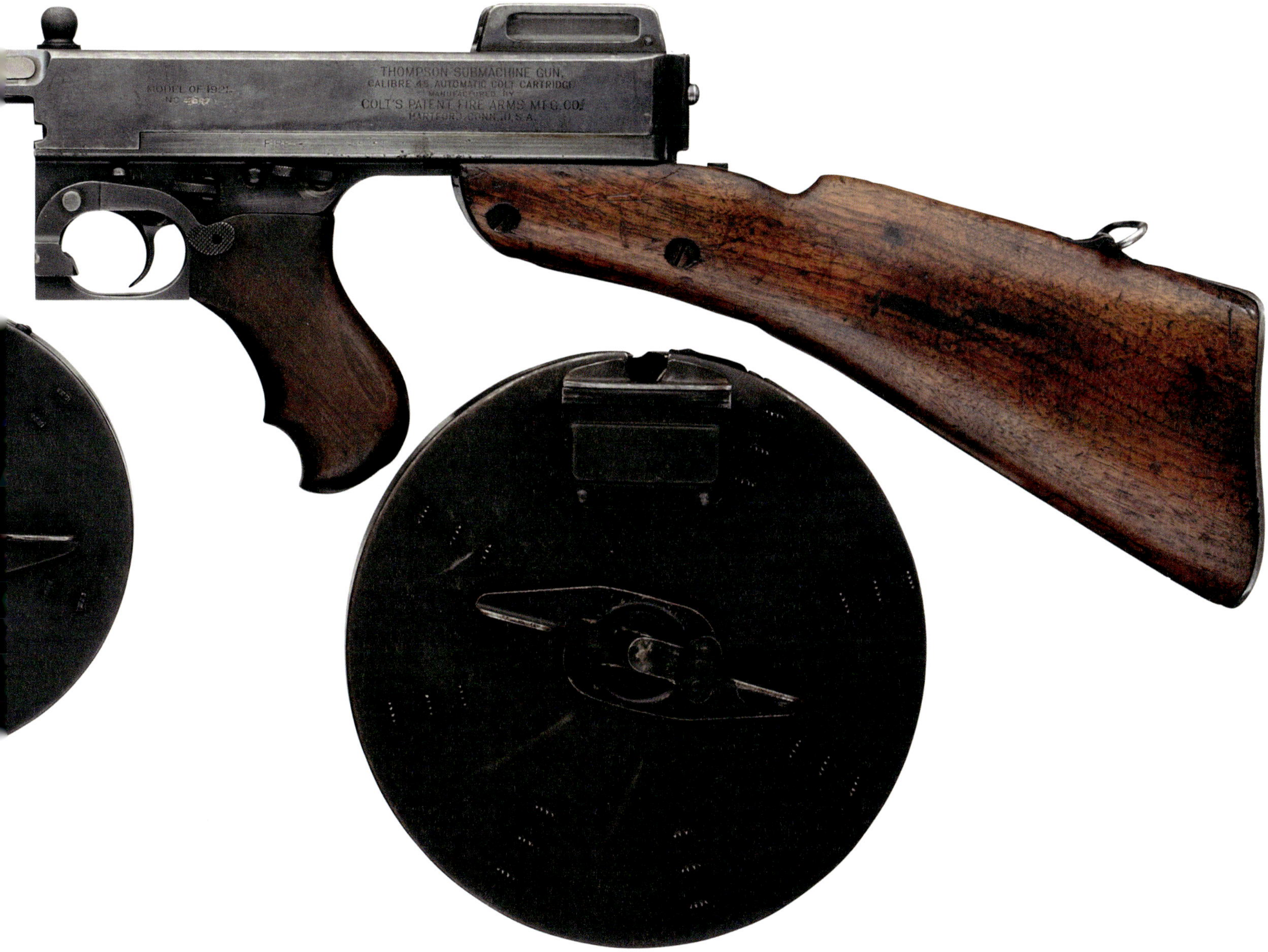
THOMPSON SUBMACHINE GUN,
COLT'S PATENT FIRE ARMS MFG. CO.

110

The 'Baby Browning' centrefire self-loading pistol

Belgium, 1931–40 · XII.11254

The Belgian state-owned *Fabrique National de Herstal* at Herstal (near Liège), founded in 1889 and known simply as FN, is one of the largest small-arms manufacturers in the world. From 1897 the company made weapons designed by John Moses Browning (1855–1926), one of the most inventive and productive gun designers of all time, who from 1897 worked for FN as Chief Designer. From 1907 the company used the Browning name for a number of products, making the brands interchangeable.

In 1905 Browning designed a small 6.35 mm automatic pistol, marketed as the 'Vest Pocket' or 'Baby' pistol, designed for personal protection. This was the basis of the pistol shown here, which also adopted the 1905 model's informal name, and was designed in the late 1920s by Browning's successor at FN, Dieudonné Saive (1888–1970). Its launch was delayed by the onset of the Great Depression in 1929, but the gun went into manufacture in 1931, selling over 50,000 until production ceased when Germany invaded Belgium in May 1940.

This example of what was normally a plain and functional product is exceptional for the richness of its decoration. The metal surfaces are blued in their entirety, compartmented into geometric fields by inlayed gold lines, within which the ground is engraved with a pattern of stylised flowers. The highlight of the decoration is a golden 'sunburst' on the top of the slide – a defining motif of Art Deco, the dominant decorative style in Europe from the eve of the First World War to the mid 1930s. Meanwhile the plainly functional plastic grips of the standard item have been replaced by mother-of-pearl, engraved with a boldly geometric FN monogram. Along the left slide the 'Slide Legend', in Art Deco *sans serif* gold capitals, reads 'FABRIQUE NATIONAL D'ARMES DE GUERRE HERSTAL BELGIQUE' ('National Manufactory of Weapons of War, Herstal, Belgium') and underneath BROWNING'S PATENT DEPOSE ('Patented by Browning').

Precisely when the gun was made is uncertain, although it is stamped with a combination of standard Liège proof marks, inspector's markings and the number '5'. The inspector's markings appear to be those of Auguste Jamart who worked at the FN from 1924 to 1959, whilst the '5' stamped on the exterior of the barrel, the inside of the slide and on the left side of the frame is almost certainly the serial number. If so, this is of great interest, as low numbers for FN pistols are rare, thanks to the frequency with which the earliest products failed at proof. It would mean, of course, that this was only the fifth FN Baby Browning to be produced, and date it to 1931.

The reason for the gun's lavish decoration is also something of a puzzle. Although those willing to pay could always obtain custom engraving from specialist suppliers, the factory offered no special finishes for the 'Baby Browning' until production restarted in 1945. However, if it is indeed the fifth 'Baby' ever made (and perhaps the earliest proof-tested example to survive) the decoration may have been applied to mark the successful launch of the new pistol. As for its authorship, the style of the engraving is, not surprisingly, very similar to that of FN's own Master Engraver Felix Funken (d.1965), who had exhibited 150 highly decorated FN firearms at the Liège World Fair in 1931 and again in the 1939 Liège World Water Exhibition, including some in an Art Deco style. Possibly this was his own work, which would give this unique and exceptional pistol a very special place in the history of decorated firearms.

FABRIQUE NATIONALE D'ARMES DE GUERRE HERSTAL BELGIQUE
BROWNING'S PATENT DEPOSE

111

Norwegian whaling cannon

Norway, 1947 · XIX.917

Whales have been hunted for millennia, firstly for subsistence – as they still are, by exception – and increasingly since the 15th century for profit, an activity largely banned by international agreement since 1986. Whale products, depending on species, have included food, soap, candles, lubricants, manufactured items (ladies' stays, combs, buttons, bristles and umbrellas), and above all lighting oil made from whale fat or blubber. Organised commercial hunting is recorded in Japan as early as the 7th century, but in Europe began in the Middle Ages in the Bay of Biscay by the Basques, who by the early 16th century had also developed deep-sea activity in the North and South Atlantic. In the 17th century dominance passed to Scandinavian countries, the Dutch and English, operating around the Arctic islands of Spitzbergen. In the last 300 years most maritime nations, notably the USA, had whaling industries of some sort, often very profitable indeed.

Ocean-going (as opposed to inshore) whale-catching was done using open boats, lowered from a whaling ship, with hand-thrown harpoons. These were only effective at very short range and required immense strength and skill, making the practice extremely dangerous, not least as whales could upset the boats or drag them under by the harpoon line; the ships, sometimes barely larger than the bigger whales, could be lost too, as in the case of the *Essex*, sunk in 1820, the inspiration for Hermann Melville's *Moby Dick* (1851).

Following the invention in 1731 of the harpoon gun, however, the rate of capture began to be increased and the danger reduced. Harpoon guns were shoulder-mounted flintlocks, fired from a standing position in the bow of the boat, although by the 1820s swivel-mounted versions allowed for larger calibres and greater range. At first these were also flintlocks, only useable in fine weather, but the introduction of percussion in the 1830s made for greater reliability. The leading British suppliers, originally based in Hull, were the gunmakers W. W. Weaver, still extant, who produced them until the demise of the British whaling industry in the late 19th century. Weaver's mounted harpoon guns, following on from his earlier shoulder-fired models, were similar to small naval railguns and of a similar calibre (40–60 mm) whilst still mounted on rowing boats. The most important development, in the 1870s, led by the Americans and Norwegians, was to mount the gun on specialist motorised 'catcher' boats which serviced a large factory ship, thus allowing the use of a far larger and more powerful weapon, properly known as a whaling cannon. The next step, developed by wealthy Norwegian whaler Svend Foyn (1809–94), was to attach a grenade to the harpoon, which exploded on impact, thus making the kill quicker, more efficient and (arguably) more humane; Foyn was based in Tønsberg, southern Norway, which was the centre of the Norwegian whaling industry from the 1850s, and his name is associated with several whaling sites in Antarctica, such as Foyn Island and the Foyn Coast. His original design, developed in 1870, took the form of a short, stubby cannon, from which its more sophisticated successors, such as the Royal Armouries' example, derived. Made by the Norwegian firm Kongsberg Vapenfabrik in 1947, at 90 mm this was the largest in their range; it used a blank firing brass shell to fire the exploding harpoon. The alternatives, of 50 mm and 75 mm calibre, are still used today to capture whales for scientific purposes.

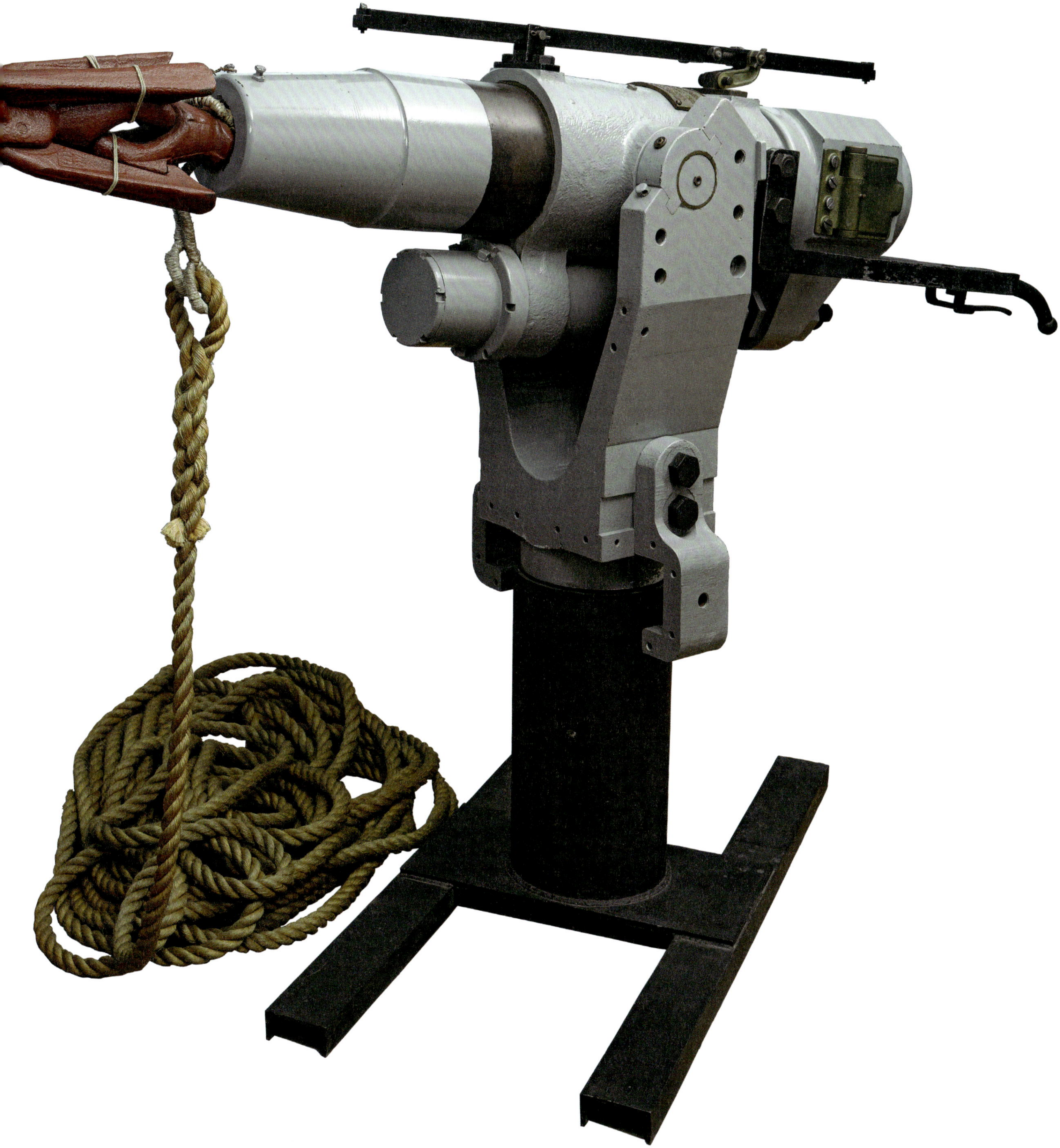

112

Russian AK47 captured in Vietnam by Captain Gregory Dillon

Russia, 1953 · PR.5428

In continuous production around the world for nearly seventy years, and now numbering at least 75 million, the *Avtomat Kalashnikova* or AK assault rifle is the single most common firearm in the world. This is due to its low cost, durability and effectiveness, and its consequent adoption by a wide variety of users including state militaries, police forces, terrorists, criminals and civilians using them for self-defence or even for hunting. Invented by former tank crewman Mikhail Kalashnikov (1919–2013) in 1947, the design has passed through various iterations and spawned numerous copies, variants and derivatives. As a product of the Cold War, it was Russian military issue for twenty years before first seeing military action in Vietnam, in the hands of the North Vietnamese Army (NVA) and the Viet Cong (VC), supplied by both Russia and China: there it was ultimately pitted against the ArmaLite AR-15 (today the second most common firearm pattern in the world), which gave the US and her allies their first chance to obtain examples for analysis and reference.

This early example, serial number GL4027, represents the second update to the original design, featuring a receiver (body) machined from solid steel. It is chambered for the standard 7.62 x 39 mm M43 cartridge, still the most common calibre for the AK family of weapons. It was captured in 1966 by US Army Captain Gregory P. Dillon, a story of interest in itself. Dillon was Operations Officer of the 3rd Brigade of the 1st Battalion, 7th Air Cavalry Regiment of the 1st Cavalry Division (nicknamed '1–7 Air Cavalry' or just '1–7 CAV' for short), commanded by Colonel Harold G. 'Hal' Moore: formed after the American Civil War, the unit is perhaps most famous for its defeat under General Custer at the Battle of Little Bighorn in 1876. Having turned in its horses in 1941, by the time of Vietnam it had regained its mobility thanks to the famous Bell UH-1 Iroquois 'Huey' helicopter, which allowed the new 'air cavalry' to deploy quickly and decisively wherever needed, and to provide its own air support by means of helicopter 'gunships'. It is best known for its exploits in the Battle of Ia Drang, made famous by the book *We Were Soldiers Once … and Young* (1992) and its movie adaptation *We Were Soldiers* (2002). Two months after that battle, in January 1966, the 1st Division formed the spearhead of Operation Masher, and battle was joined on the Bong Son plains in Bình Định Province, South Vietnam, where it wiped out an entire NVA brigade. In clearing a series of bunkers, Dillon captured the rifle and a pistol from the brigade's executive officer. As was then common practice, Dillon kept the rifle as a trophy, presenting the pistol to his commanding officer, Hal Moore. Realising that it might be commandeered for other purposes, he cut his name and unit designation into the buttstock: a fortunate move, as it was indeed taken from him for use in a covert operation requiring enemy weapons. The last he heard of it was in a newspaper article about the headquarters of the Army of the Republic of Vietnam (ARVN). Later, the rifle was transferred to the British Ministry of Defence as an example of its type and in 1971 it entered the 'Pattern Room' reference collection, given to the Royal Armouries in 2005. Curatorial staff were then able to reconstruct this very personal story – including through speaking to Colonel Dillon – of the world's most abundant weapon.

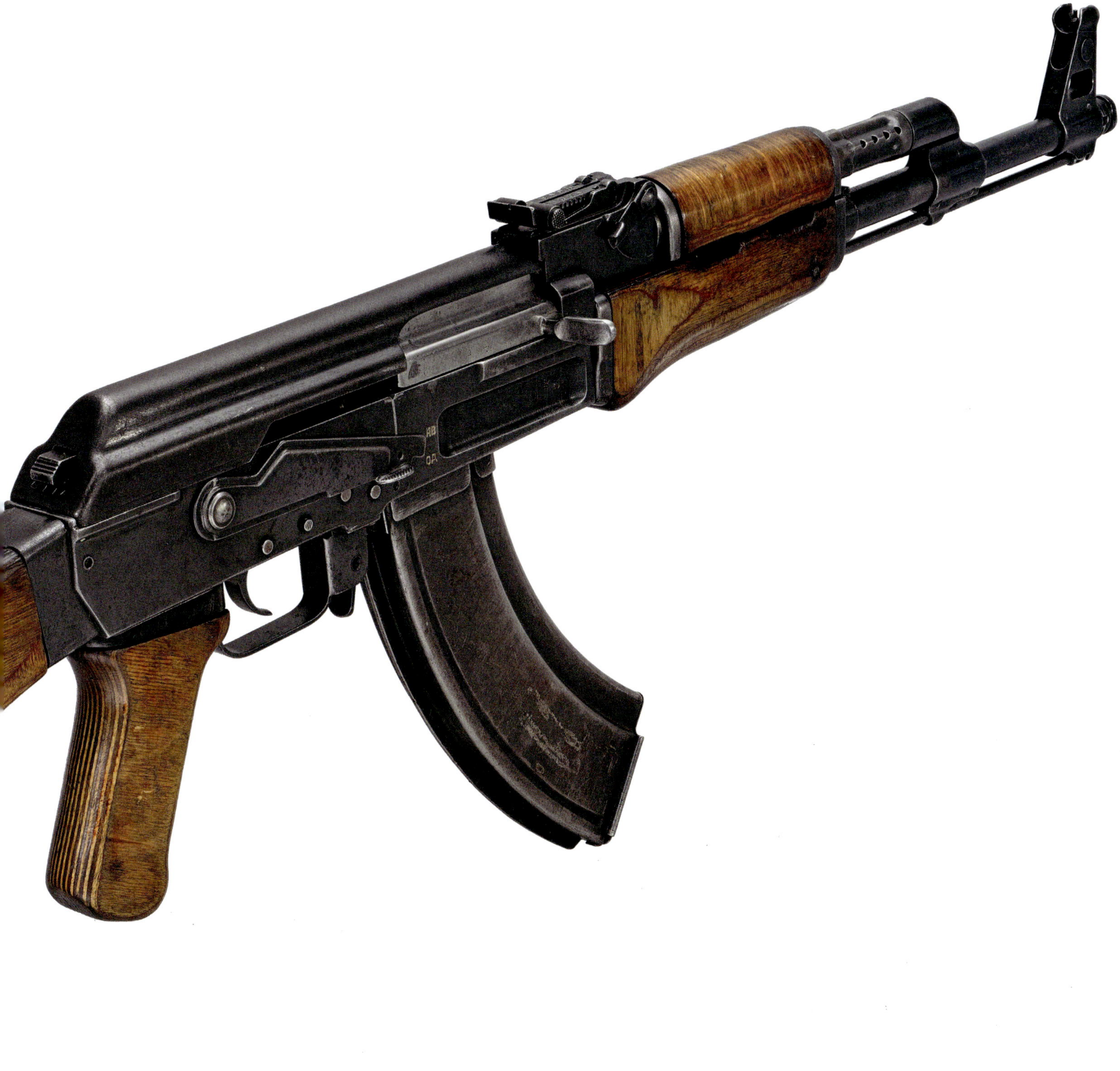

113

'M-41A Pulse Rifle', film prop for *Aliens*

England, 1986 · XII.11846

In recent decades it has become increasingly common for museums to collect contemporary objects, on the basis of their technical, aesthetic or cultural importance, and in anticipation of the historical importance likely to be attached to them in the future. This unusual object is among them, a prop item created for the Oscar-winning 1986 motion picture *Aliens*, in which it serves as the standard-issue infantry rifle of the fictional 'United States Colonial Marine Corps'. As a sci-fi design the 'Pulse Rifle' is one of the most iconic firearms in movie history thanks to its distinctive appearance, signature sound effect and prominent use on-screen by most of the main cast. In particular, the weapon is used to complete the transformation of the main character (Ellen Ripley, portrayed by Sigourney Weaver) from resourceful 'space trucker' in *Alien* (1979) to ground-breaking action heroine in this acclaimed sequel. Like much of the military equipment in *Aliens*, the M-41A was personally designed by director James Cameron, and was realised in metal by armourer Simon Atherton of the British firm Bapty & Co. Cameron's initial preference had been to use a more modern-looking MP5 submachine gun as the physical basis for the prop, but in the end he used the Second World War M1 Thompson, citing the more impressive muzzle-flash produced by the latter's larger .45 ACP cartridges. The built-in grenade launcher, showcased in Ripley's battle with the enormous Alien Queen, was created using parts of two shotguns. To disguise these various 20th-century components, a custom shroud was formed by automotive engineer Maurice Gomme.

Many film and television prop weapons are made as lower quality 'stunt' versions, often made of rubber. This example, however, was originally built as one of the few 'hero' props, which in this context means a live-firing weapon built from real firearms and finished to a standard that will hold up to close-up filming. It was rebuilt for use in the second sequel in the series, *Alien 3* (1992). What is perhaps most interesting about this design is its realistic nature. Cameron acknowledged the limitations of future technology and eschewed traditional sci-fi technology (such as laser guns) in favour of anticipated near-future features including 'caseless' ammunition, integrated under-barrel grenade launchers, high-capacity magazines, telescoping buttstocks, and coloured/camouflaged surface finishes. Most importantly, the Pulse Rifle embodied the now-ubiquitous concept of a compact rifle or carbine as a standard-issue shoulder arm. At the time, these were regarded as the preserve of Special Operations Forces or non-infantry units that did not require a full-length rifle. Moreover, in appearance the Pulse Rifle is very clearly derived from the AR-15 carbines used by Special Operations Forces in Vietnam. The helmets worn by the Marines in the film are built upon real period M1 'pots', and their camouflage is the carefully chosen 'Tiger Stripe' pattern – all nods toward the military kit of Vietnam, given a futuristic makeover. This attention to detail lent a very realistic 'gritty' and believable feel to what would otherwise be a rather fantastical production. In cinematic terms, this supported the film's Vietnam War allegory, a warning that overconfidence and high technology do not always triumph over a determined enemy fighting on its own terms. Beyond this, the M-41A reflected and even foreshadowed developments in the real world. All the above features of modern small arms have since been embraced by the world's militaries – a fascinating case of life imitating art. Perhaps as significantly, this object and the film that spawned it have also helped to inspire new generations to learn about the reality and history of military small arms and the history of popular culture alike.

114

Arms commissioned by the Royal Armouries

1984–99 · XII.5483, XII.9609, XII.11810

From the end of the First World War until the 1980s, the Tower Armouries' collecting policy excluded material from after 1900, deemed to be the preserve of the Imperial War Museum. In the 1980s, however, a new generation of curators acknowledged the need to study and collect modern arms and armour, a move encouraged by the museum's enhanced status, from 1983, as a National Museum. From this emerged the desire to celebrate modern producers and decorators of arms and armour, and there followed an entirely new idea of commissioning pieces from outstanding practitioners. These three items were among the results.

The first commission, championed by the Viscount de Lisle (first Chairman of the Board of Trustees of the Armouries) and A. V. B. Norman (Master, 1977–88), was a round-action double-barrelled shotgun by the eminent maker David McKay Brown, of Bothwell, Lanarkshire: this was the type favoured as a vehicle for his work by the chosen decorator, the artist and engraver Malcolm Appleby. The 'Raven' theme, of course, was prompted by the famous ravens at the Tower of London, and the 19th-century legend that if they should depart the castle the kingdom would fall. The decoration takes the form of detailed engraving and carving of ravens' feathers, further highlighted by the case-hardening process: head feathers cover the action, eye plumage is used on the breeches, the trigger guard has overlapping feather decoration, and the top lever and sliding safety are feathered, in addition to a single golden feather and representation of the Tower itself, also in gold. The tang is engraved 'ARMOURIES'.

The second commission was born in the late 1980s of the museum's long association with the eminent American firearms historian, the late R. L. (Larry) Wilson, then involved in encouraging Tiffany & Co., New York, to continue their practice, dating from the American Civil War, of decorating swords and firearms. At the time, the exceptionally important and historic gun-making business, Smith & Wesson of Springfield, Massachusetts, had been bought by a British company, whose chief executive was known to both trustees and senior staff of the Royal Armouries. The suggestion followed that one of their pistols be decorated by Tiffany & Co. especially for the museum, and the famous large 'N-Frame' revolver in .44 Magnum was chosen as the base model. The decoration, devised by Tiffany's designers in conjunction with the Armouries' curators and picked out in 22-carat gold, was based on the leaves and branches of the four timber species traditionally used in English guns and gun-carriages, namely ash, elm, oak and walnut, in addition to yew, representing the longbow. The work was carried out by the gifted craftsman Leonard Francolini of Corrales, New Mexico.

The creation of the third piece was initiated in the early 1990s through the interest of Giles Whittome, firearms

[272]

enthusiast and owner of a gun-making businesses, in the museum's uniquely surviving Alexander Henry side-hammer falling block breech harpoon gun of the 1880s. Prompted by this, and having already built a 4-bore rifle using the same action, Whittome proposed the creation for the Royal Armouries of a 2-bore rifle, firing a gigantic half-pound projectile, as an item to commemorate the millennium. The offer was gladly accepted, and the gun was built using modern methods and materials, but designed for black powder, as used in the 19th century, to make the recoil manageable. In this case decoration took second place, confined to classical English scrollwork and an exquisite engraving of Henry VIII's horned helmet on the nocksform.

These three items must be among the most remarkable commissioned weapons of modern times, and the 2-bore among the more unusual commemorations of the millennium.

115

The 'Iraqi Supergun'

England, *c*.1990 · XIX.842

On 11 April 1990, BBC News reported that:

Customs officers in Middlesbrough say they have seized what they believe to be the barrel of a massive gun on a ship bound for Iraq. Export of parts for a weapon to Iraq would contravene British restrictions on arms sales …

The story begins with Gerald Bull (1928–90), a brilliant Canadian physicist whose work, inspired by the German gun that had bombarded Paris during the First World War, centred on the development of long-range artillery. In 1987, working at his own Space Research Centre in Brussels, his talents came to the attention of Saddam Hussein, President of Iraq. Bull undertook to rectify problems with Iraq's SCUD missiles and to develop a self-propelled gun, but more importantly, saw the chance to return to his work on gun-launched satellites under Iraqi patronage. His project for the so-called 'Supergun' of 1000 mm calibre, supported by Saddam Hussein, became known as 'Babylon', after the ancient Mesopotamian city, while 'Baby Babylon' (a smaller version of 350 mm) was built for exhaustive testing. To disguise the purpose of the Babylon Project, procurement was arranged through the Iraqi Petroleum Authority and the orders were ostensibly 'for petrochemical use'; contracts for the tubes were placed in England with Walter Somers Ltd of Halesowen (West Midlands) and Sheffield Forgemasters. The odd nature of the order caused Forgemasters to request government approval, which was given, as Iraq – even on the brink of the First Gulf War – was considered a friendly power.

The 1000 mm barrel would be 156 m long, composed of twenty-six tubes bolted together end to end, the wall thicknesses diminishing towards the muzzle as in a conventional gun. The tubes were manufactured to exacting tolerances using special high-quality steel. The purpose of the 'Supergun' has been the subject of some debate. As a weapon, and certainly as one of 'mass destruction', its capability was very limited (although the allies destroyed all the components they found in Iraq): installed in a fixed position, impossible to aim or hide and vulnerable to air attack, it would have been an impractical weapon, and an intended use as a satellite launcher is far more likely. Either way, it was designed to launch a rocket contained in a lightweight casing, fired from the gun with sufficient velocity for the rocket motor to take over in flight and enter space. On leaving the muzzle, the outer casing would fall away, allowing the slim rocket to continue. Bull had already tried and tested the principle elsewhere, but the design work on the 'Supergun' projectile remained unfinished. Meanwhile, the SCUDs, tweaked by Bull, were proving a real threat to Israel, and it was probably for this that he was murdered, it seems by MOSSAD, in Brussels in March 1990. By then, however, Iraq had fallen from favour with the West, and trade with it restricted: a large consignment of tubes from Sheffield Forgemasters was seized by HM Customs at Teesport (North Yorkshire), and several key people at the British companies arrested, although soon released. The Royal Armouries was given some of the seized tubes by HM Customs, including the only remaining piece of the smaller calibre trials gun. These three gigantic steel tubes, on show at Fort Nelson, remain awe-inspiring examples of British engineering, and telling reminders of the events that led to the defeat of Saddam Hussein's government by the US-led coalition.

e Supergun
Gerald Bull
Codename:
Project Bab
REPUBLIC OF IRAQ
MINISTRY FOR INDUSTRIES
AND MINERALS
PETROCHEMICAL PROJECT
BAGHDAD IRAQ
GROSS WT. 7,100 KGS
NO. 52

Glossary

AKETON
Quilted coat, worn beneath mail armour, to absorb blows and make it more comfortable to wear.

ARÇONS
Collectively the bow and cantle of a saddle, respectively at the front and rear, raised to provide a firm seat and protection. Frequently armoured from the 14th to the 17th centuries.

ARMET
Modern term to describe a helmet with side-opening cheek-pieces. In the 15th and 16th centuries, a general term used to describe a helmet.

ARTILLERY
Projectile weapon too heavy to be carried and used by one person.

ARTILLERY TRAIN
Artillery weapons and all its associated equipment and personnel for a siege or battle.

AUTOMATIC
A firearm that fires continuously for as long as the trigger is operated and there remains ammunition in the feed device (magazine, belt etc).

AVENTAIL
Mail defence attached to lower edge of helmet to protect chin, neck and upper shoulders.

AXE
Bladed head with sharpened edge attached to wooden haft, of varying sizes for one or two handed use.

BACINET
Open-faced helmet, often with pointed skull and visor. A *great bacinet* had a plate throat-and-neck defence.

BACKPLATE
Solid plate defence for the back. Together with the breastplate it forms the cuirass.

BAG CHARGE
Propellant charge for a breech-loading gun contained in a bag, usually of cloth.

BARD
Horse armour.

BASELARD
A dagger, sometimes as long as a short sword, with a hilt in the form of an upper case 'I'. In use from between the 13th century and through the 15th century.

BASILISK
A large cannon, usually of brass and often of great length.

BAYONET
An edged weapon designed for attachment to a firearm. Various attachment systems exist, and blades may be of knife, sword or spike form.

BEVOR
Plate chin-and-throat defence. Synonymous with 'buffe'. From French *baver* ('to dribble').

BILL
Long wooden-hafted infantry weapon, with a sharp curved hook, deriving from the agricultural billhook. Used from middle of the 13th century.

BLOWBACK
A firearm mechanism that is operated by the recoil of the cartridge case immediately after the weapon is fired. *Delayed blowback* is a form of blowback operation in which the opening of the firearm's action is mechanically delayed to contain for longer the high-pressure gases produced on firing. This allows the use of more powerful ammunition, whilst keeping the mechanism simple to produce and maintain.

BOLT
Either a short, thick, arrow, with flattened four-sided or square-shaped iron head and usually two fletchings (of wood, parchment or leather), for a crossbow.
Alternatively the mechanical component of a firearm that seals the breech, containing the tremendous pressures generated when the cartridge is fired.

BOLT-ACTION
a firearm that is operated manually by means of a handle on the bolt. This is pushed forward and turned down to load a cartridge and lock the breech closed, and the process reversed and repeated for the next shot.

BOMB
A hollow spherical projectile or shell, filled with gunpowder and ignited by a time fuze, fired from a mortar.

BOMBARD
A large calibre stone-throwing gun.

BORE
The interior of a gun barrel, which has a constant diameter.

BOSS
Central raised part of shield or buckler often made of metal.

BOW
Missile weapon used to shoot (not 'fire') arrow or bolt, such as longbow, composite bow or crossbow.

BREASTPLATE
Solid plate defence for the chest. Together with the backplate it forms the cuirass.

BREATHS
Helmet apertures allowing ventilation.

BREECH
The rear end of a gun barrel. If the gun is a breech-loader, 'breech' may refer to 'breech mechanism' – this allows the gun to be loaded at the breech and safely closed for firing.

BREECH-LOADER
A gun loaded at the breech (the opposite end to the muzzle) or the specific technical meaning of a gun so loaded and using a bag charge (as opposed to those using a metal cartridge). The breech has to provide obturation, to prevent the leakage of explosive gasses on firing.

BRIGANDINE
Body armour of textile jacket into which are riveted small iron plates. The name seemingly derives from 'brigands' (a term for lightly armed foot soldiers) who may have first worn them.

BUCKLER
Small shield, often round, primarily for infantry use.

BUFFE
Plate chin and throat defence. Synonymous with 'bevor'.

BUFF COAT
Oil-tanned leather coat worn with or in place of plate armour.

BURGONET
Open-faced helmet used by light cavalry and infantry in the 16th century. It often bore hinged cheek-pieces and a peak (the 'fall') over the brow to protect the eyes.

BUTT, BUTT-STOCK
The rear-most component of the firearm (or portion of the stock), used to shoulder the firearm.

CABASSET
Open-faced helmet with a flat brim and a 'pear-stalk' at the apex of the skull. Known as a 'Spanish morion' in England.

CALIBRE
The diameter of the inside of the barrel or its bore.

CALIVER
A short-barrelled gun with a bore between that of a carbine and musket. Held in two hands for discharge, fired from the chest or shoulder without the aid of a rest. Comparable to a 'harquebus'.

CANNON
Originally a heavy weapon of relatively short length, it has come to be a general name for any piece of smooth-bore artillery.

CARBINE
A short-barrelled small-bore gun for use on horseback. Held in two hands for discharge, fired from the chest or shoulder.

CARRIAGE
Support for gun barrel and sometimes providing for its transport from place to place. It may also have a mechanism to control recoil.

CARRONADE
A short, large-calibre weapon introduced by the Carron Company of Falkirk in 1779. The heaviest version was the 68-pounder of 8-inch calibre known as the 'Smasher'.

CARTRIDGE
By the time of the First World War, an individual self-contained round of ammunition consisting of case (usually brass), primer (percussion cap), propellant, and projectile (bullet or shot).

CASCABEL
The projecting rear end of a cannon. The knob [button] was used for lifting.

CASE SHOT
Or canister, was an anti-personnel round used at short range. It consisted of a cylindrical container filled with metal balls, such as musket balls, but pieces of stone or scrap metal could be used.

CAST IRON
Iron containing a proportion of carbon, suitable for casting in a mould. Brittle compared with wrought iron, especially when cold.

CHAMBER
The portion of a firearm's breech that is shaped to accept a cartridge. In revolvers there is more than one chamber housed within a rotating cylinder.

CHAPE
Metal tip at end of scabbard.

CHAUSSES
Mail leggings.

CLIP
A feed device consisting of a simple metal strip or partial enclosure that is either held within the weapon during operation (*en bloc* clip) or used simply to load cartridges into the weapon's internal magazine (in which case it is known as a 'stripper clip' or 'charger clip').

CLOSE HELMET
Modern term describing a helmet enclosing the entire head with a visor and one or two bevors pivoted at the same points at either side of the skull.

COAT OF PLATES
Body armour of canvas jacket inside which iron plates are riveted. The outside usually faced with cloth or leather. Otherwise known as a 'pair of plates'.

COMB MORION
Helmet used by light cavalry and infantry in the 16th century. Formed of a skull with a broad rim which curved up to a point, front and back, and bearing a pronounced central keel (the 'comb') running along the top of the skull. Laminated cheek-pieces protected the sides of the face.

CORSLET
Half armour worn by pikemen, comprising back and breastplate and a pair of tassets.

COULOVERINE
Large type of 15th-century handgun. Fired lead or stone shot.

COUTER
Plate defence for elbow.

CRINET
Defence for neck of horse.

CROSS
The lower guard of sword or dagger hilt protecting the hand. Later became known as the quillon.

CUIRASS
Defence for the body formed of the back and breastplate.

CUISSE
Thigh defence of plate introduced in the late 13th century.

CULET
Defence for the lower back and rump.

CULVERIN
A gun long in proportion to its calibre, firing a cast-iron shot of about 20 lb. Smaller members of the culverin family include sakers and falcons.

DAGGER
Edged weapon, shorter than a sword, with two or more edges. Primarily for thrusting, there were many types such as ballock, baselard, misericorde and rondel.

DAMASCENING
The process of decorating metal with inlays of a precious metal.

DOLPHINS
Lifting handles on a cannon, often shaped like dolphin or other animals.

DRAKE
A term often used during the 17th century, usually to mean a gun lighter and/or shorter than a full-size version of the same calibre.

EMBOSSING
Mechanical process in which a design is beaten into metal which has been placed on a pliable surface such as pitch or wood, resulting in raised and sunken areas.

ENGRAVING
Mechanical process in which a chisel or pointed tool is used to create an incised design.

ETCHING
Chemical process in which a corrosive substance is used to remove metal not protected by an applied resist of wax or oil paint. A highly popular decorative technique used on both arms and armour.

FALCHION
Sword in use by the 13th century, if not before, for cutting with. During the late middle ages it had a curved blade and in the 15th century was often used as an infantry sidearm.

FALCON
Culverin type of gun, usually 2½-3 lb.

FAULD
Laminated skirt defence for lower abdomen and upper thigh.

FEEDING HEAD
An extension to the muzzle provided by the mould when casting bronze or iron guns. It collected the dross and was sawn off when cool.

FLAIL
Infantry weapon with iron-clad wooden head attached to a haft, usually by small length of chain. The head could also be studded with spikes.

FULLER
Groove, often found running along centre of sword or dagger blades. Made the blade lighter and yet retained its strength. Erroneously called a 'blood-gutter'.

FUZE
An ignition device fitted to a shell that initiates the main charge at the desired moment, using either a timing system or by percussion on striking the target. Sometimes both methods were combined.

GAMBESON
Padded coat worn over, under armour or as independent defence.

GAMBOISED CUISSE
Quilted tubular thigh defence, sometimes richly decorated.

GAS-OPERATED
A firearm mechanism that is operated by the gases released on firing.

GAUNTLET
Plate or leather defence for the hand and wrist. Some gauntlets extended to cover the forearm.

GORGET
Defence for the throat, usually formed of a front and rear plate.

GREAVE
Plate armour for the lower leg.

GRENADE
a single-use weapon containing an explosive charge that may be thrown by hand (hand grenade) or projected from another weapon (grenade launcher).

GUARD
Part of sword or dagger hilt protecting the hand. Originally a simple bar, it evolved into more complex and protective forms.

GUARD-CHAIN
Chain that was attached to breastplate or waist belt and fixed to the helm, sword or dagger to prevent loss.

GUIGE
Longer carrying strap of a shield allowing it to be slung over the neck and shoulders.

GUNPOWDER
Explosive mixture of sulphur, charcoal and saltpetre (potassium nitrate). Used to project missiles, such as bolts or shot, from handgun or cannon.

HABERGEON
Short mail shirt worn under plate armour or separately, *c*.1350–1410. Diminutive of 'hauberk'.

HALBERD
Wooden-hafted infantry weapon with a combination broad axe-blade and spearhead. Later forms had a rear edge spike ('fluke') with a reinforced spear point. From the German '*halm*' (staff) and '*barte*' (axe).

HANDGUN
Handheld firearm with a metal barrel set in a wooden stock. The gunpowder and lead or stone shot was muzzle loaded.

HARQUEBUS/ARQUEBUS
A short-barrelled gun with a bore between that of a carbine and musket. Held in two hands for discharge, fired from the chest or shoulder without the aid of a rest.

HAUBERK
Mail coat of varying lengths with sleeves and often an integral coif. The main form of body armour from the early Middle Ages until *c*.1300.

HAUTE-PIECE
Vertical plate on pauldron protecting the neck.

HILT
The part of a sword or dagger containing the guards, grip and pommel.

HOLY-WATER SPRINKLER
Long wooden hafted infantry weapon with spiked head.

HOWITZER
A short, comparatively light piece to fire a heavy shell horizontally like a gun or at high angle like a mortar.

JACK
Thickly padded jacket made from layers of linen or canvas, from the 16th century lined with small iron or horn plates, or discs.

JUPON
Tight, often padded, fabric surcoat worn over armour.

KETTLE-HAT
Open-faced helmet with round bowl shaped skull and wide brim running all around the edge.

KLAPPVISIER
Modern term for a visor attached by a single hinge to the brow of a bacinet.

LADLE
A long handled scoop used to place gunpowder in the breech of a gun. The ladle was difficult to use and could be dangerous. From early times, it appears that cartridges were preferred.

LAME
Overlapping plates of iron or steel forming a flexible defence.

LANCE
Wooden-hafted cavalry spear, up to about 4 metres long, with an iron or steel spear-head to which could be fastened a pennon. Used in mounted charges, the knightly lance was often made of ash, a strong and resilient wood.

LANCE-REST
Bracket attached to breastplate which supported the weight of the lance and prevented it running back on impact.

LOCK
The ignition mechanism of a firearm, fixed to the side of the stock.

LOCKET
Metal mouthpiece of scabbard. First appeared in early 14th century.

LONGBOW
A selfbow, the stave of which is made from a single rounded length of wood incorporating both the elasticity and resilience of the wood to create a natural spring. Many types of wood, including yew, elm and ash were used for the stave. The string was usually made from hemp.

MACE
Wooden – or iron-hafted weapon with head of metal (copper alloy, iron or steel), often flanged or with a 'knobbly' surface.

MAGAZINE
a feed device containing a spring to facilitate the feeding of cartridges. This may be an internal magazine, or a detachable 'box' magazine.

MAIL
Armour made of interlinked iron rings.

MATCHLOCK
Ignition system for a handgun using smouldering match cord held in a pivoted match-holder and operated by a trigger. Used from the early 15th century.

MORION
Open-faced helmet with a high crest or comb and an upswept brim. Sometimes known as a 'comb morion'.

MORTAR
A short-barrelled weapon firing at high angles of elevation.

MUSKET
Long-barrelled, usually large bore gun held in two hands for discharge, fired from the shoulder with the weight of the barrel sometimes supported by a rest.

MUZZLE
The open end of a gun barrel toward the target.

MUZZLE-LOADER
A firearm loaded though the muzzle rather than the breech.

NASAL
Nose-guard of helmet.

PAUNCE
Mail defence for the groin.

PAULDRON
Plate shoulder-defence.

PEASCOD
Exaggerated padded stomach which projected into a deep rounded point overhanging the waistline.

PERIER
A gun firing a stone projectile. Can be muzzle or breech loading, and often has a powder chamber smaller than bore.

PEYTRAL
Defence for chest of horse.

PIKE
Slender wooden-hafted infantry weapon, usually 5–7 m long, with a small, sharp iron head. Particularly effective when used in masses against cavalry.

PIPE-BACK
A form of blade with a thickened, rounded rod or 'pipe' along its back edge to provide extra rigidity.

PISTOL
Short-barrelled, small-bore gun held in one hand for discharge and chambering relatively low-powered ammunition.

POINT
Lace used to attach piece of armour to undergarment.

POLEYN
Plate defence for knee.

POLLAXE
Long wooden-hafted infantry weapon, with a combination axe, rear hammer-head or spike ('fluke') and reinforced spear-point.

POMMEL
Shaped component through which the *tang* of a blade passed, securing the grip. This counterbalanced the blade and could be used to strike or 'pummel' with. In firearms, the rounded end of a pistol.

PORT PIECE
A wrought-iron breech-loading gun of around 7-inch calibre. Heavy guns transformed naval warfare when gun ports were provided. In the case of Henry VIII's Mary Rose, these were a crucial modification some years after she was built in 1511.

POTT
A contemporary term for either a light open-faced cavalry helmet or a pikeman's helmet.

PUMP-ACTION
A firearm that is operated manually by means of a pump grip (or 'slide') that is pumped back and forth to load a cartridge and lock the breech closed for each shot.

QUICK-FIRING (QF) GUN
A gun loaded at the breech using a brass cartridge with primer. Usually the projectile is attached to the cartridge to form 'fixed ammunition', but in variable charge guns, the cartridge is loaded separately and is provided with a choice of propellant charges suitable for different tactical demands. The brass cartridge seals the breech on firing. A QF gun normally has full recoil control on the carriage.

QUILLON
The cross bar on the hilt of a sword.

RAPIER
Originally a sword for wear in civilian dress. Later, as fencing techniques developed and the fashionable sword became a purely thrusting weapon, the name was applied specifically to swords with long, narrow thrusting blades.

RECEIVER
The main structural component of a firearm, housing the mechanical working parts. Also known as the 'body'.

RECEIVER RING
In bolt-action rifles, the reinforced annular portion of the barrel surrounding and reinforcing the chamber.

RECOIL
The equal and opposite force on the gun and mounting generated when firing a projectile. Various means have been adopted to resist or control this potentially damaging force.

REVOLVER
A sub-category of pistol featuring a fixed barrel in front of a cylinder. The cylinder contains several chambers that are rotated sequentially into alignment with the barrel for firing.

RIFLE
A shoulder-fired firearm with a bore that is shaped ('rifled') to impart spin to the projectile.

RIFLING
Spiral grooves machined into the bore of a gun to impart spin to the projectile. Spin is necessary when firing pointed elongated projectiles to ensure that they fly point first. Rifling came into wide use in the latter of half of the 19th century.

SABATON
Plate armour for the foot.

SALLET
A light helmet the rear drawn out over the neck. Frequently worn with a bevor.

SAKER
A member of the culverin family of guns, usually a 5–6 pounder.

SCABBARD
Protective sheath for *sword*, *knife* or *dagger*, made to carry and protect the sword when not in use.

SCALE
Armour of overlapping scales secured to a backing.

SEMI-AUTOMATIC
A firearm that fires one shot for each pull of the trigger.

SHAFFRON
Defence for head of horse.

SHELL
A projectile that is hollow in order to contain a filling, such as a high explosive. Alternative payloads include propaganda, smoke or nuclear, biological or chemical weapons.

SHOT
A solid projectile. If spherical, sometimes known as a 'cannonball'. An example of a later kind of shot is 'armour-piercing'.

SHRAPNEL
A shell containing musket balls or small pieces of metal intended to be fired against troops or early aircraft. A small explosive filling is provided to burst the shell and throw the contents forward. The range is set by a time *fuze*. First termed 'spherical case', in 1852 it was named after Henry Shrapnel, the artillery officer (1761–1842) who had invented it in 1784.

SKULL
Part of helmet covering the head above ears, or simple metal cap.

SMOKELESS PROPELLANT
A group of more powerful propellants that also burned more cleanly than traditional 'black' gunpowder. It appeared during the late 19th century, starting with the French '*poudre B*' in 1886.

SMOOTH-BORE
A gun whose bore is machined smooth, that is, without *rifling*.

SPONGE
A tool consisting of a wooden rod fitted with a sheepskin or lambswool head for cleaning the bore of a gun whilst firing is in progress.

STANDARD
Mail neck-defence, usually with an upstanding collar.

STOCK
The enclosing structural component of a crossbow or firearm and the means by which it is grasped, shouldered and fired. Traditionally made from wood. The portion that is shouldered is often called the 'butt-stock', and may be a separate component.

SUB-MACHINE GUN
The modern term, of US origin, for a pistol-calibre shoulder weapon.

SURCOAT
Sleeveless cloth garment worn over armour often bearing the owner's coat of arms hence 'coat armour'.

TANG
Thinner continuation of sword, knife or dagger blade, around which the hilt components were secured, the end of the tang being hammered down over the pommel.

TASSETS
Plate defence for the upper thighs either made of numerous separate lames or of embossed solid plates.

TOUCH HOLE
Or vent, the hole through the gun barrel at the breech by which the gun was fired.

TRUNNION
A cylindrical or slightly tapered projection on each side of a gun barrel to support the barrel on its carriage and to allow it to pivot vertically. This enabled the firing angle to be elevated or depressed.

VAMBRACE
Plate defence for the arm.

VISOR
Faceplate.

WAD, WADDING
Some elastic material, such as hay or oakum (old rope teased out into fibres), loaded between projectile and propellant and in front of the projectile. The top wad was particularly necessary at sea or when firing below horizontal, to stop the shot rolling out of the barrel.

WHEELLOCK
Ignition system in which sparks were produced by the action of a piece of hardened revolving grooved steel wheel against a piece of iron pyrites.

WINDAGE
The difference in diameter between the shot and the bore of a muzzle-loading smoothbore gun. Although this gap was a cause of power loss and inaccurate shooting, it was a necessary evil. It allowed for the fact that neither gun nor shot could be made to modern precision standards. In British service, a quarter of an inch was commonly the allowance for windage; this reduced as manufacturing methods improved during the 18th century.

WINDLASS
Mechanical device which, using handles connected to a series of cords and pulleys, was used to 'span' more powerful crossbows.

Further Reading

Abbreviations

A&A: Arms & Armour

BLACKMORE, *Armouries*:
BLACKMORE, H. L. 1976. *The Armouries of the Tower of London: 1, Ordnance*, London: HMSO.

BLACKMORE, *Hunting Weapons*:
BLACKMORE, H. L. 1971. *Hunting Weapons*, London: Barrie and Jenkins.

BLAIR, *European Armour*:
BLAIR, C. 1979. *European Armour circa 1066 to circa 1700*, London: Batsford.

JAAS:
Journal of the Arms & Armour Society

NORMAN AND WILSON, *Treasures*:
NORMAN, A. V. B. AND G. M. WILSON 1982. *Treasures from the Tower of London*, London: Arms and Armour.

RICHARDSON, *East Meets West*:
RICHARDSON, T. (ED.) 2013. *East Meets West: Diplomatic Gifts of Arms and Armour between Europe and Asia*, Leeds: Royal Armouries.

RICHARDSON, *Henry VIII*:
RICHARDSON, T. 2015. *Arms and Armour of Henry VIII*, Leeds: Royal Armouries.

RIMER ET AL, *Henry VIII*:
RIMER, G., T. RICHARDSON AND J. P. D. COOPER (EDS.) 2009. *Henry VIII: Arms and the Man*, Leeds: Royal Armouries.

1

HONG, Y. 1992. *Weapons in Ancient China*, New York and Beijing: Science Press.
PEERS, C. J. 2006. *Soldiers of the Dragon: Chinese Armies 1500 BC–AD 1840*, Oxford: Osprey.

2

MERCER, M. AND T. RICHARDSON 2016. 'Greek Armour at the Tower', *A&A* 13:1, 3–13.
EVERSON, T. 2004. *Warfare in Ancient Greece*, Stroud: The History Press.

3

FEUGERE, L. M. 2002. *Weapons of the Romans*, Stroud: Tempus.
BISHOP, M. C. 2016. *The Gladius: The Roman Short Sword*, Oxford: Osprey.
JAMES, S. 2011. *Rome & the Sword: How Weapons & Warriors Shaped Roman History*, London: Thames & Hudson.

4

PIERCE, I. G. 2002. *Swords of the Viking Age*, Woodbridge: Boydell Press.
OAKESHOTT, R. E. 1964. *The Sword in the Age of Chivalry*, London: Lutterworth Press.

5

PEERS, C. J. AND D. SQUE 1992. *Medieval Chinese Armies 1260 – 1520*, Oxford: Osprey.
LA ROCCA, D. J. 2006. *Warriors of the Himalayas: Rediscovering the Arms and Armor of Tibet*, New York: Metropolitan Museum of Art.

6

FORGENG, J. L. 2018. *The Medieval Art of Swordsmanship: Royal Armouries MS I.33*, Leeds: Royal Armouries.

7

RICHARDSON, T. 2016. *The Tower Armoury in the Fourteenth Century*, Leeds: Royal Armouries.

8

EDGE, D. AND J. M. PADDOCK 1988. *Arms and Armour of the Medieval Knight*, New York: Crescent Books.
RIMER, G. 2015. 'A Rare Great Helm, Probably German, Late 13th Century', in D. A. Oliver (ed.), *The Spring 2015 London Park Lane Arms Fair*, London: David A. Oliver, 13–19.

9

ALEXANDER, D. G. 1985. 'European Swords in the Collections of Istanbul', *Waffen und Kostumkunde* 27:2.
THOMAS, C. 2011. '"King of Emirs" Pious Donations of European swords to the Arsenal of Alexandria during the time of the Viceroy Sayf al-din Aristay', in D. A. Oliver (ed.), *The Spring 2011 London Park Lane Arms Fair*, London: David A. Oliver.

10

CAPWELL, T. 2015. *Armour of the English Knight 1400–1450*, London: Thomas del Mar.
CAPWELL, T. 2011. *Masterpieces of European Arms and Armour in the Wallace Collection*, London: The Wallace Collection.

11

APPELBAUM, S. (ED.) 1964. *The Triumph of Maximilian I*, New York: Dover Publications.

12

EAVES, I. AND T. RICHARDSON 1987. 'The Warwick Shaffron', *JAAS* 12:4, 217–222, 247–252.
WOOSNAM-SAVAGE, R. C. 2017. *Arms and Armour of Late Medieval Europe*, Leeds: Royal Armouries.

13

KRAMER, G. W. 2001. 'Das Feuerwerkbuch', *JAAS* 17:1.

14

PAGGIARINO, C. 2011. *The Royal Armouries: Masterpieces of Medieval and Renaissance Arms and Armour*, volume 1, Milan: Carlo Paggiarino.
BOULTON, D'A. J. D. 2000. *The Knights of the Crown: The Monarchical Orders of Knighthood in Later Medieval Europe 1325–1520*, Woodbridge: Boydell Press, esp. 348–55.

15

REYNOLDS, V. 1999. *From the Sacred Realm; Treasures of Tibetan Art from the Newark Museum*, Munich and London: Prestel.
LA ROCCA, D. J. 2006. *Warriors of the Himalayas: Rediscovering the Arms and Armor of Tibet*, New York: Metropolitan Museum of Art.

16
FERGUSON, J. 2015. 'The Danzig gun: a rare decorated bronze handgun of the 15th century', *A&A* 12:2, 97–102.

17
SMITH, R. D. AND R. RHYNAS BROWN 1989. *Bombards: Mons Meg and her Sisters*, London: Royal Armouries.

18
BLACKMORE, *Armouries*, 172.

19
EDGE, D. AND J. M. PADDOCK 1988. *Arms and Armour of the Medieval Knight*, New York: Crescent Books, 185.
MANN, J. 1959. 'A Gothic horse armour from Anhalt in the Armouries of the Tower of London', *Waffen und Kostumkunde* 1–2, 22–27.

20
CAPWELL, T. 2015. *Armour of the English Knight 1400–1450*, London: Thomas del Mar.

21
BLAIR, *European Armour*, 70.

22
PYHRR, S. W., J. A. GODOY AND S. LEYDI 1998. *Heroic Armour of the Italian Renaissance. Filippo Negroli and his Contemporaries*, New York: Metropolitan Museum of Art.

23
RICHARDSON, T. 2015. *Islamic Arms and Armour*, Leeds: Royal Armouries.
ELGOOD, R. 1995. *Firearms of the Islamic world in the Tareq Rajab Museum, Kuwait*, London: I.B. Tauris, 23.

24
RICHARDSON, T. *Islamic Arms and Armour*, Leeds: Royal Armouries.

25
TERJANIAN, P. 2019. 'The Currency of Power: the Central Place of Armor in the Ambitions and Life of Maximilian I', in P. Terjanian (ed.), *The Last Knight. The Art, Armor, and Ambition of Maximilian I*, New York: Metropolitan Museum of Art, 17–38.
APPELBAUM, S. 1964. *The Triumph of Maximilian I*, New York: Dover Publications.

26
FORGENG, J. L. 2015. *The Art of Swordsmanship by Hans Lecküchner*, Woodbridge: Boydell & Brewer.
NORMAN, A. V. B. 1980. *The Rapier and Small Sword, 1460–1820*, London: Arms and Armour Press.

27
BLAIR, C. 1962. *European & American Arms c.1100–1850*, London: Batsford.
CAPWELL, T. 2009. *The Illustrated Encyclopedia of Knives, Daggers and Bayonets*, London: Lortenz Books.

28
ADAMS, N. 2008. 'The origins of the sabre', in B. Muhamed (ed.), *The Arts of the Muslim Knight: The Furusiyya Art Foundation Collection*, Milan: Skira Editore, 19–21.
YŪCEL, Ū. 2001. *Islamic Swords and Swordsmiths*, Istanbul: IRCICA, 93–113.

29
RIMER ET AL, *Henry VIII*.

30
RIMER, G. 2013. 'The Horned Helmet of Henry VIII: A Famous Enigma', in Richardson, *East Meets West*, 40–64.

31
RICHARDSON, *Henry VIII*.
BLAIR, C. 1965. 'The Emperor Maximilian's Gift of Armour to King Henry VIII and the Silvered and Engraved Armour at the Tower of London', *Archaeologia* 99, 1–52.

32
ELLIS, E. (ED.) 1809. *Hall's Chronicle Containing the History of England During the Reign of Henry the Fourth and the succeeding Monarchs to the end of the Reign of Henry the Eighth*, London: J. Johnson, 572–3
CAPWELL, T. 2021. *Arms and Armour of the Renaissance Joust*, Leeds: Royal Armouries.
GUNN, S. J. 1988. *Charles Brandon, Duke of Suffolk 1484–1545*, Oxford: Blackwell.

33
RICHARDSON, T. 2013. 'The King and the Astronaut', *A&A* 10:1, 3–14.
RIMER ET AL, *Henry VIII*, 116.

34
BLAIR, C. 1995. 'King Henry VIII's Tonlet Armour', *JAAS* 15:2, 85–109.
RIMER ET AL, *Henry VIII*, 116.

35
KONSTAM, A. 1996. *Pavia 1525: the climax of the Italian wars*, Oxford: Osprey.

36
RICHARDSON, *Henry VIII*, 48.
RIMER ET AL, *Henry VIII*, 248.
WILLIAMS, C. (TRANS.) 1937. *Thomas Platter's Travels in England 1599*, London: Jonathan Cape, 160.

37
BLAIR, C. 2002. 'King Henry VIII's chamber-pieces', *Royal Armouries Yearbook* 7, 22–39.
RIMER, G. 2001. *Wheellock Firearms of the Royal Armouries*, Leeds: Royal Armouries.
BLACKMORE, *Hunting Weapons*, 217.

38
PYHRR, S. W., J. A. GODOY AND S. LEYDI 1998. *Heroic Armour of the Italian Renaissance. Filippo Negroli and his Contemporaries*, New York: Metropolitan Museum of Art, 155.

39
SMITHURST, P. 2009. 'Henry VIII's Gun Shields' in Rimer et al, *Henry VIII*, 228.

40
RIMER ET AL, *Henry VIII*, 212–19.
RICHARDSON, *Henry VIII*.

41
BLAIR, C. 1981. 'The Early Basket-Hilt in Britain', in D. H. Caldwell (ed.), *Scottish Weapons & Fortifications 1100–1800*, Edinburgh: John Donald, 153–252.
WILSON, G. M. 1986. 'Notes on Some Early Basket-Hilted Swords', *JAAS* 12:1, 1–19.

42
HILDRED, A. (ED.) 2011. *Weapons of Warre: the armaments of the Mary Rose*, Volume 3, Portsmouth: Mary Rose Trust, chapter 8.

43
BOTTOMLEY, I. 2017. *Japanese Arms and Armour*, Leeds: Royal Armouries, 45–6.
BOTTOMLEY, I. 2013. 'Japanese diplomatic gifts of arms and armour to Europe of the 16th and 17th centuries' in Richardson, *East Meets West*, 37–8.

44
REVERSEAU, J.-P. 2004. *Armes et Armures de la Couronne au Musée de l'Armée*, Dijon: Faton, 220–5.
PYHRR, S. W., J. A. GODOY AND S. LEYDI 1998. *Heroic Armour of the Italian Renaissance. Filippo Negroli and his Contemporaries*, New York: Metropolitan Museum of Art, 306–8.

45
BLACKMORE, *Hunting Weapons*, 3.

46
DUFTY, A. R. AND W. REID 1968. *European Armour in the Tower of London*, London: Ministry of Public Building and Works, plates XLIV, XLV and XCIV.
PAGGIARINO, C. 2011. *The Royal Armouries: Masterpieces of Medieval and Renaissance Arms and Armour*, volume 2, Milan: Carlo Paggiarino.
BLAKELEY, E. 1997. 'Tournament Garniture of Robert Dudley Earl of Leicester', *Royal Armouries Yearbook* 2, 55–63.

47
EAVES, I. D. D. 1989. 'On the remains of a jack of plate excavated from Beeston castle in Cheshire', *JAAS* 13, 81–154.
STARLEY, D. 2005. 'Brigandine and jack plates', The Finds Research Group AD 700–1700, Datasheet 36.
BLAIR, *European Armour*.

48
WILLIAMS, A. AND A. DE REUCK 1995. *The Royal Armoury at Greenwich 1515–1649*, Leeds: Royal Armouries, 36.
MANN, J. G. 1932. 'Sir John Smythe's Armour in Portraiture', *Connoisseur* 90, 200.

49
RIMER, G. 2001. *Wheellock Firearms of the Royal Armouries*, Leeds: Royal Armouries, 41.
PAGGIARINO, C. 2011. *The Royal Armouries: Masterpieces of Medieval and Renaissance Arms and Armour*, volume 2, Milan: Carlo Paggiarino.

50
WILKINSON, F. 2002. *Those entrusted with arms: A History of the Police, Post, Customs and Private use of Weapons in Britain*, London: Greenhill, 43.
PORTER, S. 2016. *Everyday Life in Tudor London: Life in the City of Thomas Cromwell, William Shakespeare & Anne Boleyn*, Stroud: Amberley.

51
SCHILLE, C. 1957. 'Christian I', *Neue Deutsche Biographie*, Berlin: Historische Kommission, 230–1.
ANGLO, S. 2007. 'The Barriers: From Combat to Dance (Almost)', *Dance Research: The Journal of the Society for Dance Research* 25:2, 91–106.

52
DUFTY, A. R. 1977. 'Two Paintings from the Reign of Elizabeth I', *Connoisseur* 194, 20–5.

53
NORMAN AND WILSON, *Treasures*.

54
BLACKMORE, *Hunting Weapons*, 174–5.
LAVIN, J. 1992. 'The gift of James I to Filipe III of Spain', *JAAS* 14, 64–88.

55
BLAIR, *European Armour*, 136.
PATTERSON, A. 2009. *Fashion and Armour in Renaissance Europe*, London: Victoria and Albert Museum, 93.
STANTON, M. O. A. (TRANS.) 1975. *Princely Arms and Armour. A Selection from the Dresden Collection*, London: Barrie and Jenkins, 13.

56
WOOD, J. 2010. *Rubens: copies and adaptations from Renaissance and later artists: II, Titian and North Italian art*, London: Harvey Miller, 229.

SOLER DEL CAMPO, A. 2009. *The Art of Power: Royal Power and Portraits from Imperial Spain*, Madrid: Patrimonio Nacional, 96.
WOODS-MARSDEN, J. 2013. 'The Sword in Titian's Portraits of Emperor Charles V', *Artibus et Historiae* 34:67, 201–218.
JENKINS, S. 2005. '"An Inventory of His Grace the Duke of Chandos's Seat Att Cannons taken June the 19th 1725" by John Gilbert', *The Volume of the Walpole Society* 67, 93–192.

57
TRIM, D. J. B. 1999. 'Sir Horace Vere in Holland and the Rhineland, 1610–12', *Historical Research* 72, 344–6, 350–1.
CLIFTON, J. 2009. '"To showe to posteritie the manner of souldiers apparel": Arms and Armor in European Prints', in I. Sinkević (ed.), *Knights in Shining Armor: Myth and Reality 1450–1650*, Piermont, NH: Bunker Hill Publishing, 56–7.

58
BOTTOMLEY, I. 2017. *Japanese Arms and Armour*, Leeds: Royal Armouries.
BOTTOMLEY, I. 2013. 'Japanese gifts of armour to Spain in the 16th century and the Tokugawa Japanese gift armoure to James I and the European Courts', in Richardson, *East Meets West*, 1–39.

59
VAN GELDER, J. G. 1963. 'Notes on the Royal Collection – IV: The "Dutch Gift" of 1610 to Henry, Prince of "Whalis", and Some Other Presents', *The Burlington Magazine* 105, 541–5.
STRONG, R. C. 1986. *Henry, Prince of Wales and England's Lost Renaissance*, London: Thames & Hudson, 69–70, 78, 83, 176, 220.

60
BLAIR, C. AND R. C. WOOSNAM-SAVAGE 1995. *Scottish Firearms*, Bloomfield, Ont.: Museum Restoration Service, 6.
WHITELAW, C. E. 1977. *Scottish Arms Makers*, London: Arms and Armour Press, 50.

61

ELMY, D. AND N. ALLEN 1972. 'An Assassin's Crossbow', *Journal of the Society of Archer-Antiquaries* 15, 37–9.
FLEWETT, W. E. 1996. 'The "Assassin's Crossbow"?: A Reassessment', *Journal of the Society of Archer-Antiquaries* 39, 78–93.
BREIDING, D. H. 2013. *A Deadly Art: European Crossbows, 1250–1850*, New York: Metropolitan Museum of Art, 82.

62

PANT, G. N. 1989. *Mughal Weapons in the Baburnama*, New Delhi: Agam Kala Prakashan.
BORG, A. 1974. 'A Crusader in Borrowed Armour', *Country Life* (18 July 1974), 168–9.

63

TOKYO MUSEUM 2000. *Catalogue of an exhibition of treasures from the shrines and temples of Nikko held at the Edo-Tokyo Museum in 2000*, Tokyo: Tokyo Museum, 102.
BEZDEK, R. 2000. *German Swords and Sword Makers: Edged Weapon Makers from the 14th to the 20th centuries*, Boulder, CO: Paladin Press, 57.

64

BLACKMORE, *Hunting Weapons*, 83–93.
CUMMINS, J. 1988. *The Hound and the Hawk: The Art of Medieval Hunting*, London: Weidenfeld & Nicolson, 100, 124.

65

RICHARDSON, T. 1996. 'The elephant armour', *Royal Armouries Yearbook* 1, 100–106.
ELGOOD, R. 2004. *Hindu Arms and Ritual: Arms and Armour from India 1400–1865*, Delft: Eburon Academic Publishers, 55.
ROWELL, C. 1987. 'Clive of India and his family: the formation of the collection', in *Treasures from India: The Clive Collection at Powis Castle*, London: Herbert Press, 17–30.

66

BÜTTNER, N. 2018. *Rubens: Allegories and Subjects from Literature*, Turnhout: Brepols.
BÜTTNER, N. 2012. 'Rubens & son', in K. Brosens, L. Kelchtermans and K. van der Stighelen (eds.), *Family ties: art production and kinship patterns in the early modern Low Countries*, Turnhout: Brepols, 131–44.

67

DOWEN, K. 2016. 'The State of Militia and Private Armouries in England and Wales on the Eve of the Civil Wars', *JAAS* 22:2, 72–87.
DOWEN, K. 2019. *Arms and Armour of the English Civil Wars*, Leeds: Royal Armouries.
DOWEN, K. 2015. 'The Seventeenth Century Buff Coat', *JAAS* 21:5, 157–77.

68

BLAIR, C. 1996. 'Some Swords associated with Oliver Cromwell' in D. A. Oliver (ed.), *The Spring 1996 London Park Lane Arms Fair*, London: David A. Oliver, 26–33.
BOSQUECILLO 1848. 'A Visit to the United Service Institution in 1848', *Colburn's United Service Magazine and Naval and Military Journal* 3, 370–81.
MOWBRAY, S. 2013. *British Military Swords, Volume One: 1600–1660 The English Civil Wars and the Birth of the British Standing Army*, Andrew Mowbray Publishers.
BLACKMORE, D. 1996. 'Arms and the Man', *Royal Armouries Yearbook* 1, 107.

69

SCHEDELMANN, H. 1958. 'Jean Conrad Tornier, An Alsatian Gunstock-Maker', *JAAS* 2:12, 261–4.

70

FERGUSON, J. 2018. 'An important early self-rotating revolver c.1680 possibly by John Dafte', *The Antique Arms Fair at Olympia 2018*, London: Olympia Antique Arms Fair, 33–45.
BLAIR, C. 1968. *Pistols of the World*, London: Batsford, 44, 128.

71

IMPEY, E. 2019. ''A Desperat Wepon': rehafted scythes at Sedgemoor, in warfare and at the Tower of London', *The Antiquaries Journal* 99, 225–70.

72

BLACKMORE, H. L. AND C. BLAIR 1991. 'King James II's armour and Richard Holden of London', *JAAS* 13:5, 316–34.

73

HAYWARD, J. F. 1980. 'Bertrand Piraube', *Livrustkammaren: Journal of the Royal Armoury, Stockholm* 15, 119–60.
LA ROCCA, D. J. 1992. 'Sorting Out Simonin: Pattern Books for Decorated Firearms, 1684–1702', *Studies in European Arms and Armor*, 184–207.
HAYWARD, J. F. 1962. *The Art of the Gunmaker*, volume 2, London: Barrie and Rockcliff, 44, 326.

74

GUNNIS, R. 1968. *Dictionary of British Sculptors 1660–1851*, London: Odhams Press, 167.
EDWARDS, P. 2007. *Horse and Man in Early Modern England*, London: Continuum, 110–17.
WATSON, K. AND C. AVERY 1973. 'Medici and Stuart: A Grand Ducal Gift of "Giovanni Bologna" Bronzes for Henry Prince of Wales (1612)', *The Burlington Magazine* 115, 493–507.

75

RIMER, G. 2008. 'An important 17th-century English presentation sporting gun / Una importante arma esportiva do século XVII para presentear', *ICOMAM Proceedings 2008*, 117–40.
BLACKMORE, H. L. 1986. *A Dictionary of London Gunmakers 1350–1850*, Oxford: Phaidon.

76

NORMAN AND WILSON, *Treasures*, 72.

77

RIMER, G. 2017. 'Doleps for the Medici: A new study of a group of firearms by Andrew Dolep, traditionally a British royal gift to Cosimo III, Grand Duke of Tuscany', in D. A. Oliver (ed.), *The Spring 2017 London Park Lane Arms Fair*, London: David A. Oliver, 102–31.

78

BENNETT, N. 2020. 'Armour for an Age of Peace', in K. Almqvist and Y. Duke Bergman (eds.), *Japan's Past and Present*, Stockholm: Bokförlaget Stolpe, 350–67.

79

HELD, R. 1979. 'Michele Lorenzoni's Masterpiece', in R. Held (ed.), *Art, Arms and Armour: An International Anthology*, Chiasso, Switzerland: Acquafresca Editrice, 369.

HOOPES, T. 1973. 'The Function of the Perfected Lorenzoni Repeating Flintlock System', in R. Held (ed.), *Arms and Armor Annual*, Northfield, IL: Digest Books, 217.

80

BARTER-BAILEY, S. 1978. 'The Board of Ordnance', in J. Charlton (ed.), *The Tower of London: its buildings and institutions*, London: HMSO, 106–16.

BARKER, N. 1993. 'The building practice of the English Board of Ordnance, 1680–1720', in J. Bold and E. Chaney, (eds.), *English Architecture Public and Private: Essays for Kerry Downes*, London: Hambledon Press, 199–214.

IMPEY, E. AND G. PARNELL 2006. *The Tower of London: the official illustrated history*, London: Merrell, 101.

81

BLACKMORE, H. L. 1975. 'The Monlong Pistols', *Proceedings of the Huguenot Society* 22, 463–4.

NORMAN AND WILSON, *Treasures*, 84.

82

RICHARDSON, T. AND N. BENNETT 2015. *Indian Arms and Armour*, Leeds: Royal Armouries, 15–16.

HALES, R. 2013. *Islamic and Oriental Arms and Armour: A Lifetime's Passion*, London: Robert Hales, 28–97.

83

MADRA, A. S. AND P. SINGH 1999. *Warrior Saints: Three Centuries of the Sikh Military Tradition*, London: I.B. Tauris, 5–6.

COWPER, H. S. 2001. *The art of Attack and the Development of Weapons: Being a Study in the Development of weapons and Appliances of Offence from the Earliest Times to the Age of Gunpowder*, Uckfield: Naval & Military Press, 171–2.

BENNETT, N. 2019. '"Relating to a country so distant": collecting South Asian arms and armour at the Tower of London during the nineteenth century', in A. B. Peyton and K. A. Paul (eds.), *Arts of South Asia: Cultures of Collecting*, Gainesville, FL: University of Florida Press, 13–38.

84

BLACKMORE, *Armouries*.

85

NORMAN AND WILSON, *Treasures*, 85.

BLACKMORE, H.L. 1986. *Gunmakers of London 1350–1850*, York, PA: George Shumway, 143.

86

BOHLMANN, R. 1929–31. *Johann Sebastian Hauschka: Braunschweigischer Hof-Büchsenmacher*, Zeitschrift Für Historische Waffen – und Kostümkunde, Volume 12, Berlin, 187–93.

87

WILSON, G. M. 2011. 'New light on the Simpson of York gun', *A&A* 8:1, 89–95.

88

RODIMTSEVA, I. A. AND G. M. WILSON (EDS.) 1998. *Treasures of the Moscow Kremlin: Arsenal of the Russian Tsars*, Leeds: Royal Armouries, 22–3.

BERMAN, V. (ED.) 1981. *Masterpieces of the Tula Gun-Makers*, Moscow: Planeta Publishers.

89

ANDERSEN, N. A. 2014. *Gold and Coral: Presentation Arms from Algiers and Tunis*, Copenhagen: Devantier.

ELGOOD, R. 1995. *Firearms of the Islamic World in the Tareq Rajab Museum, Kuwait*, London: I.B. Tauris.

90

ANGELO, D. 1765. *The school of fencing: with a general explanation of the principal attitudes and positions peculiar to the art*, London: S. Hooper.

HILLYARD, M. (ED.) FORTHCOMING. *The School of Fencing*, Leeds: Royal Armouries.

91

KENNARD, A. N. 1986. *Gunfounding and Gunfounders: A Directory of Cannon Founders from Earliest Times to 1850*, London: Arms and Armour, 28.

BLACKMORE, *Armouries*, 137.

92

BUDDLE, A. 1990. *Tigers round the Throne: the court of Tipu Sultan (1750–1799)*, London: Zamana Gallery, 60.

ELGOOD, R. 2004. *Hindu Arms and Ritual: Arms and Armour from India 1400–1865*, Delft: Eburon Academic Publishers, 55–65.

93

RICHARDSON, T. AND N. BENNETT 2015. *Indian Arms and Armour*, Leeds: Royal Armouries, 70–1.

WIGINGTON, R. 1992. *The Firearms of Tipu Sultan: 1783–1799*, Hatfield: John Taylor Book Ventures, 11–12.

94

DELAHAYE, R.-P. 1993. 'Historique de la manufacture d'armes de Versailles (1793–1818)', in *La Manufacture d'armes de Versailles et Nicolas-Noël Boutet: manufacture nationale, impériale et royale, 1793–1818*, Versailles: Musée Lambinet, 9–49.

OPPERMAN, H. 1977. *Jean-Baptiste Oudry*, New York: Graland Publishing.

KENNARD, [A.N.] 1975. 'Un cadeau pour l'espagne', *Gazette d'Armes* 29 (July-August 1975), 34.

95

THOUMINE, R. H. 1968. *Scientific Soldier: A Life of General Le Marchant, 1766–1812*, Oxford: Oxford University Press.

KELLY, C. 1818. *A Full and Circumstantial Account of the Memorable Battle of Waterloo*, London: Thomas Kelly, 92, 94.

96

NEWNHAM-COLLINGWOOD, G. L. (ED.) 1837. *A selection from the public and private correspondence of Vice-Admiral Lord Collingwood, interspersed with memoirs of his life*, London: James Ridgeway.

SOUTHWICK, L. 1990. 'The recipients, goldsmiths and costs of the swords presented by the Corporation of the City of London', *JAAS* 13:3, 173–220.

97
DUNN, R. 2009. *The Telescope: A Short History*, London: National Maritime Museum, 23–4.
MCCONNELL, A. 2016. *Jesse Ramsden (1735–1800): London's leading scientific instrument maker*, London: Routledge.

98
RIMER, G. 2005. 'Ezekiel Baker's "cradle jigg" for the guns of King George IV', *Royal Armouries Yearbook* 5, 51.
BLACKMORE, H. 1960. 'The Prince Regent as a Gun Collector', *Connoisseur* 145, 233.

99
DARWIN, C. 1845. *Journal of Researches during the Voyage of H.M.S. "Beagle"*, London: T. Nelson & Sons, 243.
MOORHEAD, A. 1969. *Darwin and the Beagle*, London: Penguin.

100
MOORE, D. AND G. SALTER 2011. *Mallet's Great Mortars*, Fareham: Palmerston Forts Society.
BELLAMY, C. 2001. *The Oxford Companion to Military History: Crimean War*, Oxford: Oxford University Press.

101
Duggan, D. [n.d]. *The Great Gunmaker*, Newcastle: Frank Graham.
HALL, N. 2001. 'Theophilus Alexander Blakely and the revolution in Victorian gun design', *Royal Armouries Yearbook* 6, 135–49.

102
WARING, J. B. 1863. *Masterpieces of Industrial Art & Sculpture at the International Exhibition 1862*, volume 1, London: Day & Son.
NORMAN AND WILSON, *Treasures*, 96.

103
EZELL, E. C. 1993. *Handguns of the World*, New York: Barnes & Noble, 504.

SMITHURST, P. 2015. 'Samuel Colt, 1814–1862: Commemorating a Legend. Part 2', *The Rampant Colt: Journal of the Colt Collector's Association* (Spring 2015), 12–26.

104
GOLDSMITH, D. 1993. *The Devil's paintbrush: Sir Hiram Maxim's gun*, Toronto: Collector Grade Publications.
MAXIM, H. S. 1915. *My Life*, London: Methuen, 290.

105
GROGAN, E. AND A. H. SHARP 1900. *From the Cape to Cairo: the first traverse of Africa from south to north*, London: Hurst and Blackett.
WILSON, G. M. 1976. 'An African Explorer and his Elephant Gun', *Guns Review* 16:5, 252–6.

106
HALL, N. 2015. 'The French 75 mm Modele 1897 Field Gun', *A&A* 12:1, 4–21.
LELUC, S. 2006. 'Le Canon de 75 mm modele 1897', *Revue de la Sociéte des Amis du Musée de l'Armée* 132, 28–33.

107
ROBSON, B. 1996. *Swords of the British Army: The Regulation Patterns 1788 to 1914*, London: National Army Museum.
WAR OFFICE 1915. *Cavalry Training, 1912 (Reprinted with Amendments, 1915)*, London: HMSO.

108
BAILEY, J. B. A. 2004. *Field Artillery and Firepower*, Annapolis, MD: Naval Institute Press.
LE CLAIR, D. 2019. *The British Military Revolution of the 19th century: "The Great Gun Question" and the Modernization of Ordnance and Administration*, Jefferson, NC: McFarland & Co., 222.

109
HART, P. 1995. 'The Thompson submachine gun in Ireland revisited', *The Irish Sword: the Journal of the Military History Society of Ireland* 19:77, 161–70.

110
VANDERLINDEN, A. 2013. *FN Browning Pistols: Side Arms that Shaped World History*, Greensboro, NC: Wet Dog Publications, 283.

111
CHASE, O. 1999. *The wreck of the whaleship Essex: a first-hand account of one of history's most extraordinary maritime disasters*, London: Headline.
JOHNSEN, A. O. 1982. *The History of Modern Whaling*, Berkeley, CA: University of California Press.

112
CHIVERS, C. J. 2011. *The Gun*, New York: Simon & Schuster.
IANNAMICO, F. 2013. *AK-47: The Grim Reaper*, Henderson, NV: Chipotle Publishing.
MOORE, H. G. AND J. L. GALLOWAY 2002. *We were soldiers once ... and young: Ia Drang, the battle that changed the war in Vietnam*, London: Corgi.

113
MALO, J.-J. AND T. WILLIAMS 1994. *Vietnam War Films*, Jefferson, NC: McFarland & Co., 13.
DONALD, R. AND K. MACDONALD 2014. *Women in War Films: From Helpless Heroine to G.I. Jane*, Lanham, MD: Rowman & Littlefield, 180.
BRIMMICOMBE-WOOD, L. 2012. *Aliens: Colonial Marines Technical Manual*, London: Titan, 14–16, 160.

114
WILSON, G. M. 1987. 'The Raven Gun', *The Fourth Park Lane Arms Fair*, London: David A. Oliver, 23–5.
WILSON, G. M. 1988. 'Recent Acquisitions for the Royal Armouries', *The Burlington Magazine* (October 1988), 802.
RICHARDSON, T. AND G. RIMER 1997. *Treasures from the Tower in the Kremlin*, Moscow: The British Council Russia & The State Museum of the Moscow Kremlin, 166–7, 199.

115
BULL, G. V. AND C. H. MURPHY 1988. *Paris Kanonen – the Paris Guns (Wilhelmgeschütze) and Project HARP*, Bonn: E. S. Mittler & Sohn.
LOWTHER, W. 1991. *Iraq and the Supergun*, London: Macmillan.

Acknowledgements

The Royal Armouries is grateful to numerous people for providing content for, and comments on, both the introduction and the 115 entries which form the bulk of this book. In preparing the former, use has been made of the 'essays' providing perspectives on the significance of arms and armour, commissioned to support the Interpretation Strategy being developed for the redisplay of the Leeds museum. These were kindly provided by Professor John France ('Weapons, war and world history'), Dr Tiffany Jenkins and Dr Andrew Mills (separately, but both on 'Social and spiritual significance'), Dr Jeremy Warren ('The art of arms and armour'), and Professor David Williams ('Science and technology'). Discussion between members of the group convened to develop plans for the redisplay of the Royal Armouries Museum Leeds – led by Emma Carver and including Laura Bell, Bridget Clifford, Natasha Bennett, Jonathan Ferguson, Tristan Langlois, Siona Mackelworth, Dr Malcolm Mercer, Frank Riley and Henry Yallop – has also been extremely useful. Parts of the text draw on additional material generously provided by others, notably by David Williams, Dr Melanie Giles, and Dr Malcolm Mercer. Numerous other individuals have advised on particular issues, including Professor Richard Bradley, Bridget Clifford, Dr David Edge, Menno Fitski, the late Professor Jane Mellanby, Dr Malcolm Mercer, Dr Thom Richardson, Dr Jeremy Warren and Guy Wilson. Some of these have kindly read all or parts of the text in draft, and their comments and advice have been very gratefully received.

In respect of the 'entries', prepared by nineteen current or former members of staff, the Royal Armouries is grateful to those who have read all or some of them in draft and provided comments and advice, including David Edge, Professor Peter Edwards, Philip Lankester, Dr Thom Richardson, Graeme Rimer, Dr Peter Smithurst, Dr Jeremy Warren, and Guy Wilson. Help in many forms has been provided throughout by Kathryn Sibson (Royal Armouries Chief Administrator) and Stuart Ivinson (Royal Armouries Librarian). We also gratefully acknowledge that the present publication draws on an earlier list and draft entries for a projected 'Masterpieces' volume, suggested by Dr Paula Turner and drafted by Dr Thom Richardson, former Deputy Master, in the mid 1990s, although not published. Final thanks go to the Royal Armouries Head of Publishing, Dr Martyn Lawrence, who has managed the final editing and production of the volume. For errors of fact and interpretation, both in the introduction and the individual entries, the editor must take full and final responsibility. But above all, the museum extends sincere and heartfelt thanks to all those who in whatever capacity have been involved in creating and contributing to this volume. Let us hope that you – our readers – enjoy what we've produced, and are encouraged to share our fascination with this subject.

Contributors

PHILIP ABBOTT
Archives and Records Manager

LAURA BELL
Director of Collections

NATASHA BENNETT
Curator of Asian and African Collections

BRIDGET CLIFFORD
Keeper of Tower Armouries

KEITH DOWEN
Assistant Curator of Arms and Armour

JONATHAN FERGUSON
Keeper of Firearms

NICHOLAS HALL
Curator Emeritus

SCOT HURST
Assistant Curator of Arms and Armour

EDWARD IMPEY
Director General and Master

STUART IVINSON
Librarian

PHILIP MAGRATH
Curator of Artillery

MALCOLM MERCER
Curator of Tower History and Tower Special Collections

MARK MURRAY-FLUTTER
Curator of Firearms

THOM RICHARDSON,
Curator Emeritus

LISA TRAYNOR
Curator of Firearms

ROBERT C. WOOSNAM SAVAGE
Curator of Armour and Edged Weapons

HENRY YALLOP
Keeper of Edged Weapons and Armour

List of Entries

1. Chinese dagger axe (*ge*) and scabbard
2. Bronze 'Cumae' armour from southern Italy
3. Roman sword and scabbard mounts
4. A Viking sword for a child
5. Mongol helmet
6. Late medieval German fencing manual
7. Mail sleeve from the Hundred Years War
8. Great Helm
9. Sword with Arabic inscription
10. The 'Lyle' bacinet
11. Jousting saddle for the '*Hohenzeuggestech*'
12. The 'Warwick' shaffron
13. A 15th-century 'Book of Fireworks'
14. Dragon saddle from the Order of St George
15. The 'Ming' sword
16. The bronze 'Danzig' gun
17. 'Mons Meg', a 15th-century iron bombard
18. The great bronze 'Dardanelles' gun
19. Gothic armour for man and horse
20. The Writhen Hilt sword
21. Painted sallet
22. Milanese sallet belonging to a knight of the Order of St John
23. Mamluk handgun from Syria
24. The Turban helm
25. *Rennzeug* jousting armour
26. *Messer* (sword)
27. Italian 'ear dagger'
28. Mamluk sword and Ottoman scabbard
29. Henry VIII's 'Burgundian Bard'
30. The 'Horned Helmet'
31. 'Silvered and Engraved' field armour for Henry VIII
32. 'Charles Brandon's lance'
33. Foot combat armour for Henry VIII
34. Tonlet armour for Henry VIII
35. Painting of the battle of Pavia
36. 'Henry VIII's Walking Staff', a 'Holy-water Sprinkler with three guns
37. Breech-loading gun belonging to Henry VIII
38. Buffe for a burgonet by Filippo Negroli
39. Gun shield belonging to Henry VIII
40. Armour to impress a new queen: Henry VIII's garniture for field, tilt, tourney and foot combat
41. Basket-hilted sword and Wrexham buckler
42. Longbow stave from the *Mary Rose*
43. Japanese armour (*mogami haramaki*)
44. The 'Lion Armour'
45. Boar sword
46. Field and tilt armour of Robert Dudley, Earl of Leicester
47. Jack of plate with plate sleeves
48. Armour of Sir John Smythe
49. The 'Forget me not' gun
50. Extending rapier
51. Foot combat armour of Christian of Saxony
52. Portrait of Robert Radcliffe, Viscount Fitzwalter and 5th Earl of Sussex
53. Powder flask bearing the arms of the Worshipful Company of Goldsmiths of London
54. English crossbow
55. A parade burgonet from Augsburg, Germany
56. 'The Emperor Charles V holding a drawn sword' by Peter Paul Rubens
57. The 'Alexander' armour of Prince Henry Stuart
58. Japanese armour presented to James I
59. Gilt armour owned by Charles I
60. A rare Scottish flintlock long gun and a 'Fish-tail' butt pistol
61. 'Assassin's' crossbow
62. South Asian horse armour (*bargustavan*)
63. Japanese dagger (*aikuchi*) with a German blade
64. Early modern hunting spear
65. Elephant armour (*bargustavan-i-pil*) and tusk swords
66. 'Louis XIII being crowned by Victory', from the school of Peter Paul Rubens
67. Harquebusier armour of Colonel Alexander Popham
68. 'Mortuary sword', reputedly Oliver Cromwell's
69. Flintlock sporting gun with stock by Jean Conrad Tornier
70. Snaphance revolver that inspired Samuel Colt
71. Scythe blades captured from the rebel army at Sedgemoor (1685)
72. Armour of King James II
73. Flintlock sporting gun by Bertrand Piraube
74. Grinling Gibbons' wooden horse
75. Flintlock sporting gun for George Legge, 1st Baron Dartmouth
76. Partizan for Louis XIV's *Gardes du Corps*
77. Pocket set of tools for maintaining firearms
78. Japanese helmet (*harikake kabuto*)
79. Flintlock breech-loading magazine gun by John Cookson
80. Tympanum sculpture from the Grand Storehouse at the Tower of London
81. Pair of flintlock holster pistols by Pierre Monlong
82. Dagger (*khanjar*) from the Mughal empire
83. A Sikh quoit turban
84. Bronze dragon cannon
85. A sporting gun for a prisoner in the Tower
86. A sporting gun for a future king of France
87. Celebrated sporting gun signed by William Simpson of York
88. The 'Tula garniture' for Elizabeth, Empress of Russia
89. An Ottoman flintlock pistol (*kubur*) from Algiers
90. First English edition of Domenico Angelo's *The School of Fencing*
91. 'The Furies Gun': a sculptural masterpiece by Horatio Alberghetti
92. Helmet and cuirass from South India
93. Bronze tiger mortar from Mysore
94. A present from Napoleon to the king of Spain
95. Heavy Cavalry Trooper's sword, variant of Pattern 1796
96. Jewelled presentation sword for Admiral Collingwood
97. Wellington's telescope from Waterloo
98. Pistols for the Prince Regent
99. Pistols for Robert Fitzroy, Captain of HMS *Beagle*
100. A monster mortar for the Crimean War
101. The first modern artillery – the 'Armstrong gun' of 1862
102. A masterpiece for the London World's Fair
103. Presentation percussion revolvers by Samuel Colt
104. The first machine gun – the experimental Maxim 106 of 1884
105. A giant rifle and an African adventure
106. The first modern field gun – the 'Soixante-Quinze'
107. The last British cavalry sword: Sealed Pattern 1908, MKI
108. The quick-firing 18-pounder of 1903
109. Thompson machine gun
110. The 'Baby Browning' centrefire self-loading pistol
111. Norwegian whaling cannon
112. Russian AK47 captured in Vietnam by Captain Gregory Dillon
113. 'M-41A Pulse Rifle', film prop for *Aliens*
114. Arms commissioned by the Royal Armouries
115. The 'Iraqi Supergun'

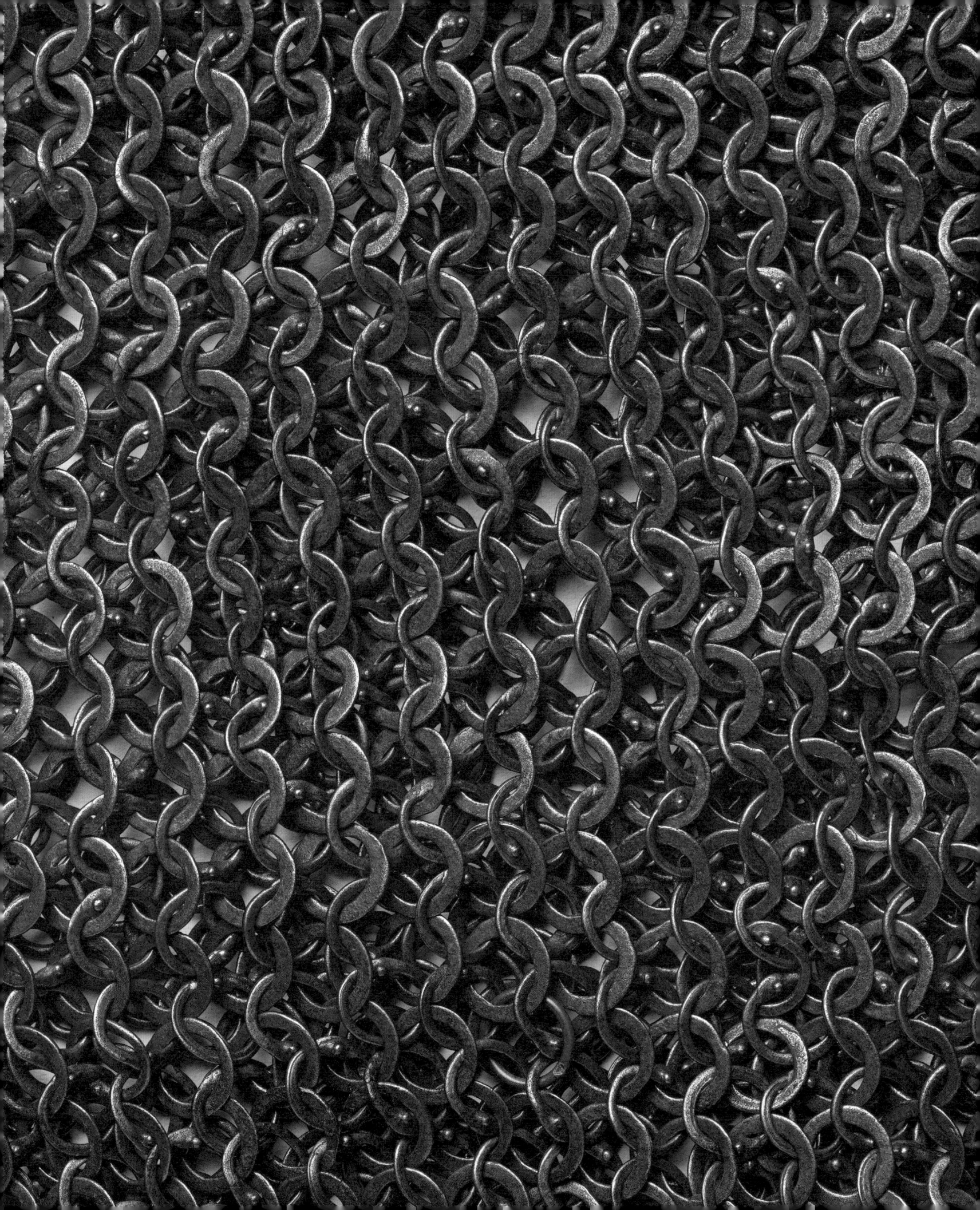

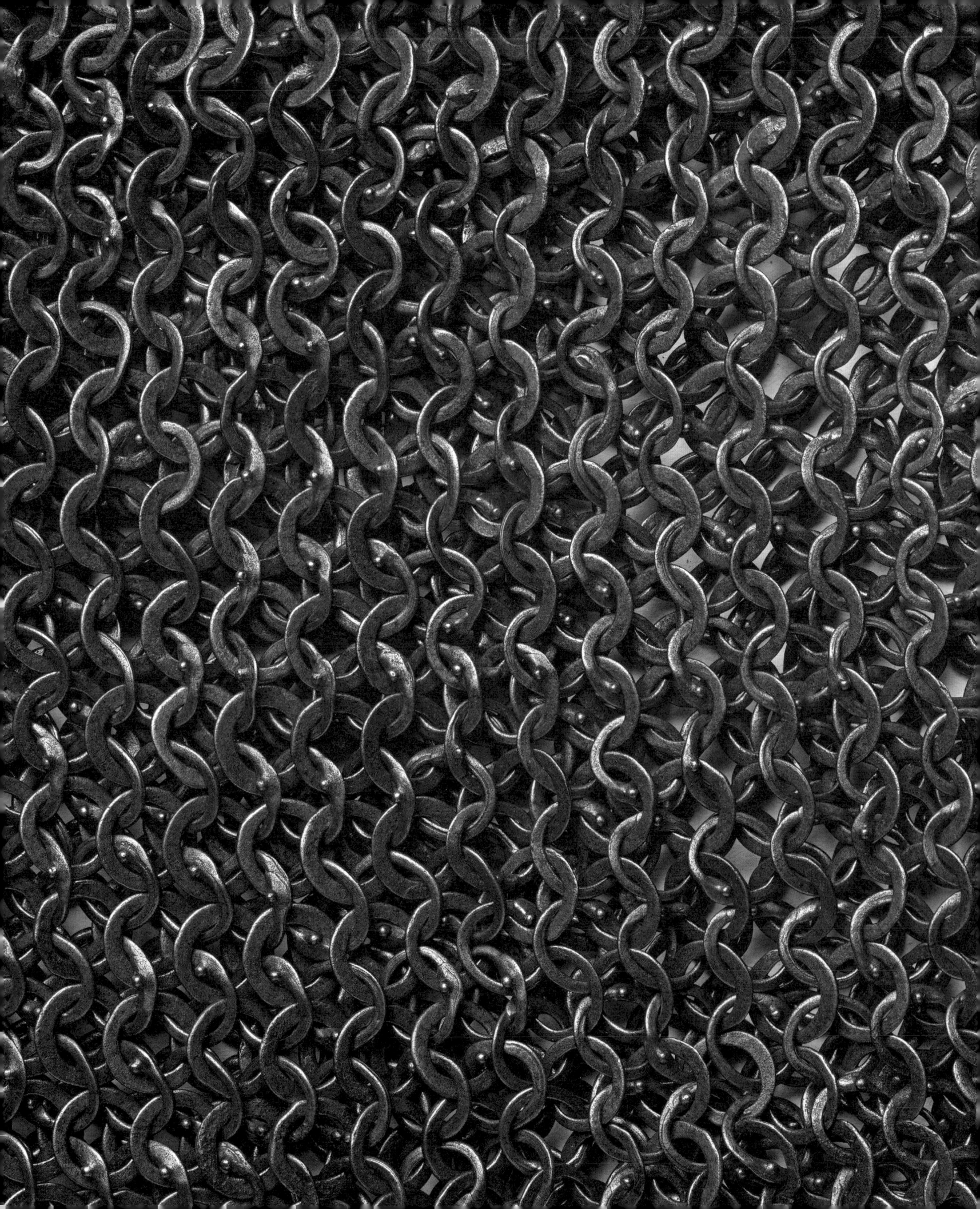